FrontPage® 2000 For Dummies®

Cheat Sheet

The FrontPage Buzzword Translator

FrontPage doesn't just come with a bucketful o' features; the program includes its very own set of obscure buzzwords! Check out the following terms:

- ✔ **FrontPage Web:** The FrontPage term for Web site, a collection of linked Web pages and files that's visible on the World Wide Web or an internal corporate network.

- ✔ **Web Page:** An individual Web site file, written in HTML. Web pages (along with other types of files) make up the content of a Web site.

- ✔ **HTML:** Short for *Hypertext Markup Language,* HTML is a set of simple text codes that defines the structure of a Web page. If you want to create Web pages, you need either to learn HTML or to use a program such as FrontPage, which cranks out the HTML for you.

- ✔ **URL:** Stands for *Uniform Resource Locator,* the technical name for an Internet site address. The URL for Microsoft's Web site is www.microsoft.com.

- ✔ **Web server:** A special type of program that knows how to deliver (serve) Web pages on request. The computer on which the web server program is installed also is called a web server.

- ✔ **Parent Web:** What FrontPage calls a top-level Web site. If you visit the Web site at www.microsoft.com, for example, you're looking at Microsoft's Parent Web.

- ✔ **Subweb:** What FrontPage calls a second-level Web site, or a complete Web site that lives in a folder on the same server as the Parent Web. If you visit the FrontPage Web site at www.microsoft.com/frontpage, for example, you're looking at the frontpage subweb.

- ✔ **Components:** Unique FrontPage features you can add to your page that simplify Web publishing tasks or add dynamic features to your Web site.

- ✔ **FrontPage Server Extensions:** A set of auxiliary programs, installed on the web server, that enables certain FrontPage-specific features to work.

Where to Go for More Help

If you have a burning question this book doesn't answer, turn to the following resources for more help:

- ✔ **FrontPage Help system:** Sometimes you just can't beat the help that comes with FrontPage. To access Help, choose Help⇨Microsoft FrontPage Help.

- ✔ **The Microsoft FrontPage Web Site:** This site contains lots of helpful articles, case studies, and other tidbits. See www.microsoft.com/frontpage.

- ✔ **Microsoft Support Online:** Home of the mammoth Microsoft Knowledge Base, a searchable database of answers to all sorts of software-related questions. See support.microsoft.com.

- ✔ **Microsoft FrontPage Newsgroup:** People just like you are posting problems and sharing solutions on the FrontPage Usenet newsgroup. Point your news reader to microsoft.public.frontpage.client and join the fun!

- ✔ **Real, live tech support people:** Your licensed copy of FrontPage comes with access to Microsoft support engineers who can help you through persistent tough spots. Check the documentation that comes with FrontPage for contact information.

IDG BOOKS WORLDWIDE

...For Dummies®: Bestselling Book Series for Beginners

FrontPage® 2000 For Dummies®

Cheat Sheet

BESTSELLING BOOK SERIES

FrontPage Toolbars You'll Use Most Often

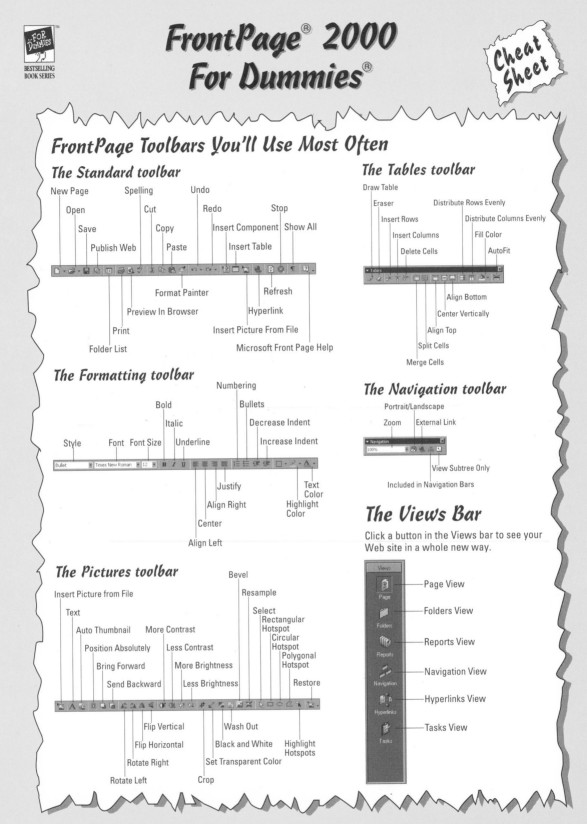

The Standard toolbar

- New Page
- Open
- Save
- Publish Web
- Print
- Folder List
- Spelling
- Cut
- Copy
- Paste
- Format Painter
- Preview In Browser
- Undo
- Redo
- Insert Component
- Insert Table
- Insert Picture From File
- Stop
- Show All
- Refresh
- Hyperlink
- Microsoft Front Page Help

The Formatting toolbar

- Style
- Font
- Font Size
- Bold
- Italic
- Underline
- Numbering
- Bullets
- Decrease Indent
- Increase Indent
- Justify
- Align Right
- Center
- Align Left
- Text Color
- Highlight Color

The Pictures toolbar

- Insert Picture from File
- Text
- Auto Thumbnail
- Position Absolutely
- Bring Forward
- Send Backward
- More Contrast
- Less Contrast
- More Brightness
- Less Brightness
- Flip Vertical
- Flip Horizontal
- Rotate Right
- Rotate Left
- Bevel
- Resample
- Select
- Rectangular Hotspot
- Circular Hotspot
- Polygonal Hotspot
- Restore
- Wash Out
- Black and White
- Set Transparent Color
- Crop
- Highlight Hotspots

The Tables toolbar

- Draw Table
- Eraser
- Insert Rows
- Insert Columns
- Delete Cells
- Distribute Rows Evenly
- Distribute Columns Evenly
- Fill Color
- AutoFit
- Align Bottom
- Center Vertically
- Align Top
- Split Cells
- Merge Cells

The Navigation toolbar

- Portrait/Landscape
- Zoom
- External Link
- View Subtree Only
- Included in Navigation Bars

The Views Bar

Click a button in the Views bar to see your Web site in a whole new way.

- Page View
- Folders View
- Reports View
- Navigation View
- Hyperlinks View
- Tasks View

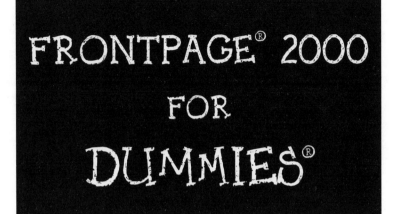

FRONTPAGE® 2000
FOR
DUMMIES®

FRONTPAGE® 2000 FOR DUMMIES®

by Asha Dornfest

IDG Books Worldwide, Inc.
An International Data Group Company

Foster City, CA ◆ Chicago, IL ◆ Indianapolis, IN ◆ New York, NY

FrontPage® 2000 For Dummies®

Published by
IDG Books Worldwide, Inc.
An International Data Group Company
919 E. Hillsdale Blvd.
Suite 400
Foster City, CA 94404
www.idgbooks.com (IDG Books Worldwide Web site)
www.dummies.com (Dummies Press Web site)

Library of Congress Catalog Card No.: 99-88799

ISBN: 0-7645-0423-1

Printed in the United States of America

10 9 8 7 6 5

1O/QW/QX/99/IN

Distributed in the United States by IDG Books Worldwide, Inc.

Distributed by CDG Books Canada Inc. for Canada; by Transworld Publishers Limited in the United Kingdom; by IDG Norge Books for Norway; by IDG Sweden Books for Sweden; by Woodslane Pty. Ltd. for Australia; by Woodslane (NZ) Ltd. for New Zealand; by TransQuest Publishers Pte Ltd. for Singapore, Malaysia, Thailand, Indonesia, and Hong Kong; by ICG Muse, Inc. for Japan; by Norma Comunicaciones S.A. for Colombia; by Intersoft for South Africa; by Le Monde en Tique for France; by International Thomson Publishing for Germany, Austria and Switzerland; by Distribuidora Cuspide for Argentina; by Livraria Cultura for Brazil; by Ediciones ZETA S.C.R. Ltda. for Peru; by WS Computer Publishing Corporation, Inc., for the Philippines; by Contemporanea de Ediciones for Venezuela; by Express Computer Distributors for the Caribbean and West Indies; by Micronesia Media Distributor, Inc. for Micronesia; by Grupo Editorial Norma S.A. for Guatemala; by Chips Computadoras S.A. de C.V. for Mexico; by Editorial Norma de Panama S.A. for Panama; by American Bookshops for Finland. Authorized Sales Agent: Anthony Rudkin Associates for the Middle East and North Africa.

For general information on IDG Books Worldwide's books in the U.S., please call our Consumer Customer Service department at 800-762-2974. For reseller information, including discounts and premium sales, please call our Reseller Customer Service department at 800-434-3422.

For information on where to purchase IDG Books Worldwide's books outside the U.S., please contact our International Sales department at 317-596-5530 or fax 317-596-5692.

For consumer information on foreign language translations, please contact our Customer Service department at 1-800-434-3422, fax 317-596-5692, or e-mail rights@idgbooks.com.

For information on licensing foreign or domestic rights, please phone +1-650-655-3109.

For sales inquiries and special prices for bulk quantities, please contact our Sales department at 650-655-3200 or write to the address above.

For information on using IDG Books Worldwide's books in the classroom or for ordering examination copies, please contact our Educational Sales department at 800-434-2086 or fax 317-596-5499.

For press review copies, author interviews, or other publicity information, please contact our Public Relations department at 650-655-3000 or fax 650-655-3299.

For authorization to photocopy items for corporate, personal, or educational use, please contact Copyright Clearance Center, 222 Rosewood Drive, Danvers, MA 01923, or fax 978-750-4470.

is a registered trademark or trademark under exclusive license to IDG Books Worldwide, Inc. from International Data Group, Inc. in the United States and/or other countries.

About the Author

On her first day of college, **Asha Dornfest** took a bold step: She replaced her broken typewriter with a PC.

Asha did not consider herself a geek; her computer was simply a tool to help her write papers and reports. But by her senior year, she had defended her clunky PC against so many insults from Mac-loving roommates that she came to regard her computer with a sense of kinship.

After graduation, Asha trudged into the real world with a liberal arts degree and strong computer skills. (Which do you think got her a job?) She soon realized that she enjoyed showing people how computers could simplify their lives, when the things weren't making life more difficult, that is.

In 1994, Asha discovered the Internet. Soon after, she and her husband Rael started a Web design business in their dining room and began hawking their electronic wares. Mind you, this venture began during the Web-publishing Stone Age; many people had never even heard of the World Wide Web. A savvy friend quipped that *...For Dummies* books about Web publishing may one day hit the shelves. Asha scoffed.

Today, Asha writes and teaches classes about Web publishing and other Internet-related topics. She welcomes visitors to her virtual home at www.ashaland.com.

ABOUT IDG BOOKS WORLDWIDE

Welcome to the world of IDG Books Worldwide.

IDG Books Worldwide, Inc., is a subsidiary of International Data Group, the world's largest publisher of computer-related information and the leading global provider of information services on information technology. IDG was founded more than 30 years ago by Patrick J. McGovern and now employs more than 9,000 people worldwide. IDG publishes more than 290 computer publications in over 75 countries. More than 90 million people read one or more IDG publications each month.

Launched in 1990, IDG Books Worldwide is today the #1 publisher of best-selling computer books in the United States. We are proud to have received eight awards from the Computer Press Association in recognition of editorial excellence and three from Computer Currents' First Annual Readers' Choice Awards. Our best-selling ...For Dummies® series has more than 50 million copies in print with translations in 31 languages. IDG Books Worldwide, through a joint venture with IDG's Hi-Tech Beijing, became the first U.S. publisher to publish a computer book in the People's Republic of China. In record time, IDG Books Worldwide has become the first choice for millions of readers around the world who want to learn how to better manage their businesses.

Our mission is simple: Every one of our books is designed to bring extra value and skill-building instructions to the reader. Our books are written by experts who understand and care about our readers. The knowledge base of our editorial staff comes from years of experience in publishing, education, and journalism — experience we use to produce books to carry us into the new millennium. In short, we care about books, so we attract the best people. We devote special attention to details such as audience, interior design, use of icons, and illustrations. And because we use an efficient process of authoring, editing, and desktop publishing our books electronically, we can spend more time ensuring superior content and less time on the technicalities of making books.

You can count on our commitment to deliver high-quality books at competitive prices on topics you want to read about. At IDG Books Worldwide, we continue in the IDG tradition of delivering quality for more than 30 years. You'll find no better book on a subject than one from IDG Books Worldwide.

John Kilcullen
Chairman and CEO
IDG Books Worldwide, Inc.

Steven Berkowitz
President and Publisher
IDG Books Worldwide, Inc.

VIII WINNER
Eighth Annual Computer Press Awards ≥1992

IX WINNER
Ninth Annual Computer Press Awards ≥1993

X WINNER
Tenth Annual Computer Press Awards ≥1994

XI WINNER
Eleventh Annual Computer Press Awards ≥1995

IDG is the world's leading IT media, research and exposition company. Founded in 1964, IDG had 1997 revenues of $2.05 billion and has more than 9,000 employees worldwide. IDG offers the widest range of media options that reach IT buyers in 75 countries representing 95% of worldwide IT spending. IDG's diverse product and services portfolio spans six key areas including print publishing, online publishing, expositions and conferences, market research, education and training, and global marketing services. More than 90 million people read one or more of IDG's 290 magazines and newspapers, including IDG's leading global brands — Computerworld, PC World, Network World, Macworld and the Channel World family of publications. IDG Books Worldwide is one of the fastest-growing computer book publishers in the world, with more than 700 titles in 36 languages. The "...For Dummies®" series alone has more than 50 million copies in print. IDG offers online users the largest network of technology-specific Web sites around the world through IDG.net (http://www.idg.net), which comprises more than 225 targeted Web sites in 55 countries worldwide. International Data Corporation (IDC) is the world's largest provider of information technology data, analysis and consulting, with research centers in over 41 countries and more than 400 research analysts worldwide. IDG World Expo is a leading producer of more than 168 globally branded conferences and expositions in 35 countries including E3 (Electronic Entertainment Expo), Macworld Expo, ComNet, Windows World Expo, ICE (Internet Commerce Expo), Agenda, DEMO, and Spotlight. IDG's training subsidiary, ExecuTrain, is the world's largest computer training company, with more than 230 locations worldwide and 785 training courses. IDG Marketing Services helps industry-leading IT companies build international brand recognition by developing global integrated marketing programs via IDG's print, online and exposition products worldwide. Further information about the company can be found at www.idg.com. 1/24/99

Dedication

To Rael, for making it possible.

Author's Acknowledgments

I'd like to thank the team of editors, software folks, family, friends, and other talented people who made this edition of *FrontPage 2000 For Dummies* run so smoothly. My thanks to Project Editor Nate Holdread, who, despite a very full plate, managed to be available whenever I needed help. I'd like to thank Lee Musick for checking the text for technical accuracy, and Elizabeth Kuball for her thorough copyediting. Many more people helped put this book together than I can list here; thank you all.

The Microsoft FrontPage and Office teams were extremely helpful and responsive. I am especially grateful to Nancy Buchanan for her help and warm vibes; Courtney Crawford, Bryan DeLuca, Paul Seymour, Yonas Seme, and Doug Dearing for their commitment to a strong beta program; and Shane Frigon for his prompt replies to my e-mails.

My thanks to the folks at Studio B Productions for their advocacy and support. I'd also like to thank DNAI (www.dnai.com) for steady-as-a-rock Internet service.

As ever, the biggest Gratitude Prize goes to my family and friends. I am so lucky to be surrounded by such warm, loving, and intelligent people.

Finally, I'd like to thank all the readers who have written me with questions, comments, and suggestions for improving the book. I appreciate that so many of you take the time to share your thoughts. My e-mailbox is always open: webpub@ashaland.com.

Publisher's Acknowledgments

We're proud of this book; please register your comments through our IDG Books Worldwide Online Registration Form located at http://my2cents.dummies.com.

Some of the people who helped bring this book to market include the following:

Acquisitions, Editorial, and Media Development

Project Editor: Nate Holdread
   (Previous Edition: Kelly Ewing)

Acquisitions Editors: Jill Pisoni,
   Steven H. Hayes

Copy Editor: Elizabeth Netedu Kuball

Technical Editor: Lee Musick

Media Development Editor: Marita Ellixson

Associate Permissions Editor:
   Carmen Krikorian

Media Development Coordinator:
   Megan Roney

Editorial Manager: Mary C. Corder

Media Development Manager:
   Heather Heath Dismore

Editorial Assistant: Alison Walthall

Production

Project Coordinator: Valery Bourke

Layout and Graphics: Linda M. Boyer,
   J. Tyler Connor, Kelly Hardesty, Angela F.
   Hunckler, Brent Savage, Brian Torwelle

Proofreaders: Kelli Botta, Jennifer Mahern,
   Nancy Price, Rebecca Senninger,
   Toni Settle, Janet M. Withers

Indexer: Infodex Indexing Services Inc.

Special Help: Publication Services

General and Administrative

IDG Books Worldwide, Inc.: John Kilcullen, CEO; Steven Berkowitz, President and Publisher

IDG Books Technology Publishing Group: Richard Swadley, Senior Vice President and Publisher; Walter Bruce III, Vice President and Associate Publisher; Steven Sayre, Associate Publisher; Joseph Wikert, Associate Publisher; Mary Bednarek, Branded Product Development Director; Mary Corder, Editorial Director

IDG Books Consumer Publishing Group: Roland Elgey, Senior Vice President and Publisher; Kathleen A. Welton, Vice President and Publisher; Kevin Thornton, Acquisitions Manager; Kristin A. Cocks, Editorial Director

IDG Books Internet Publishing Group: Brenda McLaughlin, Senior Vice President and Group Publisher; Diane Graves Steele, Vice President and Associate Publisher; Sofia Marchant, Online Marketing Manager

IDG Books Production for Dummies Press: Michael R. Britton, Vice President of Production; Debbie Stailey, Associate Director of Production; Cindy L. Phipps, Manager of Project Coordination, Production Proofreading, and Indexing; Shelley Lea, Supervisor of Graphics and Design; Debbie J. Gates, Production Systems Specialist; Robert Springer, Supervisor of Proofreading; Laura Carpenter, Production Control Manager; Tony Augsburger, Supervisor of Reprints and Bluelines

Dummies Packaging and Book Design: Patty Page, Manager, Promotions Marketing

♦

The publisher would like to give special thanks to Patrick J. McGovern, without whom this book would not have been possible.

Contents at a Glance

Introduction 1

Part I: Getting Friendly with FrontPage 7
Chapter 1: Weaving a FrontPage Web 9
Chapter 2: Web Management 101 27
Chapter 3: Playing with Web Pages 47

Part II: Creating Web Pages That Make You Look Like a Genius 67
Chapter 4: Web Design Fundamentals 69
Chapter 5: Tweaking Your Text 79
Chapter 6: Hyperlinks: Your Web Site's Ticket to Ride 103
Chapter 7: You Oughta Be in Pictures 129
Chapter 8: Creating an Image Map 159
Chapter 9: You Don't Have to Take Wood Shop to Build a Table 165
Chapter 10: Forms Aren't Only for the IRS 187
Chapter 11: I've Been Framed! 219

Part III: Nifty Web Additions 235
Chapter 12: Playing in the FrontPage Theme Park 237
Chapter 13: Eye-Popping Extras: Multimedia, Dynamic HTML, and Style Sheets . .249
Chapter 14: Cool Components 269

Part IV: Taking Your Web Site to a New Level 289
Chapter 15: Sharing Access to Your Web Site 291
Chapter 16: Making Your Worldwide Debut 307

Part V: The Part of Tens 319
Chapter 17: Ten Things You Can Do with Your Web Site 321
Chapter 18: Ten Web Spots You Don't Want to Miss 325

Part VI: Appendixes 329

Appendix A: Installing FrontPage 331
Appendix B: What's on the CD 339

Index 345

IDG Books Worldwide, Inc., End-User License Agreement 378

Book Registration Information ....Back of Book

Cartoons at a Glance

By Rich Tennant

The 5th Wave By Rich Tennant

"Excuse me — is anyone here NOT talking about FrontPage?"

page 7

The 5th Wave By Rich Tennant

"FRANKLY, I'M NOT SURE THIS IS THE WAY TO ENHANCE OUR COLOR GRAPHICS."

page 235

The 5th Wave By Rich Tennant

"I couldn't say anything. They were in here with that FrontPage program we bought them that encourages artistic expression."

page 67

The 5th Wave By Rich Tennant

"I found these two in the multimedia lab morphing faculty members into farm animals."

page 289

The 5th Wave By Rich Tennant

"He found a dog site over an hour ago and has been in a staring contest ever since."

page 329

The 5th Wave By Rich Tennant

LARRY KING LIVE

"OK LARRY, ENOUGH ABOUT THE ELECTION. LET'S TALK INTERNET BROWSERS. NEITHER ONE OF THE TWO BIG ONES ADEQUATELY REPRESENTS THE USER, WHICH IS WHY I PLAN TO LAUNCH A THIRD ALTERNATIVE—THE 'REFORM BROWSER.'"

page 319

Fax: 978-546-7747 • E-mail: the5wave@tiac.net

Table of Contents

Introduction 1
  About This Book 1
  Conventions Used in This Book 2
  What You're Not to Read 3
  Foolish Assumptions 3
  How This Book Is Organized 3
      Part I: Getting Friendly with FrontPage 4
      Part II: Creating Web Pages That Make You Look Like a Genius 4
      Part III: Nifty Web Additions 4
      Part IV: Taking Your Web Site to a New Level 4
      Part V: The Part of Tens 4
      Part VI: Appendixes 5
  Icons Used in This Book 5
  Where to Go from Here 6

Part I: Getting Friendly with FrontPage 7

Chapter 1: Weaving a FrontPage Web 9
  Exactly What Is Web Publishing? 10
  Creating Your First FrontPage Web Site 10
  Creating a New Web Site 14
      Creating a Web site by using a template 14
      Creating a Web site by using a wizard 16
      Creating a Web site from scratch 18
  Importing an Existing Web Site into FrontPage 19
  Creating a Subweb 21
  Open, Sesame! 23
  Closing a Web Site 25
  Deleting a Web Site 25
  Exiting FrontPage 26

Chapter 2: Web Management 101 27
  Taking In the Views 27
      Page View 27
      Folders View 28

Reports View 29
Navigation View 33
Hyperlinks View 37
Tasks View 39
Working with Web Site Files and Folders 39
Adding existing files and folders to a Web site 39
Creating new folders 41
Renaming files and folders 42
Converting a folder into a subweb (and vice-versa) 43
Deleting files and folders 44
Backing up Web sites 45

Chapter 3: Playing with Web Pages **47**
Creating a New Web Page 47
Using a template to create pages 48
Creating blank pages 49
Opening an Existing Web Page 49
Opening a page that's part of the current Web site 50
Opening a page stored on your computer or network 50
Opening a page from the World Wide Web 52
Converting Other Documents into Web Pages 54
Previewing a Page 57
Previewing pages using the Preview tab 58
Previewing pages using a web browser 58
Printing a Page 60
Saving a Page 61
Saving a page on your computer or network 62
Saving a page as part of a "live" Web site 64
Saving a page as a FrontPage template 65

Part II: Creating Web Pages That Make You Look Like a Genius *67*

Chapter 4: Web Design Fundamentals **69**
Clients and Servers 101 69
Cross-Platform Mania 71
Web truism #1: Your visitors use different computers 72
Web truism #2: Your visitors use different browsers 72
Web truism #3: Your visitors connect to the Internet at
different speeds 73
Web truism #4: Your visitors come from diverse cultures 74
Five Steps to a Brilliant Web Site 74
Give your site a purpose 74
Remember your visitors 75
Cultivate an image 75

Make your site easy to navigate 75
Plan for the future 76
Evidence That HTML Is Easy 76

Chapter 5: Tweaking Your Text 79
What Does the Page View Do? 79
Getting Started 81
Adding text to a page 81
Sanity-saving shortcuts 82
Keeping Web Browser and Server Compatibility in Mind 83
Foolin' with Fonts 85
Using font tools 85
Changing text font 87
Being bold (or italic or underlined) 88
Changing text size 88
Changing text color 89
Changing character spacing 91
Creating Stylish Paragraphs 92
The List of Lists 93
Bulleted and numbered lists 93
Definition lists 94
List-in-a-list 95
Collapsible outlines 96
Adjusting Paragraph Alignment, Indenting, and Spacing 96
Adding Borders and Shading 98
Inserting Symbols 101
Inserting Comments 101
Inserting Horizontal Lines 102

Chapter 6: Hyperlinks: Your Web Site's Ticket to Ride 103
The Hyperlink Two-Step 103
Linking to a page inside the current FrontPage Web site 104
Linking to a page on the World Wide Web 106
Linking to a downloadable file 107
Linking to an e-mail address 108
Editing Hyperlinks 109
Changing hyperlink text 109
Changing the destination of a hyperlink 109
Changing hyperlink color 110
Adding a rollover effect 113
Do-It-Yourself Hyperlink Repair 114
Verifying and fixing hyperlinks throughout your Web site 115
Checking individual hyperlinks 118
Unlinking Hyperlinks 119

Using Bookmarks 119
    Creating bookmarks 119
    Linking to a bookmark 120
    Dismantling bookmarks 121
Helping Visitors Find Their Way with Navigation Bars 121
    Inserting a navigation bar in your page 122
    Adding navigation bar links 124
    Changing navigation bar text 125
    Removing navigation bar links 126
    Using shared borders 126

Chapter 7: You Oughta Be in Pictures 129
Understanding the Quirks of Web Graphics 130
    Getting to know the Web-friendly graphic formats 130
    Picky palettes 132
    Keeping graphics zippy 132
    Practicing graphic restraint 133
Adding a Picture to Your Page 134
    Inserting a picture that's stored inside the current
    FrontPage Web site 135
    Inserting pictures stored elsewhere on your computer 136
    Grabbing a picture off the World Wide Web 137
    Using the Clip Art Gallery 138
Controlling How a Picture Is Displayed 140
    Aligning a picture with surrounding text 140
    Controlling how text wraps around a picture 143
    Controlling the amount of space surrounding a picture 143
    Adding (or removing) a border around a picture 144
    Setting display dimensions 144
    Specifying ALT text 146
    Placing a text label on top of a picture 148
Editing the Picture Itself 148
    Creating a transparent GIF 149
    Creating an interlaced GIF 150
    Cropping a picture 151
    Applying a special effect to a picture 152
    Launching a separate graphics program 152
Deleting a Picture 153
Using Thumbnails to Speed Up Your Page 153
    Inserting a thumbnail in your page 154
    Changing FrontPage's thumbnail settings 154
Creating a Background Image 156

Chapter 8: Creating an Image Map 159
What Is an Image Map? 159
Choosing the Right Picture 160

Creating Hotspots 161
    Drawing hotspots 161
    Drawing labeled hotspots 162
    Moving hotspots 163
    Resizing hotspots 163
    Deleting hotspots 164
  Setting the Default Hyperlink 164

Chapter 9: You Don't Have to Take Wood Shop to Build a Table . . .165
  What's a Table Good For? 165
  Creating a Table 167
    Using the Insert Table button 167
    Using the Insert Table command 168
    Drawing a table 169
    Converting existing text into a table 170
  Inserting Stuff into a Table (Including Another Table) 170
  Table Tinkering 171
    Aligning a table on the page 171
    Creating a floating table 172
    Padded cells 173
    Adding space between cells 174
    Setting border thickness 175
    Setting table height and width 175
  Fiddling with Cells, Columns, and Rows 177
    Selecting table parts 177
    Adding new columns 178
    Adding new rows 178
    Adding new cells 178
    Deleting cells, columns, and rows 178
    Aligning cell contents 179
    Changing cell, row, and column dimensions 179
    Merging and splitting cells 181
  Adding a Caption 182
  Adding Color to a Table 182
    Changing the background 183
    Changing border color 183
  Deleting a Table 185

Chapter 10: Forms Aren't Only for the IRS 187
  How Do Forms Work? 187
  Creating a Form 188
    Using a form page template 189
    Using the Form Page Wizard 189
    Adding a form to an existing page 192
  Working with Form Fields 192
    One-line text boxes 193
    Scrolling text boxes 198

Check boxes 199
Radio buttons 200
Drop-down menus 203
Specifying What Happens to Form Results 206
Adding Submit and Reset buttons 206
Designating where form results go 208
Creating a Confirmation Page 214
Using the Confirmation Form template 216
Adding confirmation fields to an existing page 217
Making Sure Your Form Works 217

Chapter 11: I've Been Framed! **219**
What Are Frames? 219
Creating a Framed Web Site: The Game Plan 220
Creating the Frames Page 221
Filling Frames with Content Pages 223
Using a new page 223
Using an existing page 224
Tweaking the Frames Page 224
Adding new frames 224
Deleting frames 225
Changing frame properties 225
Changing the target frame 228
Creating an Alternative for Browsers That Don't "Do" Frames ...231
Saving a Framed Web Site 232
Previewing a Framed Web Site 233

Part III: Nifty Web Additions 235

Chapter 12: Playing in the FrontPage Theme Park **237**
Touring the Themes Dialog Box 237
Applying a Theme to Your Web Site 240
Inserting a Page Banner 241
Modifying Themes 242
Modifying theme colors 242
Choosing different theme graphics 245
Changing theme text styles 246

**Chapter 13: Eye-Popping Extras: Multimedia, Dynamic HTML,
and Style Sheets** **249**
Fun with Multimedia 250
Fun with video 250
Music to your ears 253
Adding Pizzazz with Dynamic HTML 255

Adding a Page Transition 256
Precisely Positioning Stuff in Your Page 257
        Creating a floating object 258
        Using absolute positioning 260
        Using relative positioning 261
Working with Style Sheets 263
        Creating and modifying styles in the current page 264
        Applying styles to one or more pages in your site 266

Chapter 14: Cool Components **269**
What's a Component? 269
        Calling in the Banner Ad Manager 270
        Tracking visits with a hit counter 273
        Inserting a hover button 275
        Creating a marquee 278
        Include Page 280
        Scheduled Include Page and Scheduled Picture 282
        Substitution 284
        Adding a keyword search to your Web site 287

Part IV: Taking Your Web Site to a New Level *289*

Chapter 15: Sharing Access to Your Web Site **291**
Collaborating with a Web-Building Team 291
        Assigning pages and setting review status 292
        Using the Tasks View to keep track of workflow 294
        Checking documents in and out .296
        Automating site updates with the Categories Component 298
Keeping Your Web Site Secure 301
        Setting permissions 302
        Changing permissions 304
        Changing your password 304

Chapter 16: Making Your Worldwide Debut **307**
What "Publishing Your Web Site" Means 307
The Skinny on FrontPage Server Extensions 308
Going Public 311
        Excluding unfinished pages from publishing 311
        Publishing your Web site 312
You're Live! 315
Keeping Your Web Site Fresh 316

Part V: The Part of Tens *319*

Chapter 17: Ten Things You Can Do with Your Web Site 321

Make a Million Bucks 321
Keep in Touch 321
Impress Potential Employers 322
Impress Geeky Friends 322
"Wire" Your Company 322
Spread the Word about a Good Cause 322
Indulge Your Artistic Side 323
Incite World Revolution 323
Erect a Personal Monument 323

Chapter 18: Ten Web Spots You Don't Want to Miss 325

Microsoft FrontPage Home Page 325
Microsoft Support Online 325
Netscape Web Site 326
Know the Code: HTML For Beginners 326
Builder.com 326
Webmonkey 326
Learn the Net 327
Search.com 327
Download.com 327
Dummies.com 327
Web Publishing Online Resource 328

Part VI: Appendixes *329*

Appendix A: Installing FrontPage 331

System Requirements 331
Installing FrontPage 2000 on Your Computer 332
Using FrontPage Together with a Local Web Server 334
Using the Microsoft Personal Web Server 4.0 334
"Publishing" your Web site to a local web server 335
Creating and opening Web sites directly from the local
web server 337

Appendix B: What's on the CD .339

System Requirements 339
What You'll Find on the CD 340
FrontPage 2000 For Dummies Web Links Page 340
Bonus chapter: Can We Talk? 340
Bonus chapter: Advanced Additions 340

Internet tools 341
Utilities 341
How to Use the CD 342
If You Have Problems (Of the CD Kind) 343

Index *345*

IDG Books Worldwide, Inc., End-User
License Agreement *378*

Book Registration Information ....*Back of Book*

Introduction

● ●

A few years ago, geeks, academics, and soda-fueled computer jocks popu-
lated the Internet. Today, everyone — from CEOs to seventh-grade
students to weekend technology fiends — wants to get online. And people
don't just want to surf. They each want to carve out a unique personal space:
They want a Web site.

Until recently, only the technically gifted and artistically inclined attempted
to publish sites on the Web. If you wanted to look good on the Web, you
needed either techno-gusto or the bucks to commission someone who had it.

Not anymore. FrontPage 2000, the latest incarnation of Microsoft's popular
Web site creation tool, brings new ease to Web publishing. Without any
knowledge of HTML (the language used to create Web pages), you can use
FrontPage to build and manage a beautiful and sophisticated Web site, complete with exciting effects you see on those *other* sites.

FrontPage is a hefty, powerful piece of software. And like a lot of powerful
software, FrontPage is easy to use — *after* you figure out what all those buttons and menu items do.

Enter *FrontPage 2000 For Dummies*.

About This Book

You won't find lists of obscure technical terms or pages of unrelated details
here. I concentrate on the practical information and the FrontPage features
you need to know to build a well-designed, attractive, easy-to-navigate Web
site. I figure you're not interested in becoming a FrontPage expert; you want
to get up to speed with FrontPage 2000 quickly and easily so you can get your
project underway *now*. And why not have a little fun while you're at it?

You don't need to start at Chapter 1; just flip to the section of the book that
tells you what you want to know. If you're new to Web publishing, you may
want to skim the book first to get a sense of what building a Web site entails,
and then read the stuff that looks particularly interesting. If you're the adven-
turous type, fire up FrontPage, push all the buttons, play with all the menu
items, and refer to the book when you get stumped.

Conventions Used in This Book

I use a few text conventions throughout the book:

- ✔ A notation like "Choose File⇨Open" is a condensed version of "from the File menu, choose the Open command."

- ✔ When I say "Press Ctrl+N," it means "while holding down the Ctrl key on your keyboard, press the letter N."

- ✔ If you are trying to cut down on your mouse usage, the underlined letters in menu bar notations indicate *keyboard shortcuts*. To use a keyboard shortcut, do this: While holding down the Alt key on your keyboard, simultaneously press the first underlined letter to open the menu. Then release the Alt key and press the next underlined letter. For example, to use keyboard shortcuts instead of choosing File⇨Open, you press Alt+F and then you press O.

FrontPage often gives you more than one way to tackle a particular task. For example, choosing a menu item, clicking a toolbar button, pressing a keyboard shortcut, or right-clicking an item and then choosing an option from the pop-up menu that appears might all accomplish the same thing. In this book, I generally tell you the easiest way to carry out a particular task. If you prefer to use an alternate method, by all means, go ahead.

By the way, I wrote this book using Microsoft Windows 98. If you're a Windows 95 or NT user, not to worry. The step-by-step instructions in this book apply to both Windows 98 and Windows 95/NT. Notice, however, that some of the standard Windows dialog boxes look a little different in the book than they do on your screen. For the purposes of this book, the differences are only cosmetic; you will be able to work through all the examples just fine.

This is a sidebar

Text tucked inside a gray-shaded box is called a *sidebar*. These sidebars highlight important information that's related to the topic being covered.

What You're Not to Read

For those of you who want a little more detail, I flag discussions about advanced or technical topics with the Technical Stuff icon. These discussions are purely optional; if you're not interested, feel free to pass up the information.

Foolish Assumptions

FrontPage 2000 For Dummies helps you jump right into using FrontPage. I therefore make a few assumptions about who you are and what you already know how to do.

- ✔ **You've developed a cordial relationship with your computer and its associates: the mouse, keyboard, monitor, and modem.** You ask the computer nicely to do things by pressing keys and clicking the mouse button, and it usually complies. You're comfortable with the basic workings of Windows 98/95/NT such as using the Start menu, double-clicking items, getting around the Windows desktop, using Windows Explorer, clicking buttons in toolbars, and choosing commands from menu bars.

- ✔ **You have an Internet connection through your workplace, school, an Internet Service Provider (ISP) or an online service, and you've spent some time surfing the Web.** You don't necessarily understand how the Internet works, but you have a staff person at your Internet Service Provider, company techie, or nerdy neighbor to call when you have a problem.

- ✔ **You have FrontPage sitting in a box in a highly visible location on your desk so that passersby will see it and comment upon how technically savvy you are.** If you're brave, you've installed FrontPage on your computer (if not, I give you directions).

- ✔ **You've never tried your hand at Web publishing.** If you've tried Web publishing, you've never done it with FrontPage. If you have worked with FrontPage, you were perplexed after fiddling with the program, rushed to the bookstore, and are reading this book right now.

How This Book Is Organized

FrontPage 2000 For Dummies contains all the information you need to create great-looking Web sites with FrontPage 2000. FrontPage is no small topic, so I divide the subject into easily chewable parts.

Part I: Getting Friendly with FrontPage

Part I introduces you to FrontPage and helps you become comfortable with the program's interface and basic workings.

Part II: Creating Web Pages That Make You Look Like a Genius

Part II familiarizes you with the fundamentals of Web design and the page formatting and layout capabilities of FrontPage. You discover how to add and format text, create hyperlinks and navigation bars, insert graphics and clickable images, and build tables (the electronic kind, not the wooden kind). You find out how to create interactive forms that let your visitors communicate with you. You also become acquainted with frames and how they can make your Web site easier to navigate.

Part III: Nifty Web Additions

Part III shows you how to add optional-but-impressive capabilities to your Web site. You become familiar with FrontPage themes (collections of colors and graphics that give your Web site style and polish). You find out how to pump up your Web site with multimedia, Dynamic HTML, and Cascading Style Sheets. You get familiar with Components, sets of ready-made tools you can plop into your Web site.

Part IV: Taking Your Web Site to a New Level

Part IV shows you how to control access to your Web site and take advantage of FrontPage workgroup and collaboration features. You also discover how to make your Web site visible on the World Wide Web.

Part V: The Part of Tens

The Part of Tens is full of highly-useful-but-not-mandatory stuff. Read this part with your feet up on the desk, this book in one hand, and a tall, cool drink in your other hand. Find out about ten things you can do with your Web site and ten Web spots you don't want to miss.

Part VI: Appendixes

Read Appendix A if you haven't yet installed FrontPage and you want more help than the documentation included in the box gives you.

Appendix B describes the goodies you'll find on the CD-ROM tucked away in the back of this book, including two bonus chapters.

Icons Used in This Book

Icon-studded notes and sidebars highlight special information.

This icon points out important details you don't want to forget.

Here, you find a time-saving FrontPage shortcut. Or you may receive a design tip you can use to add oomph to your Web site.

Don't worry, your computer doesn't explode when you see this icon. The icon alerts you to a potential FrontPage or Web publishing sticky spot.

The information flagged with this icon is for those of you who want to dig a little deeper into the technical aspects of Web publishing. If you just want to get that Web site published, skip this stuff.

The World Wide Web is a veritable cornucopia of Web publishing and FrontPage information. Throughout the book, I point to Web sites that offer additional help, free software tools, and information about related topics. (To save you time and to encourage you to visit these sites, I include on the CD a Web page that contains links to each Web site. See Appendix B for details.)

Some FrontPage and Web publishing effects are only visible inside a page if the visitor uses a particular kind of web browser, or if the site is stored on a particular type of web server (I explain all this in more detail later in the book). I use this icon to point out features that require a certain type of web browser or server program to be able to work.

Where to Go from Here

Enough preamble . . . it's time to get that Web site started! If you haven't already installed FrontPage, turn to Appendix A for instructions.

It's my wish that this book gives you the confidence and skills to create whatever Web site you envision. I'd love to hear how you're doing — you can reach me by sending e-mail to webpub@ashaland.com. You can also visit my Web site at www.ashaland.com.

If the instructions listed in the book don't exactly match what you see on your screen, check to see that your computer and Internet connection are working properly. If everything checks out, you may have stumbled upon a beta change. I wrote this book using a prerelease or *beta* version of FrontPage 2000. Although several editors and I tested all the examples in this book using the final beta version, the version of FrontPage 2000 you bought at the store may contain minor differences from the version I used to write the book.

I list all beta changes and errata on the Beta Changes and Errata page, located at www.ashaland.com/webpub/errata.html. Please check this page, and if you don't see what you need listed there, send me an e-mail. Your note will help me ensure that this book is as perfect as it can be; plus, I can integrate the bug fixes into future printings of *FrontPage 2000 For Dummies.*

Part I
Getting Friendly with FrontPage

The 5th Wave   By Rich Tennant

"Excuse me – is anyone here NOT talking about FrontPage?"

In this part . . .

Faced with mastering a new piece of software, the scariest moment probably occurs after you launch the program for the first time and stare at all those unfamiliar buttons and menu items. The situation's kind of like walking into a party and not recognizing anyone.

In this part, you get fully acquainted with FrontPage. I make the introductions, pass around a few refreshments, and pretty soon you're going to feel right at home.

Chapter 1

Weaving a FrontPage Web

. . . .

In This Chapter

▶ Understanding Web publishing

▶ Creating your first Web site

▶ Simplifying site creation with templates and Wizards

▶ Using FrontPage to work with an existing Web site

▶ Creating a subweb

▶ Opening and closing a FrontPage Web site

▶ Deleting a Web site

▶ Exiting FrontPage

. . . .

*W*ith so many people jumping on the Web publishing bandwagon, you can easily feel like you've been left in the dust. Just a few years ago, many of us used our computers as glorified typewriters and calculators. Today, regular folks are hitching the dusty, old desktop machine to a modem and are cranking out publications with worldwide distribution and impact. What happened?

The World Wide Web happened. Now that the Web has come into popular use, desktop computers are no longer isolated islands of letters, recipes, and personal finance records — computers can now hook you into a new world of information and communication possibilities. You've already heard the hype: The Web is *big,* and everybody who's anybody wants to be a part of the excitement.

So where does that leave you? If you're edging your way into the Internet Age (or being dragged in, kicking and screaming, by your employer or your kids), you're in for a pleasant surprise: Creating your own Web site with FrontPage 2000 is easy and fun.

In this chapter, you get your feet wet with FrontPage. You fire up the program and experience just how easy it is to get started on your new Web site. You find out how to import an existing Web site into FrontPage, and how to open, close, and delete Web sites.

Exactly What Is Web Publishing?

Before you hang your shingle as a FrontPage Web publisher, it helps to understand what you're actually doing when you create and publish a Web site.

No doubt, you've already seen a Web site. Web sites are the places you visit as you make your way around the World Wide Web. Some folks refer to their own Web sites as their *home pages*. FrontPage refers to Web sites simply as *Webs*. A FrontPage Web is simply a Web site that was created in or is maintained with FrontPage. A FrontPage Web is no different from any other Web site, aside from the capabilities that FrontPage can add.

As a book is made up of individual pages, a Web site is made up of individual files called *Web pages*. Web pages contain the text, pictures, and other content you see when you visit a Web site.

As you construct a Web site, you create Web pages and then string them together with *hyperlinks*. Hyperlinks are the highlighted words and pictures inside the page that visitors can click to jump to a different location, page, or Web site.

After your site is complete, you *publish* it. In other words, you make the site visible to the rest of the world on the World Wide Web. This isn't automatic. For a Web site to be live, you must transfer the site's files from your computer to a host computer called a *web server*.

Many people gain access to a host web server by signing up for an account with an Internet Service Provider (or *ISP*) that makes web server space available to its users. Others use a web server maintained by their workplace or school.

Creating Your First FrontPage Web Site

If you read the previous section of this chapter, you have a general idea about how Web publishing works. You don't need more than a fuzzy sense at this point — the process will become clearer as you become comfortable with FrontPage. You're now ready to get started with FrontPage by creating your first Web site.

If this feels like getting thrown into the deep end before learning to swim, relax. Creating your first Web site — even if you don't yet know what kind of information you want the Web site to contain — is the easiest way to become familiar with how FrontPage looks and acts. As you get acquainted with the program, you can change any aspect of the Web site or even delete the Web site and start over.

To create your first FrontPage Web site, follow these steps:

1. **Launch FrontPage by clicking the Start button and then choosing** **Programs⇨Microsoft FrontPage.**

   FrontPage launches. Your screen should look like Figure 1-1. A new, blank Web page named new_page_1.htm appears in the program's main window with its cursor blinking patiently.

   (If your screen doesn't look like this, then, in the FrontPage Views bar, click the Page button.)

Views bar   Title bar   Menu bar   Standard toolbar ⌐ Formatting toolbar

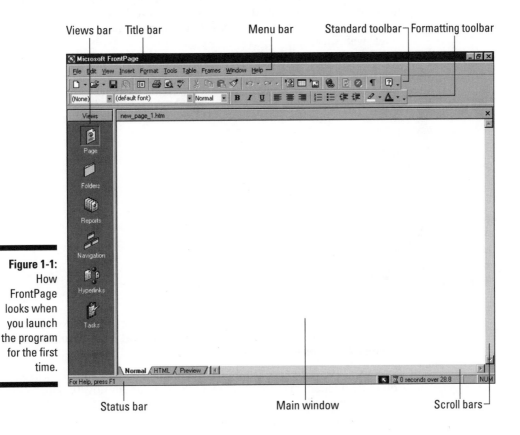

Figure 1-1:
How
FrontPage
looks when
you launch
the program
for the first
time.

Status bar   Main window   Scroll bars ⌐

2. Insert some text into the page (that is, start typing).

Not sure what to say? How about "Welcome to My First Web Site" for starters? You can always change the text later.

3. In the Standard toolbar, click Save.

The Save As dialog box appears (see Figure 1-2). The dialog box prompts you to save your new Web page in the My Webs folder. When you installed FrontPage, the Setup program created this folder specifically to hold your first FrontPage Web site.

Based on your computer's operating system or setup, FrontPage may save new Web sites in a different folder by default.

If you have a web server program installed on your computer (such as the Microsoft Personal Web Server, a web server program that comes with Windows 98), FrontPage saves new Web sites in the default location http://<servername>/myweb, where <servername> is the name of your web server. Refer to your web server program's documentation for the location on your hard drive of the web server's content directory. In Appendix A, I discuss why and how to use FrontPage in conjunction with a local web server.

Figure 1-2:
The Save As
dialog box.

4. In the dialog box's File Name text box, type index **(this is the filename most web servers recognize as a Web site's initial page, also known as the site's *home page*).**

When you save the page, FrontPage automatically adds the .htm extension to the filename you enter here. I talk more about how to name Web pages in Chapter 3.

5. To change the page title, click Change.

The Set Page Title dialog box appears.

6. **In the dialog box's Page Title text box, enter a new title.**

   Choose a title that describes the content and purpose of the page (something like *My First Web Site: Home Page*). In Chapter 3, I go into more detail about how to choose a good page title.

7. **Click OK to close the Set Page Title dialog box.**

8. **Click Save.**

   The Save As dialog box closes, and FrontPage saves the page. If it's not already visible, the Folder List appears and displays a list of the folders and files that make up your first Web site (see Figure 1-3).

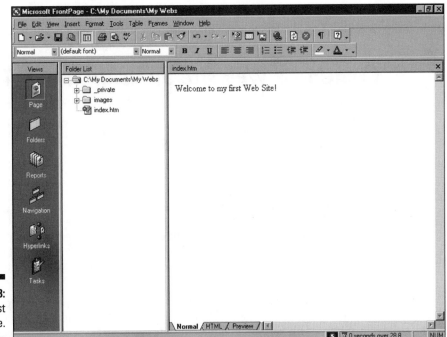

Figure 1-3:
Your first
Web site.

Congratulations — you've just laid the groundwork for your first FrontPage Web site! From here, you can do one of three things:

✔ Add more content — text, pictures, and anything else you want to display in your Web site — to the page you just started. The chapters in Part II show you how.

✔ Fill out your Web site with more new Web pages. I explain how to create new pages in Chapter 3.

✔ Set your first Web site aside and create a completely new Web site (read the next section of this chapter for details).

Creating a New Web Site

Creating a new Web site with FrontPage can be likened to sitting at a typewriter (if you still have one of those antiquated pieces of equipment) with a blank piece of paper tucked in the carriage. Sometimes brilliant concepts, fully formed, spring from your brain and land right on the page. At other times you need a little nudge to get those creative juices flowing.

FrontPage provides a comfortable balance of direction and flexibility. If you want help getting started, use a Web site template to crank out a boilerplate Web site, complete with linked pages, to which you simply add your own text and graphics. If you need hand-holding, call on a FrontPage Wizard to guide you through setting up a site. If you bristle at the prospect of an off-the-rack Web site, you can easily build your own site from scratch.

Creating a Web site by using a template

Templates lay the groundwork for "canned" Web sites you can customize to suit your own needs. Admittedly, sites created with FrontPage templates lack the flair of custom-designed Web sites, but they give you a good foundation on which to begin building.

FrontPage comes with three templates:

- **Customer Support Web:** The Customer Support Web enables companies to broadcast product help and information over the Internet. Customers access the Web site to read product news, have questions answered, brainstorm with other product users, and more. The template is geared toward the needs of software companies but can easily be adapted for any type of business.

- **Personal Web:** Use this template as the basis for a personal home page. The Personal Web template contains space for a photograph collection, personal information, and a list of favorite sites.

- **Project Web:** The Project Web tracks the status of a project and includes space for project team members, status reports, schedules, an archive, a search form, and a discussion forum. This template is well suited for use on an *intranet* — a company's internal network accessible only to employees and other insiders.

To create a new Web site by using a template, follow these steps:

1. **With FrontPage running, choose File⇨New⇨Web.**

    The New dialog box appears (see Figure 1-4).

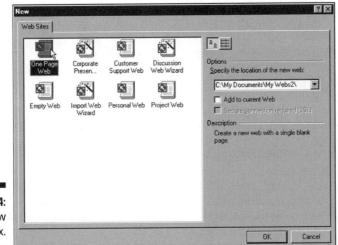

Figure 1-4:
The New
dialog box.

2. **In the dialog box's Web Sites area, click the template you want to use.**

   A description of the template appears in the Description area of the dialog box.

3. **In the Specify the Location of the New Web list box, enter the location of the new Web site.**

   To save the Web site inside a new or existing folder on your hard drive, enter the folder's file path. If you're not sure how file paths work, refer to the sidebar "File path 101" later in this chapter.

   If you save your new Web site inside an existing folder that already contains files, the files themselves are not affected, but FrontPage treats the files as part of the new Web site. If, however, you specify a folder that already contains a FrontPage Web site, FrontPage prompts you to choose a different location.

   To keep your Web site distinct (and your hard drive well organized), I recommend saving the site in its own unique folder.

4. **Click OK.**

   Depending on the file path you entered in Step 3, one of the following things happens:

   • If you're saving the Web site in a new folder, the New dialog box closes, and FrontPage saves the new Web site in the location you specified.

- If you're saving the Web site in an existing folder that doesn't already contain a FrontPage Web site, the Microsoft FrontPage dialog box appears, explaining that the program needs to convert the folder into a FrontPage Web in order to proceed. Click Yes. The Microsoft FrontPage and New dialog boxes close. FrontPage converts the folder into a FrontPage Web and then saves the new Web site in the location you specified.

After FrontPage saves the new Web site, the site's files and folders appear in the Folder List. If another Web site is already open in FrontPage when you create a new Web site, the new Web site appears in a separate FrontPage window.

Web pages that come courtesy of a FrontPage template already contain text, hyperlinks, and graphics, which you can change or rearrange to suit your own needs. Chapter 3 shows you how to open pages, and the chapters in Part II tell you everything you need to know about working with Web page content.

Creating a Web site by using a Wizard

A Wizard takes you through a process of creating a Web site by presenting you with a series of dialog boxes that prompt you to fill in and select different options. FrontPage comes with Wizards for its two most elaborate Web site templates: the Corporate Presence Web site and the Discussion Web site.

- **Corporate Presence Wizard:** The Corporate Presence Wizard sets up a corporate Web site complete with graphics. Depending on the options you choose, the site may contain anything from a product catalog to a discussion forum to company contact information.

- **Discussion Web Wizard:** The Discussion Web Wizard creates an interactive site where visitors post comments and read others' replies about a given topic. Visitors are also able to search for specific information in the text of the Discussion Web replies. Refer to "Can We Talk" on the CD to see how to create a discussion group.

To create a Web site by using a Wizard, follow these steps:

1. **With FrontPage running, choose File➪New➪Web.**

   The New dialog box appears.

2. **In the Web Sites area of the dialog box, click the Wizard you want to**

File path 101

When you create a Web site in FrontPage, the program prompts you to save the site's pages in a folder on your hard drive. You specify the location of the folder using a notation called a *file path*. The file path describes the location of a file or folder by listing the name of the drive on which the file is stored, followed by the name of the folder (or, in the case of a single file, the filename). If the folder or file is stored inside another folder, that folder name is preceded by a backslash (\). So, for example, instead of describing the location of a file by saying "the file named `index.htm` that's stored inside the My Webs folder inside the My Documents folder on the C drive," you can just say `C:\My Documents\My Webs\index.htm`.

use.

3. **In the <u>S</u>pecify the Location of the New Web list box, enter the location of the new Web site.**

   If you're not sure how to specify the new Web site's location, read Step 3 in the preceding section, "Creating a Web site by using a template."

4. **Click OK.**

   The dialog box closes, and FrontPage pauses to summon the Wizard. In a moment, the introductory Wizard dialog box appears.

   (If, in Step 3, you specified the location of an existing folder, the Microsoft FrontPage dialog box appears prompting you to convert the folder into a FrontPage Web. Click Yes to close the dialog box and proceed.)

5. **In the dialog box, click <u>N</u>ext to proceed to the next step.**

   The next dialog box asks questions about how you want the Web site to look and act.

6. **Answer the Wizard's questions and then click <u>N</u>ext to move on.**

   Proceed through each Wizard dialog box in this manner. If you change your mind a decision you made earlier in the process, return to the previous dialog boxes by clicking Back.

   When you reach the final Wizard dialog box, the Next button appears grayed out.

7. **Click <u>F</u>inish to complete the Web site.**

   Based on your choices, the Wizard creates a new Web site. This process may take a moment or two. Relax. Get a snack. Pretty soon, the Wizard disappears and the Web site appears in FrontPage. If another Web site is already open in FrontPage when you create a new Web site, the new Web site appears in a separate FrontPage window.

Another piece of the puzzle: FrontPage Server Extensions

Certain FrontPage templates and Wizards make use of unique FrontPage features such as keyword site searches and interactive discussion groups. For these and other nifty FrontPage features to function properly, the host web server on which you eventually publish your Web site must have *FrontPage Server Extensions* installed. FrontPage Server Extensions is a set of programs that works together with the host web server. Although you can just as easily publish FrontPage Web sites on servers that don't have FrontPage Server Extensions installed, you can't take advantage of certain extra-cool FrontPage goodies. Throughout the book, I point out features that require the assistance of FrontPage Server Extensions, and I talk in more detail about FrontPage Server Extensions in Chapter 16.

Creating a Web site from scratch

You may already have a vague idea about how you want your Web site to look. A glimmer of an idea is all you need. Templates and Wizards can be helpful, but you may prefer to build your site page by page.

Creating a Web site from scratch is essentially the same process as creating your first Web site (described earlier in this chapter): You create new, blank pages to which you later add text, pictures, and other content.

1. **With FrontPage running, choose File⇨New⇨Web.**

   The New dialog box appears.

2. **In the New dialog box's Web Sites area, click One Page Web.**

   This option creates a new Web site containing a single page: the home page. If you prefer to start *absolutely* from scratch, click Empty Web.

3. **In the Specify the Location of the New Web list box, enter the location of the new Web site.**

   If you're not sure how to specify the new Web site's location, read Step 3 in the section "Creating a Web site by using a template" earlier in this chapter.

4. **Click OK.**

   The dialog box closes, and FrontPage creates a new Web site. If another Web site is already open in FrontPage when you create a new Web site, the new Web site appears in a separate FrontPage window.

(If, in Step 3, you specified the location of an existing folder, the Microsoft FrontPage dialog box appears prompting you to convert the folder into a FrontPage Web. Click Yes to close the dialog box and create the site.)

The stage is now set for you to begin construction on your masterpiece.

Importing an Existing Web Site into FrontPage

If you want to use FrontPage to maintain and update a Web site that was originally assembled using a different program or coded by hand, you must first import that site into FrontPage. The easiest way to accomplish this task is by using the Import Web Wizard, a handy tool that does most of the work for you.

To import a Web site into FrontPage, follow these steps:

1. **With FrontPage running, choose File⇨New⇨Web.**

   The New dialog box appears.

2. **In the dialog box's Web Sites area, click Import Web Wizard.**

3. **In the Specify the Location of the New Web list box, enter the location of the new Web site.**

   If you're not sure how to specify the new Web site's location, read Step 3 in the section "Creating a Web site by using a template" earlier in this chapter.

4. **Click OK.**

   The dialog box closes. After a brief pause, the Import Web Wizard – Choose Source dialog box appears (see Figure 1-5). Here, you specify the location of the Web site that you want to import. The site's files may be stored in a folder on your computer or local network, or the site may already be published on the World Wide Web.

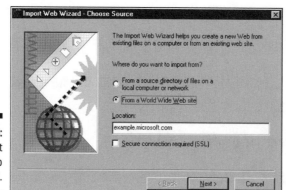

The Import Web Wizard helps you create a new Web from existing files on a computer or from an existing web site.

Where do you want to import from?

○ From a source directory of files on a local computer or network

● From a World Wide Web site

Location:

example.microsoft.com

☐ Secure connection required (SSL)

< Back | Next > | Cancel

Figure 1-5:
The Import
Web
Wizard.

(If, in Step 3, you specified the location of an existing folder, the Microsoft FrontPage dialog box appears prompting you to convert the folder into a FrontPage Web. Click Yes to close the dialog box and proceed.)

5. In the dialog box, specify the current location of the Web site you want to import.

- If the Web site is stored on your computer or local network, click the radio button marked From a Source Directory of Files on a Local Computer or Network, and then type the folder's path in the Location text box.

  If you don't know the folder's location offhand, click Browse to choose from a hierarchical list of folders on your computer or network. If you want the Import Web Wizard to import the files stored in folders *inside* the folder you specified, click the Include Subfolders check box.

- If the site is already live on the World Wide Web, click the From a World Wide Web Site radio button and then, in the Location text box, enter the site's Web address (which looks something like `www.mysite.com`).

If you're about to import a site from the World Wide Web, you must turn on your modem and activate your Internet connection.

6. Click Next.

The next dialog box that appears depends on the location of the Web site you're importing.

- If the site's files are located on your computer or local network, the Import Web Wizard – Edit File List dialog box appears, listing all the files contained in the source folder in a text box. This dialog box enables you to exclude files you don't want to import along with the rest of your Web site. To do so, click the names of the files you don't want to import and then click the Exclude button. To start over with a fresh file list, click the Refresh button.

- If the site is located on the World Wide Web, the Import Web Wizard – Choose Download Amount dialog box appears. This dialog box enables you to control how much of the Web site you want FrontPage to download and import. To limit the levels of sub-folders FrontPage imports, click the Limit to This Page Plus check box and, in the accompanying text box, enter the number of levels. To limit the amount of total file space taken up by the downloaded files, click the Limit To check box and, in the accompanying text box, enter a number of kilobytes. To tell FrontPage to import only the site's Web pages and image files, click the Limit To Text and Image Files check box.

7. **Click Next.**

   The Import Web Wizard – Finish dialog box appears, congratulating you on a job well done. If you want to double-check your choices, click the Back button, otherwise. . . .

8. **Click Finish.**

   The Import Web Wizard performs its magic and, in a moment, your Web site — now a full-fledged FrontPage Web site — appears in FrontPage. (I dare you to say "full-fledged FrontPage Web site" five times fast.) If another Web site is already open in FrontPage when you import a new Web site, the new Web site appears in a separate FrontPage window.

Your Web site is now poised for a FrontPage makeover.

Different makes and models of web servers recognize different filenames as the site's home page. Most web servers recognize the names `index.htm` or `index.html`, but others recognize `default.htm`, `welcome.htm`, and `home.htm`.

If you import a Web site into FrontPage, and the site's home page filename is something other than `index.htm`, FrontPage changes the filename when it imports the site (and updates all the page's associated hyperlinks to reflect the new name) in order for FrontPage to display the Web site properly.

I only mention this little quirk now in case you're wondering why the name change takes place. The home page filename only becomes important when it comes time to publish your Web site, so I return to this subject in Chapter 16.

Creating a Subweb

Small, straightforward Web sites are easy to maintain in FrontPage. As the Web site grows, or the number of people involved in the site's creation and maintenance increases, however, keeping track of the Web site's exploding number of pages can turn into a major pain.

If your Web site is starting to resemble an ever-expanding amoeba, consider breaking the Web site into a core *parent* Web site with second-level tiers of information called *subwebs*. A subweb is a complete Web site that lives in a folder inside the parent Web site. (Previous versions of FrontPage referred to parent Web sites as *Root Webs* and subwebs as *Child Webs*.)

The parent Web site/subweb setup works well when you are creating a large network of interrelated Web sites — for example, a main company site with subwebs for each of the company's different products. The Microsoft Web site offers a good example: Check out the Microsoft parent Web site at www. microsoft.com, and the FrontPage subweb at www.microsoft.com/ frontpage.

Another example would be a company-wide intranet site, to which members of different departments contribute material. The entire network exists inside a single parent Web site, but each department works on its own subweb. In this situation, you can take advantage of FrontPage *permissions* so that site authors from different departments must enter a user name and a password to access their respective subwebs. I talk in detail about how permissions work in Chapter 15.

The parent Web site/subweb arrangement simplifies managing a large site, because, although subwebs live inside the parent Web site, they are distinct Web sites in their own right. You can create hyperlinks between the parent Web site to its subwebs, creating a large network of interrelated Web sites, or you can keep each site separate. The choice is yours.

 If you intend to create a Web site that contains subwebs, you must publish your Web site on a host web server that has FrontPage Server Extensions installed. I talk a bit about FrontPage Server Extensions earlier in this chapter, and I go into detail in Chapter 16.

You have two choices for creating a subweb: You can either create a new subweb by using a FrontPage template, Wizard, or from scratch (the steps that follow show you how), or you can convert a folder inside a FrontPage Web site into a subweb (I explain how in Chapter 2).

1. **With FrontPage running, choose File⇨New⇨Web.**

   The New dialog box appears.

2. **In the New dialog box's Web Sites area, click the template or Wizard you want to use.**

   To create a Web site from scratch, click One Page Web.

3. **In the Specify the Location of the New Web list box, enter the location of the new subweb.**

   Enter a file path that contains the location of the parent Web site followed by a backslash (\) and then the name of the new subweb's folder. For example, a new subweb named *subweb* of the existing Web site *My Webs* stored in the My Documents folder on the C: drive would have the following file path: C:\My Documents\My Webs\subweb. If you're not sure how file paths work, refer to the sidebar "File path 101" earlier in this chapter.

   The subweb folder name you choose should use all lowercase letters and should contain only one word.

4. **Click OK.**

   The dialog box closes, and FrontPage creates the new subweb. If another Web site is already open in FrontPage when you create the subweb, the subweb appears in a separate FrontPage window. In the parent Web site, the subweb's folder appears in the Folder List with a small globe icon on top (see Figure 1-6).

   (If, in Step 3, you specified the location of an existing folder, the Microsoft FrontPage dialog box appears prompting you to convert the folder into a FrontPage Web. Click Yes to close the dialog box and create the subweb.)

You can now update and work with the subweb just like you would any other FrontPage Web site.

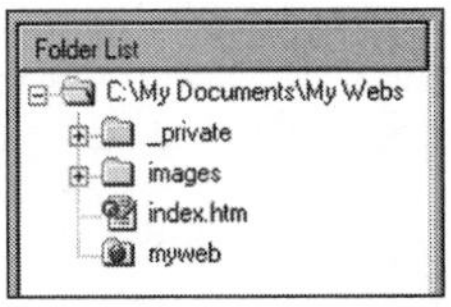

Figure 1-6:
A parent
Web site
with a single
subweb
named
myweb.

Folder List
C:\My Documents\My Webs
_private
images
index.htm
myweb

Open, Sesame!

You don't need a special incantation to open a FrontPage Web site. Just follow these easy steps:

1. **With FrontPage running, choose File➪Open Web.**

   The Open Web dialog box appears. This standard Office 2000 dialog box displays the folders on your computer or local network. The left side of the dialog box contains shortcuts to popular storage locations on your hard drive.

2. **In the dialog box, navigate your hard drive or network to the location of the folder that contains the Web site you want to open.**

   Folders containing FrontPage Web sites appear with different icons than regular folders.

3. **Click Open.**

   The Open Web dialog box closes, and then the selected Web site opens in FrontPage.

If you open more than one Web site at the same time, FrontPage opens the second Web site in a new window, enabling you to jump back and forth between the two Web sites by clicking their respective buttons in the Windows Taskbar, or by pressing Alt+Tab.

Working with Web sites that are stored on other computers

Throughout this book, I assume you do your Web-building on your own computer and then publish your finished Web site on a different computer (most likely a host web server belonging to your company or your ISP). I recommend this approach because you create Web sites in the privacy of your own hard drive and make only the perfect stuff visible to the world. This approach also minimizes the time you spend connected to the Internet, which can save you a bundle if you pay for access time.

In a few instances, however, you may need to create or open a Web site located on another web server, such as when you're working as part of a site-building team or if you want to adjust your Web site's password protection. (I discuss password protection in Chapter 15.) In FrontPage, you can create and open Web sites directly from remote web servers, as long as: a) you're connected to the Internet or local network, and b) the web server has FrontPage Server Extensions installed. (For more information about FrontPage Server Extensions, see Chapter 16.)

To create or open a Web site on a remote web server, follow the steps listed in this chapter with the following change: When you specify the Web site's location, instead of specifying a folder on your own hard drive, enter the remote server's address (it looks something like `http://www.mysite.com`). FrontPage establishes a connection to the remote server. In a moment, the Name and Password Required dialog box appears. In the dialog box, enter the user name and password required for that server, and then click OK. The dialog box closes, and the Web site opens in FrontPage. You can now update and change the site just as if it were stored on your own computer. Just remember, after you save your pages, any changes you make are immediately visible to the world, so proceed with care.

Each time you create or open a Web site on a remote Web server, FrontPage saves a shortcut to that server in the Web Folders folder on your hard drive.

Opening a subweb of the current site is a snap: In the Folder List, double-click the subweb's folder. (If the Folder List isn't visible, in the Standard toolbar, click the Folder List button or choose View➪Folder List.) You can tell if a folder inside a FrontPage Web site contains a subweb because the subweb's folder is marked with a little globe icon.

To quickly open a Web site you worked with recently, choose File➪Recent Webs, and then choose the location of the Web site you want to open. You can also tell FrontPage to automatically open your most recent Web site each time you launch the program. To do so, choose Tools➪Options to display the Options dialog box. In the General tab of the dialog box, mark the check box called Open Last Web Automatically When FrontPage Starts, and then click OK to close the dialog box.

Closing a Web Site

FrontPage enables you to open more than one Web site at a time. If you prefer to only work on a single Web site, you may want to close the current Web site before creating or opening another. To do so, choose File➪Close Web. If you haven't yet saved changes to the site's pages, the Microsoft FrontPage dialog box appears, prompting you to save each open page; click Yes. The dialog box closes, FrontPage saves the changes, and the window in which the Web site is displayed closes.

Deleting a Web Site

Remove those dusty old Web sites lurking in the corners of your computer. You know — the ones you no longer use. You're rewarded with a tidy hard drive and lots of extra disk space.

To delete a Web site that's currently open in FrontPage, follow these steps:

1. **In the Folder List, click the Web site's top-level folder, and then press the Delete key.**

   The Confirm Delete dialog box appears and warns you that deleting a Web site is a permanent action (in other words, you can't decide after you delete your Web site that you want it back — it's kaput).

2. **In the dialog box, click the radio button called Delete This Web Entirely, and then click OK.**

   The dialog box closes, and FrontPage deletes the Web site.

When you delete a Web site, you delete all its subwebs as well.

To delete a subweb, first open the parent Web site in FrontPage. In the Folder List, click the subweb's folder icon and then press Delete. In the Confirm Delete dialog box that appears, click Yes.

Exiting FrontPage

When you're done with Web-building for the day, closing up shop only takes a second or two.

To exit FrontPage, choose File⇨Exit. If any of the site's pages are currently open and unsaved, FrontPage prompts you to save the pages, and then the program closes.

The next time you launch FrontPage, the program opens in whichever view you were using when you last exited (you find out about the different FrontPage views in Chapter 2).

Screaming . . . er, I mean, calling for help

By now, I'm sure you've developed an inkling of the power and complexity of FrontPage. (No doubt that inkling motivated you to buy this book!) Never fear: Help is as close as your mouse. Choose Help⇨Microsoft FrontPage Help (or press F1) to access a nicely organized set of FrontPage crib notes. Refer to them whenever this book isn't handy and you need assistance.

If you find yourself wondering what a button or menu item does, choose Help⇨What's This?, or press Shift+F1. Then click the button or choose the menu item you don't understand. FrontPage automatically flips to the appropriate Help screen. For a quick reminder about the purpose of a particular button, pass your pointer over the button: In a moment, a yellow Tool Tip appears.

If you still can't find answers to your question, refer to the Cheat Sheet at the front of the book for more places to go for help.

Chapter 2

Web Management 101

● ●

In This Chapter

▶ Getting familiar with the different FrontPage views

▶ Creating a navigational structure for your Web site

▶ Importing and exporting files and folders

▶ Creating and renaming pages and folders

▶ Deleting files and folders

● ●

Consider FrontPage your Web publishing Command Central. Using FrontPage, you can do just about anything to change, update, or repair your Web site (assuming something needs repairing).

In this chapter, you delve into the site-management capabilities of FrontPage. You become familiar with FrontPage's six views. You also discover how to use FrontPage to manage the files that make up your Web site.

Taking In the Views

FrontPage's charm lies in its *views,* or ways of displaying information about your Web site. FrontPage contains six views, each of which illuminates your site in a different way.

To switch between views, click the appropriate button in the Views Bar (see Figure 2-1) or choose View and then select the name of the view you want to see.

Page View

You use the Page View to look at and add stuff to the individual Web pages that make up the Web site.

Figure 2-1:
The Views
Bar.

You'll spend most of your time in the Page View, so I devote most of this book to the Page View's many talents. In Chapter 3, you explore the Page View's basic features, and in the chapters in Part II, you find out how to put the Page View's tools to work.

Folders View

The Folders View displays your Web site as a group of files and folders to help you manage and organize your Web site's file system (see Figure 2-2). This view serves the same purpose for your Web site as the Windows Explorer serves for the files stored on your hard drive and local network.

The Folders View even looks and works much like the Windows Explorer:

- ✔ Click a folder in the Folder List to display its contents in the Contents area.

- ✔ To sort the list of files and folders in the Contents area, click the header label of your choice.

- ✔ To move a page into a folder, click the page icon, drag it on top of the folder, and then release the mouse button. FrontPage updates the page's hyperlinks to reflect the page's new location. (I talk more about how hyperlinks work in Chapter 6.)

Subweb   Folder list   Contents area   Header labels

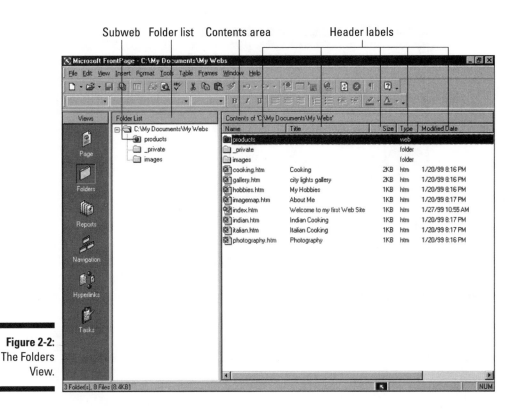

Figure 2-2:
The Folders
View.

Folders with globe icons on top denote *subwebs,* which are complete Web sites that live inside a folder of the main or *parent* Web site. To view the contents of a subweb in the Folders View, double-click the subweb's folder to open the subweb in a new FrontPage window. For more information about subwebs, see Chapter 1.

Reports View

The Reports View contains 14 different reports about your Web site, all of which help you keep track of important facts (see Figure 2-3). For example, the Slow Pages report helps you monitor your site's download speed, and the Recently Changed Files report gives you the lowdown on who updated the site and when.

The Reports View comes in especially handy if you're using FrontPage as part of a site-building team. I talk more about using FrontPage as a collaborative tool in Chapter 15.

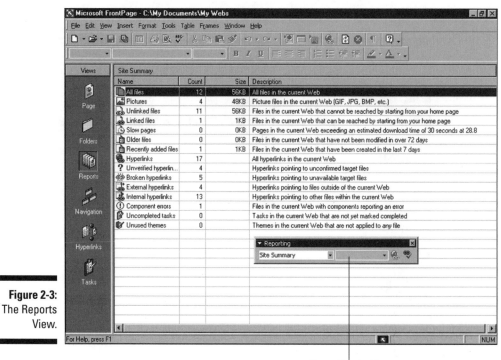

Figure 2-3:
The Reports
View.

Reporting toolbar

To switch between the reports in the Reports View, choose View⇨Reports, and then select the name of the report you want to see. Or avail yourself of the Reporting toolbar: It contains a drop-down menu of reports, plus a couple of other handy tools. If it's not already visible when you switch to the Reports View, show the Reporting toolbar by choosing View⇨Toolbars⇨Reporting.

Weird FrontPage folders

When you switch to the Folders View, no doubt you notice some unfamiliar folders lurking in your Web site. All FrontPage Web sites contain a standard set of folders, each of which has its own role:

✔ _private: Documents stored in this folder remain hidden from web browsers and from

the FrontPage Search Form Component (which you get to know in Chapter 14).

✔ images: The images folder is where FrontPage stores images that appear inside Web pages. I recommend keeping all your images in that folder, too, just so your Web site remains neat.

To open a page or file listed in any of the reports, double-click the file's icon. Read on for details about each of the FrontPage reports.

Site Summary

This report rounds up interesting tidbits of information, including how many hyperlinks and pictures the site contains, how many pages can and cannot be reached by following a link from the home page, and how many pages contain broken hyperlinks. This report contains much more information than I've listed here — see for yourself!

All Files

The All Files report lets you peruse a complete list of the files in your Web site. Use this report when you want details about your Web site files, such as the file's size or author.

Recently Added Files

This report lists the files that have been added (by you or another author) to the Web site in the last 30 days.

To change the number of days FrontPage thinks of as "recent," select a different time frame from the Reporting toolbar, or choose Tools⇨Options to display the Options dialog box. In the dialog box, click the Reports View tab, and then type a new number in the "Recent" Files Are Less Than X Days Old text box. Click OK to close the dialog box.

Recently Changed Files

This report lists the files that have been edited or have otherwise changed in the last 30 days.

To change the number of days FrontPage thinks of as "recent," select a different time frame from the Reporting toolbar, or choose Tools⇨Options to display the Options dialog box. In the dialog box, click the Reports View tab, and then type a new number in the "Recent" Files Are Less Than X Days Old text box. Click OK to close the dialog box.

Older Files

Turn to this report for a list of aging pages (that is, pages that haven't changed for at least 72 days). If a bunch of your site's pages appear in this report, it's time to spruce up your site with some new and exciting content.

To change the number of days FrontPage thinks of as "older," select a different time frame from the Reporting toolbar, or choose Tools⇨Options to display the Options dialog box. In the dialog box, click the Reports View tab, and then type a new number in the "Older" Files Are More Than X Days Old text box. Click OK to close the dialog box.

Unlinked Files

This report lists files that do not contain hyperlinks and cannot be reached by following hyperlinks from the site's home page.

Pages that appear in this report can safely be deleted, because they are effectively cut off from the rest of the site. I show you how to delete pages later in this chapter.

If you delete a page using FrontPage, you can't later change your mind. FrontPage-deleted pages don't end up in the Recycle Bin — they go to Web page heaven.

Slow Pages

Web surfers hate to wait for pages to download. This report helps you keep track of the potential slowpokes in your site. The report lists pages that take more than an estimated 30 seconds to load over a 28.8 modem. I say *estimated* because download speed depends on several factors, only one of which is page content. (Other factors include the speed of the host web server, the amount of network traffic at that given moment, and the state of the phone and data lines that make up the Internet, to name a few.)

To change this report's assumptions about download time and speed, select a new time frame from the Reporting toolbar, or choose Tools⇨Options to display the Options dialog box. In the dialog box, click the Reports View tab, and then type a new number in the "Slow Pages" Take At Least X Seconds To Download text box. Next, select a connection speed from the Assume Connection Speed Of list box. Click OK to close the dialog box.

Broken Hyperlinks

This report lists hyperlinks that are broken or have not yet been verified by FrontPage. In Chapter 6, I show you how to find and fix broken hyperlinks.

Component Errors

FrontPage Components are dynamic little programs you can insert into your site for extra dazzle (you find out about Components in Chapter 14). If you use Components in your site, and one or more of those Components runs into a problem, FrontPage lists the ailing page and a description of the problem in this report.

Review Status and Assigned To

If you're part of a Web design team, these reports list the review status and assignments for each page in the Web site. In Chapter 15, I go into detail about how these reports and other FrontPage workgroup and collaboration features work.

Categories

In FrontPage, you can create general groupings of information called *categories,* and you can then assign each page to a specific category (I talk about how and when this feature can be useful in Chapter 15). This report lists each page and the category to which it's assigned. To show only those pages assigned to a specific category, choose a category name from the Reports toolbar.

Publish Status

This report keeps track of when pages were last modified and which pages are ready to be published. I show you how to publish your Web site (and how to exclude unfinished pages from publishing) in Chapter 16.

Checkout Status

If you collaborate with a team of people to build a FrontPage Web site, FrontPage's *source control* feature can simplify the process. When you enable source control, each Web site author must check pages out before he or she can work on the pages, and only one author at a time can check out a page. (I talk in detail about source control in Chapter 15.)

This report lists the checkout status for each page in your site: A green dot signifies that the page is checked in, and a red check mark signifies that the page is checked out and can't be accessed. The report also lists the name of the person who has checked out the page, the most recent version of the page that has been checked out, and the *locked date,* or the date the page was checked out.

Navigation View

You may think that I started writing this book on Page 1, right? Wrong. I spent many hours putting together a table of contents before jotting down a single word. When it was time to write, my words flowed easily because the information was already organized.

I relate this anecdote because building a Web site is not unlike writing a book. You have information to present to an audience, and you want that information to be clear and well-organized. Here's where the Navigation View comes in handy. Using this view, you can map out a *navigational structure* for your Web site. A navigational structure is a graphic representation of the "levels" of pages in your site. Similar to a company's organization chart, which provides a picture of the leadership hierarchy within the company, a navigational structure illustrates the organization of the information in your site.

Building a navigational structure is optional unless you want to take advantage of FrontPage *navigation bars* and *page banners,* because both features make use of information in the site's navigational structure. A navigation bar is a row of text or graphic hyperlinks that lead to other pages, making it easy for your visitors to get around (I show you how to create navigation bars in Chapter 6). Page banners are decorative banner graphics that add spice to your pages (see Chapter 12 for details).

Designing a navigational structure

Creating a navigational structure is easy. Simply think about how you want your site to be structured, and then drag the site's pages from the Folder List into place in the blue area of the Navigation View. Here's how:

1. **In FrontPage, open the Web site of your choice.**

   If you can't remember how, refer to Chapter 1.

2. **If the Navigation View isn't already visible, click the Navigation button in the Views Bar.**

   The Navigation View becomes visible. The home page is already represented in the Navigation View. You construct a navigational structure by dragging pages from the Folder List and dropping them into the Navigation View. In this example, I illustrate creating a navigational structure for a simple personal Web site containing a home page, three second-level pages, and two third-level pages.

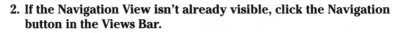

   If the Folder List isn't visible, click the Folder List button, or choose View➪Folder List.

   Note: Web sites based on FrontPage templates already have a navigational structure in place. Read on to find out how to add more pages to or change the setup of the navigational structure.

3. **In the Folder List, click the page you want to add to the navigational structure and then, while holding down the mouse button, drag the page into the blue area of the Navigation View.**

   As you drag the page into place, a line appears that connects the page you're dragging to the home page (see Figure 2-4).

4. **Release the mouse button.**

   An icon representing that page appears in the navigational structure.

Drag page icon from here...

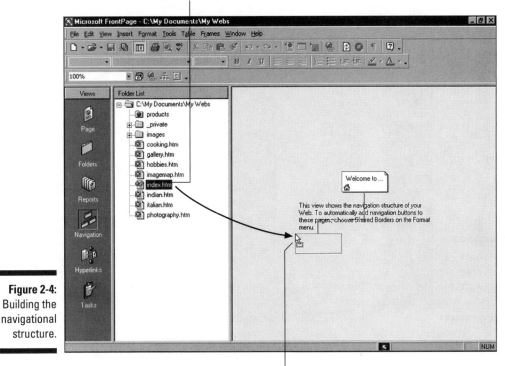

...to the place in the navigational structure where you want the page to appear.

Figure 2-4:
Building the
navigational
structure.

5. **Continue adding pages to the navigational structure until you've added all of the pages to be represented in the site's navigation bars or page banners.**

Figure 2-5 illustrates a complete navigational structure.

You don't have to add every page in your site to the navigational structure — only add those pages you want to show up in the site's navigation bars or page banners. If you're not sure how you should arrange the pages, skim the information in Chapter 6 about navigation bars. Understanding how navigation bars work may make it easier to visualize how you should lay out your Web site's navigational structure.

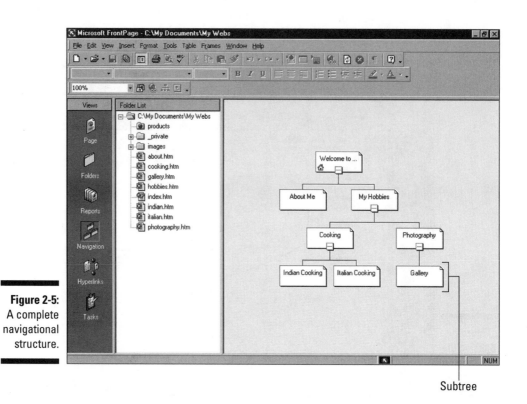

Figure 2-5:
A complete
navigational
structure.

Subtree

After you finish the navigational structure, you can easily rearrange it by
clicking any of the icons and dragging them to a new spot. As you add new
pages to your site, you can drag them into the navigational structure as well.
The navigational structure can accommodate many different organizational
schemes, including more than one top-level page. Try it out.

To remove a page from the navigational structure, click a rectangle in the
map and press the Delete key. The page disappears from the navigational
structure, but the page itself remains safely ensconced in the Web site.

You can print the navigational structure by clicking the Print button in the
Standard toolbar. To preview the printed page before you set it on paper,
choose File⇨Print Preview.

Changing the display

The Navigation toolbar contains a few gizmos that let you adjust the navigational structure display (see Figure 2-6). If the toolbar isn't already visible,
choose View⇨Toolbars⇨Navigation.

Figure 2-6:
The
Navigation
toolbar.

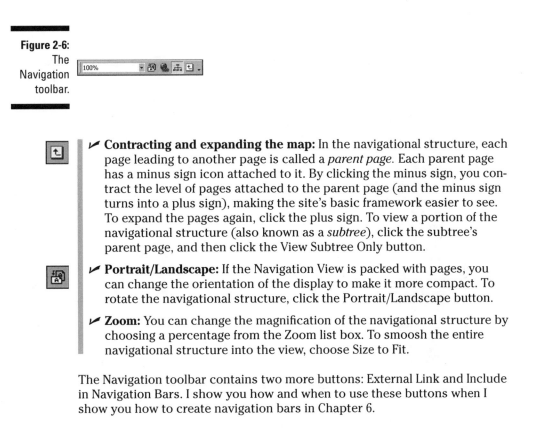

✔ **Contracting and expanding the map:** In the navigational structure, each page leading to another page is called a *parent page*. Each parent page has a minus sign icon attached to it. By clicking the minus sign, you contract the level of pages attached to the parent page (and the minus sign turns into a plus sign), making the site's basic framework easier to see. To expand the pages again, click the plus sign. To view a portion of the navigational structure (also known as a *subtree*), click the subtree's parent page, and then click the View Subtree Only button.

✔ **Portrait/Landscape:** If the Navigation View is packed with pages, you can change the orientation of the display to make it more compact. To rotate the navigational structure, click the Portrait/Landscape button.

✔ **Zoom:** You can change the magnification of the navigational structure by choosing a percentage from the Zoom list box. To smoosh the entire navigational structure into the view, choose Size to Fit.

The Navigation toolbar contains two more buttons: External Link and Include in Navigation Bars. I show you how and when to use these buttons when I show you how to create navigation bars in Chapter 6.

Hyperlinks View

The Hyperlinks View displays your Web site as a network of linked files. These links, also known as *hyperlinks,* are the glue that keeps the Web site stuck together. Hyperlinks connect Web pages to each other and to sites on the World Wide Web. When you click a hyperlink in a Web page, you are transported to another location. (In Chapter 6, I explain hyperlinks in detail.)

The links between the pages in your Web site create a path that visitors follow when they explore the site. The Hyperlinks View is like a road map; it illustrates the Web site's navigational path so you can make sure that your Web site is easy to get around.

The left side of the Hyperlinks View contains the Folder List (the same list that appears in the Page and Navigation Views). When you click a page in the Folder List, an icon representing that page appears in the Hyperlinks area of the view. Figure 2-7 shows how a Web site looks in the Hyperlinks View.

The selected page contains hyperlinks leading to these destinations.

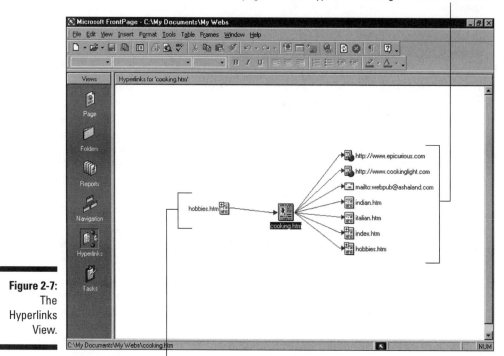

This page contains hyperlinks that lead to the selected page.

Figure 2-7:
The
Hyperlinks
View.

Small icons with blue arrows pointing to the central page icon illustrate *incoming hyperlinks,* or pages that contain hyperlinks leading to the selected page. Small icons to the right of the central page icon illustrate *outgoing hyperlinks,* or the destinations of hyperlinks inside the selected page. If the selected page contains no hyperlinks and isn't linked to from any other page in the site, the page icon appears in the Hyperlinks area of the view all by itself.

Broken hyperlinks appear as broken gray lines instead of blue arrows. I show you how to find and repair broken hyperlinks in your site in Chapter 6.

You can modify the Hyperlinks View diagram by right-clicking anywhere inside the yellow area of the view and then choosing one of the following options from the pop-up menu that appears:

 ✔ **Show Page Titles:** By default, the Hyperlinks View displays the page's filenames. Choose this option to display the page's titles instead.

 ✔ **Hyperlinks to Pictures:** Choose this option to display links to picture files.

➔ **Repeated Hyperlinks:** If the page contains more than one hyperlink to the same destination, the Hyperlinks View only displays one instance of the link. Choose this option to make repeated hyperlinks visible.

➔ **Hyperlinks Inside Page:** If the page contains hyperlinks to locations inside the same page (that is, links to *bookmarks*), the Hyperlinks View doesn't display these links. Choose this option to make the hyperlinks to locations inside the same page visible.

Tasks View

The Tasks View helps you keep track of the thousand-and-one details involved in putting together a flawless Web site. I talk about the workings of the Tasks View along with other FrontPage workgroup features in Chapter 15.

Working with Web Site Files and Folders

FrontPage gives you easy access to the files that make up your Web site. Use FrontPage whenever you want to import, move, or delete files and folders in your Web site.

Adding existing files and folders to a Web site

The easiest way to add an existing file or folder to a FrontPage Web site is to move, copy, or save that file or folder inside the Web site's folder.

For example, say you have a document stored inside your `C:\My Documents` folder that you want to add to the Web site stored in the `C:\My Documents\My Webs` folder. Using Windows Explorer, simply copy or move the file from the `My Documents` folder to the `My Webs` folder. The next time you open the Web site in FrontPage, the new file appears in the Folder List. (If the Web site is currently open in FrontPage, click the Refresh button to display the file.)

Another option is to save a document directly inside a FrontPage Web site folder. For example, if you're currently working on a Microsoft Word document, and you want to add that document to the Web site stored in the `C:\My Documents\My Webs` folder, save the document in Microsoft Word in the location `C:\My Documents\My Webs`.

If you prefer to do all your Web site work from within FrontPage, you can *import* files into your Web site instead. You can import files that are currently stored on your computer, local network, or the World Wide Web. When you import a file, FrontPage places a copy of the file inside the currently open Web site.

In this section, I show you how to add existing files to the Web site that's currently open in FrontPage. To import a complete Web site into FrontPage, take the Import Web Wizard for a spin (see Chapter 1 for details).

In the following steps, I show you how to import single files from your computer or local network into the current FrontPage Web site. At the end of this set of steps, I tell you how to import entire folders, and I also talk about how to import material that's currently stored on the World Wide Web.

1. **With a Web site open in FrontPage, choose File⇨Import.**

   The Import dialog box appears.

   (If you choose File⇨Import when no Web site is currently open, FrontPage thinks that you want to import an entire site and displays the New dialog box with the Import Web Wizard selected.)

2. **In the dialog box, click the Add File button.**

   The Add File to Import List dialog box appears. You use this dialog box to poke around your hard drive or local network to find the files that you want to import.

3. **Navigate your hard drive or local network and select the files that you want to import.**

   To select multiple files, press and hold down the Ctrl key while clicking file icons in the Add File to Import List dialog box. To select a range of files, press and hold down the Shift key while clicking the first and last file icons. If you don't see the file that you want to import, choose All files (*.*) from the Files of Type list box.

4. **Click the Open button.**

   The Add File to Import List dialog box closes, and the file appears in the import list in the Import dialog box (see Figure 2-8).

5. **To add another file to the import list, repeat Steps 2 through 4. When you're finished, click OK to close the dialog box and import the file(s).**

   If you would rather put off importing the files, click the Close button in the Import dialog box. FrontPage saves the import list and closes the dialog box, which you can later access by choosing File⇨Import.

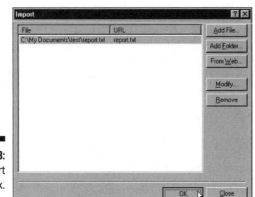

Figure 2-8:
The Import
dialog box.

To import a folder to your Web site, in Step 2 of the previous list click the Add Folder button. The Browse for Folder dialog box appears, enabling you to choose the folder that you want to import. Click the folder and then click the OK button. The Browse for Folder dialog box closes, and the folder's contents appear in the import list.

To import a single file or folder, you can also resort to the quick-and-dirty approach: Simply drag the file or folder from your desktop or Windows Explorer and drop it into the contents area of the Folders View.

To import a file or folder that's currently stored on the World Wide Web, in Step 2 of the previous list click the From Web button. The Import Web Wizard launches. Refer to Chapter 1 for directions on how to use the Import Web Wizard.

Creating new folders

You can add new folders to your Web site using the Folders View. If your site contains lots of files and pages, folders help you keep the files organized.

Say, for example, your company's Web site contains four main sections — About Acme Consulting Company, Acme Services, Acme Staff, and Contact Acme — and each section contains several files. You can store each section's files in its own folder to keep your file system spic-and-span.

Don't confuse storing files inside folders to keep the files organized with creating a subweb. Although a subweb is indeed a group of files stored inside a folder of the current Web site, it is actually a distinct and fully functional Web site in its own right. For details on how to convert a folder into a subweb, read the section "Converting a folder into a subweb (and vice versa)" later in this chapter. For more information on what a subweb is, see Chapter 1.

To create new folders, follow these steps:

1. **In the Folders View, choose File⇨New⇨Folder.**

   A new folder appears. The folder name (New_Folder) is highlighted.

2. **Type a new folder name and then press Enter.**

   FrontPage renames the folder.

Renaming files and folders

I admit it. The power of this feature makes me weak in the knees. If, for any reason, you need to change the name of a file or folder in your Web site, FrontPage automatically updates all the file's associated hyperlinks.

Renaming the home page filename involves some extra considerations. I tell you about these considerations in the Chapter 3 sidebar "File naming tips and tricks."

You can rename a file or folder several ways, but the easiest is by following these steps:

1. **In any view except the Tasks View, click the icon for the file or folder you want to rename, and then click its filename.**

   A box appears around the filename, and the filename is highlighted.

2. **Type a new name.**

   Be sure to maintain the same filename extension so that FrontPage knows what kind of file you're renaming.

3. **Press Enter.**

   If the file contains associated links, the Rename dialog box appears, asking if you'd like to update the links to reflect the new name. (The power! Be still my beating heart!)

4. **Click Yes.**

   The dialog box closes, FrontPage updates the links, and all is well.

Converting a folder into a subweb (and vice-versa)

As your site grows, and you find your site filling up with lots of folders, you may want to convert one or more of the folders into subwebs.

The advantages to this arrangement are as follows:

- ✔ A subweb is a complete FrontPage Web site in its own right. You can therefore open a subweb into its own FrontPage window and manage the Web site as you see fit. This is a great way to break an overwhelmingly big Web site into easy-to-manage chunks.

- ✔ If you're working in a collaborative environment, subwebs can have different *permissions* from the parent Web site (handy when different groups of people are contributing to different parts of the Web site). I talk about permissions in Chapter 15.

- ✔ Because a subweb is distinct from the parent Web site, the subweb can have its own theme, keyword search capability, navigation bars, and shared borders. (You find out about all these features in Part II of this book.)

Unfortunately, the parent Web site/subweb arrangement has its disadvantages as well:

- ✔ You must publish your Web site on a host web server that has FrontPage Server Extensions installed (for details, see Chapter 16).

- ✔ If the pages inside the folder you are about to convert contain FrontPage navigation bars or the Include Page Component, these features may be affected by the conversion. (More about navigation bars in Chapter 6 and Components in "Advanced Additions" on the CD.)

Should you decide the parent Web site/subweb setup is for you, follow these steps to convert a folder into a subweb:

1. **With the parent Web site open in FrontPage, right-click the folder you want to convert into a subweb, and from the pop-up menu that appears, choose Convert to Web.**

   The Microsoft FrontPage dialog box appears, warning you that pages inside the folder will be affected by the conversion. If you change your mind and decide to maintain the status quo, click No. Otherwise . . .

2. **In the dialog box, click Yes.**

   The dialog box closes, and FrontPage converts the folder into a subweb. If the folder contains lots of files, the conversion may take a few moments. You can tell the conversion has taken place because a little globe appears on top of the folder icon.

If, later, you change your mind and want to consolidate a parent Web site and its subwebs back into a single Web site, you can convert subwebs into regular folders.

Keep in mind that the conversion comes with a few consequences:

- ✔ If the parent Web site is decorated with a theme, the subweb's pages will take on that theme.
- ✔ The subweb's files will take on the permission settings of the parent Web site.
- ✔ Navigation bar hyperlinks leading from the parent Web site to the subweb will no longer work properly.
- ✔ The subweb's task list will be lost. (For more about task lists, see Chapter 15.)

To convert a subweb into a folder, with the parent Web site open in FrontPage, right-click the subweb's folder, and from the pop-up menu that appears, choose Convert to Folder. The Microsoft FrontPage dialog box appears, listing the changes that will occur in the subweb's pages as a result of the conversion. If the changes are okay with you, click Yes to close the dialog box and convert the subweb into a folder.

Converting folders isn't the only way to create subwebs. You can also use FrontPage templates and Wizards to create new subwebs; for details, see Chapter 1.

Deleting files and folders

If your Web site contains a file that has outlived its usefulness or is otherwise cluttering your Web site, you can boot the file out with one swift click. To delete a file or folder, do the following:

1. **In any view except the Tasks View, click the file or folder you want to delete.**

2. **Press the Delete key.**

   The Confirm Delete dialog box appears, making sure that you want to delete the file or folder.

3. **Click Yes.**

   If you are deleting more than one file, click Yes to All to delete them all in one step (instead of having the Confirm Delete dialog box pop up before deleting each file). If you change your mind, click No or Cancel to close the dialog box without deleting the file.

Be careful — once you delete a page or folder using FrontPage, you can't later change your mind.

Also, if you delete a file that's the destination of a link from elsewhere in your Web site, the link will break. The damage isn't irreparable — you can always use FrontPage to find and fix broken hyperlinks — but you should be aware of the problem all the same. The best way to avoid broken links caused by deleted files is to do your file cleanup using the Unlinked Files report (available by choosing View⇨Reports⇨Unlinked Files). The pages listed in this report can safely be axed, because those pages don't contain any hyperlinks, nor can the pages be reached by following links from the site's home page.

Backing up Web sites

FrontPage enables you to copy your Web site to other locations such as floppy disks or other backup media. By backing up your Web site, you not only have a clean copy in the event of a computer glitch, but you can maintain a working copy to use as a scratch pad so that you avoid making permanent changes to the original.

To back up your Web site, you follow similar steps to the ones you would follow if you were publishing your Web site:

1. **With the Web site open in FrontPage, choose File⇨Publish Web.**

   The Publish Web dialog box appears.

2. **In the Specify the Location To Publish Your Web To list box, enter the path to the location to which you want to back up the Web site.**

   Or click Browse to select a location on your computer or network.

3. **If the Web site contains subwebs, and you want to back up the subwebs at the same time, mark the Include Subwebs check box.**

4. **Click Publish.**

   The dialog box closes, and FrontPage backs up the Web site. After the work is done, the Microsoft FrontPage dialog box appears, saying your Web site has published successfully. Don't be misled — your Web site isn't live. This is just the way FrontPage lets you know the copy process went smoothly.

5. **Click Done to close the dialog box.**

Chapter 3

Playing with Web Pages

• •

In This Chapter

▶ Creating a new Web page

▶ Opening a Web page

▶ Converting another type of document into a Web page

▶ Previewing a page

▶ Printing a page

▶ Saving a page

▶ Creating a page template

• •

My artistic period took place between the ages of 6 and 10, when my teachers set aside part of each school day for creative time. I drew pictures, wrote poems, and perfected my finger-painting technique.

As I got older, my artistic ability dwindled to scribbling on cocktail napkins. One day, I discovered Web publishing and entered my renaissance. I no longer work with construction paper or tempera paints; I now use FrontPage to create stacks of colorful Web pages.

In this chapter, you get familiar with basic Web page operations: creating, opening, previewing, and saving pages. If you already feel comfy working with pages and are ready to tinker with page design tools, turn to the chapters in Part II.

Creating a New Web Page

FrontPage can whip out a Web page in milliseconds. In fact, each time you launch FrontPage, the Page View presents you with a new, empty Web page ready for filling. If the prospect of an empty page intimidates you, you can instead lean on FrontPage page templates for a push in the right direction.

Using a template to create pages

Templates are to a page what a jump start is to an engine. If your Web publishing inspiration is tapped out, templates jolt you back into action.

Templates are skeleton pages to which you add your own content and design effects. FrontPage contains templates for different page layouts, as well as pages that commonly appear in Web sites, such as lists of *FAQs* (pronounced *eff-ay-cues* or *faks,* which is Web-speak for *frequently asked questions*) and bibliographies, to name a couple.

Unlike with Microsoft Word document templates, you cannot attach a FrontPage Web page template to an already-existing page. You must use the template as the starting point for a new Web page.

To create a new page with the help of a template, follow these steps:

1. **If you intend to add the new page to an existing FrontPage Web site, open the Web site. If not, or if you're not sure, skip ahead to Step 2.**

   I explain how to open a FrontPage Web site in Chapter 1.

2. **In the Page View, choose File➪New➪Page.**

   The New dialog box appears, displaying a smorgasbord of templates (see Figure 3-1).

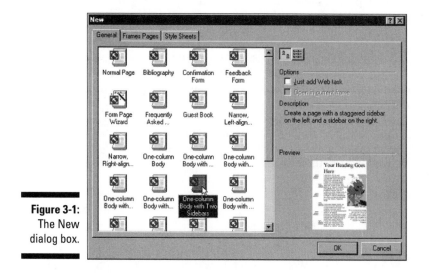

Figure 3-1:
The New
dialog box.

3. **In the dialog box's list of templates, click the name of the template you want to use.**

   A description of the template appears in the Description area of the dialog box, and a tiny version of the template appears in the Preview area.

4. **Click OK.**

   The New dialog box closes, and a new page based on the template appears in the Page View.

If the built-in FrontPage templates don't meet your needs, you can always create your own template. I explain how later in this chapter.

Some pages based on FrontPage templates appear with text sitting at the top of the page preceded by the word Comment. *Comments* are visible when you edit the page in the Page View but not when you view the page with a web browser. FrontPage uses comments to give you hints about how to customize the template. You can leave the comments there for reference, or you can delete them after you understand how the template works. To delete a comment, click anywhere on the comment and then press the Delete key. (I show you how to add your own comments to a page in Chapter 5.)

Creating blank pages

If you already have a good idea about what you want to include in the new page, forgo the templates and start from scratch. When you launch FrontPage, the Page View automatically contains a new, blank page on which you can get to work.

To create another empty page, in the Page, Folders, or Navigation View's Standard toolbar, click the New Page button.

If instead of a blank, white page, a new page appears with a colorful background and/or graphic buttons or hyperlinks in the page margins, then the current Web site sports a *theme* or *shared borders.* For more information about themes, turn to Chapter 12. If you're curious about shared borders, flip to Chapter 6.

Opening an Existing Web Page

If you already have Web pages hanging around on your hard drive, you can easily open them in FrontPage. It doesn't matter if the pages are part of a FrontPage Web site; FrontPage willingly opens any Web page.

In fact, FrontPage can open pages that aren't even stored on your computer; the pages may live somewhere on your company network or in the wilds of the World Wide Web. FrontPage can even open non-Web page files that are part of your Web site (such as graphic files or Microsoft Office documents) by launching the appropriate program for that type of file.

Opening a page that's part of the current Web site

FrontPage gives you several ways to open pages and files that make up your FrontPage Web site. I list the easiest methods here.

First, open the Web site that contains the page you want to open (if you're not sure how to open a Web site, see Chapter 1). Next, do one of the following things:

✔ Double-click a page or file icon in the Folder List, the blue area of the Navigation View, or the Hyperlinks area of the Hyperlinks View. You can also double-click a listing in any of the reports in the Reports View.

✔ Right-click a page or file icon and then choose Open from the pop-up menu.

To open a page that's part of a subweb inside the currently open Web site, in the Folder List, double-click the subweb's folder. FrontPage pops open a new window inside which it displays the contents of the subweb. From there, you can proceed as usual to open one of the subweb's files. (What's a subweb, you ask? Check out Chapter 1.)

You can open one page at a time, or you can open several pages and move between them by choosing Window and then choosing the name of the page you want to see.

While a page is open in the Page View, the page's icon in the Folder List changes from a regular page to a page with a little pencil on top.

Opening a page stored on your computer or network

You may want to open a page that's part of a FrontPage Web site, but not the Web site that's currently open in FrontPage. No problem. You can even open a page that isn't part of a FrontPage Web site — FrontPage doesn't mind.

Associating file types with editors

FrontPage recognizes many file types and generally knows which program to launch when you ask FrontPage to open a file. For example, if your site contains Microsoft Office documents, FrontPage knows to launch the appropriate Office program when you attempt to open the file. If your Web site contains a file that FrontPage *doesn't* recognize, you need to tell FrontPage which editing program to launch when you open that type of file.

To associate a file type with an editing program, follow these steps:

1. **In FrontPage, choose Tools⇨Options.**

   The Options dialog box appears.

2. **In the dialog box, click the Configure Editors tab.**

   This tab lists all the file types FrontPage recognizes along with their associated editing programs.

3. **To add a new editing program to the list, click the Add button.**

   The Add Editor Association dialog box appears.

4. **In the dialog box's File Type text box, type the filename extension that you want to associate with a program.**

   For example, type **pdf** for PDF files.

5. **In the Editor Name text box, type the name of the editing program.**

   For example, **Adobe Acrobat**.

6. **In the Command text box, enter the location of the editing program or click Browse to locate the program on your computer.**

7. **Click OK.**

   The Add Editor Association dialog box closes, and the new file type and program appear in the Configure Editors tab. You can change or remove any entry on the list by clicking the Modify or Remove buttons.

8. **Click OK to close the Options dialog box.**

To tell FrontPage to open a file with an editing program other than the one with which the file type is associated, in FrontPage, right-click the file's icon and choose Open With from the pop-up menu. The Open With Editor dialog box appears displaying a list of associated editors. In the dialog box, double-click the name of the program that you want to use to open the file.

To do so, follow these steps:

1. **In the Page View's Standard toolbar, click the Open button. Or, choose File⇨Open, or press Ctrl+O.**

   The Open File dialog box appears, displaying a list of files and folders contained in the Web site currently open in FrontPage (see Figure 3-2). If no Web site is currently open, the dialog box displays the contents of the last folder you viewed.

Figure 3-2:
The Open
File dialog
box.

2. In the dialog box, navigate to the location of the file you want to open.

The page may be stored anywhere on your computer or network. The left side of the dialog box contains shortcuts to common file locations including your desktop, your My Documents folder, or your Favorites folder.

3. In the dialog box's file list, click the file, and then click Open.

The Open File dialog box closes, and the page opens in the Page View. Be patient — the page may take a few moments to open, especially if the page contains pictures.

If the page is part of a FrontPage Web site, FrontPage opens the Web site as well, and the Web site's files and folders appear in the Folder List.

Opening a page from the World Wide Web

FrontPage enables you to open any Web page stored on just about any web server in the world. This feature is extremely useful if you want to open a Web page directly from the World Wide Web or from your company *intranet* (an internal company network based on Internet technology, but only accessible to company insiders).

To open a page stored on another web server, follow these steps:

1. Activate your Internet or network connection.

2. In the FrontPage Standard toolbar, click the Open button.

The Open File dialog box appears.

HEADS UP

A note about Web site security

Opening Web pages stored on other web servers brings up the topic of security. After all, if you can use FrontPage to open any page anywhere, what's to keep you from fooling around with someone else's Web site files (aside from your squeaky-clean conscience)?

Web servers keep files safe by using an identification system of user names and passwords. If you want to make changes to files stored on a particular server, the server's administrator must give you a unique user name and password that you must enter before you can proceed. This means that, although anyone with FrontPage can open just about any Web page, only those folks with password access can actually make changes to the pages sitting on the server and have those changes be visible on the World Wide Web.

(You can set up password protection for your own FrontPage Web sites; I show you how in Chapter 15.)

Furthermore, in order for FrontPage to be able to work with the server's password system, the server must be running a set of programs called FrontPage Server Extensions. Without FrontPage Server Extensions, FrontPage doesn't know how to access the server's list of authorized user names and passwords.

Therefore, you may only use FrontPage to edit live pages that are stored on servers to which you have password access *and* those servers must be running FrontPage Server Extensions. I discuss FrontPage Server Extensions in much more detail in Chapter 16.

3. **In the dialog box's File Name text box, enter the file's Web address.**

   A Web address (also known as a *URL* or *Uniform Resource Locator*) looks similar to the following address:

   ```
   http://www.server.com/file.html
   ```

4. **Click Open.**

   The Open File dialog box closes. If the file is part of a Web site stored on a web server that supports FrontPage Server Extensions, the Enter Network Password dialog box appears. In the dialog box, enter your user name and password, and then click OK. The dialog box closes, and FrontPage opens both the page and the Web site.

   If the host web server doesn't support FrontPage Server Extensions, FrontPage opens a copy of the page for you to edit (not the live page itself). When you later save the page, FrontPage prompts you to choose a saving location on your own computer or network.

> When you open a Web site stored on a server to which you have access, you are working on the *live version* of the Web site. Each change you make is visible to the world as soon as you save the page.

Converting Other Documents into Web Pages

Document conversion is one of the most lovable FrontPage features because much of your Web site's content may already exist in other formats. FrontPage can convert the following popular document formats into Web pages in the blink of an eye:

- Microsoft Word documents (for Windows, Versions 2.*x*, 6.0/95, 97-2000; for Macintosh, Versions 4.0-5.1) (with filename extension doc)
- Microsoft Works 4.0 documents (wps)
- WordPerfect 5.*x* and 6.*x* documents (doc, wpd)
- Microsoft Excel and Lotus 1-2-3 worksheets (xls, xlw, wk1, wk3, wk4)
- Windows write files (wri)
- RTF documents (rtf)
- Text documents (txt)

If you have information stored in a file format other than those listed here, FrontPage attempts to recover text from any file format.

When you use FrontPage to convert a word-processing or RTF file into a Web page, FrontPage maintains much of the document's text and paragraph formatting by converting the formats to the closest HTML style. (Incidentally, RTF stands for *Rich Text Format,* which is a format readable by all kinds of word-processing programs, and is often used by folks who want to share formatted documents with others who are using different types of computer systems.)

FrontPage can also convert spreadsheet worksheets into Web pages. If you've never worked with a *spreadsheet,* it's a type of program that simplifies numerical calculations. Lotus 1-2-3 and Microsoft Excel are popular spreadsheet programs loved by number-crunchers. Spreadsheet *worksheets* (what the program calls its documents) are arranged in rows and columns of information.

Conversion considerations

To convert or not to convert? It's a worthwhile question, because you have a few options when deciding how to include non-Web page files in your Web site. Here's a quick rundown:

✓ **Using FrontPage to convert the file into a Web page works well for text files and simply formatted word processing files, or files in which all you need is static data.** If you just want to grab content from a file to dump into a Web page, this is the way to go.

✓ **Importing the file into your Web site in its native format makes more sense for long or complex documents, such as reports or publications, or if you want users to have access to dynamic information in a document (such as equations and functions in a spreadsheet worksheet).** The upside is that visitors can open the documents on their own computers as long as they have programs installed that know how to read the documents. The downside is that non-Web page files can be quite large and therefore take a long time to download. For details on how to import files into a FrontPage Web site, see Chapter 2.

✓ **Many Web sites make formatted documents available as *PDF files*.** PDF files look just like the original files, but download quickly because the files are compact. Visitors can install a free PDF viewing program to view and print the file (I include this viewing program, called Acrobat Reader, on this book's CD-ROM; for more information, see Appendix B). This option is great when you want to make a complex document such as a brochure easy for your visitors to download. However, you must buy a separate program called Adobe Acrobat to be able to create PDF files.

Office 2000 users have some additional options. Word, Excel, and PowerPoint can each save documents as Web pages. The Office 2000 Web page conversion features are more sophisticated than FrontPage's, and often work better for complex or highly formatted documents (see each Office program's Help system for details). Office 2000 also contains a new feature called Web Components. Web Components enable Office users to embed in Web pages some of the Office functionality many know and love, including spreadsheets, PivotTables, and charts. For more information about Web Components, see Chapter 14.

In the past, converting worksheets into Web pages meant cutting and pasting the data into a Web page table, a painstaking and time-consuming process. (If you're not sure what a table is, check out Chapter 9.) Today, FrontPage can convert worksheets into tables with nary a thought.

Unless you use Web Components, when you use FrontPage to convert a worksheet, the resulting Web page contains static numbers — you lose the ability to use functions and equations. Web Components come with specific system requirements; I discuss them in Chapter 14.

Text documents contain no formatting whatsoever. No bold or italics, no tables or curly quotes (" ") — just regular old characters and spaces. FrontPage can convert a text document to a Web page in one of the following ways:

- **One formatted paragraph:** The Page View stuffs all the document's paragraphs into a single paragraph, to which the program applies the Formatted style. In a Web page, the Formatted style appears as a monospaced font — in most web browsers, the font appears as Courier. If your text document contains rows and columns of information separated by spaces or tabs, this style is a good choice.

- **Formatted paragraphs:** FrontPage maintains the separation between individual paragraphs and applies the Formatted style to each one. Use this style if you want the individual paragraphs in your document to remain distinct.

- **Normal paragraphs:** FrontPage applies the Normal style to each of the document's paragraphs. The Normal style is the default style for Web page text. The Normal style appears as a proportional font — most browsers display Times.

- **Normal paragraphs with line breaks:** FrontPage applies the Normal style to the document's paragraphs and retains line breaks. Use this style if you want your document's line breaks to remain intact.

- **Treat as HTML:** If the text file contains HTML tags, this option tells FrontPage to treat the tags as valid HTML and not to place the tags into the body of the Web page.

If you don't want to convert an entire document, you can cut or copy data from other programs and then paste the data into an open page in FrontPage.

Now that you know your options, here's how to proceed:

1. **In FrontPage, create a new page.**

   I discuss how earlier in this chapter.

   (If you want to place converted content inside an existing Web page, open that page and place the cursor where you want the content to appear.)

2. **Choose Insert⇨File.**

   The Select File dialog box appears.

3. **In the dialog box's Files of type list box, choose the type of file you want to convert, and then navigate your computer or network to the location of the file.**

4. **In the dialog box, double-click the file.**

   The Select File dialog box closes, and one of the following three things happens:

   - If FrontPage knows how to proceed, it converts the document's content and places the content into the Web page. (You can skip the rest of the steps in this section.)

   - If the document is a text file, the Convert Text dialog box appears. This dialog box offers you five formats in which to convert text — I describe the formats earlier in this section.

   - If FrontPage needs guidance, the Open File As dialog box appears. This dialog box prompts you to select the format in which you want FrontPage to convert the file's content. Your choices are HTML, RTF, or Text (FrontPage automatically selects the option it thinks is best).

5. **In the Convert Text or Open File As dialog box, select the option you want to use, and then click OK.**

   The dialog box closes, and FrontPage proceeds to convert the document's content according to your preference.

 FrontPage's conversion features can't reliably handle certain word-processing special effects such as annotations, footnotes, and embedded objects. In the case of embedded clip art, charts, and spreadsheets, FrontPage can convert the objects into Web-ready graphics. Other effects don't weather the conversion so well.

If in doubt, try the conversion. If you don't like the way FrontPage converts your document, close the page without saving it. Because your original document remains safely unchanged on your hard drive, you can choose a different conversion method later.

Previewing a Page

As you create pages in the Page View, the pages look similar to how they appear as viewed with a web browser. In techno-speak, this similarity is called *WYSIWYG* (pronounced *wizzy-wig*), which stands for *What You See Is What You Get*.

Even so, previewing your pages is a good idea. Previewing gives you a more accurate representation of how your pages will appear to your visitors after the site has been published. FrontPage enables you to quickly preview your pages by using two methods: by clicking the Preview tab in the lower-left corner of the Page View, or by opening the pages in a separate web browser such as Microsoft Internet Explorer or Netscape Navigator.

Previewing pages using the Preview tab

The Preview tab shows you how your page would look and act in a web browser — specifically, the version of Microsoft Internet Explorer you have installed on your computer. Unlike previewing your page with a separate browser, you don't need to first save the page to preview it, which is handy for on-the-fly previewing. The Preview tab also has the advantage of living inside FrontPage, so you don't need to launch a separate program to preview your pages.

The Preview tab only works if you have Microsoft Internet Explorer 3.0 or later installed on your computer. FrontPage doesn't have a browser built into its midst; it uses Internet Explorer to display what's inside the Preview tab. Therefore, if you don't have the program installed, FrontPage has no way of rendering a page preview.

Furthermore, the Preview tab can't accurately display working versions of certain FrontPage Web site effects.

Previewing pages using a web browser

For the extra few seconds of lag time while the program launches, I recommend previewing your pages in an honest-to-goodness web browser. By using a web browser to preview your pages as you work, you get the most accurate representation of what your visitors will see when they check out your Web site.

Even better, if you have more than one web browser installed on your computer, you can choose which browser you'd like FrontPage to launch. You can also select different window sizes so that you can see how your page looks to visitors who have monitors of lower resolution than yours.

Because FrontPage makes previewing your pages in several browsers so easy, consider downloading and installing more than one browser program (preferably ones that can display different features) if you have the room on your hard drive. The insight that you gain about how different pages may look in different browsers is worth the extra bit of effort required in installing the extra browsers.

(For more general information about browser-specific Web publishing effects, see Chapter 4. For tips on how to account for browser-specific differences in your site's design, refer to Chapter 5.)

For an overview of the display capabilities of different web browsers, visit the Browser Kit section of Webmonkey at `www.hotwired.com/webmonkey/browserkit`. You can download different web browsers from Download.com at `www.download.com`.

 To preview your page in your default web browser, click the Preview in Browser button in the Page View's Standard toolbar.

To choose the browser in which you want to open the page or to control the window size, follow these steps:

1. **Choose File⟹Preview in Browser.**

   The Preview in Browser dialog box appears (see Figure 3-3).

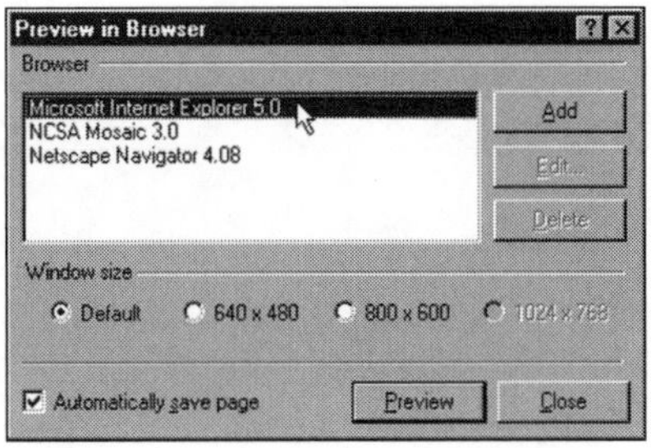

Figure 3-3:
The Preview in Browser dialog box.

Preview in Browser	? X
Browser	
Microsoft Internet Explorer 5.0	Add
NCSA Mosaic 3.0	Edit...
Netscape Navigator 4.08	Delete
Window size	
⦿ Default ○ 640 x 480 ○ 800 x 600 ○ 1024 x 768	
☑ Automatically save page Preview Close	

2. **In the dialog box's Browser list, click the name of the browser you want to use.**

3. **Click the radio button for the window size that you want to view.**

   A monitor's *resolution* refers to the number of pixels the monitor can display on-screen. The numbers listed next to each radio button represent standard resolution values. The larger the number, the higher the resolution of the picture and the more "real estate" a monitor can display.

4. **Click the Automatically Save Page check box to prompt FrontPage to save the page each time you use the Preview in Browser command.**

5. **Click the Preview button.**

   The dialog box closes, and FrontPage opens your page in the browser of your choice.

To edit the page, return to FrontPage by clicking the Microsoft FrontPage button in the Windows taskbar (or press Alt+Tab to switch between open programs). Make any changes you want and then save the page. To view changes, click the Preview in Browser button again, or switch back to your browser and click the browser's Reload or Refresh button.

You can easily add browsers to the Browser list visible in the Preview in Browser dialog box. In the dialog box, click the Add button to display the Add Browser dialog box. Also in the dialog box, type the name of the browser in the Name text box, and then click Browse to locate the browser's program icon on your hard drive.

Printing a Page

Web pages don't make the best transition to print because the concept of "a page" on the World Wide Web is tied to a chunk of information rather than to a physical piece of paper. Even so, you may, from time to time, need to print your Web pages if, say, your Net-challenged boss wants to check on your work.

Before you commit to paper, choose File⇨Print Preview to see how the Web page will look on the printed page.

To print a page, do the following:

1. **In the Page View's Standard toolbar, click the Print button.**

   If the Print button appears dimmed, in the Page View, click anywhere inside the open page.

   After you click the Print button, the Print dialog box appears.

2. **If not already visible in the dialog box's Name list box, choose the name of the printer you want to use.**

3. **In the Print Range area, click the All radio button to print all pages, or click the Pages radio button to specify a range of pages.**

   "Pages" in this case refers to the number of pieces of paper it takes to print all the information in your Web page. If you click Pages, type the number of the first page in the range in the From text box and the number of the last page in the range in the To text box.

   Unfortunately, in FrontPage, you can only print one Web page at a time. If you want to print all the pages inside your Web site, you must open each page separately and follow this set of steps.

4. **In the Number of copies text box, type the number of copies you want to print.**

5. **If you are printing more than one copy of the page and want to collate the copies, click the Collate check box.**

6. **Click OK to spur your printer into action.**

Keep in mind that FrontPage print settings affect how FrontPage prints your pages, not how your pages print after you publish them on the World Wide Web. If your visitors want to print your Web site, their web browsers' print settings determine how the finished product looks.

Saving a Page

Your Web publishing masterpiece is only as grand as the last time you saved your pages. So save your work often. My fingers instinctively press Ctrl+S every time I write a particularly brilliant sentence.

You can save a page as part of the Web site currently open in FrontPage, elsewhere on your hard drive or network, directly on the World Wide Web, or as a FrontPage template.

 If you've made lots of changes to your page but haven't yet saved the changes, you can erase all the changes and revert to the previously saved version of the page. To do so, in the Standard toolbar, click the Refresh button. After FrontPage asks whether you want to save the changes, click No.

 If you can't remember which open pages you've saved recently, click the Window menu. In the menu that drops down, filenames followed by asterisks (*) contain changes that have not yet been saved.

Filenaming tips and tricks

Here are a few tips to keep in mind as you consider what to name your Web pages:

- **Filename.** Keep your filenames short and sweet. I recommend sticking to one-word names that only use lowercase letters. This saves your visitors from having to type a long, involved filename when they want to view the page in a web browser.

- **Home page filename.** The home page filename you choose should be determined by the host web server on which you will eventually publish your Web site. Most web servers recognize the filename index.htm or index.html as the

Web site's home page, but other servers recognize different names. Before you publish your Web site, ask your system administrator or a helpful person at your ISP which home page filename you should use.

- **Filename extension.** Should you use the .htm or .html filename extension? It's up to you — they're interchangeable. FrontPage automatically appends the .htm extension to whatever filename you choose, but if you prefer to use .html, when you save the file, add .html to the filename you specify.

Saving a page on your computer or network

Follow these steps when you want to save a page anywhere on your computer or local network. Most often, you will save new pages inside FrontPage Web sites, but you can just as easily choose another location. To save a page on your computer or local network, follow these steps:

1. In the Standard toolbar, click the Save button.

The Save As dialog box appears (see Figure 3-4).

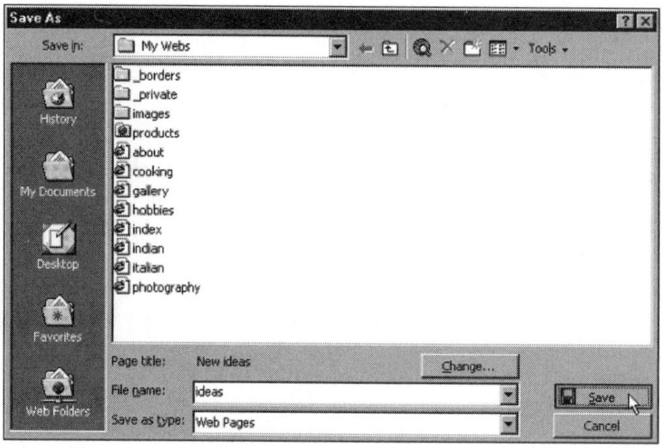

Figure 3-4:
The Save
As dialog
box.

If you're saving an existing page, no dialog box appears — the command just saves your changes. If you want to save the page in a different location, choose File⇨Save As to display the Save As dialog box.

By default, FrontPage saves pages as follows:

- If a Web site is currently open in FrontPage, and you create a new page, FrontPage prompts you to save the new page as part of that FrontPage Web site.

- If no Web site is currently open in FrontPage, and you create a new page, FrontPage prompts you to save the page as part of the last Web site that was open during the session. If you haven't yet opened a Web site, FrontPage prompts you to save the page in the My Webs folder (the default location for your first FrontPage Web site).

- When you make changes to an existing page, FrontPage saves the changes in the same location, *except* if you originally opened the page from a site on a different web server on which you don't have authoring access. In that case, FrontPage prompts you to save the page inside the last Web site that was open during the session, or in the `My Webs` folder.

2. **If you want to save the page in a different location, in the Save in list box, navigate to the location on your computer or network.**

3. **To change the page title, in the dialog box, click Change.**

   The Set Page Title dialog box appears.

When you view a Web page in a web browser, the title appears in the browser's *title bar* — the little colorful strip at the top of the browser window. Page titles also appear in Web search indexes (such as Yahoo! and Excite) and in visitors' lists of browser bookmarks. The page's title should sum up the page's content in a way that's meaningful to visitors. For example, whereas the title *My Home Page* could apply to millions of different pages all over the World Wide Web, *Asha Dornfest's Home Page* tells the visitor exactly what to expect.

4. **In the dialog box's Page title text box, type a new title, and then click OK.**

   The dialog box closes and the Save As dialog box becomes visible again.

5. **If you want to change the page's filename, enter a new name in the File name list box.**

   If you don't specify a filename extension, FrontPage adds `.htm` to the name you enter here when you save the page.

6. **Click Save.**

   The dialog box closes, and FrontPage saves the page.

   If the page you're saving contains pictures, the Save Embedded Files dialog box appears. Refer to the sidebar "Saving pages containing pictures" for details on how to use this dialog box.

If you open a page from one location and then save the page to a different location, FrontPage saves a copy of the edited page. The original, unchanged page remains in its original spot.

Saving a page as part of a "live" Web site

You can save a page as part of a Web site that's stored on another web server to which you're connected via your company intranet or the Internet. By doing so, you are, in effect, publishing the single page.

Saving pages containing pictures

If you save a page that was originally opened from a location outside the current FrontPage Web site and that page contains graphics, FrontPage is smart enough to ask if you want to save the associated graphic files as well. If FrontPage didn't take this extra step, the pictures in the page wouldn't show up, because no associated graphic file would be available to display. (You discover the mechanics of Web graphics in Chapter 7.)

After you click Save in Step 6 of the section "Saving a page on your computer or network," in addition to saving the page, FrontPage pops open the Save Embedded Files dialog box. This dialog box enables you to save the graphic file as well as change the graphic's filename and specify the folder in which it will be stored. By clicking the dialog box's Set Action button, you can even choose not to save the image file but to maintain the reference inside the page. (This action would result in a broken image reference in your page but is useful if you are using FrontPage to edit pages from a different location and the pages rely on a different file system.) After you specify your preferences, click the OK button to save the graphic.

To save a page as part of a Web site stored on a remote web server, you must have authoring access to that Web site, and the host web server must support FrontPage Server Extensions. For more information about publishing your Web site (including the importance of FrontPage Server Extensions), flip to Chapter 16.

If the host web server doesn't support FrontPage Server Extensions, you must publish your page using the steps listed in Chapter 16. Don't worry — it's just as easy.

To save your page in a Web site stored on a different web server, do this:

1. **Activate your Internet connection.**

2. **Follow Steps 1–4 in the previous section called "Saving a page on your computer or network."**

3. **In the File name list box, enter the Web address to which you want to publish the page, and then click Save.**

   The Web address you specify must include the address of the server (it looks something like `http://www.server.com`) followed by a forward slash and the filename. If the file is to be stored in a folder or subweb on the server, the folder reference must precede the filename, like this: `http://www.server.com/foldername/filename`.

   Note: File paths on web servers work just like file paths on your own computer, except that file paths on web servers contain forward slashes, not backslashes. For a crash course in file path notation, see Chapter 1.

After you click Save, the Enter Network Password dialog box appears.

3. **In the dialog box, enter your user name and password, and then click OK.**

   The dialog box closes, and FrontPage saves the page as part of the Web site.

Saving a page as a FrontPage template

You can save any page as a FrontPage page template. This feature saves countless hours if you create lots of pages with standard layouts. Even better, if you are working with a Web design team, you can create *shared templates* everyone on the team can access. (I talk more about FrontPage's collaboration features in Chapter 15.)

1. **With the page you want to save as a template open in the Page View, choose File⇨Save As.**

   The Save As dialog box appears.

2. **In the Save As type list box, choose** `FrontPage Template (*.tem)` **and then click OK.**

   (Because you're creating a template, you don't have to fill in a page title or filename.) The Save As dialog box closes, and the Save As Template dialog box appears.

3. **Enter a descriptive title in the Title text box.**

4. **In the Name text box, type a filename.**

   Just type a short word — FrontPage automatically applies the appropriate filename extension (`tem`) to the filename you choose.

5. **In the Description text box, type a short description of the template's function.**

6. **To create a shared template other site authors can use when working on the Web site, mark the Save Template In Current Web check box.**

7. **Click OK.**

   FrontPage saves the page as a template.

   If the page that you're saving contains pictures, the Save Embedded Files dialog box appears. Refer to the sidebar "Saving pages containing pictures" earlier in this chapter for details on how to use this dialog box.

The next time you choose File⇨New⇨Page in the Page View, your template appears with all its friends in the General tab of the New dialog box.

Part II

Creating Web Pages That Make You Look Like a Genius

The 5th Wave — By Rich Tennant

"I couldn't say anything. They were in here with that FrontPage program we bought them that encourages artistic expression."

In this part . . .

Mastering FrontPage is one thing. . . . Understanding how to construct a great-looking, easy-to-navigate Web site is another. Part II helps you do both.

In this part, you discover how to build Web pages from the ground up. You delve into the inner workings of the Page View, your tool for everything from creating hyperlinks to adding interactive forms to your Web site.

Chapter 4

Web Design Fundamentals

In This Chapter

▶ Clients and servers

▶ Cross-platform mania

▶ Five steps to a brilliant Web site

▶ Evidence that HTML is easy

*T*he desktop-publishing revolution of the '80s taught wannabe designers a lesson: Buying a big, fat desktop-publishing program doesn't guarantee clear, professional newsletters and reports. The crucial ingredient — design sense, or a "good eye" — isn't built into the software.

In the same way, creating great-looking Web sites by using FrontPage requires a thorough understanding of the program's capabilities *and* an eye for what makes a Web site work. This chapter pumps up your design muscles so you can build a site that's easy to navigate, loads quickly, and looks fantastic.

Clients and Servers 101

To understand Web design, you first need to understand the basic relationship between clients and servers on the World Wide Web. The client-server relationship is the yin and yang that keeps the Internet running.

A *server* is any computer that contains and distributes information. A *client* is the program that requests and processes or displays that information. Web servers store and serve Web pages, and web clients (more often referred to as *web browsers*) display the pages on your screen. Clients and servers are useless without each other, much like separate halves of a piece of Velcro.

If you're unclear about the client-server relationship, think of your television. After you turn on your TV, the device hunts for signals from a broadcast station, assembles the signals into *Ally McBeal,* and displays the show on your TV screen. In this example, the broadcast station is the server, and your TV set is the client. Without the signals sent by the broadcast station, your TV is an empty box. By the same token, without TVs to pick up and display these signals, broadcast stations have no purpose. Figure 4-1 illustrates the client-server relationship.

When you publish a site on the World Wide Web, you place all the site's linked files on a web server. The server waits patiently, listening for client requests from the Internet or company intranet. As soon as the server receives a request (a visitor types the file's URL into his or her browser), the server springs into action and delivers the requested file. How the file looks after appearing on your visitor's screen depends in large part on the particular features of the visitor's computer and Internet setup, such as the choice of browser software, operating system, and size and resolution of the monitor.

Return to the TV analogy for a moment. The broadcast station (the server) spits signals into the ether, which your TV (the client) picks up and translates into *Ally McBeal* (the file). You're watching the same show as everyone else. What you see on your color, 27-inch screen, however, looks different from what your neighbor sees on the old black-and-white set in her kitchen (see Figure 4-2).

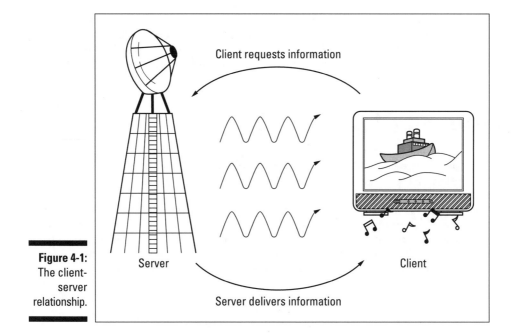

Figure 4-1:
The client-server relationship.

Client requests information

Server delivers information

Server

Client

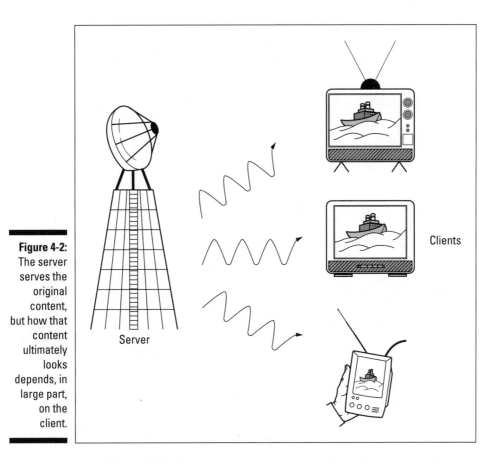

Figure 4-2:
The server
serves the
original
content,
but how that
content
ultimately
looks
depends, in
large part,
on the
client.

In a fit of mischief, you adjust the contrast setting on your TV, and Ally McBeal's face turns green. She doesn't turn green all over America — just on your set — and the broadcast station can't do a thing about it.

The moral of this story is that you have only so much control over how your Web site looks after it ends up on your visitors' screens. Read on if you want to discover more about the specific differences between clients and how to accommodate those differences in your site's design.

Cross-Platform Mania

Designing for the World Wide Web is often compared to taming a large, hairy beast. Whereas conventional design enables you to control how the finished product looks down to the finest detail, Web design can be, at times, a crapshoot. Why? Because the Web is a *cross-platform medium,* which means that people browse the Web by using any number of hardware devices, software programs, and operating systems. Each piece of the platform affects how Web sites ultimately look after the sites show up on the visitor's screen.

The challenge (or, as those less tactful may say, pain-in-the-butt) is to design sites that account for platform variations and still manage to look great. Doing so is not difficult after you accept a few truisms about the Web as a publishing medium. You soon realize that the Web design beast, although still big and hairy, is really just a teddy bear after you come to know it.

Web truism #1: Your visitors use different computers

Just as people drive to work in buses, Bugs, and BMWs, folks cruise the Net with all sorts of computers. Some drive old clunkers with tiny black-and-white monitors. Others speed along with turbo-charged processors and a big, full-color display. The beauty of the Web is that the vehicle doesn't matter — whether you use a Mac, a PC, a UNIX workstation, or even a television, all you need is a web browser and you're ready to roll. The problem, however, is that Web sites look different depending on the visitor's hardware setup.

A particular Web site viewed on different computers doesn't necessarily look so different that you wouldn't recognize the site, but slight differences such as color, text alignment, and font size are all affected (in varying degrees) by your visitor's monitor size or resolution and choice of operating system. I created my personal site on a PC running Windows 95, for example, and I gave my page a lovely lemon-yellow background color. To my chagrin, my designer friend — a Mac user — looked at my page with his Web browser and told me that my page was a sickly green. (Fortunately, this problem was easy to fix — I share the secret in Chapter 7.)

Web truism #2: Your visitors use different browsers

Not only do your visitors use different computers, they also use different programs to browse the Web. As with platform differences, Web pages appear slightly different in each web browser — and even in older versions of the same browser.

About 90 percent of the Web surfing population uses some version of Netscape Navigator or Microsoft Internet Explorer, the big guns in the battle to dominate the browser field. The other 10 percent use other browsers, such as Cyberdog, Lynx (a text-only browser), browsers designed to accommodate physical disabilities, proprietary browsers belonging to online services, or foreign-language browsers (to name a few). "Feh," you say, "why worry about a measly 10 percent?" Because 10 percent of an estimated tens of millions of Net cruisers ain't no handful.

Browser-specific design effects further complicate the situation. In an effort to encourage folks to use their products, Netscape and Microsoft each use technology that produces fantastic design effects — but only if viewed by the companies' own browsers and, even then, only by the most recent version. If you're one of the unfortunate 10 percent using another browser, or you use an older version of Internet Explorer or Navigator, too bad.

Fortunately, FrontPage gives you some level of control of browser-specific effects as you design your Web site. I show you how to use this feature in Chapter 5.

Web truism #3: Your visitors connect to the Internet at different speeds

Speed is an obsession on the Internet. A few seconds spent waiting for a Web site to appear on-screen feels like an eternity. Seconds stretch into agonizing minutes for those of your visitors using slow Internet connections.

What causes a Web site to load at tortoise speed? Some factors are beyond your control, such as the speed of the web server that hosts the Web site or the amount of traffic clogging the network at that particular moment.

Other factors are directly related to the design of the Web site itself. Graphics are the worst culprit. Big pictures with lots of colors take a long time to load and are not always worth the time spent waiting.

The length of a Web page also affects its speed. Pages containing several screens full of text load more slowly than shorter pages.

Other notorious sloths include multimedia goodies, such as sounds, videos, and embedded miniprograms called Java applets or ActiveX components. These Web publishing extras, so loved by designers with lightning-fast Internet connections, are the bane of regular folks surfing with a 28.8 Kbps modem.

Web truism #4: Your visitors come from diverse cultures

Consider your visitors' cultural backgrounds to be as central to your design as platform differences. Differences in language and outlook affect how your visitors experience your Web site just as much as do their choices of computer or browser. Beyond its appearance, your site must speak to people of different cultures, nationalities, and value systems. Keep a diverse audience in mind as you build your site. By making sure that each page is easy to navigate and is clearly written, you make your site accessible to the largest audience possible.

Five Steps to a Brilliant Web Site

If you read the preceding section, you're now aware of the Web design truisms, and you can account for these factors as you design your site. The following sections describe how to do so in five easy steps.

Give your site a purpose

As I write this book, my purpose isn't to document the Internet or even to explain every nook and cranny of Web publishing. My purpose is to show you how to use FrontPage to create a beautiful Web site — and have fun at the same time.

Your site needs a similar clarity of purpose to be effective. Focus on what you want your site to accomplish: Do you want to educate your visitors? Do you want to sell them a product? Do you just want to share your warped vision of the world? After you decide what you want your site to do, make the purpose clear to your visitors right away so that they know what to expect if they decide to stay for a while.

You can state your site's purpose directly. ("Welcome to the Hurricane-A-Day home page, your source for the latest information on tropical storms.") Or you can use a more subtle approach by listing your site's different parts, thereby enabling your visitors to know, at a glance, what kind of information they can find there.

Remember your visitors

Establishing a purpose can be daunting unless you concentrate on your most important visitors: your *target audience*. Just as *Seventeen* targets teenyboppers and *Wired* targets technology addicts, your site must target a specific group of people.

Visualize your target audience. No, don't try to divine your visitors' hair color or astrological signs. Ask yourself the following questions: "Are they technically savvy? How old are they? What kind of information do they want?" The more answers you come up with, the better you can communicate your message to your visitors.

Cultivate an image

Elvis, Nike, and Howard Stern all have something your Web site needs: an image. Your site's image is everything it says without words — in advertising and design lingo, its look and feel. So think about how you'd want your target audience to describe your site — "friendly," "cutting edge," "useful," "bizarre" — and choose your site's graphics and layout accordingly.

Make your site easy to navigate

If you've ever driven a car in San Francisco, you know it's not what one would call a user-friendly city. One-way streets, nosebleed hills, and elusive parking make driving in San Francisco a daunting experience for the first-time visitor. (Of course, you can always double-park while you hop out for a cappuccino, which more than makes up for the hassles.)

Your Web site should be just the opposite. Your site must be easy to navigate the very first time around. Guide your visitors with clearly categorized information and thoughtfully placed links. (Navigation bars help your visitors, too; check out Chapter 6 for details.) Break information into manageable bits, keeping pages short and easy to read. If your visitors get lost, give them a map containing links to all the pages in your site or, even better, set the site up so that visitors can search your site for keywords. (You can perform this task by using the FrontPage Search Form Component, which you discover in Chapter 14.)

For an excellent discussion of the merits of mapping out your site's navigational flow, read *Site Blueprints: The Key to Good Web Hygiene* by Lou Rosenfeld. You can find this useful guide on the Web at `webreview.com/design/arch/sept15/index.html`.

Plan for the future

Web sites, like little babies, grow. It's inevitable. As time goes on, you're bound to add new pages and even new sections to your site. Build some growing room into your site's organization. Minimize repetitive tasks by creating page templates and macros. Use shared borders and the Include Page Component to automate the inclusion of standard elements in your pages. (You can read about shared borders in Chapter 6 and the Include Page Component in Chapter 14.) Most important, keep the growth of your Web site in perspective by refining your site's purpose and by remaining focused on your target audience.

The Web loves to talk about itself, hence the enormous number of Web sites devoted to the topic of Web design. Here are a few of the best:

- ✔ David Siegel's Web Wonk at `www.dsiegel.com/tips`
- ✔ Builder.com at `www.builder.com`
- ✔ Web Review at `www.webreview.com`

Or, if you're looking for some good books on the topic of Web design, check out *Web Design and Desktop Publishing For Dummies* by Roger C. Parker (IDG Books Worldwide, Inc.), or *The Non-Designer's Web Book* by Robin Williams and John Tollett (Peachpit Press).

Evidence That HTML Is Easy

And you thought you'd sneak out of here without hearing anything about HTML, the language used to create Web pages. You don't need to know HTML to publish fully functional, great-looking Web sites with FrontPage. If you want to get serious about Web publishing, however, HTML fluency has no substitute. HTML evolves faster than Microsoft can crank out new versions of FrontPage, so knowing HTML enables you to integrate the latest, hottest Web design effects into your site today.

You don't need programming experience to learn HTML because HTML isn't a programming language. HTML is a *markup language,* which means that it's just a series of codes that signal your Web browser to display certain formatting and layout effects. These codes, called *tags,* are easy to pick up. Don't believe me? Keep reading: I prove my point in the following paragraphs.

Figure 4-3 shows a line of text in a Web page as it looks when viewed with a web browser.

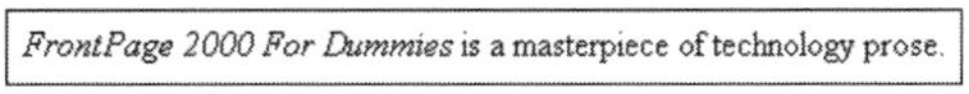

Figure 4-3:
Regular and italic text, as seen in a web browser.

FrontPage 2000 For Dummies is a masterpiece of technology prose.

Figure 4-4 shows the HTML tags behind that same line of text. The HTML tags that define italic text (`<i>` and `</i>`) surround the words `FrontPage 2000 For Dummies`. The opening tag, `<i>`, tells the Web browser where the italic text begins, and the closing tag, `</i>`, indicates where the italics end.

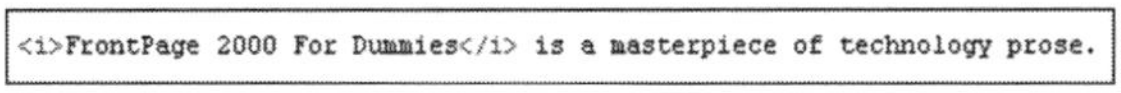

Figure 4-4:
The HTML tags behind the line of text shown in Figure 4-3.

`<i>FrontPage 2000 For Dummies</i> is a masterpiece of technology prose.`

That's the basic premise behind HTML. Not as difficult as you thought, eh? So consider taking a crack at HTML. If you're serious about becoming a Web designer and you want to keep up with the newest trends, it's the thing to do.

FrontPage contains several features that simplify working with your page's underlying HTML. To access a page's HTML tags, with the page open in the Page View, click the HTML tab (it's located next to the Preview tab in the lower portion of the Page View window). For more details about working with HTML, choose Help➪Microsoft FrontPage Help (or press F1) to access the FrontPage Help system.

No doubt my HTML teaser has captivated your imagination. Find out more by visiting one or several of the wonderful HTML tutorials on the Web. Visit `www.ashaland.com/webpub/about.html` for an overview. Or add *HTML For Dummies,* 3rd Edition (IDG Books Worldwide, Inc.), by Ed Tittel and Steve James, to your computer book library.

Chapter 5

Tweaking Your Text

● ●

In This Chapter

▶ Adding text

▶ Designing with browser and server compatibility in mind

▶ Creating stylish fonts and paragraphs

▶ Building lists

▶ Adjusting paragraph alignment, indenting, and spacing

▶ Adding borders and shading

▶ Inserting symbols, invisible comments, and horizontal lines

● ●

*Y*ou didn't buy this book just to find out how to use FrontPage. Figuring out FrontPage is simply a means to an end; your ultimate goal is to create a spectacular Web site. In this and the following chapters, I show you how to build beautiful pages using the FrontPage Page View.

The Page View contains a gazillion tools and commands that control various aspects of a Web page. In this chapter, I concentrate on the tools that affect the main ingredient of a page: text.

What Does the Page View Do?

You use the Page View to open and add stuff to the individual pages that make up your Web site.

Before programs like FrontPage hit the scene, you had to create and work with Web pages by fiddling with HTML. HTML stands for *Hypertext Markup Language,* a set of codes that defines the layout and structure of a Web page. These codes (called *tags*) control how the page looks and acts. (Figure 5-1 illustrates a bare-naked Web page with its HTML tags showing.) As you surf the Web, your web browser translates HTML tags into the nice, neat Web page you see on-screen. (Figure 5-2 shows how the page in Figure 5-1 looks as seen through the flattering lens of a web browser.)

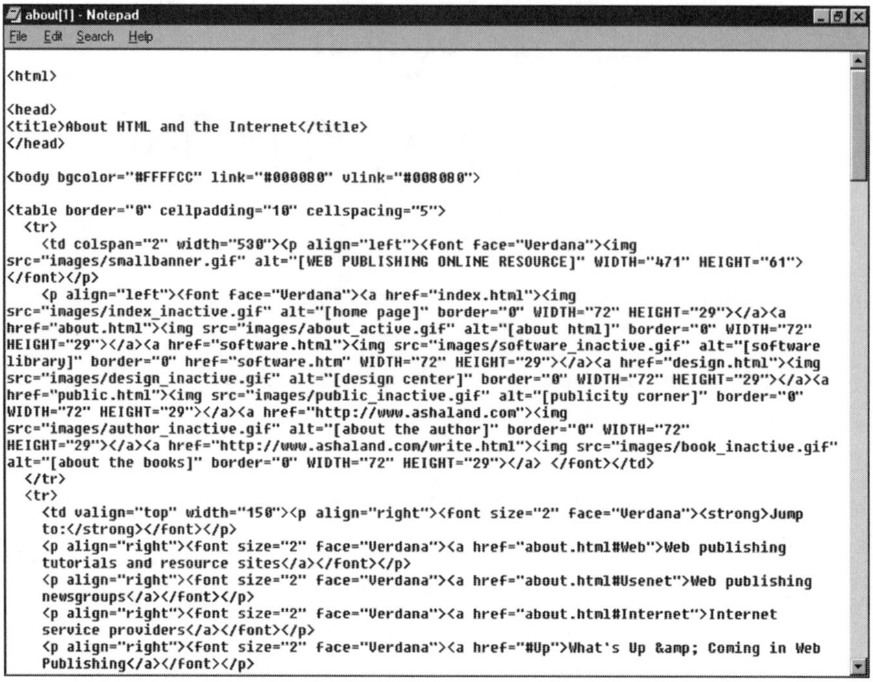

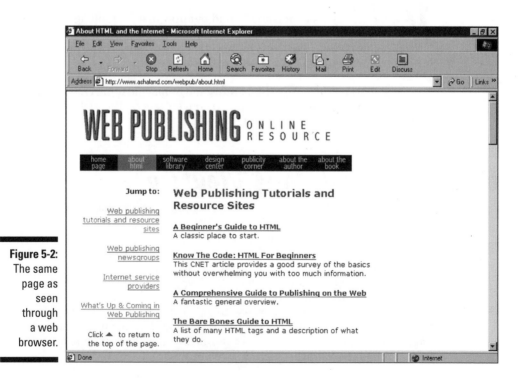

Figure 5-1:
Kindly avert your eyes; this page's HTML tags are showing.

Figure 5-2:
The same page as seen through a web browser.

HTML isn't just for geeks

Although you don't need to learn HTML to create Web pages with FrontPage, a bit of HTML knowledge certainly doesn't hurt. In fact, learning HTML is well worth your time. HTML is constantly evolving, with new tags and design effects making impressive debuts. Future versions of FrontPage are sure to support these features, but you don't want to wait for (or, heaven forbid, pay for) an upgrade so that you can use hot, new effects in your site, do you? So consider learning a bit of HTML. You gain a greater understanding of Web publishing, and you can take advantage of HTML's latest features. At the very least, you can impress your colleagues at the next staff party.

In Chapter 4, I introduce you to some elementary HTML, just to prove how easy the stuff is.

Until recently, you had to learn all the HTML tags to create a Web page. Although memorizing tags is not difficult, doing so does take time. Because most of us would rather frolic on the beach than spend weekends in front of the computer, the process of learning HTML (along with programming the VCR) stayed tucked away in the techie zone.

That is, until programs like FrontPage came along. The Page View does the HTML grunt work for you, freeing your brain cells for creative tasks such as deciding what to put on your page. You get to choose menu items and click buttons, and the Page View generates all the HTML behind the scenes — which means that you can create sophisticated Web pages without sacrificing precious beach time.

Getting Started

Words, letters, numbers, characters. Text. Seems rather humble compared to the World Wide Web's flashy graphics and interactive effects. Yet text is the most important part of each page that you create, because the text makes up the majority of the content. You may dazzle your visitors with cutting-edge visuals and multimedia tricks, but the content — fresh, interesting, useful information — keeps people coming back for more.

Adding text to a page

Enough with the lecture. I promised to get you started on a Web page, didn't I? Okay, so launch FrontPage and open your Web site, jump to the Page View, and start typing on the new, blank page sitting there. Or, open and type on an existing page. (If you're not sure how to launch or get around in FrontPage, flip through the chapters in Part I.) Type whatever you want. Better yet, type something close to what you'd like a page in your Web site to contain.

If you want more room to type, you can increase your screen real estate by hiding the Views Bar and the Folder List. To toggle the current setting, choose View↷Views Bar and View↷Folder List.

Sanity-saving shortcuts

FrontPage shares many attractive features (its ease of use, its good looks) with its Microsoft Office siblings. The Page View contains the following time-saving Office features that may tempt you to give your computer a big, affectionate squeeze:

- ✔ **Undo:** If you type (or, worse, delete) something that you didn't want typed (or deleted), the Undo button in the Standard toolbar enables you to take back what you've done, up to the last 30 actions.

- ✔ **Redo:** You can redo anything you've undone by clicking the Redo button.

- ✔ **Cut, Copy, and Paste:** You can cut, copy, and paste stuff (text, images — just about anything that you can select with your pointer) between open pages in FrontPage and between documents in different programs. Just click the Cut, Copy, or Paste button. If you want more control over how FrontPage formats the text you are about to paste into your document, choose Edit↷Paste Special.

- ✔ **Drag and Drop:** You can drag and drop text, graphics, and other elements to different locations inside pages.

- ✔ **Find and Replace:** The Edit↷Find command enables you to jump directly to the location of a character, word, or phrase. You can even replace all instances of that character/word/phrase with another character/word/phrase by using the Edit↷Replace command. Both the Find and the Replace functions work inside a single page or across the entire Web site. They can even sift through the pages' HTML tags (a useful feature if you're HTML-literate).

- ✔ **Thesaurus:** The built-in Thesaurus (accessible by choosing Tools↷Thesaurus) instantly boosts your vocabulary by thousands of words.

- ✔ **Spell checking:** Click the Spelling button to take care of last-minute typo cleanups. If you activate the spell checker while in the Page View, FrontPage spell checks the open page. If you are in any other view, FrontPage gives you the option to spell check the entire Web site in one go. FrontPage also knows how to check spelling as you type. Red squiggly lines appear inside the page beneath words that are either misspelled or unrecognizable to FrontPage. To correct a mistake, right-click the word, and then choose the correct spelling from the pop-up menu that appears. If the word is spelled correctly but is unfamiliar to FrontPage, add the word to the FrontPage dictionary by right-clicking the word and then choosing Add. (To turn on and off automatic spell checking, choose Tools⇨Page Options. In the Options dialog box that appears, click the Spelling tab, and then mark the Check Spelling As You Type check box. Click OK to close the dialog box.)

✔ **Customizable toolbars:** You can show, hide, rearrange, and customize any of the FrontPage toolbars. To show or hide toolbars, choose View⇨ Toolbars, and then choose the name of the toolbar you want to show or hide (in the Toolbars list, check marks indicate toolbars that are currently visible). To customize your toolbars, click the down-arrow on the right side of the toolbar, and then choose Add Or Remove Buttons. From the pop-up menu that appears, choose the buttons you want to show or hide, or for even more options, choose Customize. You can also "float" toolbars; pass the pointer over the left edge of the toolbar until the pointer turns into a crossed arrow. Click and drag the toolbar anywhere inside the FrontPage window, and then drop it. To dock the toolbar back in its original position, double-click the title bar on the top of the toolbar.

✔ **Right-click pop-up menus:** FrontPage contains shortcuts to commonly used commands in pop-up menus that appear after you pass the pointer over an element (a piece of text, a hyperlink, a graphic, anything) and click the right mouse button. The pop-up menu that appears contains commands pertaining to the element you just clicked.

✔ **Tool Tips:** If you can't remember a toolbar item's function, pass your pointer over the item; in a moment, a yellow Tool Tip appears telling you the item's name.

✔ **Personalized desktop setup:** The Tools⇨Customize command gives you access to all sorts of options for setting menu commands, toolbars, and other desktop settings just the way you like them.

Keeping Web Browser and Server Compatibility in Mind

Using FrontPage, you can choose a web browser platform for which you want to optimize your site, and you can also pick and choose among browser-specific design effects. You need to think about this now, *before* you embark on site-building, because, based on your choices, FrontPage makes decisions about how it carries out text formatting and other design tasks. Furthermore, FrontPage only makes those effects that will work in your chosen platform available in its menus and toolbars.

(If you're not sure what browser-specific design effects are, read Chapter 4 for a quick introduction to the Web's client-server nature and how it affects Web design.)

You'll find a handy table that summarizes browser support for different Web design effects at www.hotwired.com/webmonkey/browserkit. The BrowserCaps Web site at www.browsercaps.com contains more details about different web browsers' capabilities, but the information isn't organized to be a quick read. Even so, it's worth a look.

You can also specify the type of host web server on which you'll eventually publish your site. This feature is most helpful if you intend to publish your site on a web server that doesn't support FrontPage Server Extensions, because it automatically disables effects that require FrontPage Server Extensions to work. (I talk in detail about what FrontPage Server Extensions are and do in Chapter 16.)

To control how FrontPage uses platform-specific effects, follow these steps:

1. **Choose Tools⇨Page Options.**

   The Page Options dialog box appears. (Even though the command is called Page Options, the compatibility settings apply to the entire Web site, including the site's subwebs.)

2. **Click the Compatibility tab to make that group of options visible.**

3. **From the Browsers list box, choose the name of the web browser group for which you want to design.**

   FrontPage only lists two traditional web browsers — Internet Explorer and Netscape Navigator — because these browsers account for the vast majority of the Web browsing population.

4. **From the Browser Versions list box, choose the browser version number for which you want to design.**

   Later versions of both browsers support more design features than earlier versions.

5. **From the Servers list box, choose the name of the web server program used by your ISP or company web server.**

   If your host web server program isn't listed, or if you don't know which web server program to choose, select Custom.

6. **If the host web server has FrontPage Server Extensions installed, make sure the check box called Enabled With Microsoft FrontPage Server Extensions is marked.**

7. **If you want to enable or disable a particular type of design effect, in the Technologies section, mark or unmark the check box corresponding to that effect.**

8. **Click OK.**

   The Options dialog box closes, and FrontPage saves your compatibility settings.

From now on, FrontPage only makes available those effects that will work with the platform you've chosen. All other effects will appear dimmed in FrontPage menus and dialog boxes.

In my experience, not all browsers display certain effects the same way even though FrontPage says otherwise. For example, even though both Internet Explorer 4.0 and Netscape Navigator 4.0 support JavaScript and Dynamic HTML, each browser displays the effects slightly differently. Therefore, if you use browser-specific effects in your Web site, be sure to thoroughly preview your page using more than one web browser. If you're not sure how to preview a page, see Chapter 3.

Foolin' with Fonts

In FrontPage lingo, *font* refers to how text looks in your Web page. Characteristics such as bold or italics, size, color, and typeface all make up a character's font. Characters — the thingies that appear on-screen after you press keyboard buttons — can be an unruly bunch. FrontPage comes with an arsenal of font style tools that can rein in those rowdy . . . er, characters.

Using font tools

Font tools are stored in the Font dialog box and in the Formatting toolbar. The Font dialog box (shown in Figure 5-3) contains every tool you need to control your characters. The options in this dialog box enable you to change the font, style, color, size, and effect of text in your page. To access the Font dialog box, choose Format⇨Font.

The Formatting toolbar (shown in Figure 5-4) contains buttons for the text tools you use most often. If the toolbar isn't already visible, choose View⇨Toolbars⇨Formatting.

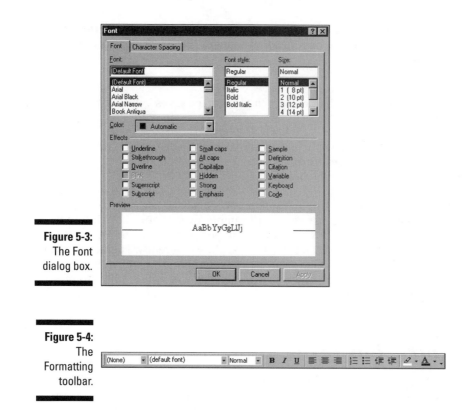

Figure 5-3:
The Font
dialog box.

Figure 5-4:
The
Formatting
toolbar.

You can use font tools in either of the following two ways:

✔ Type a bunch of text, select the text that you want to format, and then turn on the appropriate tool, either by choosing an option in the Font dialog box or by clicking a button in the Formatting toolbar.

✔ Turn on the tool first, type the formatted text, and then turn off the tool after you're done.

You can apply more than one font format to a piece of text. You can, for example, make a word both bold and italic at the same time.

The Format Painter button in the Standard toolbar enables you to copy formatting from one piece of text and then apply that formatting elsewhere. To do so, select the text that contains the formatting you want to copy, click the Format Painter button, and then select the text to which you want to apply the formatting. To apply the formatting to more than one clump of text, select the text that contains the formatting you want to copy, double-click the Format Painter button, select the text to which you want to apply the formatting, and then click the Format Painter button when you're finished.

To turn off all font styles as you type, press Ctrl+spacebar. To remove all font styles from a selected chunk of text, choose Format⇨Remove Formatting.

Changing text font

Usually, when folks talk about a document's font, they're referring to its *typeface,* or the style and shape of the characters. The right choice of font sets the tone for your document and makes the text easy to read.

Until recently, Web designers had no control over text font and had to be content with the default fonts used by most web browsers: Times and Courier. Now, because of advances in HTML and web browser technology, you can apply any font to your Web pages — with certain restrictions, of course.

If you use custom fonts in your Web pages, your visitors' computers must also have these fonts installed for your text to appear correctly on their screens. If your visitors don't have a particular font on their machines, any text you format in that font appears to them in their browsers' default font. For example, if you use the Garamond font in your pages and a visitor who doesn't have Garamond installed on her machine browses your page, she sees your page's text in Times (the default font for most browsers).

Also, font variation is visible only in recent versions of advanced browsers. In other browsers, text appears in the browser's default font.

To change text font, in the Formatting toolbar, choose a new font from the Font list box.

To set the default font for FrontPage, choose Tools⇨Page Options. In the Options dialog box that appears, click the Default Font tab, and then select the desired fonts from the Default Proportional Font and Default Fixed-width Font list boxes. Click OK to close the dialog box.

The thrill of themes

One of the most alluring features in FrontPage 2000 (and other Office 2000 programs) is its extensive collection of graphical *themes.* Themes are coordinated sets of fonts, colors, graphics, and backgrounds that you can apply to your Web site. Chapter 12 goes into detail about themes, but I mention them here because they affect each of the text-tweaking tricks covered in this chapter. For example, if you create a new Web page that is formatted using a theme, it will already have a set font. If you insert a horizontal line (mentioned later in this chapter), a custom-designed graphic line appears in place of the standard gray stripe. Keep these variations in mind as you progress through this chapter.

Being bold (or italic or underlined)

Bold and italic text make up the foundation of the font-formatting team. You pull these formats out like a trusty hammer every time you build a page. Apply these attributes for emphasis or to add variety to your text.

In addition to bold and italic, you have a bunch of other text effects at your disposal, such as subscript, superscript, strikethrough, and small caps. One effect deserves special mention: the *Blink* effect. Blink, a Netscape-specific effect, causes text to flash on and off like a faulty neon sign outside a cheap motel. Trust me — the instances are very few where the Blink effect is anything but tacky.

To apply a font effect, do one of the following things:

- ✔ Click the appropriate button in the Formatting toolbar. (Buttons are available for Bold, Italic, and Underline.)

- ✔ Choose Format⇨Font to open the Font dialog box. Choose a style from the Font Style list, or mark the check box next to the effect you want (if any). If you're not sure how a particular effect looks, mark the check box to see a preview of the effect in the Preview section of the dialog box. When you're done, click OK.

The Overline, Capitalize, Small Caps, and All Caps font effects come courtesy of *Cascading Style Sheet* commands (CSS). Browsers that are unable to display style sheets will not display these effects. Additionally, older browsers are unable to display the Strikethrough effect, because it's a relatively new addition to HTML.

Changing text size

Text size in print documents is measured in absolute units called *points* or *picas.* Because of the way HTML works, text size in Web pages is based on a relative system of *increments.*

HTML text sizes range in increments from 1 (the smallest size) to 7 (the biggest). In FrontPage, the point-size equivalents for each increment range from 8 points (for size 1) to 36 points (for size 7). The catch: The number of points each increment value turns out to be when viewed with a web browser is determined by each visitor's individual browser settings, not by FrontPage.

Here's where you run into some cross-platform prickles, because you can't assume that all of your visitors' browsers are set to display text sizes the same way. For example, by default, FrontPage creates Web pages with size 3 text, which the Page View displays as 12-point type. A nearsighted visitor browsing your site, however, may set her web browser to display size 3 text as 18-point type.

(This is a good illustration of the client-server relationship at work. Refer to Chapter 4 for more information.)

The moral of this story: Although you can control the increment size of the text in your page, you can't control each increment's point-size equivalent as it appears in visitors' web browsers. (The visitor controls his or her own browser settings.)

To change text size, in the Formatting toolbar, choose a size from the Font Size list box.

Font size is visible only in recent versions of advanced browsers. In other browsers, text appears in the browser's default font size.

Another way to change text size is to use the Heading paragraph style. I show you how to use paragraph styles in the section "Creating Stylish Paragraphs" later in this chapter.

Changing text color

You can dress up your text in any color of the rainbow (plus a few fluorescent shades that don't appear in nature). Color gives your text panache, calls attention to important words, and, if coordinated with the colors of the page's graphics, unifies design.

Cascading Style Sheet wizardry

Cascading Style Sheets (or CSS) enable you to sidestep much of the cross-platform variation inherent in Web design. A style sheet is a collection of formatting and style commands that tell the web browser how to display the page.

FrontPage contains built-in support for style sheets so you can create any font or paragraph style you like. See Chapter 13 for details.

To change the color of selected text, click the down-arrow attached to the Font Color button to display a list box of standard colors. Click the color swatch you like to apply that color to your text (see Figure 5-5).

Figure 5-5:
Using the
Font Color
button.

If you don't see a standard color you like, you can choose from a palette of 135 browser-safe colors. (I explain what I mean by *browser-safe* in Chapter 7.) You can even grab colors from any object on your screen, such as a graphic or an icon. To do so, follow these steps:

1. **Click the Font Color button, and then choose More Colors.**

   The More Colors dialog box appears (see Figure 5-6).

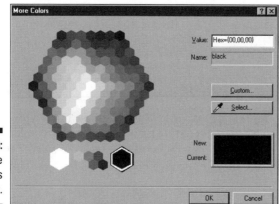

Figure 5-6:
The More
Colors
dialog box.

2. **In the dialog box's color palette, click the color you like.**

   Or, if you would rather grab a color from an existing object, click the Select button. The pointer turns into a little eyedropper. Move the eyedropper over an object on your screen that contains the color you want to use (the active color appears in the New box), and then click to select the color.

3. **Click OK.**

   The More Colors dialog box closes, and FrontPage applies the selected color to your text.

Each time you apply a color to your page, FrontPage adds that color to the Document's Colors section in all color-related list boxes (I introduce you to the list boxes later in the book). This thoughtful little extra makes it easy to apply colors elsewhere in your page, as well as helping you keep an eye on your page's overall color scheme.

You can turn the menu that drops down when you click the Font Color button into a *floating menu* so that it's visible on your screen all the time (handy if you're apply color to several items, or if you want to keep track of your page's color scheme). To do so, click the Font Color button, and then move your pointer over the solid line at the top of the menu that drops down. Once the line changes color, click and drag the menu anywhere on your screen, and then release the mouse button.

To change the body text color for the entire page, select Format⇨Background to display the Background tab of the Page Properties dialog box. From the Text list box, choose the color swatch you like, and then click OK. You can also base your page's body text color on that of another page. You discover how in Chapter 6.

(If your Web site is decorated with a theme, FrontPage prompts you to turn off the theme in order to change the background settings. You find out more about themes in Chapter 12.)

Font color variation is visible only in recent versions of advanced browsers. In other browsers, text appears in the browser's default font color.

Changing character spacing

FrontPage makes it easy to increase or reduce the amount of blank space separating selected characters. To do so, follow these steps:

1. **Choose Format⇨Font to display the Font dialog box.**

2. **In the dialog box, click the Character Spacing tab to make those options visible.**

3. **From the Spacing list box, choose Expanded or Condensed.**

4. **In the accompanying By box, enter the number of pixels by which FrontPage is to expand or contract the selected text.**

   Note: The Position options in this dialog box enable you to control the amount of space between regular text and superscript or subscript text.

5. **Click Apply to see how the spacing change looks before closing the dialog box, or click OK to close the dialog box and apply the character spacing.**

The character spacing options come courtesy of Cascading Style Sheet commands (CSS). Browsers that are unable to display style sheets will not display these effects.

Creating Stylish Paragraphs

Unlike font effects, which you can apply to individual letters and words, paragraph styles operate on entire paragraphs. Use paragraph styles if you want to make widespread changes throughout your page.

A FrontPage paragraph differs from the paragraph defined by your composition teacher. To FrontPage, every time you press the Enter key, you create a new paragraph. Even if you type only one word and then hit Enter, FrontPage considers the word a paragraph.

FrontPage contains the following paragraph styles:

- ✔ **Normal** is the default style for paragraphs. Nothing fancy — just regular old left-aligned paragraphs with a proportional font. (Times appears in most web browsers.)
- ✔ **Formatted** creates paragraphs with a fixed-width font (Courier for most browsers).
- ✔ **Address** is a holdover from the olden days of Web design (around 1993). Back then, the Address style was used to designate the page creator's e-mail address so visitors could get in touch. Today, folks format their contact information any number of ways, so the Address style has, for the most part, become obsolete. Besides, the style creates italic text just as the italic font style does, so why use the old clunker anyway?
- ✔ **Headings** help identify categories of information inside a page. Large headings, usually located at the top of the page, identify what the page is all about, and smaller headings, sprinkled throughout, divide the page's information into manageable bits. Headings in Web pages come in six sizes. Strangely enough, Heading 1 is the largest size, and Heading 6 is the smallest.
- ✔ **Lists** group related bits of information together using bullets, numbers, or special text formatting. I discuss lists in detail in the next section of this chapter.

To change the style of a paragraph, follow these steps:

1. **Place the cursor inside the paragraph you want to format, or select more than one paragraph.**

2. **In the Formatting toolbar, choose the style you want from the Style list box.**

TIP

Practicing safe styles

I remember the first time I used a word processor. I was seduced by the millions of text styles at my disposal and proceeded to use every one in my first document. (I think it was a letter to a pen pal.) The finished product looked like a cut-and-paste ransom note you might see in an old private eye movie. The text was readable, but it was a gaudy mess.

I'm not implying that *you* lack restraint. I relate the example only to illustrate how moderate use of font and paragraph styles enhances a page's readability and visual appeal, whereas overuse sends your readers screaming to a new Web destination.

The List of Lists

Lists. I love 'em and hate 'em. I love 'em because lists promote the illusion that I'm in control. I hate 'em because lists show me just how much work I still need to do.

Lists in Web pages, on the other hand, do nothing but make life easier by organizing your page's information so that your text is easy to read and understand.

Bulleted and numbered lists

Bulleted lists are not lists that were attacked with an assault weapon. Such lists are groups of items, each of which is preceded by a solid dot, called a *bullet*. A *numbered list* looks like a bulleted list, except that numbers stand in for the bullets. Numbered lists are great if you need to list a series of ordered steps.

To create a bulleted or numbered list, follow these steps:

1. **Place the cursor in the page where you want the list to begin.**

2. **Click the Bullets button or the Numbering button.**

   A bullet or number appears at the beginning of the first line.

3. **Type the first list item and then press Enter.**

   A bullet or number appears on the next line.

4. **Type your second list item (and so on).**

5. **After you're done adding items to your list, press Enter twice to end the list.**

You can convert existing paragraphs into bulleted or numbered lists by selecting the paragraphs that you want included in the list and then clicking the Bullets button or the Numbering button.

To split a long list into two separate lists, click at the end of a list item and press Enter twice. The list splits into two lists and, in the case of numbered lists, renumbers itself automatically.

If the plain dots or numbers sitting in your lists don't appeal to your aesthetic senses, dress 'em up. The List Properties dialog box enables you to change the shape of your bullets or replace the dreary black spots with pictures. If you want to give a numbered list a makeover, you can use the List Properties dialog box to apply Roman numerals or change the list's starting number.

To access the List Properties dialog box, click the cursor inside the list you want to format, and then choose Format⇨Bullets and Numbering.

Bullet and number variation is visible only in recent versions of advanced browsers. In other browsers, bullets appear as solid dots and numbers appears as regular Arabic numerals.

Here's another idea: Apply a theme to your Web site. Each theme has its own set of graphic bullets. I show you how to use themes in Chapter 12.

Definition lists

A *definition list* enables you to present information in dictionary format — with the term you want to define listed first and its definition listed on the following line, slightly indented. Definition lists turn up infrequently but can come in handy every now and then, such as for a long list of names and addresses.

Although you can create definition lists several ways (as you can the other types of lists), the easiest way is to follow these steps:

1. **Place the cursor in the location where you want the list to begin.**

2. **From the Style list box in the Formatting toolbar, choose Defined Term.**

3. **Type your first term and then press Enter.**

    FrontPage creates a new line, slightly indented.

4. **Type the term's definition and then press Enter.**

   FrontPage creates a new line, flush left.

5. **Type your second term — and so on.**

   Follow Steps 3 and 4 for each new term and its definition.

6. **To end the definition list, press Enter twice.**

List-in-a-list

Sometimes a simple list doesn't cut it. Say you need something more sophisticated, such as a multilevel outline or a numbered list with bullets following
certain items (similar to the one shown in Figure 5-7). No problem! With
FrontPage, you simply create the main list (the numbered items in Figure 5-7)
and then insert a separate list containing the secondary items (the bulleted
items in Figure 5-7).

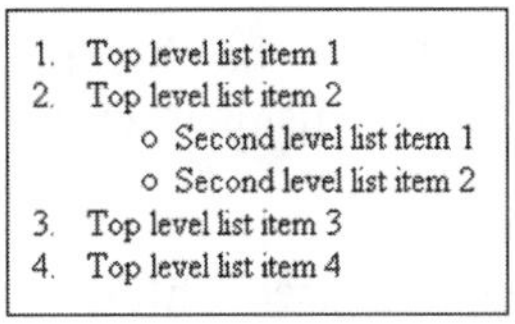

Figure 5-7:
A number-
bullet
combo list.

```
1.  Top level list item 1
2.  Top level list item 2
        ○ Second level list item 1
        ○ Second level list item 2
3.  Top level list item 3
4.  Top level list item 4
```

To create such a fancy-shmancy combo list, follow these steps:

1. **Create a list of any type.**

   The list should contain only the main, or top-level, items.

2. **Click at the end of the line above where you want to insert the second
   level of list items and then press Enter.**

   A new line appears in the list.

3. **Click the Increase Indent button.**

   The list item turns into a blank line.

4. **Click the Bullets or Numbering button (depending on the type of list
   you want to insert).**

   Depending on the style you choose, the blank line turns into a bulleted or
   numbered line.

5. **Type the list, pressing Enter each time to create new items.**

6. **After you finish, click the cursor anywhere on the page outside the list.**

   Pressing Enter twice to end the list doesn't work in this case.

Collapsible outlines

You can transform multilevel lists into *collapsible outlines*. When viewed with a web browser, the levels in a collapsible outline expand and contract when clicked.

To create a collapsible outline, follow these steps:

1. **Create a multilevel list.**

   To do so, follow the steps in the previous section, "List-in-a-list."

2. **Highlight the list, and then choose Format⇨Bullets and Numbering.**

   The List Properties dialog box appears.

3. **In the dialog box, mark the Enable Collapsible Outlines check box.**

   If you want the outline to appear initially collapsed, mark the Initially Collapsed check box.

4. **Click OK.**

   The dialog box closes. The list looks no different than before. To see how the collapsible outline works, preview the page using Internet Explorer 4.0 or later.

Collapsible outlines only work when the page is viewed with Internet Explorer Version 4.0 or later. Visitors using other browsers see a regular multilevel list.

Adjusting Paragraph Alignment, Indenting, and Spacing

By default, FrontPage paragraphs (with the exceptions of headings and lists) are single-spaced, line up with the page's left margin, and contain no indentation (that is, no extra space exists between the margin and the paragraph). Also, a little bit of space precedes and follows each paragraph. You can change these default paragraph settings one of two ways: the easy-but-basic way, and the slightly-more-involved-but-with-greater-control way.

- **Easy-but-basic way to change paragraph alignment:** Click inside the paragraph (or select multiple paragraphs) and then click the Align Left, Center, or Align Right button.

- **Easy-but-basic way to indent a paragraph:** Click inside the paragraph (or select multiple paragraphs) and then click the Increase Indent button. You may click the button as many times as you want to achieve the desired effect. To decrease the level of an indented paragraph, click the Decrease Indent button.

✔ **Slightly-more-involved-but-with-greater-control way to change paragraph alignment, indentation, and spacing:** Go through the steps that follow.

1. **Click inside the paragraph (or select multiple paragraphs).**

2. **Choose Format⇨Paragraph.**

   The Paragraph dialog box appears (see Figure 5-8).

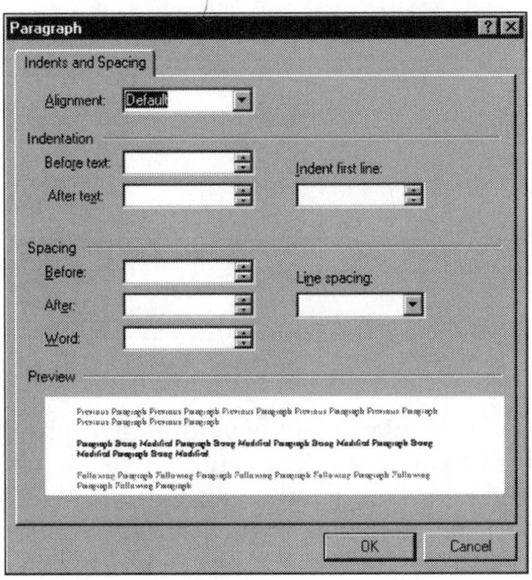

Figure 5-8:
The
Paragraph
dialog box.

3. **From the Alignment list box, choose the alignment option you want.**

   Your choices are Left, Right, Center, and Justify. (Justify creates paragraphs with neat-and-tidy text that lines up along both the left and right margins.)

4. **From the list boxes in the Indentation section, specify the amount of indentation (in pixels) you want.**

   The Before Text list box controls indentation along the left margin, and the After Text list box controls indentation along the right margin. The Indent First Line list box enables you to apply a different indentation setting to the first line of the paragraph.

5. **From the list boxes in the Spacing section, specify the amount of spacing (in pixels) you want.**

   The Before list box controls the amount of space before the paragraph; the After list box controls the amount of space after the paragraph; the Word list box controls the amount of space between words in the paragraph; and the Line Spacing list box controls (you guessed it) the space between the lines in the paragraph.

New paragraphs versus line breaks

Whenever you press the Enter key, FrontPage thinks you want to create a new paragraph. If you simply want to create a new line without creating a new paragraph, use a line break instead. To create a line break, press Shift+Enter.

To distinguish between line breaks and new paragraphs in your page, click the Show/Hide ¶ button in the Standard toolbar. Line breaks are flagged with left-pointing arrows.

---

6. **Click OK.**

   The Paragraph dialog box closes, and FrontPage applies the formatting to the selected paragraph(s).

The options in the Paragraph dialog box come courtesy of CSS commands. Browsers that are unable to display style sheets will not display these effects.

If you want more control over the placement of your paragraphs than the Paragraph dialog box can give you, consider using an invisible table (see Chapter 9), or check out the FrontPage positioning features. With positioning, you can place text anywhere inside the page you like. For details, see Chapter 13.

Adding Borders and Shading

Want to surround the selected paragraph with a box? Or give the paragraph a colorful background so it visually jumps off the page? These effects and more await you in the Borders and Shading dialog box.

To add a border to the selected paragraph, do this:

1. **Click inside the paragraph (or select multiple paragraphs) and then choose Format⇨Borders and Shading.**

   The Borders and Shading dialog box appears (see Figure 5-9).

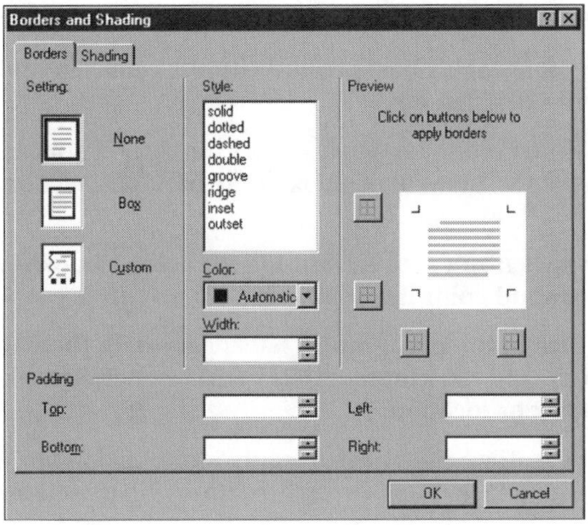

Figure 5-9:
The
Borders
and
Shading
dialog box.

2. **In the Setting area of the dialog box, click the option that corresponds to the type of border you want.**

3. **In the Style box, click the name of the border style you want.**

   A preview of the border style appears in the Preview area of the dialog box.

4. **Choose a border color from the Color list box.**

   If you choose More Colors, the More Colors dialog box appears. I explain how to use the More Colors dialog box in the previous section, "Changing text color."

5. **Enter a border width (in pixels) in the Width box.**

6. **To turn on or off individual borders, in the Preview area, click the button that corresponds to the border you want to change.**

7. **To add empty space between the paragraph text and the surrounding border, enter pixel values in boxes in the Padding area of the dialog box.**

8. **Click OK to close the dialog box and apply the border settings.**

In FrontPage, *shading* refers to the paragraph's foreground and background attributes. The paragraph's foreground attribute is its text color, and its background attributes are the color or picture that sits behind the selected paragraph's text. To add shading to a selected paragraph, do this:

1. **Click inside the paragraph (or select multiple paragraphs) and then choose Format➪Borders and Shading.**

   The Borders and Shading dialog box appears.

2. **In the dialog box, click the Shading tab to make those options visible.**

3. **To change the paragraph's background color, choose an option from the Background Color list box.**

   If you choose More Colors, the More Colors dialog box appears. I explain how to use the More Colors dialog box in the previous section, "Changing text color."

4. **To change the paragraph's foreground (text) color, choose an option from the Foreground color list box.**

5. **To place a picture in the paragraph's background, in the Background Picture text box, type the graphic file's path, or click Browse to select the file from a folder location.**

   If you click Browse, the Select Background Picture dialog box appears. If you're not sure how to use this dialog box, I provide directions in Chapter 7.

6. **To control how the picture repeats in the paragraph background, select an option from the Repeat list box.**

   By default, the picture repeats itself over and over until it fills the selected paragraph's background area. Repeat-x causes the picture to repeat horizontally, and repeat-y causes the picture to repeat vertically. No-repeat causes the picture to appear only once.

7. **To change the position of the picture relative to the paragraph, choose options from the Vertical Position and Horizontal Position list boxes.**

   For example, if you choose a vertical position of top and a horizontal position of left, the image appears in the top-left corner of the paragraph's background.

   Note: The Attachment list box controls whether the background image moves when the visitor scrolls down the page (by default, the image appears fixed in place with the text scrolling on top). Because the effect is only visible in Microsoft Internet Explorer, I recommend leaving the default setting as it is.

8. **Click OK to close the dialog box and apply the shading settings.**

 To quickly apply a background color to selected text, click the Highlight Color button.

 The options in the Borders and Shading dialog box and the Highlight Color effect come courtesy of CSS commands. Browsers that are unable to display style sheets will not display these effects. Furthermore, browsers that do support CSS don't display borders and shading consistently. If you decide to use these effects, be sure to preview your Web site in more than one browser version.

Inserting Symbols

Symbols are the odd little characters that occasionally make an appearance in Web pages. Some symbols turn up in scientific writing (Latin characters, for example), and others, such as the copyright symbol, are more commonplace.

To include a symbol in your page, follow these steps:

1. **Place the cursor in the page where you want the symbol to appear.**

2. **Choose Insert⇨Symbol.**

   The Symbol dialog box appears. If you squint, you can actually make out the tiny characters inside the dialog box.

3. **Click the character you want to insert.**

   The character appears (magnified, thank goodness!) at the bottom of the dialog box.

4. **If this character is the one you want, click Insert; if not, keep hunting and clicking until you find the right character and then click Insert.**

   The symbol appears in your page at the location of the cursor.

5. **Click Close to close the Symbol dialog box after you finish inserting symbols.**

A few (very few) browsers are unable to display certain symbols in Web pages. Keep this in mind if your Web site is symbol-heavy, and preview, preview, preview.

Inserting Comments

You can insert explanatory text and reminders to yourself (or to other members of your Web-building team) in the form of _comments_. Comments are notes that appear only in FrontPage, not as a visitor views the page with a web browser. To insert a comment, follow these steps:

1. **Place the cursor in the page where you want the comment to appear.**

2. **Choose Insert⇨Comment.**

   The Comment dialog box appears.

3. **In the Comment text box, type your comment and then click OK.**

   The dialog box closes, and the comment appears in your page as colorful text.

To edit a comment, double-click the comment. To delete a comment, click the comment and then press the Delete key.

Keep in mind that comments aren't *completely* invisible; your visitors can see the comments if they look at your page's underlying HTML tags.

Inserting Horizontal Lines

Horizontal lines are thin gray stripes that run the width of your Web page. How do they fit into a chapter about tweaking text, you ask? Because, as is true of font and paragraph styles, horizontal lines help group together bunches of related information. You can use a horizontal line if you need a quick way to divide your Web page into different sections. You can even change the line's width and height for a little variety.

Keep in mind that overusing horizontal lines can wreak design havoc on your page. A line or two can provide a much-needed visual break. Too many lines make your page look as though it's trapped behind bars.

To insert a horizontal line, place the cursor in the page where you want the line to appear and choose Insert⇨Horizontal Line. To customize how the line looks, follow these steps:

1. **In the page, double-click the horizontal line.**

   The Horizontal Line Properties dialog box appears.

2. **In the Width area of the dialog box, type a value into the text box and then click the Percent of Window or Pixels radio button.**

   You can indicate the width as a percentage of the width of the browser window, or you can specify an absolute number of pixels.

3. **In the Height text box, type the line's height (its thickness) in pixels.**

4. **In the Alignment area, click the Left, Center, or Right radio button.**

5. **Choose a color from the Color list box.**

6. **If you want the line to appear solid instead of engraved, click the Solid Line (No Shading) check box.**

7. **Click OK to close the dialog box and insert the line into the page.**

To delete a horizontal line, click the line and then press the Delete key.

Chapter 6

Hyperlinks: Your Web Site's Ticket to Ride

. . . .

In This Chapter

▶ Creating text and image hyperlinks

▶ Linking to a downloadable file and an e-mail address

▶ Editing hyperlinks

▶ Fixing broken hyperlinks

▶ Unlinking hyperlinks

▶ Using bookmarks to jump to a specific spot in a page

▶ Working with navigation bars

▶ Using shared borders

. . . .

*H*yperlinks are the gems that make the Web so addictively surfable. Click a link, and you find yourself somewhere else — maybe on another page in your Web site or, just as easily, on a page stored on a server in Sri Lanka or Cheyenne. Too bad Web surfing doesn't earn Frequent Flyer miles.

The heady nature of Web travel may lead you to believe that hyperlinks are difficult to create. Relax and discover how easily you can hitch your Web to the global conga line known as the Internet.

The Hyperlink Two-Step

Hyperlinks are bits of text or pictures that act as springboards to other locations. Hyperlinks between pages and files in a Web site *(internal hyperlinks)* transform the site from a jumble of separate files into a cohesive unit. Hyperlinks to locations outside the Web site *(external hyperlinks)* connect the site to the rest of the Internet.

After you launch FrontPage and open the Web site and/or the page you want to edit, creating a hyperlink is a two-step process. Here are the basic steps (the rest of this chapter fills in the details):

1. **In the page, select the thing you want to transform into a hyperlink.**

   I call this "thing" the *hyperlink source.* The hyperlink source is the object people click to go somewhere else. A hyperlink source can be a character, a word, a phrase, or a picture. (Chapter 7 tells you how to insert a picture into your page.)

2. **Connect the hyperlink source to the place you want visitors to end up after they click the hyperlink.**

   From now on, I call this location the *hyperlink destination.* A hyperlink destination can be a spot inside the same page, in another page or file inside the same Web site, or in a different site on the Internet. If the hyperlink destination is located inside the same page as the hyperlink source, the destination is identified with a *bookmark.* (I show you how to create bookmarks later in this chapter.) If the hyperlink leads to another page inside the Web site or on the Internet, the destination is identified with its Internet address, or *URL.*

Keep practicing these steps, and you can soon do the hyperlink two-step with the best of 'em.

Linking to a page inside the current FrontPage Web site

You can easily create links between the files that make up the Web site currently open in FrontPage.

Note: FrontPage only knows how to create internal links between pages that are part of a FrontPage Web site (that is, a site that was created in or has been imported into FrontPage). This makes sense because, by definition, internal links connect pages that are part of the same Web site. If you want to insert a hyperlink into a page that's not part of a FrontPage Web site, follow the steps in the next section of this chapter.

To create an internal hyperlink, follow these steps:

1. **In the page, select the object you want to turn into a hyperlink (the hyperlink source).**

   Highlight a bit of text, click a picture, double-click a word — whatever.

2. In the Standard toolbar, click the Hyperlink button.

The Create Hyperlink dialog box appears (see Figure 6-1). The dialog box's file list displays the files and folders that make up the Web site that's currently open in FrontPage.

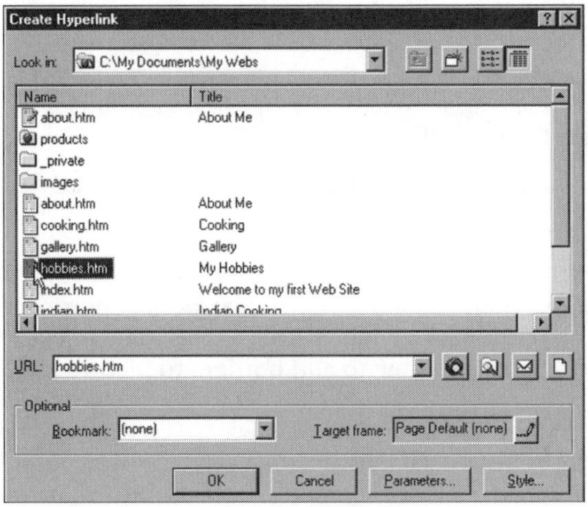

Figure 6-1:
The Create Hyperlink dialog box.

3. In the dialog box's file list, click the page or file to which you want to create a link (the hyperlink destination).

If the page is stored inside a folder or a subweb, double-click the folder or subweb to open it and then click the page.

When a page is currently open in the Page View, *two* instances of that page appear in the dialog box's file list: one preceded by a regular page icon, and the other preceded by a page-and-pencil icon. The pencil icon reminds you which pages are currently open. You can click either icon in this step.

4. Click OK.

The dialog box closes, and a hyperlink is born.

If the hyperlink source is text, that text now displays the proud markings of a link: underlining and color. (You can still apply font and paragraph styles — bold, italic, and so on — to text hyperlinks as you can to regular text.)

If the hyperlink source is a picture, the image itself looks no different than before its transformation. Trust me — the image is now a *graphic hyperlink*. If you want proof, pass your pointer over any text or graphic hyperlink, and the link destination appears in the Status Bar at the bottom of the FrontPage window.

Choosing hyperlink words wisely

Hyperlinks immediately attract attention, especially if your visitors quickly scan the page for information. Choose the clearest, most meaningful text for promotion to linkhood. Avoid the temptation to create links that say things such as "Click here to see a picture of Harold, my pet ferret." (The underlined words are the hyperlink in the previous sentence.) Instead, choose a word that clues the visitor in on what's sitting at the other end of the hyperlink. If you must immortalize Harold in your home page, you're better off using the following link text: "See a picture of Harold, my pet ferret."

To differentiate graphic hyperlinks from regular pictures in your Web pages, you can give graphic hyperlinks a border. The borders of graphic hyperlinks are the same color as text links, giving visitors a visual cue to click the picture to jump elsewhere. I show you how to add borders to pictures in Chapter 7.

The steps I list in this section aren't the only way to create internal hyperlinks. FrontPage can generate a *navigation bar* — a row of hyperlinks leading to other pages in your Web site. I explain the ins-and-outs of navigation bars later in this chapter. FrontPage can also generate a hierarchical list of hyperlinks to all the pages in your site, also known as a *table of contents*. I describe how in the sidebar "Creating a table of contents," later in this chapter.

Instant hyperlink shortcut! Drag an icon from the Folder List and drop it into the page currently open in the Page View. (If the Folder List isn't visible, in the Standard toolbar, click the Folder List button or choose View⇨Folder List.) FrontPage creates a link to the selected destination page, using the destination page's title as the hyperlink text.

Linking to a page on the World Wide Web

Linking to a page or file on the World Wide Web is just as easy as linking to a page inside your Web site. To create an external link, follow these steps:

1. **In the page, select the hyperlink source.**

2. **Click the Hyperlink button to open the Create Hyperlink dialog box.**

3. **In the dialog box's URL text box, type the URL of the hyperlink destination.**

   A World Wide Web URL looks something like this:

   ```
   http://www.microsoft.com
   ```

   If you can't remember the URL, in the dialog box, click the Use Your Web Browser to Select a Page or File button to launch your web browser. Surf to your destination, switch back to FrontPage by clicking FrontPage's button in the Windows taskbar, and — huzzah! — the URL appears in the URL text box.

4. **Click OK to close the dialog box and create the hyperlink.**

If you type an Internet URL inside the body of your page and then press the spacebar or Enter, FrontPage automatically turns the URL text into a hyperlink to that location.

If you goof while typing a Web site URL, FrontPage doesn't know that you made a mistake and creates the link anyway. You can double-check all the links in your Web site by using the Verify Hyperlinks command, or you can check individual hyperlinks one-by-one. I explain both procedures later in this chapter.

Linking to a downloadable file

Your Web site is the perfect repository for documents, programs, and other items you want to make available to visitors. Simply import the item into your Web site, and then create a hyperlink to the item you want visitors to be able to download to and save on their own computers. When a visitor clicks that link, the web browser automatically prompts the visitor to download the file.

To create a hyperlink to a downloadable file, follow these steps:

1. **Import the file you want visitors to be able to download.**

   For instructions on how to import a file into your Web site, see Chapter 2.

2. **Open the page you want to edit.**

3. **In the page, select the hyperlink source.**

4. **Click the Hyperlink button to open the Create Hyperlink dialog box.**

5. **In the dialog box's file list, click the file you want visitors to be able to download.**

6. **Click OK to close the dialog box and create the hyperlink.**

Linking to an e-mail address

The quickest way to help your visitors get in touch is to include a link to your e-mail address (also known as a *mailto link*) inside each page in your site. That way, if visitors have comments (or, dare I say it, complaints), they can click the mailto link that will pop open an e-mail window in the web browser. From there, they can fire off messages in seconds.

For mailto links to work, the visitor's browser must either have a built-in e-mail component or be able to hook up with a separate e-mail program.

The no-brainer approach to creating a link to your e-mail address is to type your e-mail address in the page followed by a tap on the spacebar or Enter key. FrontPage automatically transforms the address text into a link.

Otherwise, do this:

1. **In the page, select the hyperlink source.**

2. **Click the Hyperlink button to open the Create Hyperlink dialog box.**

3. **In the dialog box, click the Make a Hyperlink That Sends E-mail button.**

   The Create E-mail Hyperlink dialog box appears.

4. **In the Type an E-mail Address text box, enter an e-mail address.**

   It should look something like this: `webpub@ashaland.com`.

5. **Click OK.**

   The Create E-mail Hyperlink dialog box closes, and the Create Hyperlink dialog box becomes visible again.

6. **Click OK to close the dialog box and create the link.**

Linking to a file stored on your computer

FrontPage enables you to create a link from your Web page to a file stored on your computer's hard drive. Problem is, when you publish your finished Web site on a host web server, the link no longer works because the location of the hyperlink destination file is specific to your computer's file system, not the web server's.

Sometimes this feature comes in handy, such as if you're creating a local Web presentation to be

displayed only on your computer or local network (not on the World Wide Web). If you need to use this feature, follow the steps listed in "Linking to a page on the World Wide Web," except in Step 3, in the Create Hyperlink dialog box, click the Make a Hyperlink to a File on Your Computer button to select a file on your computer.

Another way to encourage visitor feedback is to provide an interactive form. I show you how in Chapter 10.

(By the way, to instantly place a link to your e-mail address at the bottom of every page in your site, place the mailto link inside a *shared border*. I show you how to use shared borders later in this chapter.)

Editing Hyperlinks

Just as you can change hair color, you can easily change hyperlinks. You can change the text that makes up the link, the hyperlink's color, and even the destination to which the link leads.

Changing hyperlink text

FrontPage enables you to change your hyperlink's text without affecting the link destination. To do so, follow these steps:

1. **Select the hyperlink text you want to change.**

2. **Type new text.**

   The new text appears in the page with its distinctive hyperlink markings intact.

If you try this trick on a URL or mailto link, in which the URL or e-mail address doubles as the link text, you only change the link text, not the underlying link destination.

Note: The steps outlined in this section work only on hyperlinks that are *not* part of a FrontPage navigation bar. In navigation bars, the title or label of the destination page determines the hyperlink text, so you must change the corresponding page label in order to change the text. I talk more about navigation bars later in this chapter.

Changing the destination of a hyperlink

If the location of a hyperlink's destination page changes, you can edit the link so that it points to the new location. (I show you how to make sure your hyperlinks work properly later in this chapter.) To change a hyperlink destination, follow these steps:

1. **In the page, click the link that you want to change.**

2. **Click the Hyperlink button to open the Edit Hyperlink dialog box.**

3. **In the dialog box, choose a new file from the file list, enter a new URL in the URL text box, or make any other change you want.**

4. **Click OK.**

   The dialog box closes, and FrontPage updates the hyperlink destination.

Note: The steps outlined here work only on hyperlinks that are *not* part of a FrontPage navigation bar. In navigation bars, the link destination is determined by the configuration of the site's navigational structure and the navigation bar properties. I talk more about navigation bars later in this chapter.

Changing hyperlink color

Hyperlinks stand out from regular text because hyperlinks appear in a different color from their ordinary text siblings. The default hyperlink color is blue, but you can change the link's color so that the hyperlink coordinates nicely with the color scheme of your page.

Hyperlinks actually have three distinct colors: the default color, the active color, and the visited color. These colors appear when a visitor views the page in a web browser.

- ✔ **The default color** is the link's color before the visitor follows the hyperlink trail. As a visitor arrives at your page for the first time, all the page's links appear in the default color, because the visitor hasn't yet followed a link.

- ✔ **The active color** is the color the link becomes "mid-click." The active color tells visitors that they are indeed activating that particular link.

- ✔ **The visited color** is the color the link changes to after visitors follow a link and then return to your page. The visited color lets visitors know which links they've already followed and which ones they haven't yet explored.

You can select unique hyperlink colors for each page you create. Or you can set up a consistent color scheme by basing the hyperlink color on the colors in another page in your site. You also can apply a theme to your Web site; each theme contains a nicely coordinated set of hyperlink colors. (I cover themes in Chapter 12.)

Creating a table of contents

A table of contents displays the titles of all your site's pages in a hierarchical list, with links to each page. The table of contents also lists any external links you added to your site's navigational structure (see Chapter 2 for information about the purpose of a navigational structure). Visitors love tables of contents for the bird's-eye view they provide, but even the best-intentioned Web designer dreads creating a table of contents for a big Web site, especially if he or she is constantly adding and changing pages.

Here's where the Table of Contents Component swoops in to the rescue. FrontPage can crank out a fully linked table of contents and keeps the list up-to-date even if pages change.

To create a table of contents, do this:

1. **In your page, place the cursor where you want the table of contents to appear.**

2. **Choose Insert⇨Component⇨Table of Contents.**

   The Table of Contents Properties dialog box appears.

3. **In the Page URL for Starting Point of Table text box, type the filename of the page that you want to appear at the top of the table of contents.**

   Or click Browse to select a page from a list of files in your Web site. By default, FrontPage specifies the site's home page as its starting point.

4. **From the Heading Font Size list box, choose the heading size for the first item in the table of contents.**

   Choosing a relatively bold heading (such as Heading 1 or Heading 2) sets the first item

apart from the rest so that the item acts as a title for the table of contents. If you'd rather the first item look like all the others, choose None.

5. **If you want each page in your site to appear in the table of contents only once, click the Show Each Page Only Once check box.**

   If you don't select this option, pages that link to more than one page in your site appear more than once.

6. **If you want the table of contents to display pages in your site that don't link to other pages, click the Show Pages with No Incoming Hyperlinks check box.**

   If you mark this check box, the only access point to the page is through the table of contents, because the page isn't linked to the rest of your Web site.

7. **If you want FrontPage to automatically update the table of contents as you edit pages and add new pages to your Web site, click the Recompute Table of Contents When Any Other Page Is Edited check box.**

   If you don't select this option and still want to update the table of contents, you need to recalculate your site's hyperlinks each time a page changes or you add a new page. (To recalculate hyperlinks, choose Tools⇨ Recalculate Hyperlinks.)

8. **Click OK.**

   The dialog box closes, and a placeholder for the table of contents appears in the page.

To see how the actual table of contents looks, preview the page in a web browser.

The link colors you choose should balance the page's design with its navigational flow. Some designers use "hot" or bright colors for new links and "cool" or muted colors for visited links. Others use the same color for new and visited links, because these designers want the page to appear uniform, no matter what. Whatever course you choose, you need to consider how you can use color to make your Web site easier and more pleasant for your visitors to explore.

Selecting unique colors

To select unique link colors for a page, follow these steps:

1. **With the page open in the Page View, choose Format⇨Background.**

   Note: If the current Web site page is formatted with a theme, this menu option appears dimmed, because themes contain a preset group of text and hyperlink colors.

   The Page Properties dialog box appears with the Background tab visible. The current link color settings appear in the list boxes labeled Hyperlink, Visited Hyperlink, and Active Hyperlink, as shown in Figure 6-2.

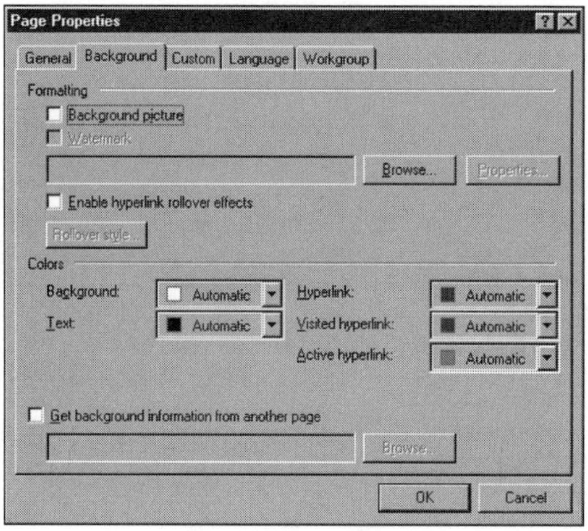

Figure 6-2:
The Background tab of the Page Properties dialog box.

2. **Choose a new color from one or all the list boxes corresponding to each hyperlink state.**

   If you choose More Colors, the More Colors dialog box appears. I explain how to use the More Colors dialog box in Chapter 5.

3. **Click OK.**

   The dialog box closes, and the page's links change color.

To see how the active and visited colors look, preview the page in a web browser.

Basing colors on another page

You can base hyperlink color (as well as the two other background attributes — the default text color and the page background color or picture) on another page in your Web site. If you choose this option, you can make background color changes to a single page and have those changes automatically appear in every page that uses those background settings.

To base background colors on those of another page, follow these steps:

1. **With the page open in the Page View, choose F<u>o</u>rmat⇨Bac<u>k</u>ground.**

   Note: If the current Web site or page is formatted with a theme, this menu option appears grayed-out, because themes contain a preset group of text and hyperlink colors.

   The Page Properties dialog box appears with the Background tab visible.

2. **Click the <u>G</u>et Background Information from Another Page check box.**

3. **Next to the corresponding text box, click the B<u>r</u>owse button.**

   The Current Web dialog box appears.

4. **In the dialog box, select the page and then click OK.**

   If the page is stored inside a folder, double-click the folder to open it, select the page, and click OK. The Current Web dialog box closes, and the file's path appears in the text box.

5. **Click OK.**

   The Page Properties dialog box closes, and the page's background and hyperlink colors change accordingly.

Adding a rollover effect

Here's an eye-catching little trick: Add a *rollover effect* to your text hyperlinks so that when visitors pass their pointers (or *roll*) over the hyperlink, something special happens to the hyperlink text. Perhaps the text turns a different color, or the text grows a couple of sizes. Whatever you choose, the effect is surprising and fun. To add a rollover effect to your page's hyperlinks, do this:

1. **Select F<u>o</u>rmat⇨Bac<u>k</u>ground to display the Background tab of the Page Properties dialog box.**

2. **In the Formatting area, check the <u>E</u>nable Hyperlink Rollover Effects check box, and then click the Rollover St<u>y</u>le button.**

   The Font dialog box appears.

3. **Choose the text effect you want the page's hyperlinks to display when a visitor rolls over the hyperlink.**

    Chapter 5 contains instructions on using the Font dialog box. (The default rollover setting turns hyperlinks bold and red.)

4. **Click OK to close the Font dialog box.**

5. **Click OK again to close the Page Properties dialog box and apply the rollover effect.**

When you preview your page, you'll see the rollover effect in action.

Hyperlink rollover effects come courtesy of Dynamic HTML, and are only visible in Microsoft Internet Explorer and Netscape Navigator, Version 4.0 or later. Furthermore, this particular effect works inconsistently when viewed with Netscape. In browsers that don't support the effect, such hyperlinks look like any other text hyperlink.

Do-It-Yourself Hyperlink Repair

Broken hyperlinks are like ants at a picnic. One or two ants are mildly annoying, but if enough ants show up, they ruin the entire afternoon.

A hyperlink breaks if the destination page the link points to becomes unreachable. A link may break because the web server on which the page is stored goes down, or the page's author renames the page. After a visitor clicks a broken hyperlink, instead of delivering the requested page, the destination web server delivers an error message stating that it can't find the page. Major Web-surfing bummer.

The most common cause of broken hyperlinks — renaming a page in your Web site and then forgetting to update the hyperlinks elsewhere in the Web site that lead to the page — is a moot point in FrontPage, because the program automatically updates hyperlinks if you rename or move a page. (I describe this feat of wonder in Chapter 2.)

Certain situations are beyond FrontPage's control, however, and cause hyperlinks in your Web site to break:

- ✔ You delete a file that is linked to from another page in the Web site.
- ✔ You import an existing Web site into FrontPage and leave out some files.
- ✔ You mistype a URL while creating a hyperlink to a site on the Internet.
- ✔ You create a link to a site on the Internet, and that site changes location or otherwise becomes unreachable.

The Verify Hyperlinks command helps you find and repair broken hyperlinks throughout your Web site. If you just want to check a few individual hyperlinks inside a Web page, you can do that as well. Read on for details on how to do both tasks.

Verifying and fixing hyperlinks throughout your Web site

The Verify Hyperlinks command performs the following miracles:

- ✔ It finds all the broken or unverified links in your Web site and lists them in the Broken Hyperlinks report.
- ✔ It checks links to external Internet sites to make sure they work properly.
- ✔ It enables you to fix individual broken links.
- ✔ It updates the corrected links in selected pages or throughout the entire Web site.

Verifying hyperlinks

You need to find broken hyperlinks before you can fix them. FrontPage is extremely helpful in this regard: It roots out broken hyperlinks for you.

Verifying hyperlinks involves locating broken internal links (links between pages and files that reside inside the Web site), and double-checking external links to make sure they work.

To verify external links, you must first activate your Internet connection.

To verify the hyperlinks in your Web site, follow these steps:

1. **Save all open pages, if you haven't already.**

2. **Choose View⇨Reports⇨Broken Hyperlinks.**

   FrontPage switches to the Reports View, and the Broken Hyperlinks report becomes visible. The report displays a list of broken internal hyperlinks and as-yet-unverified external hyperlinks (see Figure 6-3). Broken internal links (if any exist) are flagged with the status label Broken and a broken chain link, and unverified external links are flagged with the label Unknown and a question mark.

   Also, the Reports toolbar appears. (By default the Reports toolbar *floats*. To dock the toolbar with the other toolbars at the top of the FrontPage window, double-click the toolbar's title bar.)

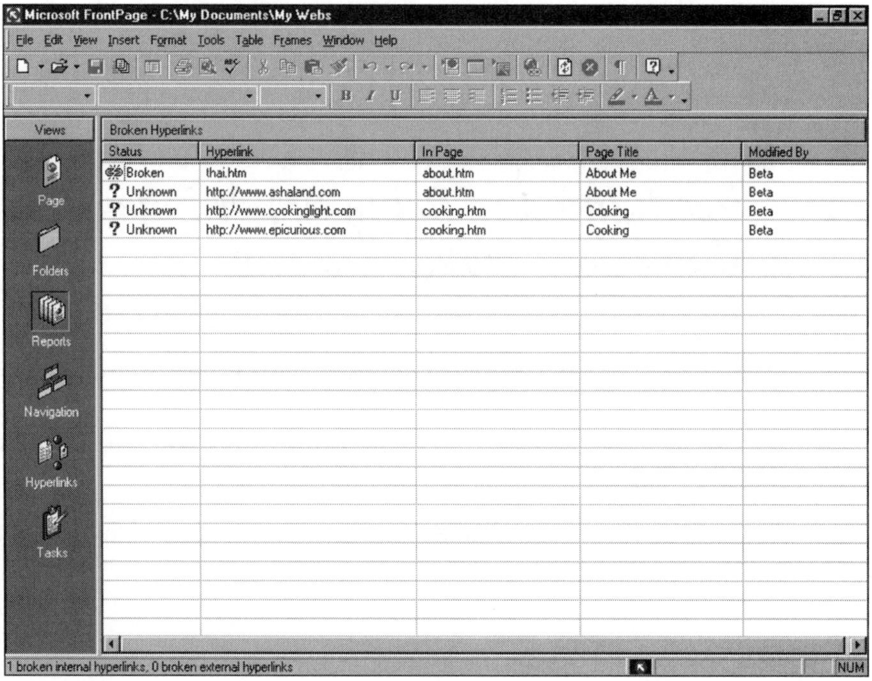

Figure 6-3:
The Broken
Hyperlinks
report.

3. **In the Reports toolbar, click the Verify Hyperlinks button.**

   The Verify Hyperlinks dialog box appears.

4. **In the dialog box, click $\underline{S}$tart.**

   If your Web site contains lots of external links, the verification process takes quite a while. Be sure that you have a few minutes to spare. (If you'd rather check links later, click Cancel to close the dialog box.)

   After you click Start, FrontPage verifies each external link by contacting the destination web server and then making sure that it can reach the page. As the verification process is going on, a progress message appears in the FrontPage Status Bar letting you know what's happening. As FrontPage checks each link, its Status label in the report changes from a question mark to either a green check mark followed by `OK` (indicating valid links) or a broken chain link followed by `Broken` (indicating broken links). When the verification process is complete, FrontPage lists a summary of its findings in the Status Bar.

   To stop the verification process, press the Esc key. To resume verifying hyperlinks, click the Verify Hyperlinks button.

Fixing broken hyperlinks

After FrontPage has unearthed the broken links, you need to fix them. To do so, follow these steps:

1. **If you haven't already, follow the steps in the preceding section, "Verifying hyperlinks."**

2. **From the Broken Hyperlinks report, double-click the broken hyperlink you want to fix.**

   The Edit Hyperlink dialog box appears (see Figure 6-4).

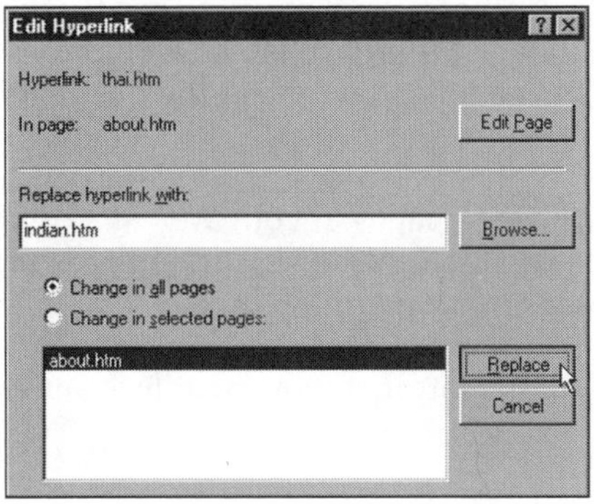

Figure 6-4: The Edit Hyperlink dialog box.

3. **Decide whether you want to edit the page containing the hyperlink or update the hyperlink destination itself; then take the appropriate action.**

   To edit the page containing the link, click the Edit Page button. The page opens in the Page View so that you can fix the ailing link. (If you're not sure how to edit the link, read the section "Changing the destination of a hyperlink," earlier in this chapter.) When you switch back to the Reports View, repaired internal links disappear from the list, and the status of repaired external links change from Broken to Edited.

   To edit the link itself, in the Edit Hyperlink dialog box, enter a new URL in the Replace Hyperlink With text box. If you can't recall the URL, click Browse to launch your web browser. Browse to the destination and then switch back to FrontPage, and the destination URL is visible in the text box. To change the link in selected pages (rather than throughout the entire Web site), click the Change in Selected Pages radio button and then click the names of the pages you want to update in the box underneath. Click Replace to fix the hyperlink and close the dialog box.

4. **Continue repairing broken hyperlinks by repeating Steps 2 and 3.**

I recommend verifying your site's hyperlinks at least every couple of weeks. Web pages move and change all the time, breaking hyperlinks in your Web site. FrontPage makes checking your links so easy — why not make it a regular habit?

Checking individual hyperlinks

If you simply want to check one or a few links while you're working on a Web page, you can easily do so in the Page View.

Following individual hyperlinks enables you to check to see that the links go where you want them to go. Although FrontPage isn't a web browser, the program approximates browsing by enabling you to visit the destinations of the links in your pages.

Note: This trick works only for links to pages in your Web site or to pages on the World Wide Web. FrontPage can't follow links to other types of Internet services, such as e-mail addresses or newsgroups.

To follow links to destinations on the Internet, you must first activate your Internet connection.

To follow individual links, switch to the Page View. In the open page, while holding down the Ctrl key, click the link you want to follow. FrontPage opens the destination page and displays it in a new window in the Page View. If FrontPage can't access the page (because the hyperlink is incorrect or the page is unreachable), a dialog box appears telling you that it couldn't open the page. Click OK to close the dialog box and then proceed to fix the broken hyperlink. (See the preceding section, "Fixing broken hyperlinks.")

You can also check individual hyperlinks using the Broken Hyperlinks report. In the report, click the link you want to verify, and then click the Verify Hyperlinks button. In the Verify Hyperlinks dialog box, click the Verify Selected Hyperlinks radio button, and then click Start. The dialog box closes, and FrontPage verifies the link.

Unlinking Hyperlinks

Suppose you became so intoxicated with the power of hyperlink creation that, looking at your page now, you see more links than text. Perhaps you overindulged. Perhaps removing a few links so that the others may shine is wise to do. To obtain forgiveness for your excesses, follow these steps:

1. **Click the link that you want to unlink.**

2. **Click the Hyperlink button to open the Edit Hyperlink dialog box.**

3. **In the dialog box, clear the contents of the URL text box, and then click OK.**

   The dialog box closes, and your link returns to regular text (or, if the link's a picture, returns to its original state).

Using Bookmarks

A *bookmark* is a location inside a Web page that is defined as the target of a link. Bookmarks enable you to more closely control where visitors end up after they click a hyperlink. A link without the benefit of a bookmark drops visitors off at the top of the destination page. When a visitor clicks a hyperlink that leads to a bookmark inside a page, the visitor jumps straight to the bookmark location.

To link to a bookmark in your page, you must first create the bookmark and then create the hyperlink that leads to the bookmark.

Creating bookmarks

A bookmark can be the current location of the cursor or any selected bit of text: a word, a phrase — even a letter. Text defined as a bookmark looks (and acts) no different from regular text; the text is simply flagged with an invisible marker that you can target with a hyperlink.

To create a bookmark, follow these steps:

1. **In the page, select the clump of text you want to turn into a bookmark.**

   Or place the cursor in the location where you want the bookmark to sit without selecting any text.

   The bookmark will eventually become the hyperlink destination.

2. **Choose Insert⇨Bookmark.**

   The Bookmark dialog box appears. If you selected text in Step 1, the text is visible in the Bookmark Name text box. (FrontPage wisely assumes that you want to give the bookmark the same name as the text it's made of.) Otherwise, the text box is empty.

3. **If the text box is empty (or if you want to choose a different name), in the <u>B</u>ookmark Name text box, enter a brief name.**

   Type a name describing the bookmark's function or location.

4. **Click OK.**

   The dialog box closes. If the bookmark is made of text, a dotted line appears underneath the selected text. If the bookmark is a single point, a flag icon appears at the location of the bookmark. (In real life, bookmarks are invisible. Surfers viewing your page with a browser can't distinguish bookmarks from regular text.)

Linking to a bookmark

Bookmarks are like ballroom dancers: They need a partner to do their thing. Without a hyperlink, a bookmark is as lonely as a wallflower.

Linking to bookmarks inside a page helps visitors find their way around long pages that otherwise require lots of scrolling and searching to navigate.

You can create a link at the top of the page to bookmarks in the interior of the same page so that visitors can jump around with swift clicks of the mouse. Likewise, you can create a link at the bottom of the page to a bookmark at the top of the page so that visitors don't need to scroll to return to the beginning of the page.

Any bookmark on any page in your Web site is an eligible candidate for a link. To forge this link, follow these steps:

1. **In the page, select the hyperlink source.**

   This step is the same as that for creating a regular link: Select the word, phrase, or picture you want to turn into a hyperlink.

2. **Click the Hyperlink button to open the Create Hyperlink dialog box.**

3. **If you're linking to a bookmark in another page in the Web site, in the dialog box's file list, click the page that contains the bookmark to which you want to link.**

4. **From the <u>B</u>ookmark list box, choose the bookmark to which you want to link.**

5. **Click OK.**

   The dialog box closes, and the bookmark and hyperlink live happily ever after. (Trumpets sound.)

Dismantling bookmarks

Dismantle any bookmarks that outlive their usefulness. The procedure is quick and painless (for both you and the bookmark). If the bookmark is made up of text, click inside the bookmark you want to dismantle, and then choose Insert⇨ Bookmark. In the Bookmark dialog box, click Clear. If the bookmark is marked with a flag icon, double-click the flag icon and then press the Delete key.

Helping Visitors Find Their Way with Navigation Bars

As I was thinking of a way to describe navigation bars, a scene from a Saturday morning cartoon popped into my head: Bugs Bunny is lost in the desert, and while searching for an oasis, he comes upon a signpost stuck into sand. The signpost contains markers pointing every which way: "This way to Cairo," "This way to New York," "This way to Mars."

Navigation bars give your visitors a similar array of choices. Navigation bars contain hyperlinks leading to the other pages inside your Web site. By placing a navigation bar inside each page of your site, you help your visitors find their way around. Think of navigation bars as signposts: "This way to the home page," "This way to the feedback form." With a single click, visitors are whisked off to the destination of their choice.

To take advantage of this feature, you must first create a navigational structure using the Navigation View. The chart needn't be complete — you can add pages as you go along — but it should at least reflect the site's core structure. For details on how to use the Navigation View, see Chapter 2.

Inserting a navigation bar in your page

FrontPage creates navigation bars based on the settings in the Navigation Bar Properties dialog box, shown in Figure 6-5. (I show you how to access this dialog box in a moment.) The Hyperlinks To Add To Page section of the dialog box enables you to select the level of hyperlinks that appear in the navigation bar. Here's where the layout of the navigational structure makes a difference, because the layout determines which pages appear in each level.

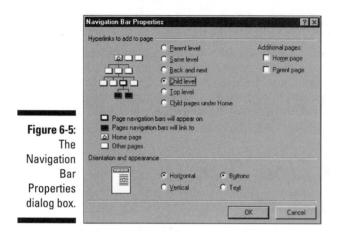

Figure 6-5:
The
Navigation
Bar
Properties
dialog box.

Your choices are as follows:

- ✔ **Parent Level.** This option lists hyperlinks leading to the pages in the level above the current page.

- ✔ **Same Level.** This option lists hyperlinks leading to the pages in the same level as the current page.

- ✔ **Back and Next.** In Web sites that rely on a linear, slideshow-like flow of information, this option lists hyperlinks to the previous page and the next page, both of which are on the same level as the current page.

- ✔ **Child Level.** This option lists hyperlinks leading to the pages in the level below the current page.

- ✔ **Top Level.** This option lists hyperlinks leading to pages that sit at the topmost level of the site.

- ✔ **Child Pages under Home.** This option lists hyperlinks leading to pages in the level beneath the site's entry page, regardless of the level of the current page.

You also can include links to two additional pages:

- ✔ **Home Page.** The home page is the site's entry page.

- ✔ **Parent Page.** The parent page sits in the level above the current page and contains a link to that page.

You control the look of the navigation bar by selecting options in the Orientation and Appearance section of the dialog box. You can choose a horizontal or vertical navigation bar, and you can specify text hyperlinks or graphic buttons. If you create a text-based navigation bar, you can also change the text formatting using any of the FrontPage font tools (see Chapter 5 for details).

To use graphic buttons, you must apply a theme to the page or site (I show you how in Chapter 12). FrontPage inserts the theme's corresponding button graphic and superimposes the page title on top of the graphic to create the button. If you specify graphic buttons inside a page that doesn't use a theme, FrontPage inserts regular text links.

To insert a navigation bar into your page, do this:

1. **In the page, place the cursor where you want the navigation bar to appear.**

   If you want the navigation bar to appear in the same position inside more than one page in your Web site, place the navigation bar inside a *shared border*. I show you how to create and use shared borders later in this chapter.

2. **Choose Insert➪Navigation Bar.**

   The Navigation Bar Properties dialog box appears.

3. **In the Hyperlinks to Add to Page section of the dialog box, choose the option(s) you want.**

   When you choose an option, a representation of the corresponding hyperlinks appear highlighted in the dialog box's navigational structure diagram.

4. **In the Orientation and Appearance section of the dialog box, choose the options you want.**

5. **Click OK.**

   The dialog box closes, and the navigation bar appears in the page. Figure 6-6 illustrates a typical image-button-based navigation bar (this one is based on the Capsules theme).

Figure 6-6:
A horizontal navigation bar based on the Capsules theme.

If an italicized notation appears in the page where the navigation bar buttons should be, some sort of problem exists. Chances are you chose a navigation bar layout that conflicts with the page's placement in the navigational structure. For example, the page sits at the bottom level of the chart, and you specified that the navigation bar contain Child level links — none of which exist. Or you may have attempted to insert a navigation bar into a page that hasn't yet been added to the navigational structure, and therefore FrontPage has no way to construct the navigation bar. The notation only appears in FrontPage to alert you to a navigation bar problem; when you preview the page using a web browser, the notations are invisible.

To change the configuration of the navigation bar, double-click the notation to display the Navigation Bar Properties dialog box, choose new options, and then click OK. You may also switch to Navigation View to reshuffle the navigational structure or to add or remove navigation bar links (I show you how to do so in the following section).

Adding navigation bar links

Although the main purpose of navigation bars is to help visitors get around inside your Web site, FrontPage gives you the option to add navigation bar links that point to external Web sites as well. To do so, follow these steps:

1. **In the Views Bar, click the Navigation button to switch to the Navigation View.**

2. **Click anywhere inside the navigational structure, and then, from the Navigation toolbar, click the External Link button.**

   Don't confuse the External Link button in the Navigation toolbar with the Hyperlink button in the Standard toolbar. They look the same, but they do very different things.

   After you click the External Link button, the Select Hyperlink dialog box appears.

3. **In the dialog box, specify the page or file to which you want to link.**

   The options in this dialog box enable you to select any page or file inside the current Web site or its subwebs, or specify a URL pointing to an external site. The Select Hyperlink dialog box works very much like the Create Hyperlink dialog box; for details, see the previous section in this chapter, "The Hyperlink Two-Step."

4. **Click OK.**

   The dialog box closes, and an icon corresponding to the new link appears in the navigation structure. To change the icon's placement, drag it to a new location inside the structure.

Changing navigation bar text

If your navigation bar is made up of graphic buttons, you might find that some of the page titles are too long to fit on top of the image. To change the text labels that FrontPage uses for the navigation bar links, do this:

1. **In the Navigation View, click the icon that corresponds to the label you want to change.**

   The icon turns blue.

2. **In the icon, click the text label.**

   The text label becomes highlighted.

3. **Type a new text label and then press Enter.**

4. **Switch back to the Page View and, if necessary, click the Refresh button in the Standard toolbar to display the label change.**

When you change a page label in the Navigation View, FrontPage uses the label as the page title.

FrontPage navigation bars contain four standard text labels: Home (for the home page), Up (for the Parent page), Back (for the previous page), and Forward (for the next page). To change these standard labels, follow these steps:

1. **Choose Tools⇨Web Settings.**

   The FrontPage Web Settings dialog box appears.

2. **In the dialog box, click the Navigation tab to make that set of options visible.**

3. **Enter different text labels in the appropriate text boxes, and then click OK to close the dialog box.**

Removing navigation bar links

You may eventually want to add a page to the navigational structure, but not have a link to the page appear inside the site's navigation bars. For example, you may want a page to appear in the navigational structure so you may insert a decorative *page banner* inside the page (you find out about page banners in Chapter 12). Here's how to exclude pages from navigation bars:

1. **In the Navigation View, click the icon in the navigation structure that corresponds to the page you want to exclude from navigation bars.**

2. **In the Navigation toolbar, click the Included In Navigation Bars button to toggle the navigation bar setting.**

   The icon turns from yellow to gray indicating that a link to the page no longer appears in the site's navigation bars.

When you exclude a page from navigation bars, FrontPage automatically excludes that page's Child pages as well. If you want to restore those pages' positions in navigation bars, click their respective icons and then click the Included In Navigation Bars button.

Using shared borders

Well-designed Web sites are easy to get around. Navigation bars help in this regard, but to be truly effective, navigation bars must appear in every page in the Web site — ideally in the same spot in each page. Consistently designed pages help visitors familiarize themselves with your site's layout. The more they explore, the easier it becomes for them to find their way.

To help you maintain a consistent layout in your Web pages, FrontPage provides a feature called *shared borders.* Shared borders enable you to place items — navigation bars, page banners, copyright notices, logos, or anything else — in the margins of your pages, and have those items automatically appear in the same position in every page in your Web site.

You can use shared borders for any type of standard inclusion in a page, but I find that shared borders really show their stuff when paired with navigation bars and page banners (you find out about page banners in Chapter 12). By placing a navigation bar inside a shared border, you avoid having to manually add a navigation bar to each page. Not only that, but FrontPage also automatically updates the navigation bar throughout the site as you add to and change the site's navigational structure.

To apply shared borders to your Web site, follow these steps:

1. **In any view, choose Format⇨Shared Borders.**

   The Shared Borders dialog box appears (see Figure 6-7).

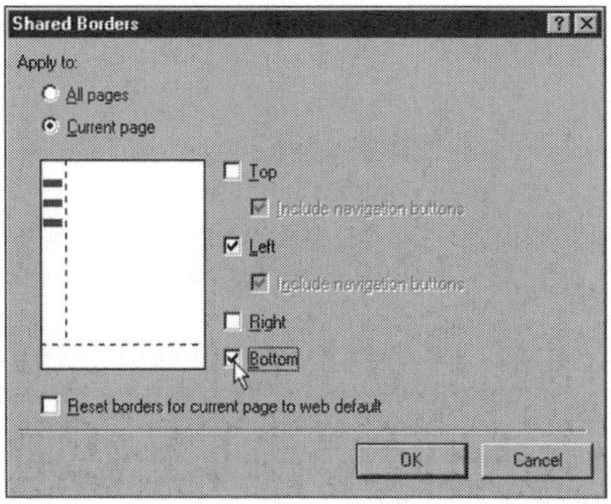

Figure 6-7:
The Shared
Borders
dialog box.

2. **In the dialog box's Apply To section, click the All Pages radio button, and then click the check boxes that correspond to the areas in your page where you want to place shared items.**

   For example, if you want a navigation bar to appear on the left side of every page in your Web site, click the Left check box.

   If you want FrontPage to include standard navigation bars in the top or left borders, mark the corresponding Include Navigation Buttons check boxes. I find it easier to add navigation bars by hand, but if you'd rather let FrontPage pick up some of the work, by all means, try this feature out. You can always change the navigation bar settings later.

3. **Click OK.**

   The dialog box closes, and FrontPage applies the selected borders to each page in your site.

When you next open the pages in the Page View, you see dotted lines demarcating the shared borders inside the page (see Figure 6-8). The area inside the shared border acts no differently than the rest of the page, except that when you place anything inside a shared border, that item appears in the same position in every page in the Web site.

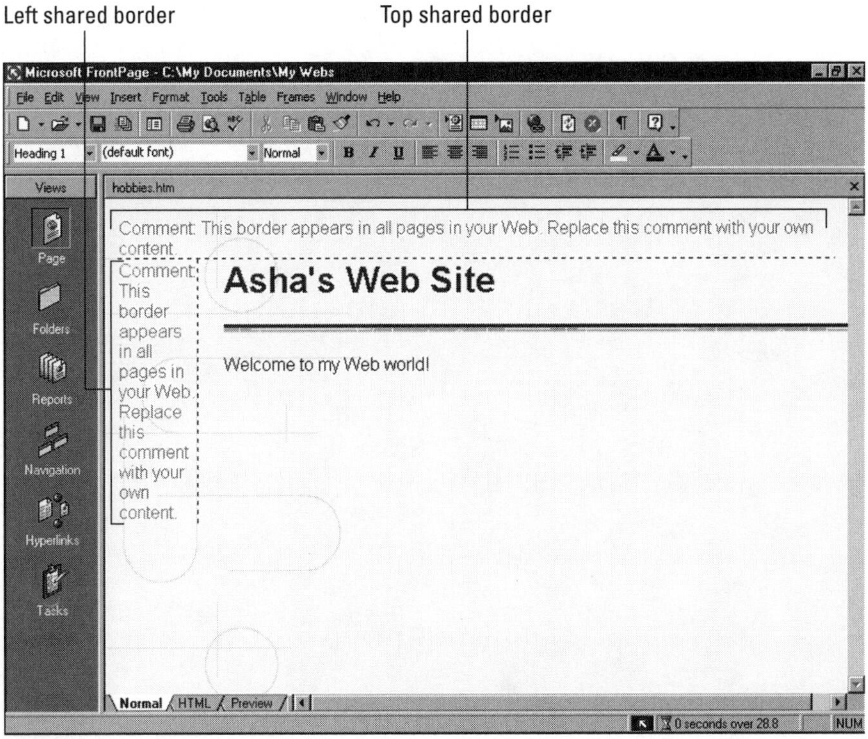

Figure 6-8: How shared borders look in the Page View.

When you look at the page using a web browser, the dotted lines disappear, and only the shared border content is visible.

You can change or turn off shared border settings for individual pages. For example, you may want navigation bars to appear in every page of your site except the home page. In that case, you can turn off the shared borders for the home page, but maintain shared borders in the rest of your site.

To change the shared border settings for an individual page, do this:

1. **To change shared border settings in the page currently open in the Page View, click the cursor anywhere inside the page. To change shared border settings in more than one page in this site, switch to the Folders View and then select the pages you want to edit.**

2. **Choose Format⇨Shared Borders.**

   The Shared Borders dialog box appears.

3. **In the dialog box's Apply To section, click the Current Page radio button (if you've selected more than one page, the Selected Page(s) radio button appears there instead), and then click the check boxes that correspond to the shared borders you want to turn on or off.**

   To return to the Web site's original shared border settings, click the Reset Borders For Current Page To Web Default check box.

4. **Click OK.**

   The dialog box closes, and FrontPage changes the border settings accordingly.

Chapter 7

You Oughta Be in Pictures

. . . .

In This Chapter

▶ Understanding the quirks of Web graphics

▶ Adding a picture to your page

▶ Controlling how pictures are displayed

▶ Editing the picture itself

▶ Deleting pictures

▶ Using thumbnails

▶ Creating a background image

. . . .

*T*ext is important. Text is, in fact, the foundation of your Web site, the basic building block of a page, and blah, blah, blah. Although that statement is essentially true, let's be honest — the World Wide Web hasn't achieved global fame because of a bunch of words. The pairing of information and pictures is what transforms the Web from a heap of data into a colorful adventure.

Web graphics, when used correctly, create a mood and help visitors navigate your site. High-quality, well-chosen images lend style and legitimacy. But, as with all Web design effects, too much of a good thing can be toxic. Cheesy clip art detracts from the site's overall image and, worse, slows its load time.

In this chapter, I let you in on tricks to keep your graphics looking good and loading fast. And, of course, I show you how to use the graphics capabilities of FrontPage.

Understanding the Quirks of Web Graphics

Web graphics can bewilder the novice Web publisher. No need to worry. As long as you follow the simple rules in this chapter, you should have a graphic-filled, stress-free Web publishing career.

Getting to know the Web-friendly graphic formats

The alphabet soup of graphic file formats is enough to send anyone into fits of intimidation. Good news: Web-friendly graphics come in only three formats: GIF, JPEG, and PNG. GIF is the oldest and most commonly used format on the Web. JPEG (pronounced *jay-peg*) can stuff a wide range of color into a small file size. PNG (say *ping*) is the new kid on the block that surpasses both GIF and JPEG in many ways.

Which format do you choose? The definitive answer is . . . it depends. GIF displays a maximum of 256 colors and is therefore best suited to high-contrast, flat color pictures, such as logos and cartoons. JPEG can display thousands of colors, so that format is your best choice for pictures containing subtle color changes or a wide range of color, such as photographs and complex digital art.

Chuck Dale's Paint Shop Pro site (a shareware graphics program included on this book's CD) sheds light on the different Web graphic formats in their excellent graphics tutorial at www.pspro.ml.org/wg/file_formats.html. Another good resource: *Web Graphics 101* at builder.com/Graphics/Graphics101/index.html.

The GIF format has a few extra cards up its sleeve: transparency and interlacing, both of which I discuss later in the chapter. Another impressive GIF trick — simple animation — is described in the accompanying sidebar, "Movin' and shakin' with GIF animation."

Is it pronounced GIF or JIF?

A dispute rages in the Web publishing community over the pronunciation of the acronym GIF. Is GIF pronounced with a hard G, as in *graphic*, or is the term pronounced *jif*, like the peanut butter brand? I say GIF with a hard G (after all, GIF stands for *Graphic Interchange Format*), but know-it-alls exist in both camps, so no matter how you say it, prepare to be corrected.

Movin' and shakin' with GIF animation

Remember those tiny "flip books" that were popular when you were a kid? Each page contained a cartoon in a suspended state of movement, and as you quickly flipped the book's pages, the cartoon looked like it was moving — just as though you were watching a movie.

The GIF format enables you to do something similar with individual graphics. You create individual frames of animation, save the frames as GIF files, and then string them together into a single file. Advanced web browsers automatically "play" the animation, displaying the graphics in quick succession and creating the illusion of a moving picture.

You can create your own GIF animation with the help of a GIF animation tool. Several tools exist,

but Microsoft GIF Animator works hand-in-hand with Microsoft Image Composer, the graphics program that comes with the stand-alone version of FrontPage. (GIF Animator installs automatically when you install Image Composer.)

For instructions and tips on how to create animated GIFs, as well as a long list of other GIF animation programs, point your browser at members.aol.com/royalef/gifanim.htm.

GIF animation is only one method of adding animation to your Web site; I discuss others in Chapter 13.

What about PNG? This new graphic format, developed specifically for Web use, is the wave of the future. PNG is able to display more colors than GIF, and it contains more transparency options than both GIF and JPEG, to name only two of its virtues.

PNG is destined to replace GIF and JPEG as the standard image format on the Web. Unfortunately, browser support for PNG files is just beginning to take hold. Only recent versions of advanced browsers such as Netscape Navigator (Version 4.0 or later) and Microsoft Internet Explorer (Version 4.0 or later) can display the format. Older or less sophisticated browsers are left in the dust. Therefore, until most Web surfers use a PNG-compatible browser, you're wise to stick with GIF and JPEG for now. But keep your eye on PNG: It's hot.

Want to know more about PNG? Check out the dense PNG Specification at www.boutell.com/boutell/png.

FrontPage takes the guesswork out of file formats because it automatically converts most Web-unfriendly formats into GIF or JPEG. I talk more about the conversion process later in this chapter.

Picky palettes

In Chapter 4, I relate a harrowing episode from early in my Web publishing career: I colored my Web site with what I thought was a soothing lemon-yellow background, but when my friend looked at the page on his computer, the same color appeared pallid green. I made the mistake of ignoring an important Web graphic rule: Stick to the browser-safe palette of colors.

As I said in the preceding section, GIFs can display a range, or *palette,* of 256 colors. The tricky thing about color palettes, however, is that the colors are operating-system-specific. In other words, colors appear slightly different when you view them on a PC running Windows than when you view them on a Mac. Bright colors look about the same, but unusual or pastel colors may appear shockingly different on different platforms.

If your graphic contains a color that isn't present in your visitor's system palette, your visitor's web browser attempts to display the color by *dithering* — that is, by mixing other colors together to approximate the color in the graphic. Dithered graphics, although better than nothing, lack clarity and definition.

You can reduce dithering by using the *browser-safe* palette for your Web graphics. This palette gives you a range of 216 colors available to most of your visitors. If you create graphics by using these colors or apply this palette to the graphics that you convert to GIF, the dithering problem shrinks considerably. And you don't have your friends calling and asking why you used such a gross color for the background of your page.

For more information about the browser-safe palette, visit `www.webreference.com/dev/graphics/palette.html`. Refer to your graphics program's documentation for instructions on how to apply the palette to your graphics.

Keeping graphics zippy

Web truism #3 states, "Your visitors connect to the Internet at different speeds." (I discuss the four Web truisms in Chapter 4.) If your visitors must wait more than a few seconds for the page to appear in their browsers, your site risks falling victim to *clickitis,* the chronic condition that causes surfers to click elsewhere whenever they must wait a moment for something to download to their machines. Clickitis is 100 percent preventable by keeping load times brief. Here are some ways to ensure that your graphics don't drag:

- ✔ **Reduce image dimensions.** Wherever possible, keep the picture file's dimensions small.

- ✔ **Limit colors.** You can shave precious seconds off the download time while maintaining your picture's quality if you use a graphics program to reduce the number of colors in your pictures.

- ✔ **Keep resolution low.** Save your graphic files at a resolution of 72 ppi (pixels per inch). This resolution, while too low for high-quality print images, works just fine for images that are displayed on a computer monitor. Anything higher and you're adding unnecessary bulk to your graphic's file size.

- ✔ **Repeat pictures.** As much as possible, use the same pictures throughout your site. Web browsers *cache* graphic files, which means that the browser saves a copy of the picture on the visitor's hard drive. The first time someone visits your site, the browser downloads the graphic files from the host server; after the initial download, the browser displays the cached files instead — which load almost instantly.

If you'd like to find out more about the nuts-and-bolts of Web graphics, pick up a copy of *Web Graphics For Dummies* by Linda Richards (IDG Books Worldwide, Inc.). That book contains lots of helpful tips and techniques for creating useful and speedy Web-ready graphics.

FrontPage displays the page's estimated download time in a box on the right side of the Status Bar. If you click the time estimate, you can select a different connection speed and watch the time estimate change. Keep an eye on the download time as you add graphics to your page.

Practicing graphic restraint

Pictures are the road hogs of the Information Superhighway, but pictures also make the Web such a pleasant drive. A conscientious Web publisher balances these opposing forces by using pictures judiciously and firing the bulk of the creative power into the site's content.

The "more is better" trap is easy to fall into when adding pictures to your site. I urge you, however, to practice restraint. Each additional picture increases the overall load time of the page and should only be added if seeing the picture is worth the wait. Use only those pictures that communicate your site's purpose and make getting around in the site easier or more pleasant for your target audience.

Finally, make sure that visitors can understand your page without the pictures. Some surfers turn off their browser's image-loading option to speed up browsing sessions. (I show you how to deal with this situation in the upcoming section called "Specifying ALT text.")

Adding a Picture to Your Page

When you insert a picture in a Web page, FrontPage adds a reference inside the page's HTML tags that points to the location of the graphic file. The reference tells the visitor's browser to display the picture inside the page at the location of the reference. In other words, when you look at a Web page that contains pictures, you're actually looking at more than one file simultaneously: the Web page (the file that contains the text and the references to the pictures) and each individual graphic file.

Inserting a picture is not unlike creating a hyperlink, because you simply link two different files: the Web page and the graphic file. So, similar to a hyperlink, a picture reference can point to a graphic file located inside the current FrontPage Web site, to a file elsewhere on your computer, or to a file stored on a remote web server.

If the graphic files you want to display in your Web site aren't already stored in a Web-friendly format, you're in luck: FrontPage automatically converts BMP, TIF, WMF, RAS, EPS, PCX, PCD, and TGA files to GIF or JPEG. (FrontPage converts graphics with 256 or fewer colors into GIF, and it converts graphics with more than 256 colors into JPEG.) FrontPage also knows how to convert graphics into PNG, but because many browsers don't yet support PNG, I don't recommend using this option.

If you want greater control over the conversion process, you should first open and convert your graphic file in a program specifically geared toward graphic work, and then import the converted image file into your FrontPage Web site.

Most graphics programs enable you to tweak any aspect of the graphic file and then save the file in the Web-friendly format of your choice. Don't have a graphics program? You do now! Microsoft Image Composer comes with the stand-alone version of FrontPage, Microsoft PhotoDraw comes with the version of FrontPage bundled with Microsoft Office, and Paint Shop Pro comes on the CD included with this book. (See Appendix B for a complete list of what's on the CD.)

Image Composer and PhotoDraw are sophisticated software programs in their own right. If you want to know more about these programs, consider picking up *Microsoft Image Composer For Dummies* by Brian Johnson (IDG Books Worldwide, Inc.).

Inserting a picture that's stored inside the current FrontPage Web site

If you have already imported into your Web site the pictures you want to use, plopping the pictures into a page is easy. (For instructions on how to import files into a FrontPage Web site, see Chapter 2.)

The easiest method is to drag the picture's icon from the Folder List and drop it into the page. Otherwise, follow these steps:

1. **In the page, place the cursor where you want the picture to appear.**

   FrontPage only knows how to place the cursor inside a line of text or at the bottom of the page. If the cursor location doesn't exactly correspond to where you want the picture to sit inside your page, just do the best you can. I talk about other ways to position pictures in the upcoming sidebar "Placing graphics right where you want them."

2. **In the Standard toolbar, click the Insert Picture From File button.**

   The Picture dialog box appears (see Figure 7-1).

   The dialog box displays a list of your Web site's graphic files and folders.

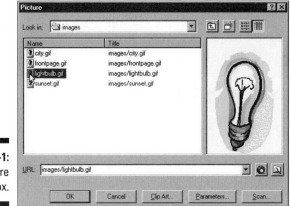

Figure 7-1:
The Picture
dialog box.

3. **In the dialog box's file list, click the icon for the picture you want to insert.**

   If you don't see any graphic files, double-click the `images` folder; they may be stored in there. After you click a file icon, a preview of the picture appears in the preview area of the dialog box.

4. **Click OK.**

   The dialog box closes, and the picture appears inside the page.

Inserting pictures stored elsewhere on your computer

You also can insert into a Web page a picture that is not part of the current Web site and is stored elsewhere on your hard drive or local network. Doing so saves you the step of first importing graphics into your Web site, because when you next save the page, FrontPage offers to import the graphics for you. To insert a picture that is currently stored elsewhere on your computer, follow these steps:

1. **In the page, place the cursor where you want the image to appear.**

2. **Click the Insert Picture From File button.**

   The Picture dialog box appears.

3. **In the dialog box, click the Select a File On Your Computer button.**

   The Select File dialog box appears. The dialog box lists the folders and files on your computer and local network. Navigate to the location of the graphic file.

4. **Click the icon for the file you want to insert and then click OK.**

   Both dialog boxes close, and the picture appears in the page.

When you next save the page, the Save Embedded Files dialog box appears and asks whether you want to import the inserted graphic into the Web site (see Figure 7-2). Click OK to import the file. See Chapter 3 for more details on how this dialog box works.

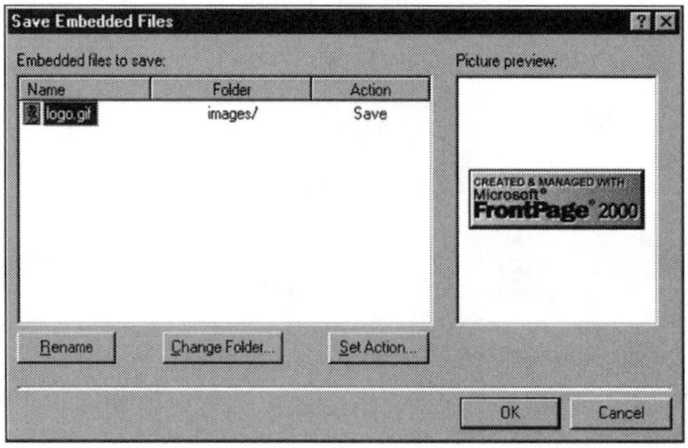

Figure 7-2:
The Save
Embedded
Files
dialog box.

You can copy a picture from another application and paste the picture into your page directly from the Clipboard. You can also drag a graphic file from your desktop or the Windows Explorer and drop it into the page. FrontPage coverts a copy of the picture into GIF or JPEG (if necessary) and then imports the copy into your Web site when you next save the page.

The steps in this section work properly only if the Web page is part of the Web site currently open in FrontPage. If you originally opened the page from a location elsewhere on your hard drive, FrontPage uses the graphic file's location on your hard drive to create the Web page reference to the graphic file. When you publish your finished Web site, the reference doesn't work because the graphic file's location is specific to your computer's file system, not the web server's. For more insight into the publishing process, turn to Chapter 16.

Grabbing a picture off the World Wide Web

Because, on the HTML level, pictures in Web pages are really only references to graphic files, you can display in your page pictures that dwell on a web server on the other side of the world.

If the web server hosting the graphic file goes down or the filename or location of the graphic file changes, the picture won't appear properly in your page. Instead, when viewed with a web browser, the page will contain a broken image icon where the picture should have appeared. To avoid this problem, first copy the picture from its original location to your computer (with permission of the host site's author and/or the creator of the artwork, of course) and then insert the picture into your page by following the steps in the preceding sections. Most web browsers enable you to right-click any picture on the Web and then save a copy of the file on your hard drive.

To insert a picture from the Web, follow these steps:

1. **In the page, place the cursor where you want the picture to appear.**

2. **Click the Insert Picture From File button.**

   The Picture dialog box appears.

3. **In the URL text box, type the complete URL of the picture that you want to display.**

   The URL should look something like the following example:
   ```
   http://www.server.com/picture.gif
   ```

If you can't remember the URL, launch your web browser by clicking the button in the dialog box marked Use Your Web Browser to Select a Page or File. In your browser, surf to the location of the picture and then switch back to FrontPage by clicking the program's button in the Windows taskbar. The picture's URL appears in the URL text box. (Keep in mind you must use the *picture file's* URL, not the URL of the page in which the picture is displayed.)

4. Click OK.

The dialog box closes. In a moment, the picture appears in the page.

In the FrontPage Page View, the Broken Picture icon appears in your page whenever the reference to a graphic file doesn't work properly. If this icon appears after you click OK in Step 4 in the preceding steps, it means that the URL you typed in Step 3 is unreachable. (Either you entered an invalid URL or the web server hosting the graphic file is down.) To correct the URL, double-click the icon to display the Picture Properties dialog box. In the Picture Source text box, type the correct URL and then click OK. After you click OK, the picture should appear in your page after a few seconds. If the Broken Picture icon is still visible, the host web server is down or the graphic file has been renamed, moved, or deleted — which is beyond your control.

Using the Clip Art Gallery

At the time you installed FrontPage, the program quietly slipped a bunch of clip art onto your hard drive. FrontPage gives you access to a bevy of colorful images you can use to adorn your Web site.

Note: Use FrontPage clip art only if you originally opened the Web page from within the current Web site. Refer to the warning at the end of the section "Inserting pictures stored elsewhere on your computer," earlier in the chapter, for details.

To insert FrontPage clip art into a Web page, follow these steps:

1. In the page, place the cursor where you want the clip art to appear.

2. Choose Insert⇨Picture⇨Clip Art.

The Clip Art Gallery dialog box appears. The Clip Art Gallery lets you store all of your clip art in a single location and then organize the graphics into searchable categories. Other Microsoft programs, including the Office suite, can work with the Clip Art Gallery. To get the most out of this program, including how to download additional clip art, sounds, photographs, and videos from the World Wide Web, click the Help button in the dialog box.

3. **At the top of the dialog box, click the tab that corresponds to the type of clip art you want to see.**

4. **In the category list, click a category name to see different groups of clip art.**

   After you select a category, that clip art group appears in the main area of the dialog box.

5. **Click the picture that you want to insert, and from the pop-up menu that appears, choose the Insert clip icon (see Figure 7-3).**

   The Clip Art Gallery dialog box closes, and the picture appears in the page. (Many of the clip art pictures are quite large. Later in this chapter, I show you how to adjust the dimensions of a picture.)

Figure 7-3:
Inserting a piece of clip art stored in the Clip Art Gallery.

Gobs of graphics

Where do you find ready-made pictures to plop into your Web site? In addition to the Clip Art Gallery, plenty of excellent Web galleries encourage you to grab their pictures for your own personal use. Try the Microsoft Images Gallery at www.microsoft.com/gallery/images/default.asp, or the Webreference.com graphics collection at www.webreference.com/authoring/graphics/collections.html.

Or decorate your Web site with a FrontPage theme. Themes contain nice-looking banner and button graphics and can easily spice up an entire Web site. I talk about themes in Chapter 12.

When you next save the page, the Save Embedded Files dialog box offers to import the clip art file into your Web site. Click OK to import the file. (For more details on how to save pages containing pictures, refer to Chapter 3.)

Controlling How a Picture Is Displayed

After you insert a picture into your page, you have some control over how it is displayed there. For example, you can specify how it gets along with surrounding text, you can change its display dimensions, and more. Read on for details.

Aligning a picture with surrounding text

When you insert a picture in the same line as text, you can control how the picture aligns with that text. Follow these steps:

1. **In the page, right-click the picture and then, from the pop-up menu that appears, choose Picture Properties.**

   The Picture Properties dialog box appears.

2. **In the dialog box, click the Appearance tab to make those options visible (see Figure 7-4).**

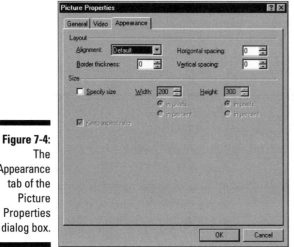

Figure 7-4:
The Appearance tab of the Picture Properties dialog box.

3. **In the Layout area, choose an option from the Alignment list box.**

   Here are your choices:

- **Left** places the picture in the left margin and wraps surrounding text around the right side of the picture (see Figure 7-5). For details on how text wraps around pictures, read the following section of this chapter.

    Right places the picture in the right margin and wraps surrounding text around the left side of the picture (see Figure 7-5).

    Note: You can right-align a picture by selecting the picture and then clicking the Align Right button in the Format toolbar, but text doesn't wrap around the picture as it does if you use the Right alignment option.

- **Top** aligns the top of the picture with the text.

- **Texttop** aligns the top of the picture with the top of the tallest text in the line.

- **Middle** aligns the middle of the picture with the text.

- **Absmiddle** aligns the middle of the picture with the middle of the tallest text in the line.

- **Baseline** aligns the picture with the text baseline. (The *baseline* is the invisible line that the page's text sits on, something like the lines on a piece of binder paper.)

- **Bottom** aligns the bottom of the picture with the text.

- **Absbottom** aligns the picture with the bottom of the text in the line.

- **Center** works just like the Middle option.

4. **Click OK.**

    The dialog box closes, and the picture alignment changes accordingly.

Figure 7-5:
The results
of the Left
and Right
alignment
options.

Placing graphics right where you want them

New Web designers (especially those who are used to working with page layout programs, such as PageMaker or Quark) are often frustrated by how difficult it is simply to place a picture where they want on the page. In Web pages, graphics sit in line with the page's text flow, which means that you have limited control over the picture's position.

Fortunately, Web design has a loophole: the table. By structuring the layout of your text and graphics inside a table and then turning off the table's borders, you can create beautifully laid-out pages. You find out more about tables in Chapter 9.

Another option is positioning, which enables you to place a picture in any spot on the page, independent of the page's text or other content. Positioning even makes possible *layering* of text and pictures in your pages. Positioning can nudge your Web site toward the cutting edge of design, but only for those visitors using state-of-the-art web browsers. (Older browsers don't know how to display positioned elements.) I explain the ins and outs of positioning in Chapter 13.

Controlling how text wraps around a picture

If you use the Left or Right option to align a picture (as outlined in the preceding section), adjacent text flows, or *wraps,* around the picture.

You can control the amount of text that wraps around the picture by inserting a *line break* where you want the wrapping to stop. A line break creates a new, blank line and moves all the text following the line break beneath the picture.

Pressing Shift+Enter creates a normal line break. (I discuss this type of line break in Chapter 5.) The line breaks described in this section work specifically with left- and right-aligned pictures.

To insert a line break, follow these steps:

1. **Position the cursor in the page where you want to insert the line break.**

2. **Choose Insert⇨Break.**

   The Break Properties dialog box appears.

3. **Click the radio button next to the type of line break you want.**

   The type of line break you select depends on how the picture is aligned:

   - **Clear Left Margin.** If the picture is left-aligned, choose this option to cause text after the line break to shift to the first empty space in the left margin below the picture.

   - **Clear Right Margin.** If the picture is right-aligned, choose this option to cause text after the line break to shift to the first empty space in the right margin below the picture.

   - **Clear Both Margins.** If the page contains several pictures — some that are left-aligned and others that are right-aligned — choose this option to cause text to shift to the first empty space where both margins are clear.

4. **Click OK to close the dialog box and insert the line break.**

Controlling the amount of space surrounding a picture

You can control the amount of breathing room surrounding each picture. By adjusting horizontal and vertical spacing, you set the amount of space that separates a picture from its surroundings. To adjust picture spacing, follow these steps:

1. **Right-click the picture and then, from the pop-up menu that appears, choose Picture Properties.**

   The Picture Properties dialog box appears.

2. **In the dialog box, click the Appearance tab.**

3. **In the Horizontal Spacing text box, type the number of pixels of blank space you want to insert to the left and right of the picture.**

4. **In the Vertical Spacing text box, type the number of pixels of blank space you want to insert above and below the picture.**

5. **Click OK to close the dialog box and adjust the spacing.**

Adding (or removing) a border around a picture

Borders are useful only if the picture in question is the basis of a hyperlink. Although you can place a black border around a regular picture by using this feature, in my humble opinion, it looks darn ugly.

Borders around graphic hyperlinks, on the other hand, can make your site easier to navigate. Graphic hyperlink borders are the same color as the page's text link colors, cueing neophyte Web surfers to click the picture to activate the link. On the *other* other hand, borders may cause visual clutter and, worse, may clash with the colors in the picture.

You can solve this design dilemma by choosing your hyperlink graphics carefully — use pictures that implicitly whisper "click me." That way, even the greenest of visitors knows to click the picture to activate its associated hyperlink.

To give your picture a border, or to remove the border surrounding a graphic hyperlink, follow these steps:

1. **Right-click the picture and then, from the pop-up menu that appears, choose Picture Properties.**

   The Picture Properties dialog box appears.

2. **In the dialog box, click the Appearance tab.**

3. **In the dialog box's Border Thickness box, type the thickness, in pixels, of the picture border.**

   I recommend nothing thicker than 2 pixels. Anything much thicker tends to look gaudy, but be sure to experiment to see what you prefer. To remove borders from graphic hyperlinks, specify a border thickness of 0 pixels.

4. **Click OK to close the dialog box and apply the border setting.**

The best way to add a border to regular (non-hyperlinked) pictures is to open the graphic file in a graphics program and edit the file itself. Later in this chapter, I explain how to launch your graphics program from within FrontPage.

Setting display dimensions

FrontPage enables you to specify the width and height of a picture as it appears when viewed with a web browser. By doing so, you don't affect the size of the graphic file itself; you affect only the dimensions of the picture as they appear inside a Web page. (It's kind of like looking at a small object through a magnifying glass; the glass makes the object look bigger, but the size of the object doesn't change.)

You can use FrontPage to adjust the dimensions of your Web graphics, either in pixels or as a percentage of the browser window size.

To resize a graphic quickly, in the page, click the graphic and then drag the size handles that appear around the graphic.

For more precise control over dimensions, follow these steps:

1. **Right-click the picture and then, from the pop-up menu that appears, choose Picture Properties.**

   The Picture Properties dialog box appears.

2. **In the dialog box, click the Appearance tab.**

   The Width and Height text boxes already contain the picture's dimensions.

3. **To change the picture's dimensions, click the Specify Size check box, and then type new numbers in the Width and Height text boxes.**

   You can specify a number of pixels, or you can choose a percentage of the browser window. To maintain the correct proportion, click the Keep Aspect Ratio check box.

4. **Click OK to close the dialog box and adjust the picture's dimensions.**

Resampling a picture

In the steps of the section "Setting display dimensions," I tell you that by changing dimension settings, you don't affect the dimensions of the graphic file itself, only the size as it appears inside a Web page. Well, I'm about to go back on my word.

If you decide you prefer the new size of the picture, you can tell FrontPage to *resample* or optimize the picture to match its new size. Resampling doesn't perform magic, but it can smooth out the rough edges that sometimes appear when you resize a picture, and it can reduce the file size a bit. To resample a picture,

click the picture, and then, in the Pictures toolbar, click the Resample button. (The Pictures toolbar appears at the bottom of the FrontPage window whenever you click a picture inside your page. Alternatively, choose View➪ Toolbars➪Pictures.)

Keep in mind that when you resample a picture, FrontPage prompts you to save the changed graphic when you next save the page. Later in this chapter, I explain how to save a changed graphic as a separate file so you can revert back to the original if you change your mind.

Specifying ALT text

Some Web surfers, desperate to save seconds, turn off their browsers' capability to display pictures automatically. Instead of a graphically exciting Web site, as embodied in the example shown in Figure 7-6, the result is a no-nonsense, fast-loading, text-only site, with empty placeholders where the pictures normally sit, as shown in Figure 7-7.

Visitors who want to dispense with pretty pictures to get just the facts love this feature. But what about you? You painstakingly designed your site's graphics only to discover that some of your visitors never even see them!

This is just a Web publishing reality you must accept. All you can do is specify for each of your pictures *alternative text* (known in Web design circles as *ALT text*). ALT text appears inside the placeholder where the original graphic would have appeared if image-loading were turned on. Generally, you use ALT text to describe the graphic, giving visitors an idea of what the graphic contains and enabling visitors to decide whether the graphic is worth the load time.

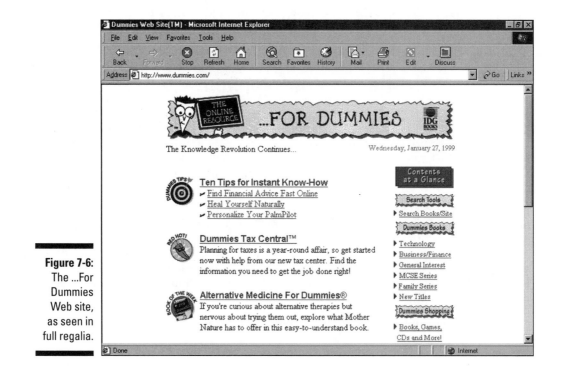

Figure 7-6:
The ...For Dummies Web site, as seen in full regalia.

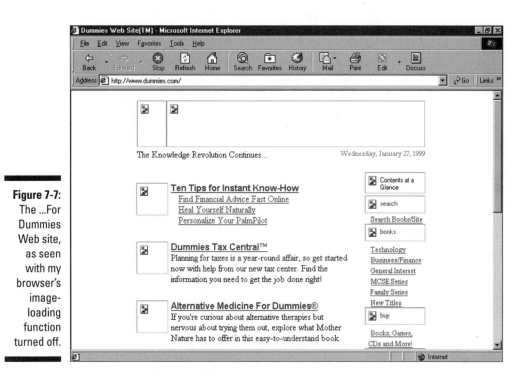

Figure 7-7:
The ...For
Dummies
Web site,
as seen
with my
browser's
image-
loading
function
turned off.

ALT text comes with a bonus: Some browsers display ALT text as a caption of sorts, popping the text up in a little box when the visitor hovers the pointer over a picture. A nice touch, to be sure.

Give every picture in your Web site meaningful ALT text. By doing so, you give visitors yet another way to enjoy your Web site (a thoughtful touch that many Web surfers appreciate).

To specify ALT text, follow these steps:

1. **Right-click the picture and then, from the pop-up menu that appears, choose Picture Properties.**

   The Picture Properties dialog box appears, with the General tab visible.

2. **In the Alternative Representations section of the dialog box, in the Text box, type a brief, descriptive blurb.**

3. **Click OK to close the dialog box.**

   Although nothing appears to have changed in your page, FrontPage has inserted the ALT text into your page's HTML tags.

Placing a text label on top of a picture

If a picture in your page needs a descriptive caption, or if you want to transform your favorite pictures into buttons or banners, you can easily do so by placing a bit of text on top of the picture.

The tool you use for this effect resides in the Pictures toolbar, as shown in Figure 7-8. You can make this toolbar visible by clicking a picture in the page or by choosing View➪Toolbars➪Pictures.

Figure 7-8:
The Pictures
toolbar.

To create a text label, follow these steps:

1. **In the page, click the picture you want to edit.**

2. **In the Pictures toolbar, click the Text button.**

   After you click the Text button, an empty rectangular area with a flashing insertion point appears in the center of the picture.

3. **Type your desired text and then click anywhere outside of the picture.**

   The picture is deselected, with the new text label sitting at the center of the picture.

To reposition the text label inside the picture, click the picture. A rectangular box appears around the text label. Click inside the rectangular box and then drag the label to a new position.

You can also format the text by using any of the text tools in the Font dialog box (available by choosing Format➪Font) and the Formatting toolbar.

Editing the Picture Itself

FrontPage has limited image-editing capabilities that can save you the hassle of launching a separate program for little touch-ups.

When you edit a graphic file by using FrontPage, the next time you save the page, the Save Embedded Files dialog box appears and prompts you to save the new, changed version of the picture. If you click OK to save the picture, you overwrite the original picture. To be safe, consider renaming the changed picture (which prompts FrontPage to save the picture as a separate file) so that you can revert to the original picture if you change your mind. To do so, in the Save Embedded Files dialog box, click the Rename button, enter a new filename, and then click OK to close the dialog box and save the file.

Creating a transparent GIF

The concept of a transparent GIF is more easily demonstrated than explained, so I'm going to show you one first and then tell you about the concept in a moment. Figure 7-9 shows the difference between a regular GIF and a transparent GIF. The graphic on the left is a regular GIF. See how the background color of the graphic wrestles with the background color of the page? This problem disappears if you make the GIF's background color transparent, as in the graphic on the right. The transparent GIF blends nicely with the rest of the page — with no unsightly clashing.

Figure 7-9:
A regular GIF on the left, and a transparent GIF on the right.

Regular GIF   Transparent GIF

A transparent GIF has one of its colors erased (generally the background color) so that the color of the page shows through. The Pictures toolbar contains a "magic eraser" that can make regular GIFs transparent with a couple of clicks.

A GIF can have only one transparent color. Whichever color you slate for erasure disappears throughout the graphic. Unless the color you choose is unique, your GIF resembles Swiss cheese, because see-through spots appear throughout the picture. To avoid this problem, make sure that the GIF's background color does not appear anywhere else in the graphic. If you're working with ready-made graphics, you may need to first alter them in a graphics program.

To transform a regular GIF into a transparent GIF, follow these steps:

1. **Insert the GIF of your choice into your page.**

2. **Click the picture.**

3. **In the Pictures toolbar, click the Set Transparent Color button and then, in the picture, move the pointer over the color you want to erase.**

   As you move the pointer over the picture, the pointer turns into a little pencil eraser with an arrow sticking out of the top.

4. **Click the mouse button.**

   The color disappears!

To change a picture's transparent color, click the Set Transparent Color button and then click a different color inside the picture. The original color reappears, and the newly chosen color becomes transparent.

To turn a transparent GIF back into a regular GIF, click the Set Transparent Color button and then click the transparent area. The old color comes back.

If you try this trick on a JPEG graphic, FrontPage prompts you to convert the picture to GIF format. (GIF and PNG are the only Web graphic formats that can be made transparent.) Proceed with care, however, because the GIF format can't accommodate as many colors as JPEG can, and your picture's quality and file size may suffer as a result.

Creating an interlaced GIF

Web surfers' greed for speed is so well documented that many Web designers resort to a sleight-of-hand called an *interlaced GIF*. When viewed in a web browser, an interlaced GIF appears on-screen gradually, starting as a fuzzy haze and clearing up as the picture loads. Interlacing creates the illusion that the picture loads faster than does a regular GIF (which downloads in full clarity from the top of the picture to the bottom). This effect is actually a tiny act of psychological subterfuge, because interlaced GIFs take just as long to load as regular GIFs. A little trickery is okay, in this case, because your visitors usually don't mind waiting quite so much if they have something to look at in the meantime. To turn a regular GIF into an interlaced GIF, follow these steps:

1. **Right-click the picture and then, from the pop-up menu that appears, choose Picture Properties.**

   The Picture Properties dialog box appears.

2. **In the Type area of the dialog box's General tab, click the Interlaced check box.**

3. **Click OK to close the dialog box.**

The picture doesn't appear to have changed; however, it is now an interlaced GIF. To see the interlacing effect in action, preview the page in a web browser. (For more information about previewing pages, refer to Chapter 3.)

Cropping a picture

Cropping a picture involves trimming parts of the picture away, leaving only the stuff you like. To crop a picture, do this:

1. **In the page, click the picture you want to crop.**

2. **In the Pictures toolbar, click the Crop button.**

   A dashed border appears inside the selected picture — this border defines the area to be cropped (see Figure 7-10). After you crop the picture, the stuff inside the border stays, and the stuff outside the border goes.

   To change the shape of the cropping border, click and drag one of its size handles. Keep reshaping the cropping border until it completely surrounds the area that you want to keep intact. You can also click inside the cropping border and drag the border around without reshaping it.

Figure 7-10:
Cropping a
picture.

Cropping removes everything
outside the cropping border.

3. **After you get the cropping border right where you want it, click the Crop button again.**

   Snip! The unwanted portion of the picture goes away.

If you decide you don't like the newly cropped picture, in the Standard toolbar, click Undo.

Applying a special effect to a picture

The Picture toolbar contains a few goodies that let you apply special visual effects to your pictures. To use any of these effects, click the picture you want to change, and then click the corresponding button:

- ✔ **Rotate Left and Rotate Right.** These options rotate the picture 90 degrees to the left or right.

- ✔ **Flip Horizontal and Flip Vertical.** These options flip the picture horizontally and vertically.

- ✔ **More Contrast and Less Contrast.** These options increase or decrease the picture's contrast.

- ✔ **More Brightness and Less Brightness.** These options increase or decrease the picture's brightness.

- ✔ **Black and White.** This option turns a color picture black and white.

- ✔ **Wash Out.** This option fades the picture to a ghost of its former self. Useful when you want inactive graphic hyperlink buttons to look inactive.

- ✔ **Bevel.** This option bevels the picture's border (if the picture has one). The resulting picture looks like it's raised on a platform.

 If you're not happy with any of the effects, click the Restore button to return the picture to its original state. (Just be sure *not* to save the changes first; otherwise the Restore button won't work.)

Launching a separate graphics program

Want to add some finishing touches to your graphic? You can launch a separate graphics program right from within FrontPage. To do so, you must first associate your graphics program with FrontPage. (Refer to Chapter 3 for instructions.) After FrontPage knows which graphics program to launch, in the page, double-click any graphic to open the file in the graphics program.

Deleting a Picture

Erasing a picture from your page hardly takes a thought. Just click the picture and then press the Backspace or Delete key. It's gone!

Using Thumbnails to Speed Up Your Page

As I discuss earlier in this chapter, adding pictures to a Web page increases the page's overall load time. Because Web surfers' annoyance level rises with every second they must wait for a page to appear on-screen, you're wise to limit the number of pictures to keep the site loading fast.

But what if your site *relies* on pictures? Let's say you're building an online catalog or a Web-based art gallery. For these sites, the pictures are the main attraction. Are you (and your visitors) doomed to a slow-moving site?

Thankfully, no. Your salvation is called a *thumbnail*. A thumbnail is a tiny version of the picture you want to display in your page. Because small pictures load faster than large pictures, thumbnails take only moments to appear on-screen. The thumbnail is hyperlinked to the full-sized picture, so if visitors want to see more detail, they can click the thumbnail. (Presumably they are willing to wait the few moments it takes for the full-sized version to appear.) Figure 7-11 shows you how thumbnails work.

Figure 7-11: Using thumbnails to speed up a picture-laden page.

city lights gallery
1111 main street, ashaland, california 91121

nighttime, original photograph by shutter bug.
$250.00

Click the thumbnail...

sunset, original photograph by shutter bug.
$250.00

...to display the full-sized picture

Thumbnails are wonderful, because visitors wait only for the pictures they really want to see. Furthermore, you can insert several thumbnails into a page while keeping the load time minimal.

Keep in mind that loading a page with bunches of graphics, no matter what their size, will slow the page down. Keep an eye on your page's download time and, if necessary, break hefty pages into several, more sparsely filled, pages.

Inserting a thumbnail in your page

For the FrontPage-less Web designer, thumbnails take time to produce. The poor soul must create the thumbnail in a graphics program, import the file into the Web site, insert the thumbnail into the page, and then hyperlink the thumbnail to the original graphic. But for you, blessed with FrontPage as you are, thumbnails take only moments to create.

Follow these steps:

1. **In the page, insert the picture you wish to turn into a thumbnail.**

 2. **Click the picture, and then, in the Picture toolbar, click the Auto Thumbnail button.**

   Note: If the Auto Thumbnail button appears faded, it means the picture you selected cannot be used as a thumbnail.

   After you click the Auto Thumbnail button, the picture shrinks, and a colorful border appears around the picture, indicating it is now a graphic hyperlink.

To see the thumbnail in action, preview the page and click the thumbnail.

The following types of pictures can not be used as thumbnails: pictures that are already hyperlinked, pictures that have text labels, pictures whose original dimensions are smaller than the thumbnail, and image maps. (I introduce you to image maps in Chapter 8.)

Changing FrontPage's thumbnail settings

You can control the dimensions, border thickness, and bevel setting FrontPage uses to create thumbnails. Follow these steps:

1. **Choose Tools⇨Page Options.**

   The Page Options dialog box appears.

2. **In the dialog box, click the AutoThumbnail tab to make those options visible (see Figure 7-12).**

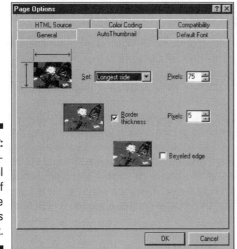

Figure 7-12:
The Auto-
Thumbnail
tab of
the Page
Options
dialog box.

3. **From the Set list box, choose the picture dimension you want to control.**

   Your choices are Width, Height, Shortest Side, and Longest Side. For example, if you want all the thumbnails to have the same width, choose Width. (FrontPage maintains the proper ratio so the thumbnail won't appear distorted.)

4. **In the accompanying Pixels box, type the number of pixels you want.**

   For example, if you want all your thumbnails to be 75 pixels wide, in Step 3, choose Width, and then enter 75 in the Pixels box.

5. **To change the border thickness, enter a new number in the accompanying Pixels box.**

   To turn off borders around thumbnails, unmark the Border Thickness check box.

6. **To give each thumbnail a beveled edge (turning square or rectangular pictures into something that looks like a button), mark the Beveled Edge check box.**

7. **Click OK to close the dialog box.**

From now on, thumbnails you create in FrontPage will conform to the new settings.

Creating a Background Image

You can use a picture as the background of your page, with the page's text sitting on top. How the background image appears as viewed with a browser depends on the dimensions of the graphic file itself. The web browser *tiles* the picture — repeating the picture over and over until it fills the browser window — which creates a consistent background for the text.

You also may turn your background into a *watermark.* Watermarks are the same as regular backgrounds, except that watermarks appear fixed in place if viewed with a web browser — when a visitor scrolls around the screen, the text appears to float above the fixed background. (With regular background images, the background and text move together when a visitor scrolls around the page.) As of this writing, Microsoft Internet Explorer is the only browser that can display watermarks.

Each FrontPage theme contains a background pattern that you can use in your pages. (I show you how to work with themes in Chapter 12.) You also can use the backgrounds that come with the Clip Art Gallery, or you can download backgrounds from the World Wide Web. You can also create your own backgrounds in a graphics program.

If you decide to use a background image, choose one that harmonizes with the colors in your site. If the picture is too busy, the background may obscure the text, making the page difficult to read. Additionally, background images, as do regular pictures, add time to your page's total download speed. The smaller and simpler your background image is, the faster the page loads.

To insert a background image, follow these steps:

1. **With a page open in FrontPage, choose F<u>o</u>rmat⇨Background.**

   The Page Properties dialog box appears, with the Background tab visible.

   Note: If the page uses a theme, this menu option is unavailable because all background options are determined by that theme.

2. **In the dialog box, click the Background P<u>i</u>cture check box.**

3. **In the corresponding text box, type the graphic file's path.**

   Or click Browse to select the file from a list of files in your Web site, your computer or local network, or the Clip Art Gallery.

4. **If you want the background to appear fixed, click the <u>W</u>atermark check box.**

5. **Click OK to close the dialog box.**

   The background image appears in your page.

TIP

What browser offsets are and why you should care

If you intend to line up pictures and text in your page's foreground with the page's background image, you need to find out about pesky things called *browser offsets*.

If you place a word or picture at the top of your Web page, the place in which the element actually appears on-screen depends on which web browser your visitors use. Each browser nudges these elements a few pixels over from the left edge of the browser window and a few pixels down from the top of the browser window. The amount of offset depends upon the browser. If you want to place an element precisely over a specific spot on your page's background image, the offset variation wreaks havoc because the alignment is usually a few pixels off if viewed with another browser.

Right now, Microsoft Internet Explorer is the only browser that enables you to control the amount of offset by setting the margins in your Web page. (You may do so by choosing File⇨Properties to display the Page Properties dialog box, then clicking the Margins tab, typing pixel values for the top and left margin of your page, and then clicking OK.)

Web designer David Siegel discusses browser offsets in detail and has even invented a simple test that you can use to see different browser offsets in effect. Visit www.dsiegel.com/tips/wonk14.

If the background image is stored elsewhere on your computer, when you next save the page, the Save Embedded Files dialog box offers to import the graphic file to your Web site. Click OK to import the file.

You can choose a solid color as your page background instead of a picture. Solid background colors load instantly and are often easier to coordinate with the color scheme of the page. To specify a background color, choose Format⇨Background to display the Page Properties dialog box. Choose the color of your choice from the Background list box (or choose More Colors to pick a color from the More Colors dialog box) and then click OK.

Alternatively, you can base the page's background color or image on that of another page in your Web site. For instructions on how to do so, refer to Chapter 6.

In the Background list box, the Default color is displayed in FrontPage as white. This display is a bit misleading because, by choosing this option, you tell the visitor's web browser to display the *browser's* default background color, which is often set to gray. Therefore, if you want your pages to consistently appear with a white background, choose White from the Background list box.

Chapter 8

Creating an Image Map

● ●

In This Chapter

▶ Understanding what image maps do

▶ Choosing the right graphic

▶ Creating and working with hotspots

● ●

*I*mage maps are the stuff of which Web designers' dreams are made. Image maps look just like regular pictures, except that visitors can click different parts of the picture to activate a hyperlink and go somewhere else. Image maps pack a big visual punch while retaining the utility of a bunch of text hyperlinks. In this chapter, I show you how easily you can transform a regular picture into an image map.

What Is an Image Map?

An *image map* is a picture that contains more than one hyperlink. Unlike a regular graphic hyperlink, which leads to only one destination, an image map can lead to several. Visitors activate different hyperlinks by clicking different places inside the picture (see Figure 8-1).

The clickable areas of the picture are called *hotspots*. Hotspots work just like regular hyperlinks; they can link to another location in the Web site or on the Internet, an e-mail address, or a downloadable file. Most often, however, image maps contain links to other places inside the Web site.

FrontPage enables you to turn pictures into image maps by "drawing" hotspots on the picture of your choice by using simple tools. Hotspots are visible to you as you work with the image map in FrontPage, but when viewed with a Web browser, hotspots are invisible. (Visitors see only the image map graphic.)

Figure 8-1:
The
"buttons"
on Yahoo's
image map
show visi-
tors where
to click to
activate a
hyperlink.

If you use an image map in your Web site, consider including a list of match-ing text hyperlinks somewhere else in the page. Visitors who surf the Web with their browsers' image-loading functions turned off (or who use text-only browsers) cannot see both regular pictures and image maps and, therefore, must rely on the text hyperlinks to move around. If you're not sure how to create a text hyperlink, refer to Chapter 6.

Choosing the Right Picture

You don't want to turn just any old picture into an image map. Because hotspots are invisible to the visitor, the picture you choose should clearly indicate where to click, either with the help of a visual metaphor (the exam-ple pictured in Figure 8-1 uses buttons, for example) or with text labels. The ideal image map picture doesn't require more explanation — the clickable areas should be obvious.

If you can't get your hands on the perfect image map graphic, don't worry too much. Even though, when viewed with a web browser, image map hotspots are invisible, when the visitor hovers the pointer over a hotspot, the pointer changes shape, and the hotspot's destination address appears in the browser's Status Bar. These clues are enough to prompt most visitors to click away.

After you choose your picture, open the page in which you want the image map to appear and then insert the picture into the page. (Refer to Chapter 7 if you're not sure how to insert a picture.)

Creating Hotspots

Here's the fun part of building an image map: creating the hotspots. Read on to find out how.

Drawing hotspots

You use tools available in the Pictures toolbar to draw hotspots; you can draw rectangles, circles, and multisided shapes (also known as *polygons*) around the areas that you want to make clickable. The Pictures toolbar automatically appears when you click a picture inside a page, or you can make the toolbar visible by choosing View⇨Toolbars⇨Pictures.

To draw hotspots, follow these steps:

1. **Open the page containing the image map graphic and then click the picture.**

    The Pictures toolbar appears at the bottom of the FrontPage window.

2. **In the Pictures toolbar, click the Rectangular Hotspot, Circular Hotspot, or Polygonal Hotspot button, depending on the shape of the area that you want to define.**

    Pick the shape you think best approximates the shape of the area you want to turn into a hotspot. You can always move or reshape the hotspot later — or delete the hotspot and start again.

3. **Move the pointer over the picture.**

    The pointer turns into a little pencil.

4. **Click the hotspot area and drag the cursor until the resulting hotspot surrounds the area.**

    *   If you're drawing a rectangular hotspot, click the corner of the hotspot area and drag the rectangle until the shape surrounds the area.

    *   If you're drawing a circular hotspot, click the center of the hotspot area and drag. (The circle expands from its center point.)

    *   If you're drawing a polygonal hotspot, creating a hotspot is like playing connect the dots, only you decide where the dots are: Click the first point, release the mouse button, and then drag the pointer. (This action produces a line.) Stretch the line to the second point — click, stretch, click, stretch — until you enclose your hotspot area. After you've finished defining the hotspot, click the hotspot's starting point, and FrontPage closes the hotspot for you.

You can overlap hotspots. If you do so, the most recent hotspot is on top, which means that this hotspot takes priority if you click the overlapped area.

After you draw the hotspot, the hotspot border appears on top of your picture, and the Create Hyperlink dialog box appears, enabling you to associate a hyperlink with the hotspot.

5. **Create a link for the hotspot, just as you would a regular hyperlink.**

   Refer to Chapter 6 if you're not sure how to create hyperlinks.

6. **Keep creating hotspots until you define all the clickable areas inside the picture.**

   Areas not covered by a hotspot don't do anything if clicked unless you specify a *default hyperlink*. (I show you how to do this later in this chapter.)

7. **When you're finished, click anywhere outside the picture to hide the hotspot borders.**

For a quick look at all the hotspots inside the picture, in the Pictures toolbar, click the Highlight Hotspots button. The picture becomes blank, and only the hotspot borders are visible. To return to the regular display, click the Highlight Hotspots button again.

If you later want to change a hotspot's hyperlink, click the picture to make the hotspots visible and then double-click the hotspot to open the Edit Hyperlink dialog box. Make any changes you want and then click OK to close the dialog box.

Drawing labeled hotspots

Hotspots are most effective when it's obvious to visitors where in the picture to click. If the clickable area isn't readily apparent, you may need to label a hotspot with descriptive text. To draw a labeled hotspot, do this:

1. **In the page, click the picture.**

   The Pictures toolbar appears.

2. **In the Pictures toolbar, click the Text button.**

   A rectangular hotspot with a flashing insertion point appears in the center of the picture.

3. **Type a descriptive text label.**

4. **Click anywhere outside of the hotspot to deselect it.**

   Now you need to specify the hotspot's hyperlink.

5. **Double-click the text hotspot.**

   The Create Hyperlink dialog box appears.

6. **Create a link for the hotspot and, when you're finished, click anywhere outside the picture.**

To change the text label, click the hotspot to select it, click inside the text label, and then type new text. You can also format the text by using any of the text tools in the Formatting toolbar or in the Font dialog box (available by choosing Format⇨Font).

Because a text hotspot is essentially a rectangular hotspot with some text on top, you can resize the hotspot as you would a non-labeled rectangular hotspot. (Read on for details.)

Moving hotspots

If the placement of a hotspot isn't just so, move the hotspot by following these simple steps:

1. **Click the image map to make its hotspots visible.**

   Don't worry — image maps aren't modest.

2. **Click the hotspot you want to move.**

   You can tell whether you selected a hotspot because size handles that look like little square points appear on its border after you select the hotspot.

3. **Drag the hotspot to a new location inside the picture and drop it there.**

Resizing hotspots

Hotspots are as malleable as taffy. Adjusting their shapes and sizes is easy. Just follow these steps:

1. **Click the image map to make its hotspots visible.**

2. **Click the hotspot you want to resize.**

   Size handles appear on the hotspot border.

3. **Click a size handle and drag the handle until the hotspot is the size or shape you want.**

Size handles act differently depending on the shape of the hotspot. Working with handles, unfortunately, is not a precise science. Just keep clicking, dragging, and stretching until you're happy with the results.

Deleting hotspots

Sometimes, no amount of coaxing gets a stubborn hotspot into shape. Those times call for drastic action — so delete the recalcitrant hotspot and draw a new one. Just follow these steps:

1. **Click the image map to make its hotspots visible.**

2. **Click the hotspot you want to delete.**

3. **Press the Backspace or Delete key.**

Setting the Default Hyperlink

The final (and optional) step in creating an image map is setting the image map's *default hyperlink*. Visitors jump to the destination of the default hyperlink if they click anywhere on the image map not defined by a hotspot. If you forgo the default hyperlink, clicking an undefined area does nothing. To set an image map's default hyperlink, follow these steps:

1. **Right-click the image map and then, from the pop-up menu that appears, choose Picture Properties.**

   The Picture Properties dialog box appears.

2. **In the Default Hyperlink area of the dialog box, enter the default hyperlink's URL in the Location text box.**

   If you can't remember the URL, click the Browse button to display the Edit Hyperlink dialog box. Chapter 6 contains complete instructions for using this dialog box.

   After you specify the URL, click OK to close the Edit Hyperlink dialog box. The Picture Properties dialog box becomes visible again, with the URL appearing in the Location text box.

3. **Click OK to close the dialog box.**

   FrontPage applies the default hyperlink to the image map.

To test-drive the image map, preview your page. (Refer to Chapter 3 if you're not sure how.) Alternatively, in FrontPage, hold down the Ctrl key and click one of the hotspots. In a moment, the destination page opens in the Page View.

Chapter 9

You Don't Have to Take Wood Shop to Build a Table

. . . .

In This Chapter

▶ Figuring out what a table is good for

▶ Creating a table

▶ Inserting stuff into a table (including another table)

▶ Selecting part or all of a table

▶ Changing table layout and alignment

▶ Adding color to a table

▶ Deleting a table

. . . .

*P*ut away that hacksaw! True, after you finish this chapter, you can build a table — but not the kind at which you play cards with your buddies. No, in this chapter, I introduce you to the wonders of the Web page table, a lovable layout tool that shows up in the best-designed pages on the World Wide Web.

What's a Table Good For?

Both left- and right-brained Web designers love tables.

Left-brained, well-organized types use tables to create grids of information, similar in layout to a spreadsheet. Tables cordon off individual bits of data into *cells,* which are arranged in horizontal rows and vertical columns (see Figure 9-1).

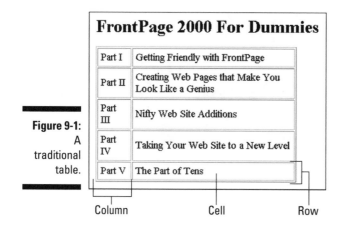

Figure 9-1:
A
traditional
table.

Column   Cell   Row

Right-brained, creative types use tables to structure the layout of the page. Tables without visible borders create a framework into which you can place chunks of text, images, and even other tables (see Figure 9-2). The result is a layout similar to what you can achieve by using a desktop-publishing program. Invisible tables are a boon for designers who feel constrained by the traditional one-paragraph-after-another Web page layout.

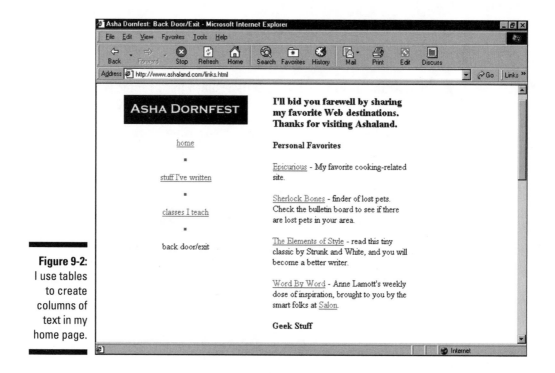

Figure 9-2:
I use tables
to create
columns of
text in my
home page.

(For excellent examples of how invisible tables can be used to structure page layout, take a look at one of the many FrontPage page templates. In Chapter 3, I show you how to create a page by using a template.)

The HTML coding required to build tables gets rather convoluted, causing newbie Web publishers to shy away from using tables in their pages. FrontPage eliminates all cause for alarm because table creation in FrontPage is a snap. And the only power tool you need is your mouse.

Tables work well as a page-layout tool. *Positioning* is another option. FrontPage positioning features enable you to place elements in your page with more precision than is possible with an invisible table. However, only advanced web browsers are able to display positioned elements, whereas most browsers are able to display tables. I talk more about positioning in Chapter 13.

Creating a Table

FrontPage bends over backward to make tables accessible to the neophyte Web publisher. FrontPage offers no less than four methods — all of them easy — for creating a table.

Choose the table creation method that suits your personality:

- **You like instant gratification.** Use the Insert Table button.

- **You are a perfectionist.** Use the T*a*ble⊏>*I*nsert⊏>*T*able command.

- **You are creative.** Use table-drawing tools.

- **You would rather be using a word-processing program right now.** Convert regular text into a table.

Using the Insert Table button

The Insert Table button suits people who want fast results. Two clicks of the mouse, and you have a perfectly good table. Try this:

1. **Place the cursor in the page where you want the table to appear.**

   FrontPage only knows how to place the cursor inside a line of text or at the bottom of the page. If the cursor location doesn't exactly correspond to where you want the table to sit inside your page, just do the best you can; you can more precisely position the table later by using alignment options (described later in this chapter) or positioning (described in Chapter 13).

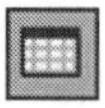

 2. In the Standard toolbar, click the Insert Table button.

A grid of white boxes representing table rows and columns appears underneath the button.

3. Click and drag your pointer on the grid until the number of high-lighted boxes equals the number of rows and columns you want your table to contain (see Figure 9-3).

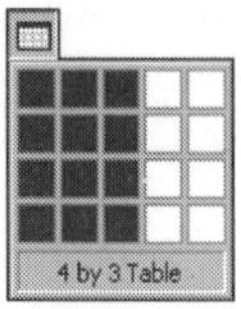

Figure 9-3:
Highlight the squares that corre-spond to the table dimensions you want.

As you highlight boxes, the table dimensions appear at the bottom of the grid. If you drag past the last box in a column or row, the grid expands.

If you don't know exactly how many rows or columns you need, just pick something close. You can always add or delete rows and columns later.

4. Release the mouse button.

A new, empty table appears in your page.

Using the Insert Table command

If you like everything to be just so, you may prefer to create your table by using the Table➪Insert➪Table command. With this method, you first set all of the table's attributes — number of rows and columns, border size, width, and so on — and *then* stick the table inside the page. To do so, follow these steps:

1. Place the cursor in the page where you want the table to appear and then choose Table➪Insert➪Table.

The Insert Table dialog box appears (see Figure 9-4).

2. In the dialog box, specify the table's size, layout, and width.

I explain each attribute in "Table Tinkering," later in this chapter.

3. Click OK.

The dialog box closes, and the table appears in the page.

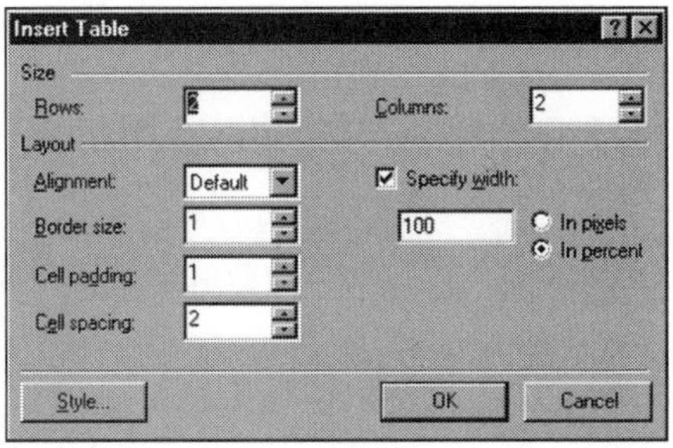

Figure 9-4:
The Insert
Table
dialog box.

Drawing a table

If you view table creation as an inspirational act, you can sketch your table's layout by using drawing tools. To draw a table, follow these steps:

1. **Choose Table➪Draw Table.**

   The Tables toolbar appears, and the pointer turns into a pencil.

   Note: The Tables toolbar *floats;* to dock the toolbar at the top of the window, double-click the toolbar's title bar.

2. **Click the pointer in the page where you want the table to appear and then, while holding down the mouse button, drag the cursor from left to right.**

   A dotted line appears, marking out the table's external boundary.

3. **Release the mouse button.**

   A one-celled table appears in the page.

Next, you draw in the rows and columns. Follow these steps:

1. **Click inside the table and then drag the pencil pointer to the left or right.**

   A horizontal dotted line appears, marking out a row boundary.

2. **Release the mouse button.**

   A new row appears.

3. **Click inside the table and then drag the pencil pointer up or down.**

   A vertical dotted line appears, marking out a column boundary.

4. **Release the mouse button.**

   A new column appears.

5. **Keep drawing rows and columns until the table looks the way that you want it to look.**

6. **When you're finished, click the Draw Table button to turn off table drawing.**

Don't worry if the rows and columns aren't spaced properly. You can adjust the spacing later.

Converting existing text into a table

If you're more comfortable with your trusty word processor than you are with FrontPage, you can convert text separated with tabs, commas, or any other character, into a table. To do so, follow these steps:

1. **In the page, insert the text you want to appear inside the table.**

   Separate each line of text you want to appear in its own row by placing the text inside its own paragraph. Section each row into "columns" by separating the text with tabs, commas, or some other character. Don't worry if the spacing is uneven — when you convert the text into a table it will all line up nicely.

2. **Highlight the text and then choose Table⇨Convert⇨Text to Table.**

   The Convert Text to Table dialog box appears.

3. **Click the radio button next to the text separator you want FrontPage to recognize when creating columns.**

   If the text separator in your page isn't a tab or comma, click the Other radio button and then, in the accompanying text box, enter the text separator character.

4. **Click OK.**

   The dialog box closes, and a table materializes around the selected text.

FrontPage can also convert Microsoft Word tables and Excel or Lotus 1-2-3 worksheets into Web page tables. Just cut and paste portions of a Word, Excel, or Lotus 1-2-3 file into an open page in FrontPage.

Inserting Stuff into a Table (Including Another Table)

You can insert anything into a table cell that you can into a regular page: text, pictures, and even other tables. Simply click inside a cell and proceed as usual. By default, cell height and width stretch to accommodate whatever you place inside.

Text entered into a cell *wraps* as you type, which means that, when the text reaches a cell boundary, the word being typed jumps down to a new line. You enter new paragraphs in a cell by pressing Enter and enter line breaks by pressing Shift+Enter.

If you're ready to type text in another cell, press Tab until the cursor ends up in the destination cell — and type away. If you press the Tab key when the cursor is sitting in the last cell in the bottom row of the table, a new table row appears, and the cursor jumps to the first cell in that row so that you can continue to add to the table. To move the cursor backward through a table, press Shift+Tab.

Table Tinkering

After you plug stuff into your table, you can tinker with the table's layout until the thing looks just the way you want it to look.

Aligning a table on the page

You can left-align, right-align, or center a table on the page. Just follow these steps:

1. **Right-click the table and, from the pop-up menu that appears, choose Table Properties.**

   The Table Properties dialog box appears (see Figure 9-5).

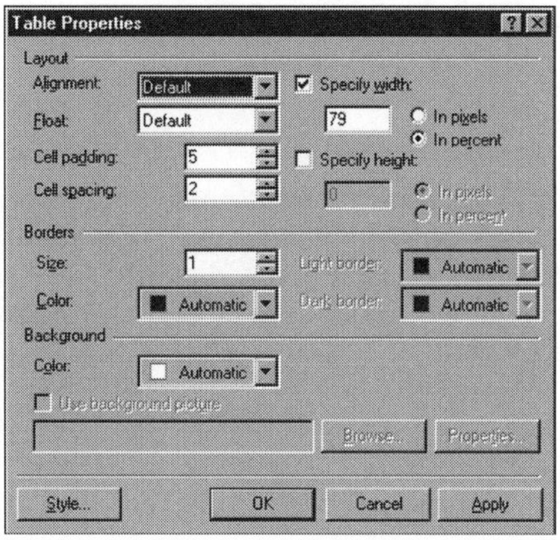

Figure 9-5: The Table Properties dialog box.

2. **In the dialog box, choose an option from the Alignment list box.**

   Your choices are Default, Left, Right, Center and Justify. The Default option uses the visitor's default browser alignment setting, which is left-aligned.

3. **Click the Apply button to see how the change looks before you close the dialog box.**

   If you like what you see, click OK.

   If you don't like what you see, choose a new option from the Alignment list box or click Cancel to close the dialog box without making any changes.

   After you click OK, the dialog box closes, and the table alignment changes accordingly.

Creating a floating table

No levitation occurs during this operation, but the effect is impressive just the same. Similar to a picture, adjacent text can wrap around the right or left side of a table. This effect is referred to as *floating* (see Figure 9-6).

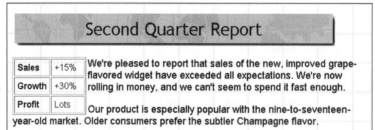

Figure 9-6:
A floating
table.

The effect looks a bit awkward when the floating table contains borders, because the surrounding text juts up right against the table; unfortunately, you can't adjust the amount of space that sits between the table and surrounding text. If the table is invisible (that is, the border setting is turned off), the floating effect looks elegant.

To make your table float, do this:

1. **Right-click the table and, from the pop-up menu that appears, choose Table Properties.**

   The Table Properties dialog box appears.

2. **In the dialog box, choose an option from the Float list box.**

   The Default setting creates no floating effect. The Left setting causes the table to float over to the left margin, with adjacent text wrapping around its right side. The Right setting causes the table to float over to the right margin, with adjacent text wrapping around its left side.

3. **Click OK to close the dialog box and change the table's floating setting.**

Older browsers aren't able to display floating tables; the table appears left-aligned with no text wrapping.

Padded cells

What do mental institutions and tables in Web pages have in common? I'll spare you the answer to that one. Suffice it to say that adding space between the contents of table cells and the cell borders is called *cell padding*. Padded cells open up a table by placing white space around the contents of each cell. Figures 9-7 and 9-8 illustrate the difference that a little padding makes.

Figure 9-7:
A table with no cell padding.

Part I	Getting Friendly with FrontPage
Part II	Creating Web Pages that Make You Look Like a Genius
Part III	Nifty Web Site Additions
Part IV	Taking Your Web Site to a New Level
Part V	The Part of Tens

Figure 9-8:
A table with 5 pixels of cell padding.

Part I	Getting Friendly with FrontPage
Part II	Creating Web Pages that Make You Look Like a Genius
Part III	Nifty Web Site Additions
Part IV	Taking Your Web Site to a New Level
Part V	The Part of Tens

To pad cells, follow these steps:

1. **Right-click the table and, from the pop-up menu that appears, choose Table Properties.**

   The Table Properties dialog box appears.

2. **In the dialog box's Cell Padding text box, type the desired amount of white space (in pixels) that you want to separate cell contents from cell borders.**

3. **Click OK to close the dialog box and change the cell padding setting.**

Adding space between cells

Cell spacing determines how much space exists between cells and also affects the appearance of table and cell borders. Figures 9-9 and 9-10 illustrate how changes in cell spacing affect the look of a table. To change cell spacing, follow these steps:

Figure 9-9:
A table
with a
1-pixel
border and
no cell
spacing.

Part I	Getting Friendly with FrontPage
Part II	Creating Web Pages that Make You Look Like a Genius
Part III	Nifty Web Site Additions
Part IV	Taking Your Web Site to a New Level
Part V	The Part of Tens

Figure 9-10:
A table
with a
1-pixel
border and
5 pixels
of cell
spacing.

Part I	Getting Friendly with FrontPage
Part II	Creating Web Pages that Make You Look Like a Genius
Part III	Nifty Web Site Additions
Part IV	Taking Your Web Site to a New Level
Part V	The Part of Tens

1. **Right-click the table and, from the pop-up menu that appears, choose Table Properties.**

   The Table Properties dialog box appears.

2. **In the dialog box's Cell Spacing text box, type the desired amount of space (in pixels) separating table cells.**

3. **Click OK to close the dialog box and change the cell spacing setting.**

Setting border thickness

In FrontPage, tables are born with 1-pixel-thick borders. If you turn off the borders, you transform the table from a traditional grid into an invisible framework you can use to arrange text, pictures, and other elements in your page.

Tables have two types of borders: those surrounding individual cells and those surrounding the entire table. Cell borders can be only 1 pixel thick. Table borders, however, can be of any thickness. To change a table's border setting, follow these steps:

1. **Right-click the table and, from the pop-up menu that appears, choose Table Properties.**

   The Table Properties dialog box appears.

2. **In the dialog box's Size text box, type the desired border thickness in pixels.**

   The number you type refers to the thickness of the border surrounding the table; the borders inside the table remain at 1 pixel. If you want to make table and cell borders invisible, enter **0** in the Border Size text box.

3. **Click OK to close the dialog box and change the border setting.**

Borders look different depending on which browser you use. Some browsers display borders as solid black lines. Others display raised lines, similar to what you see in the Page View. When in doubt, preview your page in more than one browser. (I provide directions in Chapter 3.)

If you turn off your table's borders, the solid border lines shown in the Page View are replaced with dotted lines. These lines appear only in FrontPage — when viewed with a web browser, the borders are invisible.

Setting table height and width

You can control the dimensions of your table. You have two options: You can give the table *absolute measurements* (a fixed size) or *proportional measurements* (the particulars of which are based on the size of the visitor's browser window).

You may be tempted to opt for absolute measurements so you can retain total control over the table size. Consider, however, the unfortunate visitor who must view your page by using a tiny or low-resolution monitor. That visitor may need to scroll all over the place to see the table in its entirety and may curse the inconsiderate person who created such a table.

By using proportional measurements, you enable the visitor's browser window to determine the dimensions of the table. You give up precise control, but your visitor gets to see the entire table inside the browser window, no matter what the monitor or window size.

Which option is best? The choice depends on how you intend to use your table. If the table's overall structure is more important than the precise placement of its contents, use proportional measurements. If you require control, use absolute measurements.

Another option is to forgo specifying the table's height and width altogether. If you do this, the table stretches to accommodate the dimensions of whatever sits inside the table's cells, and no more.

A good middle ground is to specify the dimensions of each column instead of the dimensions of the table as a whole. In this way, you can give some columns an absolute width and others a proportional width, creating a more flexible table. I show you how to change column dimensions in the upcoming section "Changing cell, row, and column dimensions."

To eyeball your table's absolute dimensions, click one of the outer table borders and drag the border to the desired size.

Otherwise, follow these steps:

1. **Right-click the table and, from the pop-up menu that appears, choose Table Properties.**

   The Table Properties dialog box appears.

2. **In the dialog box, mark the Specify Width check box, and in the corresponding text box, type the width of the table.**

   To specify a proportional width, type the width of the table as a percentage of the width of the browser window. For example, if you type **50**, FrontPage sets the width of the table at 50 percent, or half the width of the browser window.

   To specify an absolute width, type the table width in pixels.

   To turn off table width specifications, unmark the Specify Width check box.

3. **Click the radio button that corresponds to the measurement you specified in Step 2.**

   If you specified a proportional width, choose the In Percent radio button. If you specified an absolute width, choose the In Pixels radio button.

4. **If you want to specify a table height, mark the Specify Height check box; in the corresponding text box, enter the table's height in pixels or as a percentage value, and then click the corresponding radio button.**

5. **Click OK to close the dialog box and change the table size.**

Fiddling with Cells, Columns, and Rows

In addition to tinkering with the table as a whole, you can fiddle with the layout and structure of individual table cells, rows, and columns.

Many of the operations in this section take advantage of buttons on the Tables toolbar (shown in Figure 9-11). To make the Tables toolbar visible, choose View⇔Toolbars⇔Tables.

Figure 9-11:
The Tables
toolbar.

Selecting table parts

Selecting table parts. . . . It sounds like something you do at a hardware store. I'm not about to discuss buying lumber or wood screws; I talk about how to highlight, or select, different parts of your table in order to format those parts in some way.

At times throughout the rest of the chapter, I instruct you to select cells, columns, and rows. Here's how you do it:

- ✔ **Cells:** To select a cell, click inside the cell and then choose Table⇔Select⇔Cell. To select more than one cell, after selecting the first cell, press and hold down the Shift key as you click other cells.

- ✔ **Columns:** To select a column, click inside the column and then choose Table⇔Select⇔Column. Or, pass the cursor over the table until the cursor hovers just above a column. The cursor turns into a stubby down-pointing arrow. Click once to select the column. To select more than one column, select the first column and then drag until you highlight the area you want.

- ✔ **Rows:** To select a row, choose Table⇔Select⇔Row or pass the cursor over the left side of the table until the cursor hovers just to the left of a row. The cursor turns into a stubby arrow pointing to the right. Click once to select the row. To select more than one row, select the first row and then drag until you highlight the area you want.

Adding new columns

Here's how to add a new column to your table:

1. **Place the cursor anywhere inside the column to the right of where you want the new column to appear.**

2. **In the Tables toolbar, click the Insert Columns button.**

   A new column appears to the left of the selected column.

Adding new rows

Adding new rows involves a similar procedure. To add a new row to an existing table, follow these steps:

1. **Place the cursor anywhere inside the row beneath where you want the new row to appear.**

2. **Click the Insert Rows button.**

   A new row appears above the selected row.

Adding new cells

If you want to add a single cell rather than an entire row or column, you can do that, too. Just follow these steps:

1. **Click inside the cell to the right of where you want the new cell to appear.**

2. **Choose Table⇨Insert⇨Cell.**

   A new cell appears.

When you insert a single cell, the cell dislocates the other cells in the row creating a somewhat lopsided table. That's okay, if that's the effect you're looking for. However, if you want to add a cell to a table and, at the same time, maintain the table's grid-like structure, consider splitting an existing cell into two. I show you how to do this later in the chapter.

Deleting cells, columns, and rows

Want to shave a cell, row, or column off your table? No problem. Just follow these steps:

1. **Select the cell(s), row(s), or column(s) you want to consign to oblivion.**

2. **Click the Delete Cells button.**

   The selected cells, rows, or columns and their contents disappear. (Had you pressed the Delete key instead, only the cell contents would have disappeared; the cells would have remained in place.)

Aligning cell contents

You can control the vertical (up and down) and horizontal (left and right) alignment of the stuff inside table cells. By selecting several cells, a row or column, or even the entire table, you can apply alignment controls to a group of cells in one fell swoop.

To change vertical alignment, select the cells, rows, or columns you want to format, and then click the Align Top, Center Vertically, or Align Bottom button.

To change horizontal alignment, select the cells, rows, or columns you want to format, and then, in the Formatting toolbar, click the Align Left, Center, or Align Right button.

The Cell Properties dialog box contains an extra vertical alignment option that lines cell contents up along the baseline (the invisible line on top of which text sits) and an extra horizontal alignment option that justifies cell contents. To access the Cell Properties dialog box, right-click the selected cells and from the pop-up menu that appears, choose Cell Properties.

Changing cell, row, and column dimensions

Controlling the dimensions of table cells (and by extension, columns and rows) is similar to working with table dimensions: You can set an absolute size in pixels or a proportional size based on the size of the entire table. (Refer to the section "Setting table height and width," earlier in this chapter, for a detailed discussion of the pros and cons of absolute and proportional measurements.)

If you want to use absolute measurements, the easiest way to adjust the dimensions of cells, rows, and columns is to click on a border and drag it to a new position.

To adjust the height and/or width for a cell, column, or row by using proportional measurements (or for more control over the dimensions), follow these steps:

1. **Select the cells, columns, or rows you want to format.**

2. **Right-click the selection and, from the pop-up menu that appears, choose Cell Properties.**

   The Cell Properties dialog box appears (see Figure 9-12).

3. **In the dialog box's Specify Width text box, type the desired width.**

   (If the text box appears dimmed, be sure the Specify Width check box is marked.)

   If you are specifying a proportional width, type the width of the cell or column as a percentage of the width of the table. For example, if you type **50**, FrontPage sets the width of the cell or column at 50 percent, or half the width of table.

   If you are specifying an absolute width, type the width in pixels.

   To turn off width specifications, click to deselect the Specify Width check box. (If you do this, the size of the selected area is determined by the size of its contents.)

4. **Click the radio button that corresponds to the measurement you specified in Step 3.**

   If you are specifying a proportional width, click the In Percent radio button. If you are specifying an absolute width, click the In Pixels radio button.

5. **Click the Specify Height check box; in the corresponding text box, enter the desired height in pixels or as a percentage value and then click the corresponding radio button.**

   To turn off height specifications, unmark the Specify Height check box.

6. **Click OK to close the dialog box and change the dimension settings.**

 To distribute the rows and/or columns equally in the table, select the row or column and then click the Distribute Rows Evenly or the Distribute Columns Evenly button.

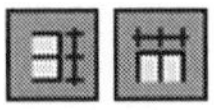

To adjust the dimension of columns and rows to fit their contents precisely, click inside the table and then click the AutoFit button.

Merging and splitting cells

When you merge cells, you erase the borders between the cells, creating one big, combined cell. Splitting cells divides one cell into two or more, arranged in rows or columns.

To merge cells, select the cells you want to merge and then click the Merge Cells button.

Or, click the Eraser button and swipe over the borders you want to erase.

To split cells, follow these steps:

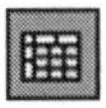

1. **Select the cell (or cells) you want to split and then click the Split Cells button.**

   The Split Cells dialog box appears (see Figure 9-13).

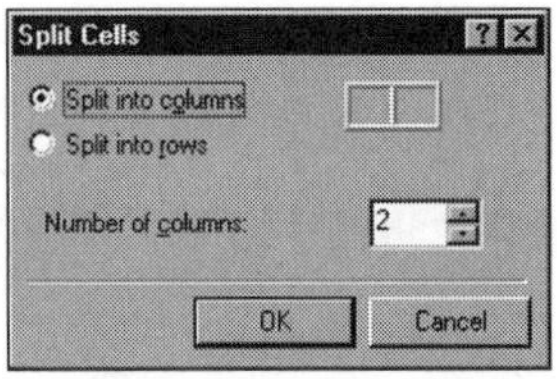

Figure 9-13:
The Split
Cells
dialog box.

2. **Click the Split into Columns radio button to split the cell(s) vertically, or click the Split into Rows radio button to split the cell(s) horizontally.**

   Depending on which option you click, the diagram next to the radio buttons shows a representation of how the cell will look after it is split.

3. **In the Number of Columns text box (or Number of Rows text box, depending on your selection in Step 2), type the number of cells into which you want to divide the selected cell(s).**

4. **Click OK to close the dialog box and split the selected cells.**

Tables and tribulations

FrontPage contains a bug (or is this quirk actually a feature?) that makes it possible to set the width of table columns to a number not equal to the total width of the table. For example, if you set the width of a two-column table to 100 pixels, you can also set the width of the table's columns to a number totaling more or less than 100.

FrontPage's display also gets confused if you set different widths for individual table cells (as opposed to entire columns of cells), especially if the table is complex.

The solution is to keep your tables relatively simple. At the very least, preview your page in a web browser (preferably more than one model) to see how your table looks to your visitors.

Adding a Caption

You can easily add a *caption* to your table — a bit of descriptive text that sits just above or below the table. To add a caption, follow these steps:

1. **Click anywhere inside the table and then choose Table⇨Insert⇨Caption.**

   The cursor hops to an empty space above the table.

2. **Type the caption text.**

If you want the caption to appear beneath the table, follow these steps:

1. **Right-click the caption and, from the pop-up menu that appears, choose Caption Properties.**

   The Caption Properties dialog box appears.

2. **Click the Bottom of Table radio button and then click OK.**

   The cursor moves to an empty space beneath the table.

Adding Color to a Table

Here's a nifty design effect: You can apply color to the background of your table, down to the individual cell. You can also change the color of table and cell borders.

Changing the background

You can apply a solid background color or a background image to a table or cell, just as you can to an entire page. (I show you how to change your page's background in Chapter 7.)

To add a background color to a table or cell, follow these steps:

1. **Select the cells you want to color (or select the entire table).**

2. **Click the little down-arrow next to the Fill Color button and then select the color you want.**

   The Fill Color button works just like the Text Color button, which I describe in Chapter 5.

To add a background image to a table or cell, follow these steps:

1. **If you're changing the background of the entire table, right-click the table and, from the pop-up menu that appears, choose Table Properties.**

   If, instead, you're changing the background of selected cells, choose Cell Properties from the pop-up menu. Depending on your choice, the Table Properties or Cell Properties dialog box appears.

2. **In the dialog box, click the Use Background Picture check box.**

3. **In the accompanying text box, type the URL of the background image.**

   If you don't remember the URL, click Browse to display the Select Background Picture dialog box. (Refer to the steps outlined in Chapter 7 if you're not sure how to select a graphic file from this dialog box.) After you select the file, the dialog box closes, and the picture's URL appears in the text box of the Table Properties (or Cell Properties) dialog box.

4. **Click OK to close the dialog box and apply the background setting.**

Only advanced browsers, such as Internet Explorer (Version 3.0 or greater) or Netscape Navigator (Version 4.0 or greater), are able to display table background color and images.

Changing border color

You can also change the color of table and cell borders. Keep in mind, however, that the same caveat applies to border colors as to background colors: Only advanced browsers, such as Internet Explorer (Version 3.0 or greater) or Netscape Navigator (Version 4.0 or greater), can display these effects.

To further complicate things, these versions of Explorer and Navigator display border colors differently — be sure to preview your page in each browser (plus a browser that can't display colored borders) for the most accurate representation of what visitors will see after you publish your site.

You can use color to create two different visual effects: a flat table with solid borders or a raised table, in which you use light and dark colors to simulate shadows.

To change table border color, follow these steps:

1. **Right-click the table and, from the pop-up menu that appears, choose Table Properties.**

   The Table Properties dialog box appears.

2. **Choose a border color from the list boxes in the Borders area of the dialog box.**

   Note: If the page uses a theme, these list boxes are unavailable, because table border colors are determined by that theme.

   To create a flat table, choose a color from the Color list box. To create a raised table, choose colors from the Light Border and Dark Border list boxes.

   If, in any of the list boxes, you choose More Colors, the More Colors dialog box appears. I explain the workings of this dialog box in Chapter 5.

3. **Click OK to close the dialog box and apply the border color.**

To change cell border color, follow these steps:

1. **Select the cells, columns, or rows you want to format.**

2. **Right-click the selection and from the pop-up menu that appears, choose Cell Properties.**

   The Cell Properties dialog box appears.

3. **Choose a border color from the list boxes in the Borders area of the dialog box.**

   As with table border color, you may choose either a solid border color or light and dark border colors.

4. **Click OK to close the dialog box and apply the border color.**

Deleting a Table

Building the perfect table takes some work, but deleting a table is effortless. You can either preserve the table's contents by converting the contents to regular paragraphs, or you can erase the table completely.

To convert the contents of a table into regular paragraphs, click inside the table and then choose Table⇨Convert⇨Table to Text.

To *really* delete a table, follow these steps:

1. **Click inside the table and then choose Table⇨Select⇨Table.**

2. **Press the Backspace or Delete key.**

   Your table goes off to table heaven.

Chapter 10

Forms Aren't Only for the IRS

. . . .

In This Chapter

▶ Understanding how forms work

▶ Creating a form

▶ Working with form fields

▶ Saving form results

▶ Creating a confirmation page

. . . .

*W*hat's the first thing that pops into your mind when I say *forms?* Let me guess: bureaucracy-perpetuating pieces of paper — or worse, multipage monstrosities in triplicate. Well, put those thoughts aside for a moment, because I'd like to introduce you to the wonders of the *interactive form.* Interactive forms transform your Web site from a showpiece into a workhorse. Here are a few of the amazing things you can do with forms:

✔ Survey your visitors and ask their opinions about things.

✔ Enable visitors to search the contents of your site for keywords.

✔ Host a discussion group in which visitors post their thoughts on a continuously updated Web page.

✔ Promote community by providing a guest book visitors can "sign" by submitting a form.

All this, and you don't need to hire an accountant to help you.

How Do Forms Work?

Before you build a form, it helps to understand the basics of how forms work. If this stuff seems a little tricky, don't worry. FrontPage takes care of the hard part. All you need to do is decide how you want to use forms in your Web site.

As do paper forms, interactive forms collect different types of information. Web site visitors fill in *fields,* either by typing information or selecting an item from a list (see Figure 10-1). After visitors complete the form, they click a button to submit the information.

The information submitted from forms is organized into a list of *field names* and *field values.* The *field name* is a unique identifying descriptor assigned to each field in your form. The field name is invisible to your visitors; it exists inside the form's HTML and is visible only to the person receiving the information submitted from the form. The pieces of text you see in Figure 10-1 — `Name`, `Your favorite ice cream flavor`, and so on — are not field names; they are bits of regular text sitting inside the page, prompting the visitor to fill in the accompanying field.

The *field value* is the information submitted by the visitor. Depending on the type of field, the value is either the stuff the visitor types or an item the visitor chooses from a list you define. (In Figure 10-1, for example, the value of the first field is `Asha Dornfest`.)

What happens to that information after a visitor submits the completed form depends on the type of *form handler* assigned to the form. A *form handler* is a program that resides on the host web server. This program receives the form data and then does something with it. Depending on the type of form handler, the program may save the data (also known as the *form results*) in a text file, format the results as a Web page, or even send the information back to the site administrator in an e-mail message.

Creating a Form

After that rah-rah introduction, no doubt you're pumped up and ready for some serious form creation. FrontPage is happy to oblige with three different methods: You can use a prefab form-page template; you can tag along with the Form Page Wizard; or you can build your own form.

Using a form page template

FrontPage contains templates for forms that often show up in Web sites:

- **Feedback Form:** This template creates a form that visitors use to send comments, questions, or suggestions.

- **Guest Book:** This template also collects comments, but it saves the submissions in a public Web page that other visitors can read.

- **Search Page:** This template works with the Search Form Component to create a searchable keyword index of your Web site. You find out how to use this feature in Chapter 14.

- **User Registration:** The User Registration template creates a registration page that enables you to track or restrict who visits the Web site. For more information about registration systems, refer to the FrontPage Help system by choosing Help➪Microsoft FrontPage Help.

To create a form by using a form page template, follow the directions in Chapter 3.

Inside the pages created by using form templates, the form consists of all the stuff inside the form boundary — a box surrounded by dashed lines. The colorful comments at the top of the page give you hints as to how to customize the form. The rest of what appears on-screen is a regular old Web page. Treat the entire page (including text inside the form boundary) just as you would any Web page: Format the text, insert a few graphics — whatever you want.

Using the Form Page Wizard

The Form Page Wizard possesses magical powers — at least, that's what I thought when I discovered how easy this Wizard makes creating a form. The Wizard walks you through the entire process of creating a customized form, including choosing form fields, suggesting questions to prompt visitors for different types of information, setting up the layout of the page, choosing a form handler, and deciding how to format form results.

Unless you have a Web form or two under your belt, you may not understand some of the Form Page Wizard's options at first glance. For that reason, before you activate the Wizard, you might want to skim the rest of this chapter to familiarize yourself with forms. The form-creation process makes more sense after you do so, and you realize just how ingenious the Form Page Wizard really is.

To create a form with the help of the Form Page Wizard, follow these steps:

1. Choose File➪New➪Page to make the New dialog box visible.

2. **In the dialog box's template list, double-click Form Page Wizard.**

   The dialog box closes, and the Form Page Wizard launches. The Wizard's initial dialog box explains what the Wizard is about to do. As you can with all Wizards, click Next to advance to the next screen or Back to return to a previous screen. You can also click Cancel at any time to close the Wizard.

3. **In the Form Page Wizard dialog box, click Next.**

   The next screen appears. Here, you decide what kind of information to include in your form.

4. **Click the Add button.**

   In the list box called Select the Type of Input to Collect for This Question, the Wizard lists several categories of information commonly collected with forms (as shown in Figure 10-2). Scroll down the list to see all your options.

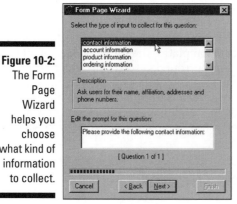

Figure 10-2:
The Form Page Wizard helps you choose what kind of information to collect.

5. **In the list box, click the first category of information you want your form to contain.**

   A description of the category appears inside the Description area. The text question that prompts visitors to fill in the field appears in the Edit the Prompt for This Question text box.

6. **If you like, in the Edit the Prompt for This Question text box, change the wording of the text question and then click Next.**

   The screen that appears next depends on the category you selected in Step 5. In this screen, you choose the specific types of information that you want the form to collect (see Figure 10-3). If some options don't seem to make sense to you yet, keep this book close at hand as you work and skim the rest of this chapter to clear things up.

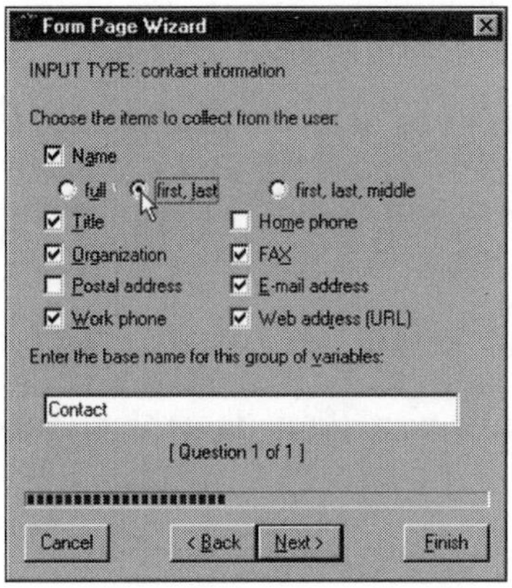

Figure 10-3:
Specify the
information
you want
the form to
contain.

7. **After you choose the items you want the form to contain, click Next.**

   You return to the section of the Wizard in which you add more questions to the form. The question you chose in the previous steps appears inside the list box. To add more questions to your form, click Add and repeat Steps 5 through 7. To change the order in which questions appear inside the form, click an item in the list and then click Move Up or Move Down. To modify or remove any item in your form, select the item and then click Modify or Remove. To erase everything and start again, click Clear List.

8. **When you finish adding questions, click Next.**

   The Presentation Options screen appears. Here, you decide how you want FrontPage to arrange the questions and form fields on the page: as a series of paragraphs or as a list of items. (Refer to Chapter 5 for a description of each type of list.) You can also include in the form page a Table of Contents that contains links to each section of the form. Finally, you can tell the Wizard to use an invisible table to align form fields. (Chapter 9 tells you all about tables.)

9. **Click the radio button next to the presentation options you want to use and then click Next.**

   The Output Options screen appears. Here, you decide what happens to the information contained in form submissions. (I explain each output option — plus a couple of options not included in the Wizard — later in this chapter.) You also choose a filename for the file in which the information submitted from forms will eventually be stored.

10. **Choose an output option and then click Next to advance to the final screen of the Form Page Wizard.**

11. **Click Finish to create the form page.**

    The Wizard disappears after it generates a new page containing a form based on your specifications.

Adding a form to an existing page

A form is nothing more than a special type of HTML that sits inside a page. You can, therefore, add a form to any Web page. To do so, you can rely on the assistance of the Form Page Wizard, or you can create your own form from scratch.

If you want the help of the Form Page Wizard but want to add the resulting form to an existing page, follow the steps in the preceding section to create a new form, and then copy and paste the form (including the form boundary) into an existing page.

To build your own form, follow the directions in the next section of this chapter.

Working with Form Fields

If the FrontPage form templates and Form Page Wizard don't create the kind of form you want, you can easily build your own form by adding individual form fields to a page.

Form fields are the collection plates into which visitors drop bits of information. The kinds of fields you include in your form depend on the kinds of information you want to gather. Do you want visitors to select from a predefined list of choices? Would you rather let them fill in whatever information they like? The answers to these questions determine the types of fields you should use in your form.

To create your own form, you add one or more fields to a page and then customize the fields so that they look and act the way that you want them to. By *customize,* I mean that you assign the field a name; in some cases, a value; and you adjust how the field looks. (I explain what field names and values are in the section "How Do Forms Work?" earlier in this chapter.) You can also create data entry rules for certain fields that restrict the kind of information visitors can enter there.

The first time you add a form field to a page, FrontPage sets aside a space for the form (indicated by a box with dashed lines) and inserts Submit and Reset buttons. (Visitors click these buttons to submit completed forms and to clear form contents; I talk more about how these buttons work later in this chapter.) You add fields to the form by inserting one or more fields inside the form boundary. You can add as many fields as you like to your form. You can cut, copy, and paste fields. You can also drag and drop fields to different locations.

To add fields to your page, you use the Insert⇨Form command. You can more quickly build a field-laden form by *floating* the Insert⇨Form menu, transforming the menu into a toolbar. To do so, choose Insert⇨Form, and then move your pointer over the thin stripe at the top of the menu that appears. When the stripe appears highlighted, click and drag the menu elsewhere inside the FrontPage window.

When you add fields to a form, you must insert the field *inside* the form boundary. If you insert a form field outside the form boundary, FrontPage thinks that you want to create a second form and creates a new form boundary, complete with its own Submit and Reset buttons. These two forms will then work independently of each other. Although it's technically okay for one Web page to contain more than one form, I assume that your intention is to create a single form.

As you create your form, be sure to preview the page to get a more accurate picture of how the page will look after it's published. If you're not sure how to preview a page, refer to Chapter 3.

One-line text boxes

One-line text boxes are plain-vanilla fields into which visitors enter a single line of text. Use a one-line text box when you want to collect small bits of information, such as a name or e-mail address. Figure 10-4 shows a filled-in one-line text box, as seen with a web browser.

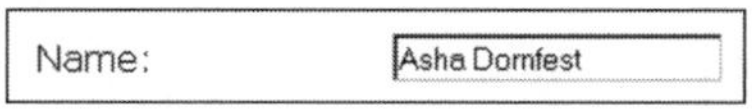

Figure 10-4:
The one-line text box.

Name:	Asha Dornfest

Creating a one-line text box

To add a one-line text box to your page, follow these steps:

1. **Place the cursor in the page where you want the field to appear (for a new form, anywhere in the page, or to add a field to an existing form, inside the form boundary), and then choose Insert⇨Form⇨One-Line Text Box.**

   A one-line text box appears in your page.

Form design tips

Here are a few simple tricks to make your home-grown forms easy for visitors to fill out:

- **Place helpful descriptors next to each field.** If, for example, you include a field in your form for the visitor's e-mail address, use the text descriptor `E-mail address` `(username@server.com)` to make absolutely clear what information you want.

- **Help visitors provide you with the correct information.** If your form contains mandatory fields or fields that require information to be entered in a certain way, include a note that demonstrates the correct format or at least that reads `This field is required`.

- **Use an invisible table to keep the form's layout neat and tidy.** (Chapter 9 explains how to build a table.) Insert the first form field in the page. Inside the form boundary, create a two-column invisible table, and then drag and drop the field into the top right table cell. Next, place text descriptors in the left column and more form fields in the right column.

- **Pay attention to the order of the fields.** Most web browsers enable visitors to use the Tab key to advance to the next field. You, therefore, should arrange fields in sequential order.

- **Use initial text in text box fields to save visitors' time and typing effort.** For example, if your form asks the visitor's country of origin, and most of your visitors are American, use USA as the field's initial text.

- **Consider rewarding visitors for taking the time to fill out the form.** Enter them in a drawing (with their permission) or give them access to free downloadable goodies.

---

2. **In the page, double-click the text box field.**

   The Text Box Properties dialog box appears.

3. **In the dialog box's Name text box, type the field name.**

   Choose a one-word, generic name that describes the information collected by the text box. If, for example, you're creating a text box to collect a visitor's e-mail address, type **E-mail** or **E-mail_address**.

   Always keep your field names restricted to one word. (You can use the underscore character to cheat a bit, as I did in the preceding example.) Some web servers aren't able to process forms with longer field names. Also, the name you choose does not need to match the text descriptor you insert in the page to identify the field to visitors.

4. **If you want the text box field to appear with text inside (instead of empty), type the text in the Initial Value text box.**

5. In the <u>W</u>idth in Characters text box, type the visible width of the text box field.

The number you type affects the visible size of the text box, not the amount of text a visitor can enter in the text box. To limit the amount of text a visitor can type into a text box, use a validation option, as described in the following section.

If you prefer to adjust the width of a text box by hand, skip this step. Instead, after you're finished defining the text box's properties, click the text box in the page and then drag the field's size handles until you're satisfied with its new width.

6. Optionally, enter a number in the <u>T</u>ab Order text box.

The *tab order* is the order in which the cursor advances to the next field when a visitor presses the Tab key. By default, the tab order is sequential; the visitor fills out the first form field and then presses Tab to advance to the next field in the form. By entering a number in the Tab Order text box, you can control the sequence in which the cursor moves. For example, type **1** in the Tab Order text box if you want the current field to be the first field in which the cursor appears, even if that field isn't the first field in the page.

As of this writing, only Internet Explorer (Version 4.0 or later) can display changes in tab order. In other browsers, the tab order is sequential, starting with the first field in the form.

7. Specify whether the text box is a password field.

Password fields are no different from regular text boxes except that, if viewed with a browser, text that someone types into a password field appears on-screen as dots or asterisks so that nosy passersby can't see what's typed. (If they could see what is typed, the password would be compromised.)

Including a password field in your form does not automatically add password protection to your Web site. I show you how to work with passwords in Chapter 15.

8. To restrict the type of information visitors can enter into the text box, click the <u>V</u>alidate button.

The following section explains how to use validation options. If you don't want to restrict the information visitors can enter, skip this step.

9. Click OK.

The dialog box closes, and any initial text you specified appears inside the text box. If you changed the width of the text box, it stretches or shrinks accordingly.

Validating information entered into a one-line text box

FrontPage enables you to make certain form fields mandatory. Unless visitors complete these fields, they can't submit the form. You can also control the format of information that visitors type into text boxes. This control is especially helpful if you want to standardize the format of form results.

Before you use FrontPage validation features, you must first specify how you want FrontPage to create the data rules. See the sidebar "Setting up FrontPage form validation," later in this chapter, for details.

After you click the Validate button in the Text Box Properties dialog box, the Text Box Validation dialog box appears (see Figure 10-5).

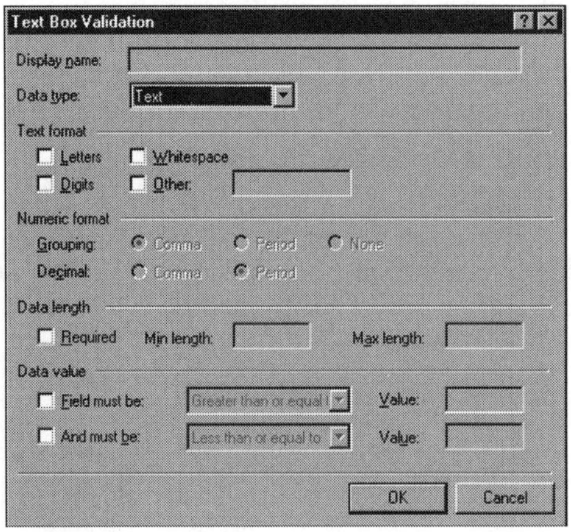

Figure 10-5:
The Text
Box
Validation
dialog box.

To validate information entered into text boxes, follow these steps:

1. **To restrict the type of data that can be entered into the text box, choose an option from the Data Type list box.**

   Choose one of the following options: No Constraints (no restrictions on data type), Text (letters, characters, or numerals), Integer (whole numbers only), or Number (all numbers, both whole and decimal).

2. **Depending on the option you chose in Step 1, choose an option from either the Text Format or the Numeric Format area of the dialog box.**

   • If you chose the Text data type, choose options from the Text Format area of the dialog box.

      The Letters check box creates a text box that can contain only alphabetic characters. The Digits check box creates a text box that can contain only numeric characters. The Whitespace check box creates a text box that can contain white space (such as spaces, tabs, and line breaks). If you want to allow other types of characters (such as commas or hyphens, for example), click the Other check box and type the characters in the corresponding text box.

- If you chose the Integer or Number data type, choose options from the Numeric Format area of the dialog box.

  The Grouping radio buttons enable you to control how visitors punctuate numbers greater than or equal to 1,000: with a comma, as in 1,000; with a period, as in 1.000; or with no punctuation, as in 1000. The Decimal radio buttons enable you to choose which punctuation character visitors can use as a decimal point: a period or a comma.

3. **To control the amount of information typed into a text box or to make a text box mandatory, choose options from the Data Length area of the dialog box.**

   Click the Required check box to make the text box mandatory.

   Type a number of characters in the Min Length and Max Length text boxes to control the length of information entered into the text box.

4. **To place restrictive conditions on the content of text box data, choose options from the Data Value area.**

   If you choose the Text or No Constraints data type, these options compare the information that visitors type into the text box against the order of the alphabet. If you specify that the field must be greater than *E*, for example, all information entered into the text box must start with the letter *F* or any other letter later in the alphabet (such as *H, Q,* or *Z* — but not *A, C,* or even *E*).

   If you choose the Integer or Number data type, these options make a numerical order comparison. If you specify that the field must be less than or equal to 10, for example, a visitor may type 10 or any lesser number in the text box.

5. **Click OK to close the dialog box.**

If a visitor enters information that doesn't stick to the validation rules, the visitor will be presented with a *validation warning message*. The warning message identifies the offending field to the visitor by using the field name you entered in the Name text box in the Text Box Properties dialog box. If the field name you used wouldn't make sense to a visitor (say, the field collects phone numbers and you chose field name `phon_num`), you can specify a friendlier display name (such as `Phone Number`) for the purposes of the validation warning. To do so, type the display name text in the Display Name text box at the top of the Text Box Validation dialog box.

Scrolling text boxes

Scrolling text boxes are just like one-line text boxes, except that this type of field holds more than one line of text. (See Figure 10-6 for an example of how a scrolling text box looks as seen with a web browser.) Scrolling text boxes are perfect for verbose visitors who want to send lots of comments. To create a scrolling text box, follow these steps:

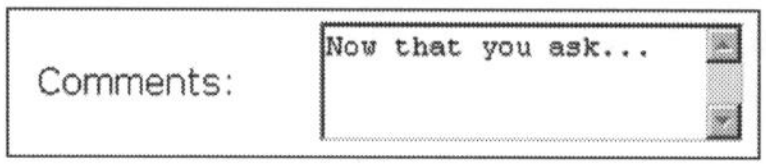

Figure 10-6:
A scrolling text box field.

Comments: | Now that you ask...

1. **Place the cursor in the page where you want the field to appear (for a new form, anywhere in the page, or to add a field to an existing form, inside the form boundary), and then choose Insert⇨Form⇨Scrolling Text Box.**

   A scrolling text box appears in the page.

2. **In the page, double-click the scrolling text box.**

   The Scrolling Text Box Properties dialog box appears (see Figure 10-7).

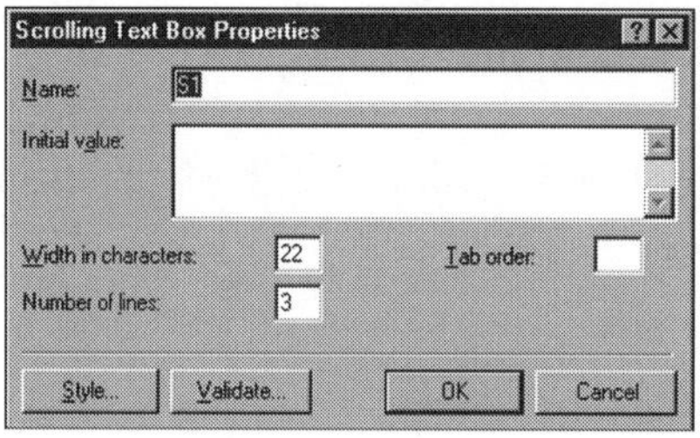

Figure 10-7:
The Scrolling Text Box Properties dialog box.

Scrolling Text Box Properties

Name: S1
Initial value:
Width in characters: 22   Tab order:
Number of lines: 3
Style...   Validate...   OK   Cancel

3. **In the Name text box, type the scrolling text box's field name.**

   The name you choose does not need to match the text descriptor you insert in the page to identify the field to visitors.

4. **If you want the scrolling text box to appear with text inside, type that text in the Initial Value text box.**

5. **In the Width in Characters text box, type the visible width of the scrolling text box.**

6. **In the Number of Lines text box, type the number of lines of text the scrolling text box can hold.**

   Effectively, this option controls the field's height. You can also adjust the height and width by hand (after you finish defining the field's properties) by clicking the scrolling text box and dragging the size handles until the field is the size you want.

7. **Optionally, enter a number in the Tab Order text box.**

   You can find out more about the tab order under Step 6 in the section "Creating a one-line text box," earlier in this chapter.

8. **To restrict the type of information that visitors can type into the scrolling text box, click the Validate button.**

   Refer to the preceding section, "Validating information entered into a one-line text box," for details on how to use validation options. If you don't want to restrict this information, skip this step.

9. **Click OK.**

   The dialog box closes, and any initial text you specified appears inside the scrolling text box. If you changed the size of the scrolling text box, it stretches or shrinks accordingly.

Check boxes

Check boxes are like teenagers: They're independent but prefer to hang around in groups all the same. (Figure 10-8 shows how a group of check boxes looks as seen with a web browser.) Use check boxes if you want visitors to select as many items from a predefined list as they want. You can include one check box or several in your form. To insert a check box, follow these steps:

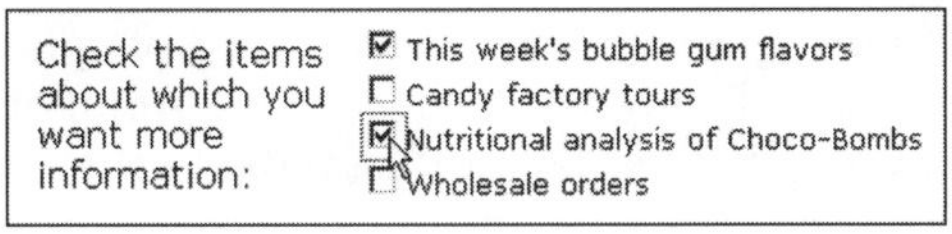

Figure 10-8:
A gang of check boxes.

Check the items about which you want more information:
☑ This week's bubble gum flavors
☐ Candy factory tours
☑ Nutritional analysis of Choco-Bombs
☐ Wholesale orders

1. **Place the cursor in the page where you want the field to appear (for a new form, anywhere in the page, or to add a field to an existing form, inside the form boundary), and then choose Insert⇨Form⇨Check Box.**

   A check box appears in your page.

2. **In the page, double-click the check box.**

   The Check Box Properties dialog box appears.

3. **In the Name text box, type the check box's field name.**

   The name you choose does not need to match the text descriptor you insert in the page to identify the field to visitors.

4. **In the Value text box, type a word or two that describes what the marked check box means.**

   For example, suppose you're using a check box to enable visitors to request more information about a particular product. Using the first check box in Figure 10-8 as an example, More_info is a good name choice, and Flavors is a good value choice because if visitors mark that check box, their choice means "I want more information about bubble gum flavors."

5. **If you want the check box to appear initially marked, click the Checked radio button.**

6. **Optionally, enter a number in the Tab Order text box.**

   You can find out more about the tab order under Step 6 in the section "Creating a one-line text box," earlier in this chapter.

7. **Click OK to close the Check Box Properties dialog box.**

To add more check boxes, repeat the preceding steps until you have all the check boxes you want.

Radio buttons

If check boxes are independent teens, *radio buttons* are a giddy high school clique. Radio buttons are never seen alone and base their identity solely on the others in the group.

Use a group of radio buttons to present visitors with a list of options in which only one option may be chosen. Figure 10-9 shows how a group of radio buttons looks as seen with a web browser. To create a radio button group, follow these steps:

Figure 10-9:
A gathering of radio buttons.

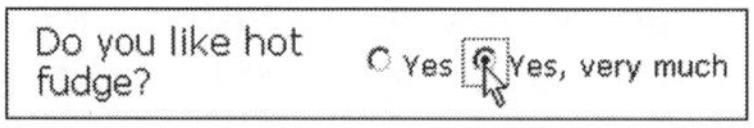

Do you like hot fudge?   ○ Yes ◉ Yes, very much

Setting up FrontPage form validation

If you use FrontPage form validation, FrontPage takes down all the data-entry requirements you specify as a set of rules. You can tell FrontPage to store these data rules in one of two locations: either as a script that sits inside the HTML of your Web page, or as a script stored on the host web server. Why do you care? Because, if you choose the wrong method, a few of your visitors may be able to slip past your data rules. Here's why.

By default, FrontPage stores the data rules as a script inside the Web page. The advantage to this method is the speed at which the browser is able to check the information. If a visitor enters information that doesn't conform to a data rule into the form, a pesky dialog box pops up right away prompting the visitor to change the entry. Unfortunately, this approach comes with a big downside: If a visitor using an older browser fills in the form, the validation doesn't work, because the browser doesn't know how to process the script and simply ignores the data rules.

Your other option is to tell FrontPage to store the data rules on the host server. If you choose this method, after a visitor fills in the form and clicks the Submit button, the form handler checks the submission against the data rules. If everything checks out, the server sends back a response letting the visitor know all is well. If not, the visitor gets an error message and is returned to the form to try again. This method is more clunky for visitors, but it ensures that all visitors, regardless of browser choice, must comply with the form's data rules. The only requirement is that you publish your Web site on a host web server that has FrontPage Server Extensions installed.

To choose the method or scripting language FrontPage uses to create data rules, follow these steps:

1. **Choose Tools⇨Web Settings to display the Web Settings dialog box.**

2. **At the top of the dialog box, click the Advanced tab.**

3. **From the Client list box, choose the appropriate option.**

   To store data rules inside the Web page, choose JavaScript or VBScript. (Only Internet Explorer 3.0 or later understands VBScript, whereas recent versions of Internet Explorer and Netscape Navigator both understand JavaScript.)

   To store the data rules on the host web server, choose <None>.

4. **Click OK to close the dialog box.**

   The Microsoft FrontPage dialog box appears, prompting you to recalculate the Web site.

5. **Click Yes.**

   The dialog box closes, and FrontPage recalculates the site. You can now set up data rules for your form.

1. **Place the cursor in the page where you want the field to appear (for a new form, anywhere in the page, or to add a field to an existing form, inside the form boundary), and then choose Insert⇨Form⇨Radio Button.**

   A single radio button appears in your page.

2. **In the page, double-click the radio button.**

   The Radio Button Properties dialog box appears.

3. **In the Group Name text box, type a name that applies to the entire group (even though you've only created one radio button so far).**

   In the example shown in Figure 10-9, the Group Name is `Like_fudge`.

   The group name you choose does not need to match the text descriptor you insert in the page to identify the list of radio buttons to visitors.

4. **In the Value text box, type the value for the individual radio button.**

   In the example shown in Figure 10-9, the value for the first radio button is `Yes`.

5. **If you want the radio button initially to appear unmarked, click the Not Selected radio button.**

   By default, the first radio button in a group appears selected.

6. **Optionally, enter a number in the Tab Order text box.**

   You can find out more about the tab order under Step 6 in the section "Creating a one-line text box," earlier in this chapter.

7. **Optionally, to require visitors to choose one of the items in the list of radio buttons, click the Validate button.**

   Before you use FrontPage validation features, you must first specify how you want FrontPage to create the data rules. See the sidebar "Setting up FrontPage form validation" for details.

   (In this case, validation applies only to a radio button group in which none of the radio buttons appears initially selected.) The Radio Button Validation dialog box appears. Click the Data Required check box. If you want the validation warning message to identify the radio button group by a name other than the group name you specified in Step 3, type a display name in the Display Name text box. (The "Validating information entered into a one-line text box" section earlier in the chapter explains the purpose of the display name.) Click OK to close the Radio Button Validation dialog box.

8. **Click OK to close the Radio Button Properties dialog box.**

Now you must create at least one more radio button to complete the group. To do so, follow these steps:

1. **Place the cursor inside the form boundary (ideally, near the first radio button field) and then choose Insert⇨Form⇨Radio Button.**

   A second radio button appears in your page, to the right of the first one.

2. **In the page, double-click the second radio button.**

   The Radio Button Properties dialog box appears. The Group Name is the same as for the first radio button. (I told you they stick together.) All you need to do is give the second radio button a unique value. In the example shown in Figure 10-9, the value for the second radio button is `Very Much`.

3. **Choose the radio button's initial state.**

   If you want the second radio button to appear initially selected, click the Selected radio button. (By default, the first radio button in a group appears selected; because only one radio button may be selected at any given time, if you choose this option, the first radio button in the group appears initially empty.) If you want the second radio button to appear empty, click the Not Selected radio button.

4. **Optionally, enter a number in the Tab Order text box.**

5. **Click OK to close the Radio Button Properties dialog box.**

   Validation options apply to the entire radio button group, so whatever you specify for the first radio button applies to all the radio buttons in that particular group.

Drop-down menus

Drop-down menus are so named because, after you click the field, a list of choices "drops down." Figure 10-10 shows how a drop-down menu works when viewed with a web browser. Drop-down menus are similar in function to radio button groups — this field type also lets visitors choose from a predefined group of options. In some cases, though, drop-down menus have their advantages, as follows:

Figure 10-10:
A drop-down menu field.

- Drop-down menus save space in your page by popping open only after a visitor clicks the down-pointing arrow next to the option.
- You can set up a drop-down menu to accept more than one choice at a time.

To create a drop-down menu, follow these steps:

1. **Place the cursor in the page where you want the field to appear (for a new form, anywhere in the page, or to add a field to an existing form, inside the form boundary), and then choose Insert⇨Form⇨Drop-Down Menu.**

   A drop-down menu field appears in your page.

2. **In the page, double-click the drop-down menu.**

   The Drop-Down Menu Properties dialog box appears (see Figure 10-11).

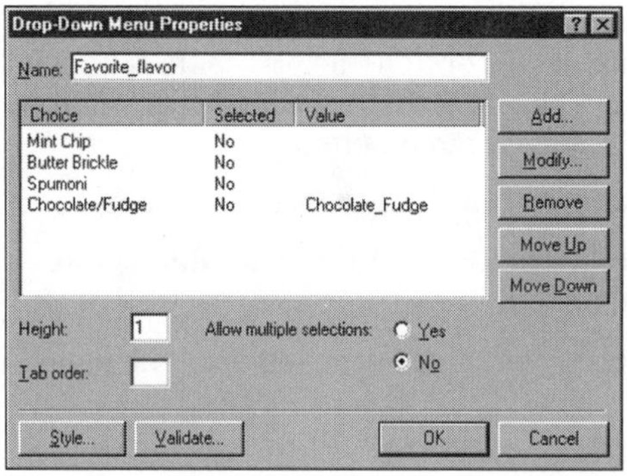

Figure 10-11: The Drop-Down Menu Properties dialog box.

3. **In the Name text box, type the field name.**

   In the example in Figure 10-11, the name is `Favorite_flavor`.

   REMEMBER: The name you choose does not need to match the text descriptor you insert in the page to identify the field to visitors.

4. **To add menu choices, click the Add button.**

   The Add Choice dialog box appears (see Figure 10-12).

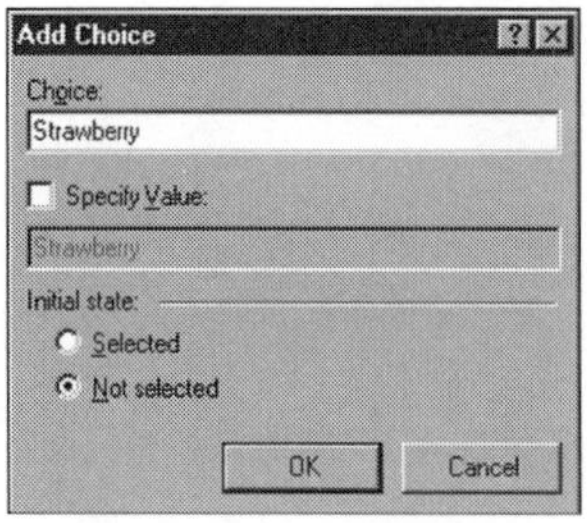

Figure 10-12: The Add Choice dialog box.

5. **In the Choice text box, type the text that you want to appear in the drop-down menu.**

   In the example in Figure 10-11, the choices are Mint Chip, Butter Brickle, and so on. (Although `Choose one` appears in the drop-down menu in Figure 10-11, it isn't a valid menu choice; I explain how to disallow the first item of a drop-down menu as a choice in Step 13.)

6. **If you want the choice's value to be something other than the information you type in the Choice text box, click the Specify Value check box and then type the value in the accompanying text box.**

   For example, if you transfer the form results from the example in Figure 10-14 into a database and the database program is unable to process the / character (as in the Chocolate/Fudge menu choice), you can instead specify a value of `Chocolate_Fudge`. That way, visitors select an item from the drop-down menu that reads Chocolate/Fudge, whereas the database receives the value `Chocolate_Fudge`.

7. **If you want the choice to appear initially selected, click the Selected radio button.**

8. **Click OK to close the Add Choice dialog box.**

9. **Repeat Steps 4 through 8 to add more menu choices until the drop-down menu is complete.**

   You can rearrange, modify, or remove menu items by selecting the item in the list and then clicking the Move Up, Move Down, Modify, or Remove button.

10. **In the Height text box, type the number of menu choices visible before a visitor clicks the drop-down menu and causes it to "drop down."**

    You can also manually adjust the height and width of a drop-down menu (after you're finished defining the field's properties) by clicking the drop-down menu in your page and dragging its size handles.

11. **To enable visitors to select more than one item from the list, in the Allow Multiple Selections area of the dialog box, click the Yes radio button.**

    As visitors view the form with a web browser, they select more than one option by pressing and holding the Ctrl or Apple Command (⌘) key as they click their selections.

12. **Optionally, enter a number in the Tab Order text box.**

    You can find out more about the tab order under Step 6 in the section "Creating a one-line text box," earlier in this chapter.

13. **Optionally, click the Validate button.**

    The Drop-Down Menu Validation dialog box appears.

Before you use FrontPage validation features, you must first specify how you want FrontPage to create the data rules. See the sidebar "Setting up FrontPage form validation" for details.

To require that visitors choose an item from the list, click the Data Required check box. (In the case of multiple selection menus, you can specify a minimum and maximum number of choices.) To disallow the first menu choice as a valid selection, click the Disallow First Item check box. Click OK to close the Drop-Down Menu Validation dialog box.

14. Click OK to close the Drop-Down Menu Properties dialog box.

The first menu choice becomes visible in the drop-down menu in your page. (If you specified that more than one menu choice is initially visible, the drop-down menu expands to display the specified number of choices.)

Specifying What Happens to Form Results

Here's where all the action occurs — *after* a visitor submits the form. What happens to the form results is up to you; you get to decide how to handle form results and where the information eventually ends up. FrontPage contains a brilliant built-in form handler that can format the information visitors fill into your form and then dump the information into a text file, Web page, or e-mail message. If, for some reason, the FrontPage form handler doesn't fit the bill, you can use FrontPage to hitch your form to a custom form-handling script.

Adding Submit and Reset buttons

When you first insert a form field into a page, the field appears along with two hangers-on: the *Submit button* and the *Reset button*. The Submit button is the linchpin of the entire operation. After visitors click this powerful little tool, their browsers activate the form handler program, which takes over from there, processing the form results.

If a gray Submit button is too boring for your taste, you can replace it with a *picture field*. Rather than a staid button, you can insert a snazzy picture. Clicking the picture submits the form results, just as a Submit button would.

The Reset button is another handy form tool. After visitors click the Reset button, their browsers clear all the information they entered into the form so that they can start over fresh. Alas, Reset buttons cannot be replaced by picture fields and are fated to look like little gray rectangles.

FrontPage automatically places a Submit button and a Reset button inside every form you create. In case you accidentally delete the buttons, here are instructions for manually inserting the buttons (as well as inserting a picture field).

Inserting a Submit or a Reset button

To insert a Submit button or a Reset button, follow these steps:

1. **Place the cursor inside your form, and then choose Insert⇨Form⇨ Push Button.**

   A push button field appears in your page.

2. **In the page, double-click the push button field.**

   The Push Button Properties dialog box appears.

3. **In the Name text box, type** Submit **or** Reset, **depending on the kind of button you're creating.**

4. **If you want the text on top of the button to read something other than the word Button, type new text in the Value/Label text box.**

   How about something vivid? A Submit button could read Come to Mama! and a Reset button could read I changed my mind.

5. **In the Button Type area, click the Submit or Reset radio button.**

6. **Optionally, enter a number in the Tab Order text box.**

   You can find out more about the tab order under Step 6 in the section "Creating a one-line text box," earlier in this chapter.

7. **Click OK to close the Push Button Properties dialog box.**

Another push button field type sits quietly inside the Push Button Properties dialog box: the Normal push button. You can program these types of buttons to do just about anything. You can, for example, include a button in your Web page that, after a visitor clicks the button, plays a sound clip or opens a new Web page.

For such a feature to work, however, you need to either write a script (a mini-program that gets embedded into the page's HTML code), or you must write the custom program to perform the operation and then store the program on the host web server. This task requires advanced programming expertise, plus coordination with your ISP or system administrator. If you want to proceed, speak to your Internet gurus first.

Inserting a picture field

To use a picture field in place of a Submit button, follow these steps:

1. **Choose Insert⇨Form⇨Picture.**

   The Picture dialog box appears, because you can use any graphic file as the basis for a picture field.

2. **Insert the picture of your choice into your page.**

   If you're not sure how to use this dialog box, refer to Chapter 7.

3. **In the page, right-click the picture field and, from the pop-up menu that appears, choose Form Field Properties.**

   The Picture Properties dialog box appears with the Form Field tab visible.

4. **In the Name text box, type a field name (such as** Submit**).**

5. **Click OK to close the dialog box.**

Designating where form results go

The Submit button is useless unless it knows where and in what form to send the form results. In the following sections, I describe the ways in which you can save the information submitted from your form.

The built-in FrontPage form handler described in this section works only if the host web server on which you publish your site supports FrontPage Server Extensions. If your web server doesn't support FrontPage Server Extensions, jump ahead to the section called "Sending form results to a custom script." If you're not sure what FrontPage Server Extensions are, see Chapter 16.

Saving form results as a file in your Web site

By default, FrontPage saves form results in a text file stored in your Web site. The first time a visitor submits a form, FrontPage creates the file and stores the information inside that file. From then on, each time a new visitor submits a form, FrontPage appends the new form results to the file.

After visitors submit the form, they are greeted by a *confirmation page* (a page that tells them that the form was successfully submitted) or a *validation failure page* (a page that appears if data they entered into the form didn't obey a server-based data rule), in which case they must return to the form and enter new information.

To control how FrontPage saves form results in a file, follow these steps:

1. **Right-click inside the form and, from the pop-up menu that appears, choose Form Properties.**

   The Form Properties dialog box appears (see Figure 10-13).

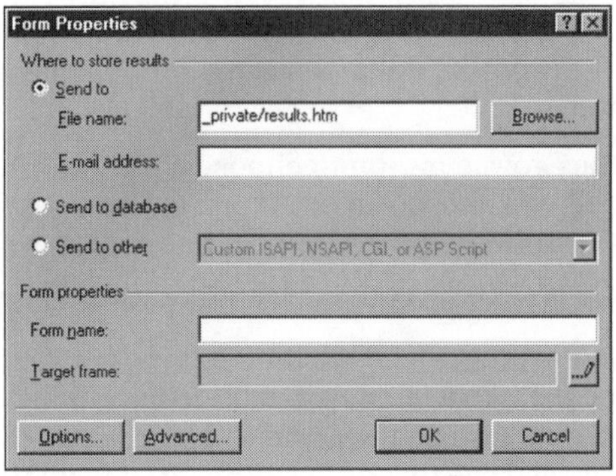

Figure 10-13: The Form Properties dialog box.

In the dialog box, the Send To area contains options that let you choose where you want form results to go. FrontPage's default setting saves form results in a text file, the location and filename of which appear in the File Name text box.

2. **In the dialog box, click the Options button.**

   The Options for Saving Results of Form dialog box appears, with the File Results tab visible (see Figure 10-14).

   This dialog box enables you to customize the results page.

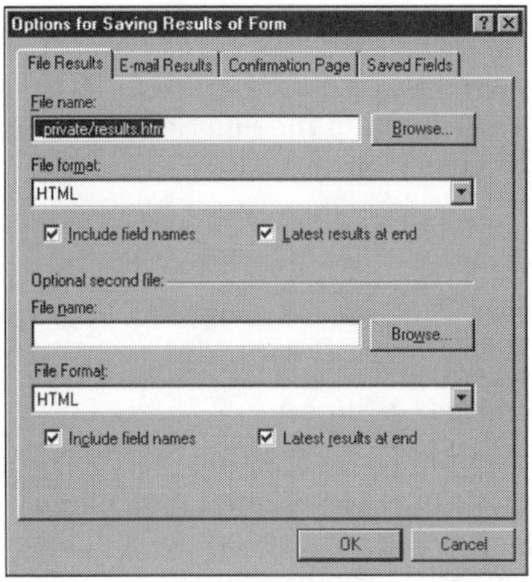

Figure 10-14: The Options for Saving Results of Form dialog box.

3. **If you want form results to be stored in a different file, enter the different filename or location in the File Name text box.**

   You can enter the filename for a text file (for example, `results.txt`) or a Web page (for example, `results.htm`). If you want the results file to be stored inside a Web site folder, type the folder name followed by a / and the filename (for example, `_private/results.htm`).

   Documents stored in the `_private` folder remain hidden from web browsers and from the FrontPage Search Form Component (which you get to know in Chapter 14).

   Alternatively, click the Browse button to choose a file that already exists inside your Web site. If you choose an existing file, FrontPage appends the form results to the bottom of the file each time a form is submitted.

4. **In the File Format list box, choose your desired page format.**

   You can save the results file as an HTML file (that is, as a Web page) or as a text file. You can format HTML files as definition lists, bulleted lists, numbered lists, or formatted text. (Refer to Chapter 5 for descriptions of each type of list.) You can save text files as formatted plain text (a nicely laid-out list of field names and values) or as a file with commas, tabs, or spaces separating names and values. (This latter format is handy if you want to later import the data into a database or spreadsheet.)

   Be sure the results filename visible in the File Name text box uses the filename extension that corresponds to the file type you choose here. HTML files should be named with the filename extension `.htm` or `.html` and text files should be named with the extension `.txt`.

5. **If you want the field names as well as the field values to appear in the results file, check the Include Field Names check box.**

6. **If you want the most-recent form results to appear at the bottom of the file instead of the top, check the Latest Results at End check box.**

   Note: If the results file is a new file, this check box appears dimmed.

7. **If you want to save form results in a second file as well, in the Optional Second File area, type the file path in the File Name text box or click Browse to choose a file in your Web site.**

   This option is handy if you want FrontPage to generate one file for, say, import into a spreadsheet and another file for your own private viewing.

8. **At the top of the dialog box, click the Confirmation Page tab.**

   The Confirmation Page tab becomes visible. (I skipped the E-mail Results tab because I cover it in the next section.)

   This tab enables you to specify custom confirmation and validation failure pages. (You discover how to create confirmation pages later in this chapter.) If you leave this section empty, FrontPage automatically creates generic pages (and you can skip ahead to Step 11).

9. **In the URL of Confirmation Page text box, enter the URL of the confirmation page (or click Browse to choose a page in your Web site).**

10. **In the URL of Validation Failure Page text box, enter the validation failure page URL (or click Browse to choose a page in your Web site).**

   Note: This text box is only available if your form uses server-based data validation rules.

11. **At the top of the dialog box, click the Saved Fields tab.**

   The Saved Fields tab becomes visible. If you only want the results of certain form fields to appear in the results page, you can say so here. You can also save additional information in the results file.

12. **In the Form Fields to Save text box, delete the names of the fields for which you don't want results saved.**

13. **In the Date and Time Area, choose options from the Date Format and Time Format list boxes.**

   By doing so, you tell FrontPage to affix a date and/or time stamp to each form submission.

14. **In the Additional Information to Save area, click the check boxes next to the other types of information that you want the results file to contain.**

   FrontPage can track the visitor's network user name, the name of the computer from which the form was submitted, and the type of web browser the visitor was using at the time.

15. **Click OK to close the Options for Saving Results of Form dialog box.**

16. **Click OK to close the Form Properties dialog box.**

Keep in mind that FrontPage will create and save the results file you just specified on the host server on which you publish your Web site, *not* on your local computer's hard drive.

Sending form results to an e-mail address

Sometimes, keeping track of form results as they arrive in your e-mailbox is easier and more fun than checking a separate results page. FrontPage makes it easy to route form results directly to you (or anyone else) as e-mail messages.

Before you proceed, check with your ISP or system administrator to be sure that the host web server on which you will eventually publish your site is set up to handle e-mail form submissions.

You can set up your form to send results via e-mail by following these steps.

1. **Right-click inside the form and, from the pop-up menu that appears, choose Form Properties.**

   The Form Properties dialog box appears.

2. **In the E-mail Address text box, enter the e-mail address of the person you want to receive form results.**

   Presumably that person is you. If so, enter your e-mail address here. (It should look like `username@domain.com`.)

   If both the File Name and the E-mail Address text boxes are filled in, FrontPage saves form results in the specified file *and* sends individual submissions via e-mail.

3. **In the dialog box, click the Options button.**

   The Options for Saving Results of Form dialog box appears.

4. **At the top of the dialog box, click the E-mail Results tab.**

   The E-mail Results tab appears. These options enable you to customize the particulars of the e-mail message format.

5. **In the E-mail Format list box, choose the desired e-mail format.**

   The default value is Formatted text, but you can choose other document formats as well.

6. **If you want the field names as well as the field values to appear in the e-mail message, check the Include Field Names check box.**

7. **In the Subject Line text box, enter the text you want to appear in the Subject line of the e-mail message.**

   You might want to choose something descriptive such as `Web Site Visitor Fan Mail`.

   If you check the Form Field Name check box, you can specify a field name here instead of static text. That way, visitors can specify what appears in the subject line of the e-mail message by filling out the corresponding form field inside the Web page. For example, say you add a one-line text field to your form and name the field `Subject`. In this step, you would click the Form Field Name check box and enter **Subject** in the Subject Line text box.

8. **In the Reply-to Line text box, specify the information you want to appear in the reply-to line of the e-mail message.**

   Here's where using a form field name really makes sense, especially if you use your form to collect visitor feedback. For example, you can tell FrontPage to replace the reply-to line in the form results e-mail message with the contents of a form field that collects visitors' e-mail addresses. Then, when you receive a form result message, you simply reply to that message, and it goes directly to the person who sent you the feedback (assuming that person entered her e-mail address correctly in the appropriate field).

9. **Click OK to close the Options for Saving Results of Form dialog box.**

10. **Click OK to close the Form Properties dialog box.**

After you click OK, you may see the very intimidating dialog box pictured in Figure 10-15.

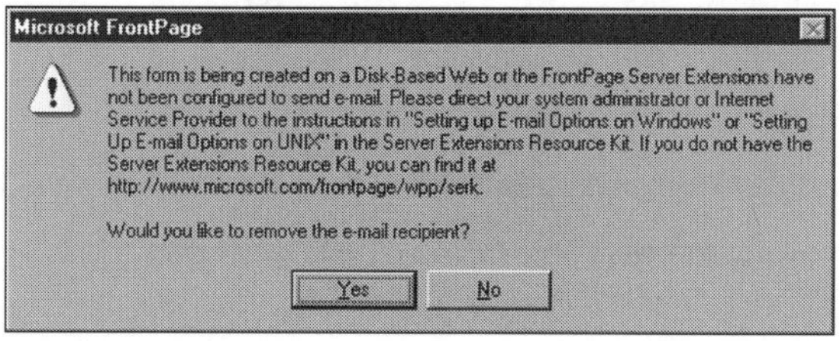

Figure 10-15:
This dialog
box may
appear
when you
set up your
form to
submit
results to an
e-mail
address.

Don't be alarmed. This dialog box pops up because FrontPage noticed you are creating a form that requires certain conditions on the host web server to be able to work (namely, that the web server has FrontPage Server Extensions installed, and that the web server knows how to process form results as e-mail messages). If you haven't already, check with your ISP or system administrator to be sure that the host web server can handle e-mail form submissions. If the answer is yes, you can ignore this dialog box (click No to close the dialog box and proceed on your merry way).

If the answer is no, you're out of luck; click Yes to close the dialog box and remove the e-mail recipient from your form.

Sending form results to a custom script

If your host web server doesn't support FrontPage Server Extensions or if you need special data-processing capabilities the FrontPage form handler can't accommodate, you can process form results by using a custom *form-handling script.* A custom script does the same job as the FrontPage form handler: It receives and processes form data and then outputs the results. The script's internal programming determines how form results are formatted and where they are sent.

Chances are good that your ISP or system administrator has a form-handling script already in place on the web server. (After all, folks were submitting Web forms long before FrontPage was born!) Speak to your ISP or administrator to discover the script's capabilities and find out where the script is located on the server (that is, the script's URL).

To write a custom form-handling script, you need programming experience or, better yet, a programmer friend who owes you a big favor.

To use a custom script as your form handler, follow these steps:

1. **Right-click inside the form and, from the pop-up menu that appears, choose Form Properties.**

   The Form Properties dialog box appears.

2. **Click the Send to Other radio button.**

   The corresponding list box comes into view, with the `Custom ISAPI, NSAPI, CGI, or ASP Script` option visible.

   If you must know, ISAPI stands for *Internet Server Application Programming Interface;* NSAPI stands for *Netscape Server Application Programming Interface;* CGI stands for *Common Gateway Interface;* and ASP stands for *Active Server Pages.*

3. **In the dialog box, click the Options button.**

   The Options for Custom Form Handler dialog box appears.

4. **In the Action text box, type the URL of the form handler.**

   If you don't know the URL, ask your ISP or system administrator.

5. **If it's not already visible, choose POST from the Method list box.**

   The majority of Web forms use this method to submit data to a script.

6. **Leave the Encoding Type text box alone.**

7. **Click OK to close the Options for Custom Form Handler dialog box.**

8. **Click OK to close the Form Properties dialog box.**

Creating a Confirmation Page

A *confirmation page* is the Web page that appears after visitors submit a form. This page lets visitors know that the form submission was successful and

TECHNICAL STUFF

Hitching your form to a database

With FrontPage, you can direct form results into a database program such as Microsoft Access or any other ODBC-compliant database. The implications are powerful: After the information is stored in a database, you can manipulate the information however you like. You can also use FrontPage to set up a form that enables visitors to search a database and display the search results in a Web page.

For database integration features to work, you must publish your Web site on a web server that

has FrontPage 2000 Server Extensions installed *and* supports Active Server Pages. (One such server is Microsoft NT Server 4.0 with Option Pack.)

The FrontPage Help system contains detailed instructions about working with databases. To access Help, choose Help➪Microsoft FrontPage Help. Another good source of information is the Microsoft FrontPage Web site at www.microsoft.com/frontpage.

(depending on how you set up the page) confirms the information that they entered in the form. A confirmation page is a nice way to reassure visitors that the information they just sent didn't float off into the ether after they clicked the Submit button.

For all forms except those submitted to custom scripts, FrontPage automatically generates plain-Jane confirmation pages. If you want your confirmation page to blend in nicely with the rest of your site's design, you can create your own page. (If you submit your form to a custom script, the script's programming determines whether it can work in conjunction with a confirmation page; your ISP or system administrator can fill you in on the script's capabilities.)

The confirmation page can be as simple as a polite acknowledgment and a hyperlink back to the Web site's home page ("Thank you for filling out our survey. Click here to return to the Acme home page."), or the page can display some or all of the information that visitors entered into the form so that the visitors can note the information for future reference. How does the confirmation page know to display visitors' form entries? Because you can insert into the confirmation page little jewels called *confirmation fields*.

Confirmation fields are simply references to the existing fields in your form. If used as part of a Web page, confirmation fields display the information the visitor typed into the corresponding form fields.

As always, FrontPage steps in to help with a handy Confirmation Form template. You can also create your own confirmation form by adding confirmation fields to an existing Web page.

Using the Confirmation Form template

The Confirmation Form template is a good place to begin building your own confirmation page.

Before you create a confirmation page based on the Confirmation Form template, you must know the names of the form fields that you want to confirm.

To create a confirmation page based on this template, follow these steps:

1. **Choose File⇨New⇨Page.**

   The New dialog box appears.

2. **In the dialog box's template box, double-click Confirmation Form.**

   A generic confirmation page opens in the Page View. This page is a boiler-plate confirmation page for a feedback form.

3. **Change the page to suit your needs.**

   This Web page is just like any other; you can format and rearrange the page any way you like. Add or change text, change the color scheme, and add your own graphics.

   The words that appear inside brackets (such as [UserEmail] and [UserTel]) are the page's confirmation fields. The word inside the brackets corresponds to the name of a form field. (The confirmation fields in this template correspond to the field names in the form created by using FrontPage's Feedback Form page template.)

4. **To change a confirmation field so that it corresponds to a field in your form, double-click the confirmation field in the page.**

   The Confirmation Field Properties dialog box appears.

5. **In the Name of Form Field to Confirm text box, type the name of the field you want to confirm.**

   Pay attention to uppercase and lowercase letters while typing the field name.

6. **Click OK to close the dialog box.**

   The word inside the selected confirmation field changes to the specified field name.

7. **Press Ctrl+S to save the changes to the page.**

After you create a custom confirmation page, you must specify its URL when you choose the form's handler. Refer to the section "Designating where form results go," earlier in this chapter, for details.

Adding confirmation fields to an existing page

You can add confirmation fields to any page in your Web site and then use that page as your form's confirmation page. To do so, follow these steps:

1. **Create or open the Web page that you want to use as your confirmation page.**

2. **Place the cursor at the point in the page where you want the first confirmation field to appear.**

3. **Click the Insert Component button, and then choose Confirmation Field.**

   The Confirmation Field Component Properties dialog box appears.

4. **In the Name of Form Field to Confirm text box, type the name of the field that you want to confirm.**

   Pay attention to uppercase and lowercase letters while entering the field name.

5. **Click OK to close the dialog box.**

   The confirmation field appears in the page.

6. **Press Ctrl+S to save the changes to the page.**

After you create a custom confirmation page, you must specify its URL when you choose the form's handler. Refer to the section "Designating where form results go," earlier in this chapter, for details.

Making Sure Your Form Works

After you finish your form, you might as well check to see if the darn thing works. Unfortunately, if you preview the page in a web browser, fill out your form fields, and then click the Submit button, FrontPage returns the message pictured in Figure 10-16.

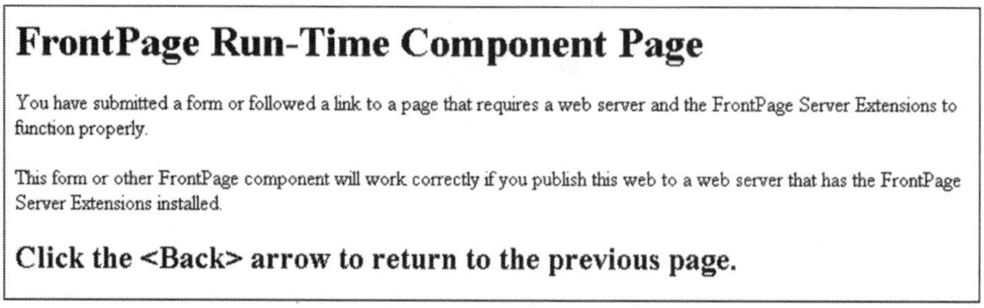

Figure 10-16:
You get this
message if
you attempt
to test your
form without
the services
of a web
server.

FrontPage Run-Time Component Page

You have submitted a form or followed a link to a page that requires a web server and the FrontPage Server Extensions to function properly.

This form or other FrontPage component will work correctly if you publish this web to a web server that has the FrontPage Server Extensions installed.

Click the <Back> arrow to return to the previous page.

Because forms require a form handler to be able to work, you must go a step beyond simply previewing the page: You must call upon the services of a web server.

You have two options, as follows:

- ✔ You can publish your Web site and then preview and test the "live" version of the form. (For directions on how to publish your site, see Chapter 16.)

- ✔ You can test the form without having to publish by using FrontPage together with a local web server (that is, a web server program running on your own computer).

In Appendix A, I talk about how to use FrontPage in conjunction with a local web server.

Chapter 11

I've Been Framed!

In This Chapter

▶ Understanding frames

▶ Building a framed Web site

▶ Tweaking the frames page

▶ Creating an alternative for browsers that can't display frames

▶ Saving a framed Web site

▶ Previewing a framed Web site

*O*f the newfangled design effects to arrive on the Web publishing scene, few have changed the face of the Web more than *frames*. Frames don't just make something happen on a page — frames, in fact, change the way that visitors experience the Web site as a whole.

In this chapter, I show you how to create a framed Web site.

What Are Frames?

Frames are dividers that separate the web browser window into sections. Each section contains a separate Web page, enabling you to display more than one page at the same time, as shown in Figure 11-1.

In this example, the browser window contains three frames, each of which displays a separate page. The top frame contains a decorative heading, the left frame contains a list of navigational hyperlinks, and the frame on the right contains the site's main content.

Sure, frames look slick. Looks are nothing, however, compared to frames' navigational power. Behold — in the site shown in Figure 11-1, when you click a hyperlink in the left frame, the link's destination page appears in the right frame. In this way, you can use frames to keep certain elements visible all the time (as the decorative heading and navigational links are in Figure 11-1), while allowing the rest of the site's content to change based on where the reader wants to go (as the content page in the right frame in Figure 11-1 changes based on which link is clicked).

Figure 11-1:
A typical framed Web site.

 You should know that not all web browsers can display frames. As of this writing, the two most popular frames-capable browsers are Netscape Navigator (Version 2.0 or later) and Microsoft Internet Explorer (Version 3.0 or later). Older and frames-challenged browsers can't even display an approximation of a framed site — the visitor sees only a blank page. The good news is that most Web surfers use a frames-capable browser. For those who don't, FrontPage sidesteps the problem by creating an alternative for browsers that can't display frames.

Creating a Framed Web Site: The Game Plan

Creating a framed site involves the following three basic steps:

- ✔ Creating the frames page
- ✔ Filling the frames with content pages (and, if necessary, modifying the pages to work inside frames)
- ✔ Adjusting the overall layout and properties of each individual frame

A *frames page* is a special type of Web page that defines the size, placement, and properties of the site's frames. A frames page can display as many frames as you want, in whatever layout you want.

After you create a frames page, you fill the frames with *content pages.* Content pages are regular old Web pages that appear inside each frame as a visitor views the frames page with a web browser. (The frames page itself is transparent, except for the placement of each frame.) *Initial pages* are the first content pages that appear as a visitor views the frames page with a web browser. You can either use an existing Web page as a frame's initial page, or you can fill the frame with a new, blank page. You then must adjust the layout and properties of the individual frames so that the site functions the way you want.

If your pages contain FrontPage-generated navigation bars or use shared borders, remove these features before using the pages in a framed site. Because of the way these features work, they can't coexist peacefully with frames and don't always display properly. For details about navigation bars and shared borders, see Chapter 6.

After you finish creating the framed site, you save and preview the whole package by using the Preview tab or a frames-capable browser. By previewing your site, you can see how the site's hyperlinks and frames work together, and you can be sure that the links work correctly.

Ah, but I get ahead of myself. The easiest place to begin is at the beginning . . . with the frames page.

Creating the Frames Page

The hardest part about creating a framed Web site can be deciding on the layout of the frames in the first place. FrontPage anticipates this problem by providing templates for popular frames page layouts. After you create the frames page by using a template, you can modify the page's layout by adding, deleting, or resizing the page's frames.

To create a new frames page, follow these steps:

1. **Choose File⇨New⇨Page.**

   The New dialog box appears.

2. **In the dialog box, click the Frames Pages tab to display FrontPage's frames page templates (see Figure 11-2).**

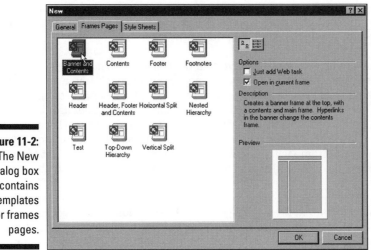

Figure 11-2:
The New
dialog box
contains
templates
for frames
pages.

3. **In the template list, click one of the template icons.**

   A description of the frames page template appears in the Description area, and a mini-preview of the frames page layout appears in the Preview area.

4. **After you find a template that resembles the frame layout you want, click OK.**

   If no template looks exactly the way that you want your frames page to look, choose the closest approximation — you can adjust the layout later.

   The New dialog box closes, and a new frames page appears in the Page View (see Figure 11-3).

In addition to the frames page, two new tabs appear at the bottom of the Page View window: No Frames and Frames Page HTML. You use the No Frames tab to create a message for those of your visitors whose browsers can't display frames. (I explain how to do this later in this chapter.) The Frames Page HTML tab displays the frames page's HTML code. (The HTML tab displays the HTML code for the site's content pages.)

Now you need to fill the frames page with content pages.

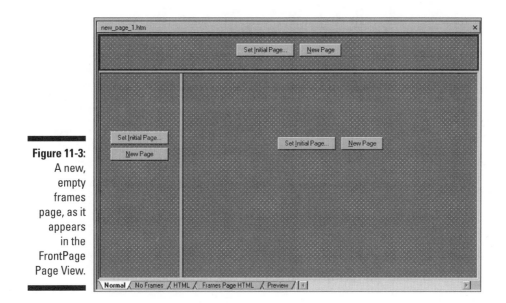

Figure 11-3:
A new,
empty
frames
page, as it
appears
in the
FrontPage
Page View.

Filling Frames with Content Pages

As with frames around fine paintings, the frames in your Web site exist only to enhance the contents. Right now, the frames page is empty — you need to fill each frame with an *initial page*. You can either create a new, blank page, or you can choose one of the pages already sitting in your Web site.

If you would rather adjust the frames page layout *before* working with content pages, skip ahead to the section called "Tweaking the Frames Page," later in this chapter. After you've made your changes, return to this section for instructions on how to insert content pages into each frame.

Using a new page

To fill a frame with a new page, in one of the frames, click the New Page button. A new, empty page appears inside the frame.

To add stuff to the new page (text, graphics, and anything else you would add to a regular Web page), click inside the page and proceed as usual. If the page is sitting inside a narrow frame and you feel cramped, right-click the page, and from the pop-up menu that appears, choose Open Page in New Window. FrontPage pops open a new, full-sized window so that you can have a little elbow room while adding content to the page.

Using an existing page

To fill the frame with an existing page, follow these steps:

1. **In one of the frames, click the Set Initial Page button.**

   The Create Hyperlink dialog box appears.

   The appearance of the Create Hyperlink dialog box makes sense because, on the HTML level, you actually are creating a special type of hyperlink between the frames page and the content page.

2. **In the dialog box, select the page that you want to use as the frame's initial page.**

   If the initial page you want to use is stored elsewhere on the World Wide Web, enter the page's URL in the URL text box.

3. **Click OK.**

   The dialog box closes, and the page appears inside the frame.

To edit the page, click inside the page and proceed as usual, or right-click the page, and from the pop-up menu that appears, choose Open Page in New Window to display the page in a full-sized window.

Tweaking the Frames Page

The frames page templates in FrontPage represent the most popular frame layouts in use on the Web today. That's great if you're the type who sticks to tried-and-true conventions. But if you're a renegade, you're probably itching to rearrange the frames page. In this section, I show you how.

Adding new frames

To add new frames to a frames page, you actually need to split existing frames. Just as splitting a table cell divides the cell in two, splitting a frame divides the frame in two. (Refer to Chapter 9 for information about tables.)

A word to the wise: More is not better when it comes to frames. Framed sites containing four or more frames can be difficult to navigate and visually overwhelming. Lots of convoluted frames not only obscure your site's design, they annoy your visitors to no end (many of whom may not return). I'm not stating an indisputable fact here; I simply encourage you to design your site with your visitors in mind.

To split a frame, you hold down the Ctrl key, click a frame border (including the outer borders), drag the border to a new position, and then release the mouse button. As soon as you release the mouse button, a new, empty frame appears.

Alternatively, follow these steps:

1. **Click inside the frame you want to split.**

   A colorful border appears around the frame, indicating that the frame is selected.

2. **Choose Frames⇨Split Frame.**

   The Split Frame dialog box appears.

3. **Click the Split into Columns or Split into Rows radio button, and then click OK.**

   The dialog box closes, and the frame splits accordingly.

If you create a frames page that you'd like to use for future Web sites, save the page as a FrontPage page template. (I explain how to do this in Chapter 3.)

Deleting frames

If the frames page looks too convoluted, delete a frame or two. By deleting a frame, you don't delete the content page inside; you simply remove the frame from the frames page. The content page remains untouched. To delete a frame, click inside the frame and then choose Frames⇨Delete Frame.

Changing frame properties

In addition to changing the overall layout of the frames page, you can change the following details:

- ✔ Frame name
- ✔ Presence of scrollbars
- ✔ Frame size
- ✔ Amount of space separating frame content from frame borders
- ✔ Presence of frame borders
- ✔ Amount of space between frame borders

To change any or all of these properties, follow these steps:

1. **Right-click inside the frame you want to edit, and from the pop-up menu that appears, choose Frame Properties.**

   The Frame Properties dialog box appears (see Figure 11-4).

   Note: The following steps describe how to change every frame property. Choose only those steps that apply to the property you want to adjust.

2. **In the Name text box, type a frame name.**

   The frame's name acts as an identifying label. If the frame is to contain a table of contents page, for example, you could type the name **TOC**. Or, if you prefer to identify the frame by its position, type a frame name, such as **Left**.

3. **To change the initial page, in the Initial Page text box, enter a new page filename, path, or URL.**

4. **In the Column Width and Height boxes, type dimension measurements.**

   As with table dimensions, you can specify an absolute pixel value or a relative percentage based on the size of the browser window. (Refer to Chapter 9 for information about how table dimensions work.)

   You can choose Relative if you want the browser to set the frame's dimension relative to the other frames in the page. For example, if the frames page contains two frames, and the width of the first frame is set to 100 pixels, and the width of the second frame is set to Relative, the second frame will expand to fill the rest of the browser window, whatever the window's size.

5. **In the Width and Height boxes, type the number of pixels with which you want to separate the content page text from the frame borders.**

The effect works in a similar way to cell padding inside a table. (See Chapter 9 for details.)

6. **If you want to lock the position of the frame so that visitors can't resize the frame as they view the site, be sure the Resizable in Browser check box is unmarked.**

If this check box is marked, when visitors view the framed site with a web browser, they can adjust the position of frame borders to work with the size of their monitors. By doing so, they don't affect the frames page, just how the framed site appears on their screens. If this check box is unmarked, frame position is locked in place.

7. **In the Show Scrollbars list box, choose an option that describes when you want the scrollbars to appear inside the frame.**

   - **If needed:** If the visitor's browser window is too small to display the entire contents of a frame, scrollbars appear so that visitors may move around inside the frame.

   - **Always:** Scrollbars are visible at all times, even when they aren't necessary.

   - **Never:** Scrollbars never appear, no matter what.

8. **Click the Frames Page button.**

The Page Properties dialog box appears, with the Frames tab visible. When you change the settings inside this tab, the changes apply to the entire frames page.

9. **In the Frame Spacing text box, enter the frame border width (in pixels).**

This option works similarly to cell spacing in tables — by changing this setting, you change the appearance of the frame borders. (Refer to Chapter 9 for more information about tables.)

10. **To make frame borders invisible, unmark the Show Borders check box.**

11. **Click OK.**

The Page Properties dialog box closes, and the Frame Properties dialog box becomes visible again.

12. **Click OK to close the Frame Properties dialog box.**

The dialog box closes, and the selected frame's settings change accordingly.

Changing the target frame

Each frames page template assigns a *target frame* to the page that's visible inside each frame. The target frame is the frame in which hyperlink destination pages appear. In Figure 11-1, for example, after a visitor clicks a navigational link inside the left frame, the corresponding page appears in the right frame. The right frame, therefore, is the target frame for the links visible in the left frame.

Each frame page template contains default target frame settings. (To determine a frame's default target frame, in the Page View, click a hyperlink inside the frame while holding down the Ctrl key. The frame in which the destination page appears is that frame's default target frame.) In the following sections, I show you how to change the target frame setting.

Changing the target frame for all the hyperlinks in a page

To change the target frame for all the hyperlinks in a page (also referred to as changing the *default target frame*), follow these steps:

1. **Right-click inside the frame, and from the pop-up menu that appears, choose Page Properties.**

   The Page Properties dialog box appears with the General tab visible. The Default Target Frame text box contains the name of the current target frame. (If the text box is empty, hyperlink destination pages appear inside the same frame.)

2. **In the dialog box, click the Change Target Frame button.**

   The Target Frame dialog box appears (see Figure 11-5).

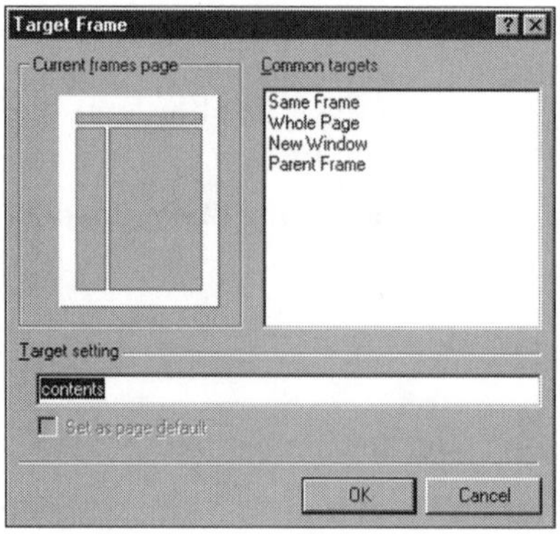

Figure 11-5:
The Target
Frame
dialog box.

Special target frame options

You can use the following four common target frame options (available in the Target Frame dialog box) to create different effects:

✔ **Same Frame:** This setting causes the hyperlink destination page to open inside the same frame in which the hyperlink source page is located.

✔ **Whole Page:** This setting causes the hyperlink destination page to replace the frames page in the browser window.

✔ **New Window:** This setting causes the hyperlink destination page to open inside a new web browser window.

✔ **Parent Frame:** If you really want to get fancy with frames, you can use a second frames page as the content page for one or more frames in your site. The result is a _nested frames page:_ A secondary level of frames appears inside one of the frames in the top-level (or _parent_) frames page. When you choose the Parent target frame setting, links in the secondary frames page load inside the parent frame. If you use nested frames, be sure to keep the site simple enough to navigate easily.

3. **In the Current _F_rames Page area of the dialog box, click the frame you want to target, or, in the _C_ommon Targets area, click the name of the target you want to use.**

   (I describe what each Common Target option does in the nearby sidebar called "Special target frame options.")

   The frame name appears in the Target Setting text box.

4. **Click OK to close the dialog box.**

   The Page Properties dialog box becomes visible again.

5. **Click OK to close the Page Properties dialog box.**

Changing the target frame for a single hyperlink

If you want to change the target frame setting for only a single hyperlink (leaving the other links in the page using the default target frame setting), follow these steps:

1. **In the content page, create a new hyperlink or click an existing hyperlink and then, in the Standard toolbar, click the Hyperlink button.**

   The Create Hyperlink or Edit Hyperlink dialog box appears. (Refer to Chapter 6 if you're not sure how to create a new hyperlink.)

2. In the dialog box, click the Change Target Frame button to choose a frame from the Target Frame dialog box.

Refer to the steps in the preceding section, "Changing the target frame for all the hyperlinks in a page," for detailed instructions on how to use the Target Frame dialog box.

3. Click OK to close the dialog box.

Specifying the target frame for form results

If one of your content pages contains a form, you can specify a target frame for form results. (If you're not familiar with forms, take a look at Chapter 10.)

To specify a target frame for form results, follow these steps:

1. Right-click inside the form, and then choose Form Properties from the pop-up menu that appears.

The Form Properties dialog box appears.

 2. In the dialog box, click the Change Target Frame button to choose a frame from the Target Frame dialog box.

Refer to the steps in the previous section, "Changing the target frame for all the hyperlinks in a page," for detailed instructions on how to use the Target Frame dialog box.

3. Click OK to close the dialog box.

Specifying the target frame for image maps

If one of your content pages contains an image map, you can specify a default target frame for the image map's hotspots. (If you're not sure what an image map or a hotspot is, refer to Chapter 8.)

To do so, follow these steps:

1. Right-click the image map and then choose Picture Properties from the pop-up menu that appears.

The Picture Properties dialog box appears with the General panel visible.

 2. In the dialog box, click the Change Target Frame button to choose a frame from the Target Frame dialog box.

Refer to the steps in the previous section, "Changing the target frame for all the hyperlinks in a page," for detailed instructions on how to use the Target Frame dialog box.

3. Click OK to close the dialog box.

You can also specify a target frame for individual hotspots inside the image map. To do so, double-click a hotspot to display the Edit Hyperlink dialog box. Then follow Steps 2 and 3 listed in the previous section called "Changing the target frame for a single hyperlink."

Creating an Alternative for Browsers That Don't "Do" Frames

Web Truism #2 states that your visitors use different types of web browsers. (The four Web Truisms are listed in Chapter 4.) The majority of your visitors surf the Web by using advanced, frames-capable browsers, but a few people continue to use browsers that can't display frames.

How do you accommodate such visitors? With a _No Frames message._ When visitors with frames-impaired browsers attempt to view the frames page, they see the No Frames message instead. The No Frames message looks and acts like a separate Web page — it can contain text, graphics, hyperlinks, and so on — but, in reality, it's a chunk of HTML sitting inside the frames page.

To create a No Frames message, click the No Frames tab in the Page View, and then proceed as though you are creating a regular Web page.

Frames forethought

If you want to give visitors the choice of viewing your site with or without frames, you must place a hyperlink that points to the frames page in another page in your site. Or you can specify the frames page as the site's home page so that the frames page is the first thing visitors see when visiting your site. (The FrontPage Help system explains how to do this; choose Help➪Microsoft FrontPage Help.) Because FrontPage knows how to set up a No Frames alternative for browsers that can't handle frames, you're in the clear. Almost.

You need to make sure that visitors who are viewing the site without frames can still get around. To understand what I mean, imagine if the site in Figure 11-1 had no frames and a copy of the main body page was used as the No Frames message. How would visitors navigate the site when that page contains no navigational links?

You can make sure that your visitors can navigate your site by reproducing in the main body page all the links found in the navigational page. Or you can create a separate set of pages for browsers that can't display frames. _Or_ you can create a No Frames message that requires visitors to use a frames-capable browser to view your site and provides links to the download sites of these browsers. Whatever you decide, test, test, and test again to be sure that your site is accessible to _all_ your visitors.

FrontPage's default No Frames message, "This page uses frames, but your browser doesn't support them," states the obvious but doesn't help the visitor solve the problem. A friendlier No Frames message offers an alternate method for exploring the site, such as providing hyperlinks to the site's content pages. A polite invitation to download a frames-capable browser (plus links that lead straight to the download sites) would be a nice touch, too.

Saving a Framed Web Site

When you work with a framed Web site, you can easily forget that you're working with several Web pages at the same time — the frames page plus its content pages. Because of this page-juggling, saving a framed Web site involves a couple of extra steps. To save a framed Web site, do this:

1. **Click the Save button.**

   The Save As dialog box appears (see Figure 11-6). The right side of the dialog box contains a diagram of the frames page. If the content pages are new, one of the frames in the frames diagram appears highlighted. The highlighted frame indicates which content page you are currently saving.

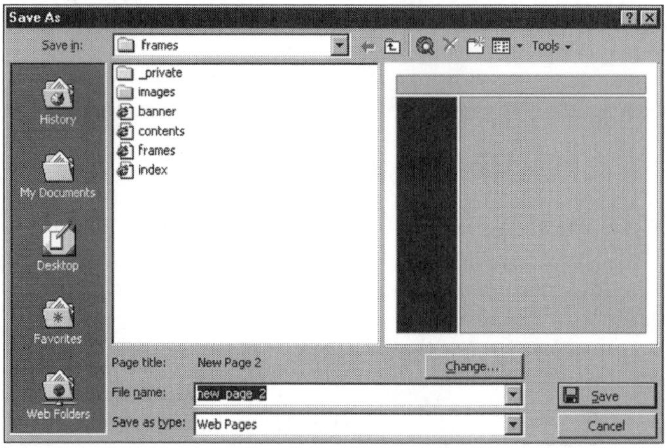

Figure 11-6:
The Save As
dialog box.

2. **Type a filename in the dialog box's File Name text box.**

3. **If you like, change the page's title by clicking the Change button to show the Set Page Title dialog box, typing a new title, and then clicking OK to close the dialog box.**

4. **Click Save.**

   The dialog box closes, and FrontPage saves the content page. In a moment, the Save As dialog box appears again, this time with a different frame in the frames diagram highlighted.

5. **Repeat Steps 2 through 4 for each content page.**

After you save the last content page, the Save As dialog box appears a final time, this time with the entire frames page diagram highlighted, indicating that you are now saving the frames page itself.

6. **Type a filename and choose a page title.**

In a framed site, the title of the frames page is the only one visible as a visitor views the site with a web browser. The titles of the individual content pages don't appear. Make sure that you choose a descriptive title for the frames page.

7. **Click Save.**

The dialog box closes, and FrontPage saves the frames page.

In the future, when you click the Save button, FrontPage saves all changes to the frames page and the content pages. To save changes in a single content page, click the page's frame and then choose Frames⇨Save Page.

Previewing a Framed Web Site

After your site is in order, be sure to preview your site by checking out the Preview tab or by clicking the Preview in Browser button. (For more information about how to preview, see Chapter 3.) Test the links in each frame to be sure that they work the way that you expect them to. If you preview your site by using a web browser, change the browser window size to see how the frames rearrange themselves. If something is amiss, return to FrontPage and keep tweaking until everything works.

Part III
Nifty Web Additions

The 5th Wave   By Rich Tennant

@RICHTENNANT

"FRANKLY, I'M NOT SURE THIS IS THE WAY TO ENHANCE OUR COLOR GRAPHICS."

In this part . . .

After you build a sturdy, attractive Web site, you may feel the urge to add on to it. Perhaps you want to embellish your Web site with a graphical theme. Or you want to enable visitors to search your site for keywords. All are easy to construct with FrontPage. And you don't need to hire a contractor.

Chapter 12

Playing in the FrontPage Theme Park

● ●

In This Chapter

▶ Applying a theme to your Web site

▶ Inserting a page banner

▶ Modifying themes

● ●

*I*f you've spent much time on the Web, you can probably tell the difference between a professionally designed Web site and a home-grown operation. Professionally designed sites look smooth and polished, with matching graphics and custom fonts. Web sites built by non-designers are no less worthwhile, but are sometimes, um, lacking in the looks department. Face it: Most people don't have the expertise to create their own graphics, the time to track down individual pieces of clip art, or the money to pay a designer. Nor should someone need these things to create an attractive Web site.

The FrontPage programmers agree with me, and they got together with professional designers to create *themes*. Now, after a few mouse-clicks, your Web site can have the style and distinction usually reserved for big-budget Web sites.

Touring the Themes Dialog Box

Themes transform a Web site by applying a coordinated set of text and link colors, fonts, background graphics, table borders, navigation bar buttons, horizontal lines, and bullets to the site's pages. Each theme generates a different look or feel: For example, the Sumi Painting theme projects peace and serenity, and the Expedition theme creates an earthy, safari look.

For a hint at what themes can do, look at Figures 12-1 and 12-2. Figure 12-1 shows a rather dowdy page — perfectly functional but visually uninteresting. Figure 12-2 shows the same page after a theme makeover. Vavoom!

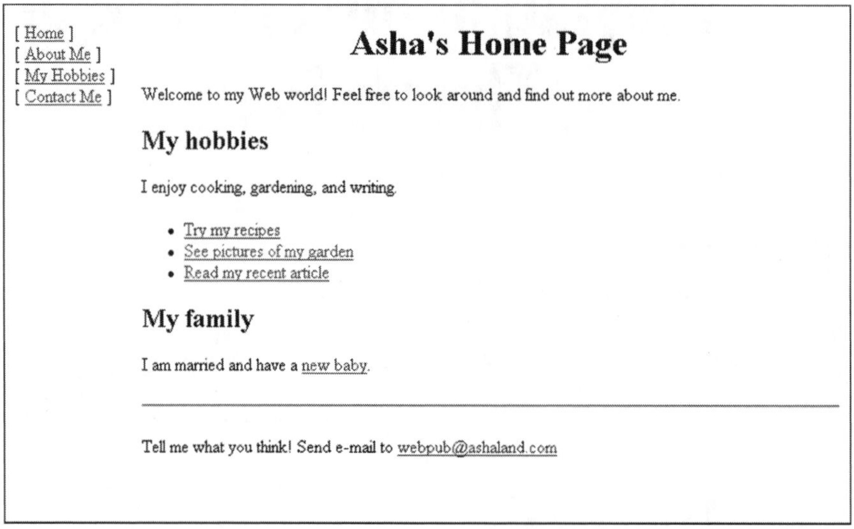

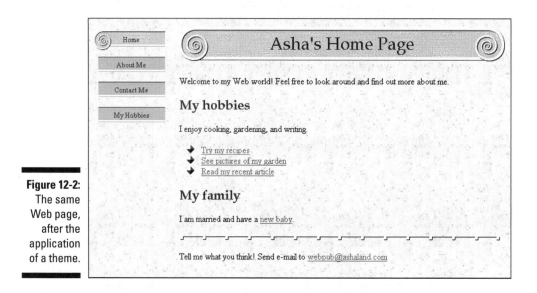

Figure 12-1:
A service-able, but plain, Web page.

Figure 12-2:
The same Web page, after the application of a theme.

You can check out FrontPage themes by touring the Themes dialog box (see Figure 12-3). To display the Themes dialog box, choose Format➪Theme.

The Themes dialog box lets you preview the many themes included with FrontPage. To preview a theme, click a name in the themes list. A representation of the theme's elements appears in the Sample of Theme area. The preview contains text fonts and colors, bullets, a custom horizontal line, hyperlink colors, navigation bar buttons, a background graphic, and a decorative page banner.

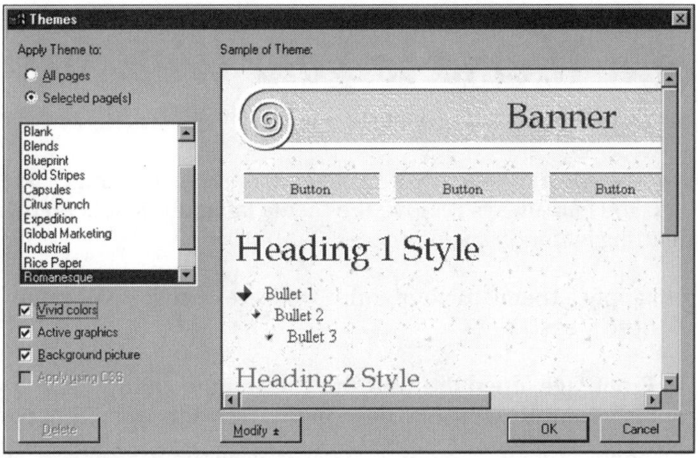

Figure 12-3:
The
Themes
dialog box.

If you're not familiar with some of the elements I just mentioned, flip through the following chapters for more information: Text color, text font, bullets, and horizontal lines are covered in Chapter 5; navigation bars and hyperlink colors are covered in Chapter 6; and background graphics are covered in Chapter 7. I talk about page banners later in this chapter.

Three check boxes sitting underneath the themes list give you some control over the standard appearance of theme elements:

✔ **Vivid Colors:** Mark this option if you want to use a brighter set of text, links, and graphic colors. Unmark this check box if you prefer more muted colors.

✔ **Active Graphics:** Active graphics add a bit of spunk to your site. FrontPage creates navigation bar buttons that change color or shape when clicked. Some themes also contain different page banners and animated bullets instead of stay-still graphic bullets.

Some of the active graphic effects in FrontPage are powered by JavaScript and, therefore, don't show up in older web browsers. Visitors using non-JavaScript-compliant browsers instead see a static version of the active graphic.

✔ **Background Picture:** This option lets you turn on or off the theme's background graphic.

Later in the chapter, I show you how to modify the theme itself, including its colors, graphics, and text styles.

Applying a Theme to Your Web Site

So now you're excited to use a theme in your Web site, right? Follow me.

When you apply a theme to your Web site, the theme changes your site's formatting. You can always remove the theme later, but just keep this reformatting in mind as you proceed.

You can apply a theme to your entire Web site or to a single page. To do so, follow these steps:

1. **In FrontPage, open the Web site you want to change. If you want to apply a theme to a single page in the Web site, open that page.**

   To apply a theme to more than one page without having to open each page, switch to the Folders View and, while holding down the Ctrl key, click the pages to which you want the theme applied.

2. **Choose Format⇨Theme.**

   The Themes dialog box appears.

3. **In the dialog box's Apply Theme To area, click the appropriate radio button.**

   You can apply the theme to all pages in the Web site or to the selected page(s). (If no pages are selected, this option applies the theme to the page currently open in the Page View.)

4. **In the list box, click the name of the theme you want to use.**

5. **Depending on the options you want to use, mark one or more of the Vivid Colors, Active Graphics, and Background Picture check boxes.**

   If you later decide you don't like any aspect of the theme, you can change it.

6. **Optionally, click the Apply Using CSS check box.**

If you mark this check box, FrontPage uses style sheet commands to apply the theme to your site. The theme looks no different to your visitors, however the method FrontPage uses to apply the theme effects to your pages changes. The upside: Style sheets can later be edited outside of FrontPage. In other words, if you later want to modify the theme elements by using a program other than FrontPage (or by hand, assuming you know HTML and style sheet syntax) you can. The downside: Several theme elements don't appear properly in older browsers that don't understand style sheets. I talk in detail about what style sheets are and how they work in Chapter 13.

7. Click OK.

The dialog box closes, and FrontPage applies the theme to your Web site. (This takes a few moments.)

Now for the fun part. Open one of your formerly plain pages to see what a difference a theme makes.

If you don't like what you see, return to the Themes dialog box and change the theme's settings. Or, if you want to remove the theme from your Web site, in the dialog box's list box, click [No Theme], and then click OK to apply the changes to your site.

The FrontPage/Office program CD comes with a bunch of additional themes; to install them on your computer, in the dialog box's list box, double-click [Install Additional Themes], and then follow the directions that appear on your screen.

Inserting a Page Banner

If you're impressed by themes, watch this. FrontPage knows how to create a decorative *page banner* you can use in place of a page header. FrontPage superimposes the page's navigational structure label on top of the theme's banner graphic to create the banner. (If you're not sure what a navigational structure is or how it works, refer to Chapter 2.)

Here's how to insert a page banner:

1. Open the page into which you want to insert a page banner.

If you haven't already, in the Navigation View, add the page to the navigational structure. (See Chapter 2 for instructions on how to work with the Navigation View.)

2. In the page, place the cursor where you want the banner to appear.

3. **Choose Insert⇨Page Banner.**

   The Page Banner Properties dialog box appears.

4. **In the dialog box, mark the Picture radio button.**

   If you prefer a plain text banner, click the Text radio button.

5. **If you want a different text label to appear on top of the banner, in the Page Banner Text text box, type the text.**

   When you change a banner label, FrontPage changes the label in the site's navigational structure and also uses the label as the page title.

6. **Click OK.**

   The Page Banner Properties dialog box closes, and the banner appears in the page.

If the message [Add this page to the Navigation view to display a page banner here] appears in place of the page banner, the page in which the banner sits is not yet part of the site's navigational structure. To fix the problem, add the page to the navigational structure in the Navigation View, and then switch back to the Page View. The page banner now displays the correct label.

To include a page banner in every page in your Web site automatically, take advantage of *shared borders*. I discuss shared borders in Chapter 6.

Modifying Themes

You can easily modify the colors, graphics, and text styles of any of the FrontPage themes. With a little creativity and a few custom graphics, you can even create your own personalized theme.

The following sections show you how to modify existing FrontPage themes. To create your own theme, start with an existing theme, modify it to suit your taste, and then save the theme under a different name. (Read on to find out how.)

Modifying theme colors

To change the theme's color scheme, follow these steps:

1. **Choose Format⇨Theme.**

   The Themes dialog box appears.

2. **In the dialog box's list box, click the name of the theme you want to modify, and then click <u>M</u>odify.**

   New buttons appear inside the Themes dialog box, enabling you to customize different aspects of the theme (see Figure 12-4).

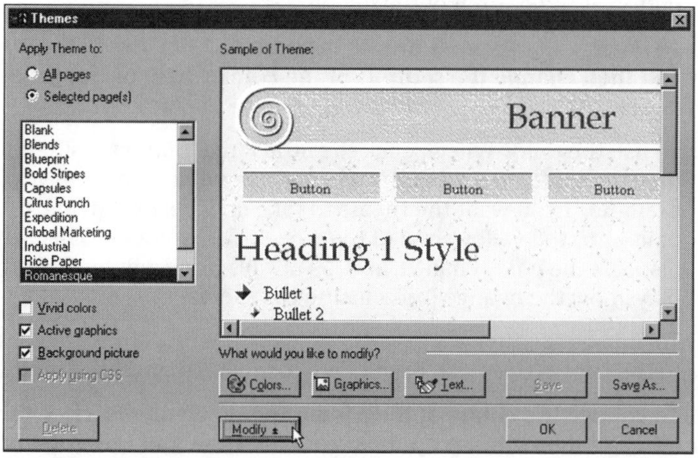

Figure 12-4:
New buttons in the Themes dialog box enable you to modify the theme.

3. **Click the C<u>o</u>lors button.**

   The Modify Theme dialog box appears (see Figure 12-5). This dialog box contains options for changing the theme's colors.

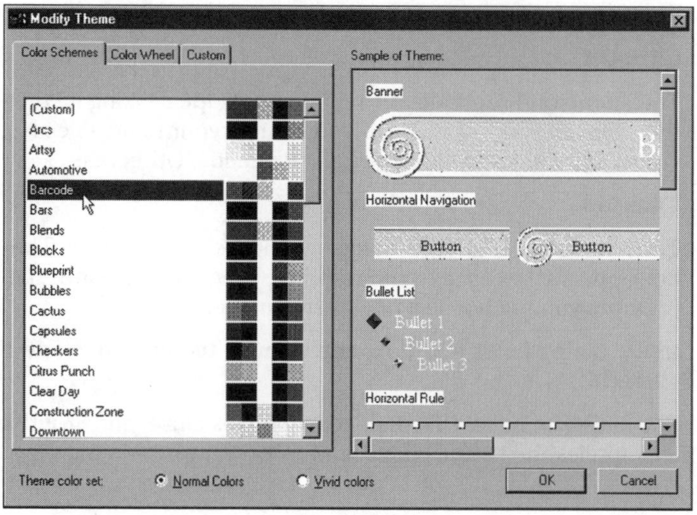

Figure 12-5:
Modifying the theme's colors.

4. **To change the theme's overall color scheme, in the dialog box's Color Schemes tab, click the color scheme you like.**

   After you click a color scheme, you can get an idea for how the theme will look by looking at the preview in the Sample of Theme box. If you prefer a more vivid version of the color scheme, click the Vivid Colors radio button at the bottom of the dialog box.

5. **To change the theme's hue or brightness, click the Color Wheel tab, and then change the settings of the color wheel or the Brightness meter.**

   To use the Color Wheel, click the little circle pointer inside the wheel, and then drag it to an area of the wheel that contains the hue you want. For example, if you want the theme to take on a yellowish hue, drag the circle pointer to the yellow area of the wheel. The Colors in This Scheme grid displays the color change, and, as always, the Sample of Theme box displays how the change looks inside the theme.

   To change the theme's brightness, click the Brightness meter and drag it to the left (to decrease brightness) or right (to increase brightness).

6. **To change the colors of individual theme elements, click the Custom tab, and then choose options from the Item and Color list boxes.**

   For example, if you want to change the theme's Heading 1 color, from the Item list box, choose `Heading 1`, and from the Color list box, choose the color you want, or choose `More Colors` to display the Color dialog box. (For details on how to use this dialog box, see Chapter 5.)

7. **Click OK to close the Modify Theme dialog box.**

   The Themes dialog box comes into view again.

8. **Click OK.**

   The Microsoft FrontPage dialog box pops open asking if you want to save the changes you just made. If you change your mind, click No, and FrontPage will forget any changes you made. Otherwise . . .

9. **Click Yes.**

   The Microsoft FrontPage dialog box closes, and the Save Theme dialog box appears. Because each FrontPage theme is read-only, the dialog box prompts you to choose a new theme name.

10. **In the dialog box's text box, enter a new theme name, and then click OK.**

    The Save Theme and Themes dialog boxes close, and FrontPage saves and applies the theme changes.

If you later decide you want to return to the theme's original color scheme, follow the directions listed in this section, and in Step 4, click the color scheme associated with the theme, and then click OK.

Choosing different theme graphics

You can replace any of the theme's graphics with your own. Say you want a theme to display a page banner of your own design, or a custom horizontal rule graphic. No problem. You can also change the characteristics of the text that appears on top of page banners and navigation bar buttons. To do so, follow these steps:

1. **Choose Format⇨Theme to display the Themes dialog box.**

2. **In the dialog box's list box, click the name of the theme you want to modify, and then click Modify.**

3. **Click the Graphics button.**

   The Modify Theme dialog box appears, this time containing options that control the theme's graphics.

4. **From the Item list box, choose the name of the graphic you want to replace.**

   Based on the graphic you choose, options pertaining to that graphic appear in the dialog box's Picture tab. Also, a sample of the graphic element you selected pops to the top of the theme preview visible in the Sample of Theme box.

5. **At the bottom of the dialog box, click the radio button that corresponds to the graphic set you want to modify.**

   You can modify either the Normal graphics set or the Active graphics set.

6. **In the appropriate text box(es), enter the filename and location of the graphic you want to use, or click Browse to select a graphic by using the Select Picture dialog box.**

   If you're not sure how to use the Select Picture dialog box, see the Chapter 7 section "Adding a picture to your page."

7. **To change the style of the text that appears on top of page banners and navigation bar buttons, click the Font tab, and then choose the options you want.**

   Note: If the options in the Font tab appear dimmed, it means the type of graphic visible in the Item list box doesn't have associated text. From the Item list box, choose an option that has associated text (such as Banner or Global Navigation Buttons) and proceed.

8. **Click OK to close the Modify Theme dialog box.**

9. **In the Themes dialog box, click OK.**

   The Microsoft FrontPage dialog box prompts you to save the changes you just made.

10. **Click Yes.**

    The dialog box closes, and the Save Theme dialog box appears.

11. **In the dialog box's text box, enter a new theme name, and then click OK.**

    The Save Theme and Themes dialog boxes close, and FrontPage saves and applies the theme changes.

Changing theme text styles

You can easily change a theme's choices of body and heading text font. To do so, follow these steps:

1. **Choose Format➪Theme to display the Themes dialog box.**

2. **In the dialog box's list box, click the name of the theme you want to modify, and then click Modify.**

3. **Click the Text button.**

   The Modify Theme dialog box appears, this time containing options that control text style.

4. **From the Item list box, choose the text element you want to change.**

5. **From the Font list box, click the name of the font you want to use for the element visible in the Item list box.**

   If you choose an unusual or custom font, keep in mind that only those visitors with that particular font installed on their computers will see the font change. (To the rest, text will appear in the browser's default font.) As a backup, consider choosing a second, similar font that will display if the first font isn't present on the visitor's computer. To do so, in the Font text box, type the first font choice followed by a comma, and then the second font choice (for example, **Arial, Helvetica**).

6. **Click OK to close the Modify Theme dialog box.**

7. **In the Themes dialog box, click OK.**

   The Microsoft FrontPage dialog box prompts you to save the changes you just made.

8. **Click Yes.**

   The dialog box closes, and the Save Theme dialog box appears.

9. **In the dialog box's text box, enter a new theme name, and then click OK.**

   The Save Theme and Themes dialog boxes close, and FrontPage saves and applies the theme changes.

You can, in fact, change any aspect of a theme's text style by clicking the More Styles button in the Modify Theme dialog box. By doing so, you call forth the powerful Styles dialog box, which I explain in Chapter 13.

Chapter 13

Eye-Popping Extras: Multimedia, Dynamic HTML, and Style Sheets

- -

In This Chapter

▶ Adding videos and sound to your Web site

▶ Getting fancy with Dynamic HTML

▶ Positioning objects in your page

▶ Working with style sheets

- -

*N*ot so many years ago, all Web pages looked like flat, gray screens full of text, with maybe a picture or two to liven things up. The most exciting design effect back then was the horizontal line.

Times have certainly changed. The Internet, formerly the domain of techies, is now a mainstream information source, shopping mall, and playground all rolled into one. Today's Internet brings sound, video, animation, and stunning design to computer screens the world over.

Unfortunately, cutting-edge design effects generally rely on sophisticated technology — advanced HTML knowledge and sometimes programming expertise — which puts these effects out of the reach for novice Web design-ers. Even accomplished Web designers must slog through new and meagerly documented HTML code with little direction and lots of willingness to experi-ment. Not a task for the faint of heart or the time-challenged.

Once again, FrontPage comes to the rescue with a slew of exciting design goodies, all usable with a few points and clicks. You can add sound effects and video clips to your Web site, you can tap into the power of Dynamic HTML, and you can even design your pages using style sheets.

As sexy as these extras are, they're entirely optional. The most effective Web sites use special effects to enhance already-strong content and good design. Too many bells and whistles can dull the site's overall impact.

Fun with Multimedia

Multimedia is the ubiquitous term used to lump together the jumble of electronically transmittable media formats. More often than not, when used on the Web, multimedia refers to video and sounds. In this section, I show you how to include both in your Web site.

Keep in mind that only advanced browsers are able to display multimedia files. Some older browsers are able to work with multimedia by launching a separate program called a *helper application* to play the file, but other browsers are unable to deal with multimedia at all.

One last detail to remember: Because they pack so much information, multimedia files tend toward chubbiness and, therefore, take a long time to load. For an indication of how much load time each addition tacks onto your page, glance at the Estimated Time to Download box on the right side of the FrontPage Status bar.

Fun with video

If a picture says a thousand words, a video clip . . . well, you know. A *video clip* is a moving picture you insert into your page for added zing.

Even though Netscape Navigator is perfectly able to play multimedia files, the HTML tags FrontPage adds to your page are specific to Internet Explorer. In the following sections, I describe cross-browser workarounds. Admittedly, the workarounds are a bit tedious, but they are worthwhile, because they enable more of your visitors to enjoy your site in its full glory.

Inserting a video for Netscape Navigator and Internet Explorer users

To insert a video clip that is visible to users of both Internet Explorer (Version 2.0 or later) and Netscape Navigator (Version 3.0 or later), you must use FrontPage's Insert⇨Advanced⇨Plug-In command. This command works for all sorts of multimedia file types that have corresponding *plug-ins* (little programs embedded in the web browser) that can play the file. I show you how to use this command in "Advanced Additions" on the CD. See Appendix B for details on how to access this chapter.

If you insert videos using this method, you can use any video file format either web browser is able to display (two popular formats are AVI and QuickTime).

Another option is to simply import the video file into your Web site and then create a hyperlink to the file. That way, only those visitors who want to see the video will click the link and wait for the download. Chapter 2 explains how to import files, and Chapter 6 shows you how to create hyperlinks.

Inserting a video for Internet Explorer users only

The steps in this section explain how to insert a video clip visible only to users of Internet Explorer (Version 2.0 or later). The only time you'd want to use such a browser-specific effect is if you're sure all your visitors use the same browser, as may the case for a corporate intranet site (a site that is only accessible by company insiders).

Note: If you insert a video into your page using the following method, your video must be stored as an AVI, ASF, or RealMedia (RA or RAS) file.

1. **In the page, place the cursor where you want the video to appear.**

2. **Choose Insert⇨Picture⇨Video.**

   The Video dialog box appears. This dialog box works just like the Picture dialog box that I explain in Chapter 7.

3. **Choose the video file you want to display and then click OK.**

   The dialog box closes, and the video appears in your page. (The video doesn't move when viewed in the Page View; to see the animation, preview the page using the Preview tab or Internet Explorer.)

After you insert a video into your page, you can tinker with some of its properties, such as how many times the video repeats and when the video begins playing. To adjust a video's properties, follow these steps:

1. **In the page, right-click the video, and from the pop-up menu that appears, choose Picture Properties.**

   The Picture Properties dialog box appears with the Video tab visible (see Figure 13-1).

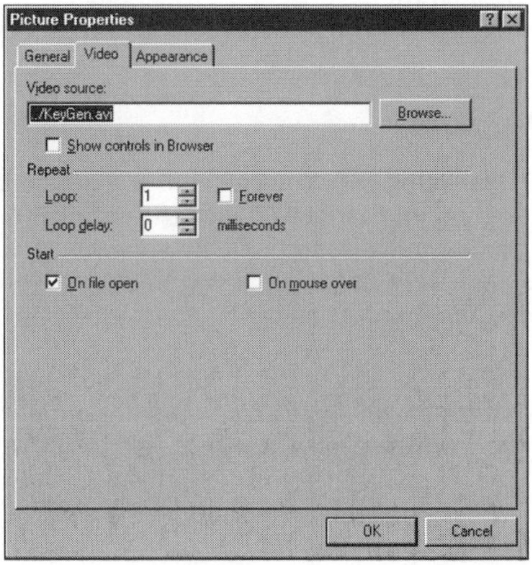

Figure 13-1:
The Video tab of the Picture Properties dialog box.

2. **To display Play and Stop buttons underneath the video, mark the Show Controls in Browser check box.**

   By showing the controls, you enable the visitor to stop and start the video.

3. **In the Loop text box, specify the number of times you want the video to repeat.**

   If you want the clip to keep playing until the visitor leaves the page, mark the Forever check box.

4. **In the Loop Delay text box, specify the number of milliseconds you want the video to pause before repeating.**

   I know, it's hard to conceive of the length of a millisecond. Just do your best. A good reference point: 500 milliseconds equals half a second, and 1,000 milliseconds equals a second.

5. **In the Start area, click the check box next to the event that triggers the video to start playing.**

   The On File Open option causes the video to play as soon as a visitor arrives. The On Mouse Over option causes the video to play as soon as the pointer passes over the video. Mark both check boxes to have the video begin playing when the visitor arrives and then repeat as soon as the pointer passes over the video.

6. **Click OK to close the dialog box.**

To see the video in action, preview your page using the Preview tab or Internet Explorer.

If the video file is stored outside the Web site, the Save Embedded Files dialog box appears the next time you save the page. Refer to Chapter 3 for instructions on how to use this dialog box.

Music to your ears

By using the Page Properties dialog box, you can embed a sound into your page that plays as soon as someone arrives (hence the moniker *background sound*). This feature can be charming if (and only if) you choose a short, pleasant sound bite. Choose wisely, because forcing loud, grating music onto your visitors annoys more than it entertains.

Last heard in the Microsoft Web Gallery: a toilet flushing, a train whistle, and various whooshes, bloops, and bangs. Listen for yourself (and download your favorites to use in your own Web site) at www.microsoft.com/gallery/sounds/default.asp.

To hear background sounds, your visitors must have sound equipment (a sound card and speakers) installed on their computers along with an advanced web browser that is able to play sounds. The two most popular choices are Internet Explorer (Version 3.0 or later) and Netscape Navigator (Version 3.0 and later).

As with video, even though Netscape Navigator can play sounds, the sound-related HTML tags FrontPage adds to your page are specific to Internet Explorer. In the following sections, I explain how to insert sounds in two ways: The first method creates background sounds that can be heard using both browsers, and the second method is limited to an Internet Explorer-only audience. Choose the method that fits your target audience.

Inserting a background sound for Netscape Navigator and Internet Explorer users

In order for both Internet Explorer and Netscape Navigator users to be able to hear background sounds, you must first import the sound file into your Web site (see Chapter 2 for instructions). Be sure your sound file is saved using the WAV, AIFF, or AU format, because both Internet Explorer (Version 3.0 or later) and Netscape Navigator (Version 3.0 and later) can play these types of files.

Next, you must add a snippet of HTML code to your page. It's easy; just do this:

1. **Place the cursor anywhere inside the page, and then choose Insert⇨Advanced⇨HTML.**

   The HTML Markup dialog box appears.

2. **In the HTML Markup To Insert box, type the following bit of code:**

   ```
   <EMBED SRC="sound.wav" HIDDEN="true" AUTOPLAY="true"
   AUTOSTART="true">
   ```

   where `sound.wav` **is the name and location of your sound file.**

   Note: My example assumes the sound file is stored in the same folder as the Web page in which you're inserting the sound. If not (say the sound file is stored in a subfolder), indicate the file location by listing the name of the subfolder followed by a slash and then the filename (for example, `foldername/sound.wav`).

3. **Click OK.**

   The dialog box closes, and all is well.

Be sure to preview the page using both browsers to make sure the sound plays properly. (This action works only if you have sound equipment installed on your computer.)

Inserting a background sound for Internet Explorer users only

If you follow the steps in this section, the HTML tags FrontPage inserts into your page only work when the page is viewed using Internet Explorer. To insert a background sound using this method, follow these steps:

1. **With the page open in the Page View, choose File⇨Properties.**

   The Page Properties dialog box appears. You specify the page's background sound using options in the Background Sound section of the General tab.

2. **In the dialog box's Location text box, type the filename and location of the sound file you want to use.**

   Or click Browse to choose a sound file from the Background Sound dialog box.

3. **If you want to control how many times the sound plays, click to unmark the Forever check box and enter a number in the Loop text box.**

   I don't recommend using the Forever option. Having a sound play over and over until the visitor leaves the page drives visitors nuts.

4. **Click OK.**

   The Page Properties dialog box closes.

To hear the sound, preview your page using the Preview tab or Internet Explorer. (This action works only if you have sound equipment installed on your computer.)

If the sound file is located elsewhere on your computer, the Save Embedded Files dialog box appears the next time you save the page. Refer to Chapter 3 for instructions on how to use this dialog box.

Adding Pizzazz with Dynamic HTML

Dynamic HTML is a new technology that enables you to apply exciting effects and animation to just about any object in your page. For example, you can use Dynamic HTML to cause a word to change color when a visitor passes the pointer over the word. Or when a visitor clicks a picture, Dynamic HTML can cause a different picture to appear.

Dynamic HTML effects are truly impressive. Unfortunately, the effects are visible only in Internet Explorer Version 4.0 or later and Netscape Navigator 4.0 or later. Furthermore, Netscape's interpretation of Dynamic HTML differs in fundamental ways from Microsoft's, resulting in browser-specific differences. If you use Dynamic HTML in your site, be sure to preview using both browsers to make sure everything works as you expect.

To use Dynamic HTML in your site, follow these steps:

1. **In the page, select the object to which you want to apply a Dynamic HTML effect.**

   Highlight a word, click a picture, or select any other object you want to jazz up.

2. **Choose Format⇨Dynamic HTML Effects.**

   The DHTML Effects toolbar appears.

3. **In the DHTML Effects toolbar, from the On list box, choose the event that triggers the effect.**

   Your choices are Click, Double Click, Mouse Over (when the visitor passes the pointer over the object), or Page Load (when the page first opens in the visitor's browser window).

   Note: Only those options that work with the object you selected in Step 1 are visible in the list box.

4. **From the Apply list box, choose the effect you want to apply to the object.**

   The effects visible in this list box change based on the selected object type and trigger event. If you're not sure how an effect looks, try it out! You can always change the setting later.

   If the effect you choose requires additional settings (not all do), the <Choose Settings> list box comes into view on the DHTML Effects toolbar.

5. **From the <Choose Settings> list box, choose your desired setting.**

And that's it! Save and preview that page to watch Dynamic HTML in action. (Be sure to preview using both Internet Explorer and Netscape Navigator to see how the effect looks in both browsers.)

To easily distinguish between regular objects in your page and those spiffed up with Dynamic HTML, in the DHTML Effects toolbar, click the Highlight Dynamic HTML Effects button. Those objects embellished with DHTML appear color-coded with a light blue background. (This effect is only visible in FrontPage. When viewed with a web browser, nothing changes.)

To remove Dynamic HTML effects from an object, click the object and then click the Remove Effect button.

For more information about what Dynamic HTML is and what it can do, visit www.microsoft.com/workshop/author/default.asp.

Adding a Page Transition

Page transitions are another breed of Dynamic HTML effect. These effects apply to the entire page and occur when a visitor enters or leaves the page or site.

Page transitions are consistently visible only in Internet Explorer 4.0 or later. Try previewing your pages in Netscape Navigator (Version 4.0 or later) to see if the transitions appear, but don't be surprised if they don't.

To apply a page transition, follow these steps:

1. **With the page open in the Page View, choose Format⇨Page Transition.**

   The Page Transitions dialog box appears (see Figure 13-2).

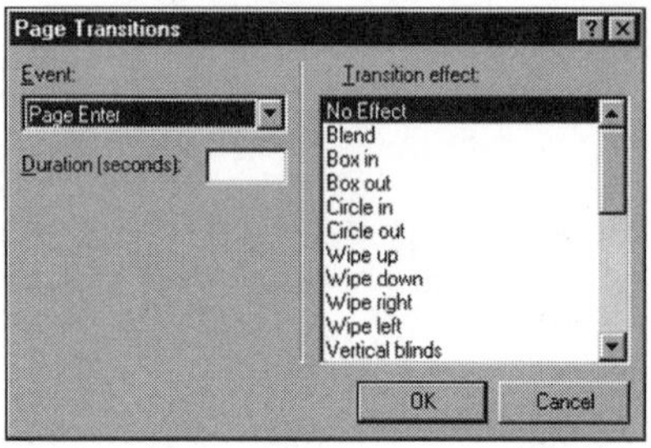

Figure 13-2: The Page Transitions dialog box.

2. **From the dialog box's Event list box, choose the event you want to trigger the transition.**

   Your choices are Page Enter, Page Exit, Site Enter, and Site Exit.

3. **In the Duration text box, enter the number of seconds you'd like the transition to last.**

4. **In the Transition Effect list box, choose the effect you want to apply, and then click OK.**

   The dialog box closes.

To see how the transition effect looks, preview the page.

Precisely Positioning Stuff in Your Page

One limitation above all others gets the collective goat of novice and professional Web designers alike: the inability to precisely position an object inside a page. If you want to stick, say, a picture in the middle of the page, you either have to wrestle with invisible tables (which are, themselves, rife with limitations), or you have to play fast-and-loose with HTML, commandeering tags that produce effects for which they were never intended.

The spirits of the technology heavens heard our prayers (or was it our banging fists?), and came up with a set of positioning commands that control object placement. Objects, be they paragraphs, pictures, or any other thing sitting inside a Web page, will never look the same way again.

Of course, like other emerging Web design technologies, positioning comes with major strings attached. Positioning requires that the visitor's browser know how to process a relatively new version of cascading style sheet commands known as CSS 2.0. (I talk more about Cascading Style Sheets later in this chapter.) As of this writing, the two most popular choices are Microsoft Internet Explorer (version 4.0 or later) and Netscape Navigator (version 4.0 or later). Older browsers ignore the positioning commands and place the object in line with other objects in the page.

Furthermore, Netscape and Internet Explorer interpret certain positioning commands differently, resulting in browser-specific variations. If you use positioning in your Web site, be sure to preview your pages using both browsers, and prepare yourself for different results.

The other option is to stick to using invisible tables as layout guides (see Chapter 9 for details about tables). Because more browsers are able to display tables properly, this option works more consistently.

The bottom line is this: Use positioning features at your own risk. Because positioning represents the cutting edge of Web design, browser companies have only begun to build positioning support into their browsers (read: Watch out for bugs). As browsers evolve, however, positioning effects promise to become the standard for layout control inside Web pages, far surpassing tables in flexibility and features.

You have several choices for how to position an object. You can use positioning commands to create *floating objects*. You can also position objects *relative* to the object's initial position, or *absolutely* (without regard for the object's initial position). Read on to find out more about your options.

Creating a floating object

A floating object sits in the left or right margin of the page, with surrounding text and page objects wrapping around it (see Figure 13-3). You can float just about anything: a sentence, a paragraph, a picture, or any other object you can insert into a page.

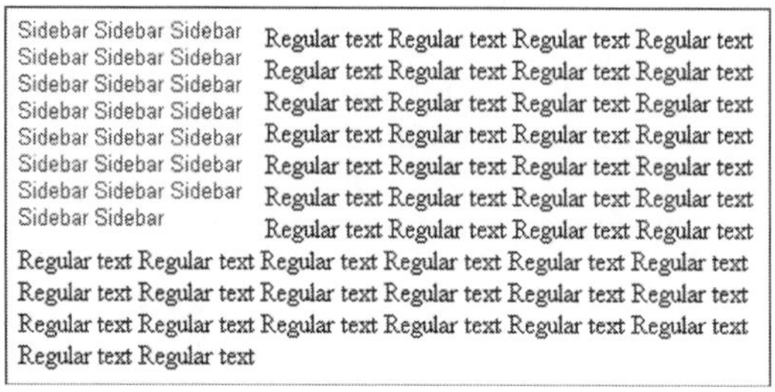

Figure 13-3: The sidebar in this page is positioned as a floating object.

To make an object float, do this:

1. **In the page, select the object you want to position.**

   The object can be some text, a picture, a table, whatever.

2. **Choose Format⇨Position.**

   The Position dialog box appears (see Figure 13-4).

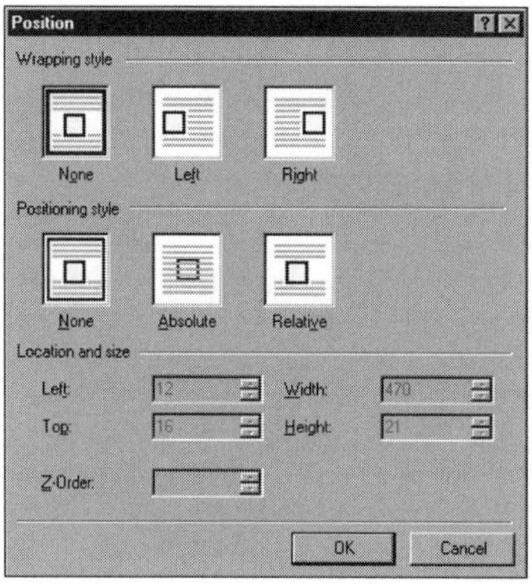

Figure 13-4: The Position dialog box.

3. **In the Wrapping Style area of the dialog box, click the option that looks like the wrapping style you want.**

   Left floats the object over to the left margin, with the rest of the page content wrapping around the right side of the object, and Right floats the object over to the right margin, with the rest of the page content wrapping around the left side of the object.

4. **Click OK.**

   The dialog box closes, and, in the page, size handles appear around the object (look closely: They may be hard to see). The size handles define the *position box* that now surrounds the object. A position box is a like an invisible container inside which positioned objects sit.

5. **In the page, resize the position box by clicking on one of the size handles and dragging it until the object is the size you want.**

   If you prefer to use more precise measurements, show the Positioning toolbar by choosing View➪Toolbars➪Positioning, and then enter pixel values into the toolbar's Width and Height boxes.

The Page View is not always able to display positioned objects correctly. To see positioning in effect, I recommend previewing the page using both Internet Explorer and Netscape Navigator to see how the page looks in both browsers.

Using absolute positioning

When you absolutely position an object, FrontPage uses the page's top and left margins as its reference points. For example, if you tell FrontPage to absolutely position a picture 50 pixels from the top of the page and 100 pixels from the page's left margin, FrontPage places the picture at that location no matter what. If another object already occupies the spot (say the page is filled with text), the picture plops itself on top of the current occupant (see Figure 13-5).

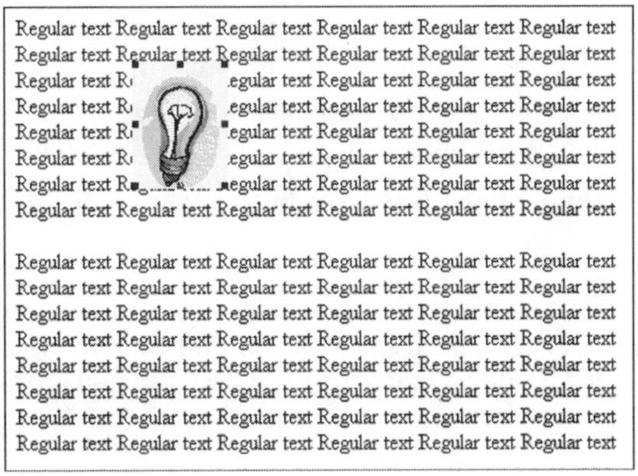

Figure 13-5:
The picture in this page is absolutely positioned.

The implications are exciting: Imagine layering several objects, one on top of the other. What about laying a descriptive paragraph over a picture, creating a sort of electronic montage?

You can even control the order in which objects stack up (known in Web lingo as the object's *z-index*). By default, the most recently placed object sits on top, but you can easily change the setting.

In the following steps, I demonstrate the easiest way to absolutely place an object: by dragging it into place using your pointer.

1. **In the page, select the object you want to position.**

2. **If it's not already visible, show the Positioning toolbar by choosing** **<u>V</u>iew⇨<u>T</u>oolbars⇨Positioning.**

3. **In the Positioning toolbar, click the Position Absolutely button.**

   A position box with size handles appears around the selected object, and any surrounding objects move to fill in the spot where the selected object previously sat.

   When you absolutely position an object, the object now sits "on top" of the other objects in the page. (It's as though you lifted the object onto a transparent level sitting above the other objects.)

4. **If you like, resize the position box by clicking one of the box's size han-dles and then dragging it to the desired size.**

5. **Move the pointer over a position box boundary until the cursor turns into a four-pointed arrow, and then click and drag the object to what-ever position in the page you want.**

6. **To change the object's z-index, in the Positioning toolbar, enter a value in the Z-Index box, or click the Bring Forward or Send Backward buttons.**

   When you stack objects on top of each other, you can specify which item sits on top of the layering order by specifying the object's z-index. A nega-tive number moves the object deeper in the stack, and a positive number moves the object higher in the stack. A z-index of 0 places the object in the same layer as the rest of the page's content.

   If the concept of a z-index is a little too abstract to grasp, click the Bring Forward or Send Backward buttons to achieve the desired effect.

7. **When you're finished, click elsewhere in the page to deselect the object.**

The Page View is not always able to display positioned objects correctly. To see positioning in effect, I recommend previewing the page using both Internet Explorer and Netscape Navigator to see how the page looks in both browsers.

Furthermore, be sure to check how the page looks in browser windows of different sizes. Because the placement of an absolutely positioned object is fixed on the page, but the rest of the page content rearranges itself depending on the size of the browser window, you might see some effects you don't expect.

To change the positioning properties of an object, select the object you want to change, and then enter new values in the appropriate places in the Positioning toolbar.

Using relative positioning

Relative positioning means that FrontPage determines the placement of an object based on its initial position in the page's text flow instead of based on the margins of the page. An example will help illustrate the concept. The page in Figure 13-6 contains no relatively positioned objects. Like any other Web page, each item sits inside the page after the item before it.

Figure 13-6:
A Web page with no relatively positioned objects.

> # Relative Positioning
>
> Relative Positioning
>
> Regular text Regular text Regular text Regular text Regular text Regular text
> Regular text Regular text Regular text Regular text Regular text Regular text
> Regular text Regular text Regular text Regular text Regular text Regular text
> Regular text Regular text Regular text Regular text Regular text Regular text
> Regular text Regular text Regular text Regular text Regular text Regular text
> Regular text Regular text Regular text Regular text Regular text Regular text
> Regular text Regular text Regular text Regular text Regular text Regular text
> Regular text Regular text Regular text Regular text Regular text Regular text
>
> Regular text Regular text Regular text Regular text Regular text Regular text
> Regular text Regular text Regular text Regular text Regular text Regular text
> Regular text Regular text Regular text Regular text Regular text Regular text
> Regular text Regular text Regular text Regular text Regular text Regular text

In Figure 13-7, however, I applied relative positioning to the first instance in the page of the words *Relative Positioning*. I told FrontPage to move those words 65 pixels down from their original position. Not only did FrontPage nudge the words down, causing them to sit on top of the second instance of the words, it left a blank spot in the page where the words used to sit.

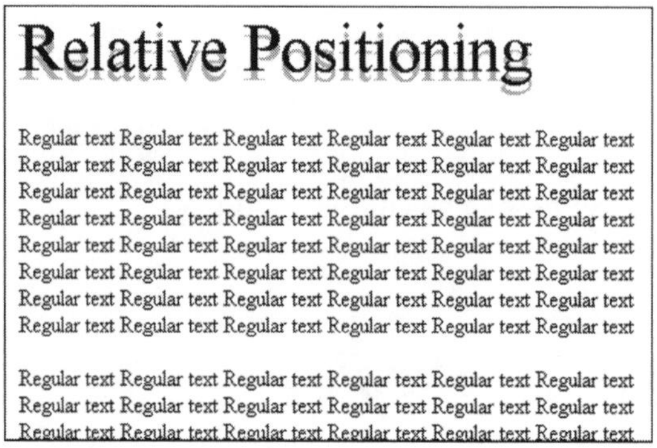

Figure 13-7:
Using
relative
positioning,
I caused
the first
instance of
the words
*Relative
Positioning*
to overlap
the second
instance of
the words.

Relative Positioning

Regular text Regular text Regular text Regular text Regular text Regular text
Regular text Regular text Regular text Regular text Regular text Regular text
Regular text Regular text Regular text Regular text Regular text Regular text
Regular text Regular text Regular text Regular text Regular text Regular text
Regular text Regular text Regular text Regular text Regular text Regular text
Regular text Regular text Regular text Regular text Regular text Regular text
Regular text Regular text Regular text Regular text Regular text Regular text
Regular text Regular text Regular text Regular text Regular text Regular text

Regular text Regular text Regular text Regular text Regular text Regular text
Regular text Regular text Regular text Regular text Regular text Regular text
Regular text Regular text Regular text Regular text Regular text Regular text

Relative positioning is less flexible than absolute positioning (described in the previous section), but can create interesting visual effects even so.

To relatively position an object, do this:

1. **In the page, select the object you want to position.**

2. **Choose Format⇨Position.**

   The Position dialog box appears.

3. **In the Positioning Style section of the dialog box, click Relative.**

4. **In the Left box, enter the number of pixels you want to move the object to the left.**

   If you would rather eyeball the object's position, skip Steps 4 and 5, and later, enter values into the Left and Top boxes of the Positioning toolbar.

5. **In the Top box, enter the number of pixels you want to move the object down from its original position.**

   Entering a positive number moves the object down, and entering a negative number moves the object up.

6. **To resize the position box surrounding the object, enter new numbers in the Width and Height boxes.**

   Or skip this step and, after you're finished working in this dialog box, resize the position box by hand by dragging the box's size handles.

7. **In the Z-Order box, enter a value that moves the object's placement in the layering order.**

   Or when you're finished, change the object's layering order by selecting the object in the page and clicking the Bring Forward or Send Backward buttons in the Positioning toolbar.

8. **Click OK.**

   The dialog box closes, and FrontPage positions the object in the page.

The Page View is not always able to display positioned objects correctly. To see positioning in effect, I recommend previewing the page using both Internet Explorer and Netscape Navigator to see how the page looks in both browsers.

To change the positioning properties of an object, select the object you want to change, and then enter new values in the appropriate places in the Positioning toolbar.

Working with Style Sheets

I've saved the most powerful extra for last: *Cascading Style Sheets* or *CSS* (in FrontPage, referred to simply as *style sheets*). Style sheets enable you to create new styles and to modify the standard HTML style definitions that come with FrontPage.

If you're a Microsoft Word user, styles may not seem so exciting. After all, word-processing styles have been around for years. Styles in Web pages, on the other hand, are relatively new. Until recently, Web designers were stuck with the standard effects produced by HTML. Style sheets open every HTML tag to modification, taking you beyond each tag's inherent abilities.

For example, if you're not satisfied with the staid appearance of the Heading 1 paragraph style (big, bold, plain text), you can use style sheets to define the Heading 1 style however you like. If you want all text formatted with the Heading 1 style to appear as magenta, 36-point, underlined, and blinking text, so be it.

Style sheets are especially useful if more than one author works on a site. Because the site's formatting instructions are stored in the style sheet, individual authors can concentrate on the page's content and can later apply the style sheet to take care of the stylistic details.

Style sheets are capable of much more than I demonstrate here. FrontPage gives you powerful access to style sheets, but to use style sheets to their fullest potential, you must be fluent in both HTML and style sheet syntax. So, think of this section as an introduction to the wonders of style sheets . . . you may very well be seduced into finding out more.

For more information about style sheets, turn to the World Wide Web. Go to `www.microsoft.com/workshop/author/css/css.asp` and `webreview.com/wr/pub/Style_Sheets` (for starters). Also, be sure to look at the style sheet coverage in the FrontPage Help system (available when you choose <u>H</u>elp⇨Microsoft FrontPage <u>H</u>elp).

Creating and modifying styles in the current page

The Style dialog box (shown in Figure 13-8) enables you to embed a style sheet in the page currently open in the Page View. You access the Style dialog box by choosing F<u>o</u>rmat⇨<u>S</u>tyle.

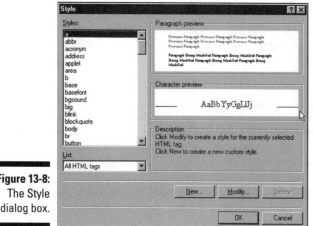

Figure 13-8:
The Style dialog box.

In the dialog box, the Styles list box contains all the HTML tags you can modify using style sheet commands. I realize you probably don't know HTML, nor are you interested in learning it this very moment. So, in Table 13-1, I list a few of the tags that control the elements you most likely want to change. For example, after you modify the style of the b tag (the tag that creates bold text), each time you tell FrontPage to apply the Bold format to text, FrontPage will refer to your style sheet for instructions on how to display that style.

Table 13-1	Quickie HTML Tag Reference
This HTML tag . . .	*. . . controls this aspect of the page*
a	Hyperlink color
b	Bold text
body	Default text color, background color
h1–h6	Heading 1 through Heading 6 paragraph styles
i	Italic text
ol	Numbered lists
p	Default paragraph text
ul	Bulleted lists

To embed a style sheet inside the page currently open in the Page View, do this:

1. **With the cursor sitting anywhere inside the page, choose Format⇨Style.**

   The Style dialog box appears.

2. **In the Styles list box, click the tag you want to modify, and then click Modify. Or to create a new style, click New.**

   Depending on which button you click, either the Modify Style or the New Style dialog box appears. Aside from their names, the dialog boxes are identical, so the instructions that follow apply to both.

3. **In the dialog box's Name (Selector) text box, enter a one-word name. (If you are modifying the style of an existing HTML tag, skip this step).**

4. **To define the style, click the Format button, and from the pop-up menu that appears, choose the category of style change you want to create.**

   Your choices are Font (affects typeface, font size, attributes, letter spacing, and font color), Paragraph (affects alignment, indentation, and word/line spacing), Border (affects borders, white space around paragraphs, and background and foreground colors), or Numbering (affects the appearance of bulleted or numbered lists).

   The category you choose determines the resulting dialog box that appears.

5. **From the dialog box, select the options you want, and then click OK.**

   If you're not sure how to use the dialog box, see Chapter 5; these are the same dialog boxes that appear if you choose corresponding commands in the Format menu.

   After you click OK, the dialog box closes, and the Style dialog box comes back into view.

6. **If you like, define more styles by repeating Steps 2–5, or click OK to close the dialog box.**

    FrontPage applies the new style definitions to the current page.

If you later want to change the style definitions you've set up, choose Format⇔Style. In the Styles dialog box, from the List list box, choose User-Defined Styles. Then, in the Styles list box, click the style you want to change, and follow Steps 2–6 in the previous set of steps.

Applying styles to one or more pages in your site

The technique for applying a style sheet to more than one page in your site (or across the entire site) is different from embedding a style sheet inside a single page. In this case, you must create or have access to a separate style sheet file, which you then link to all the pages to which you want the style sheet to apply.

Creating the style sheet

If you already have access to a style sheet file — say your company provides a standard style sheet to everyone building company-sponsored pages — import the file into your Web site, and skip to the next section (see Chapter 2 for details on how to import an existing file into a Web site).

If you don't have access to a ready-made style sheet, thankfully, you don't have to start from scratch. FrontPage contains templates for several style sheets, all of which coordinate with different FrontPage themes. To create a new style sheet by using a template, do this:

1. **Choose File⇔New⇔Page to display the New dialog box.**

2. **In the dialog box, click the Style Sheets tab to display the list of style sheet templates, and then double-click the template you want to use.**

    The dialog box closes, and the style sheet appears in the Page View. Also, the Style toolbar (containing a single button: Style) appears floating inside the FrontPage window.

Don't be put off by all the style sheet's codes and brackets; you don't need to type anything into the page at all. You can modify the style sheet using the Style dialog box (to access the dialog box, in the Style toolbar, click the Style button; see the previous section of this chapter for instructions on how to use the Style dialog box). When you're done, save the page as part of your Web site (the process is the same as saving a regular Web page).

If you know HTML and style sheet syntax, the more straightforward course is to create a new page in the Page View, type up your own style sheet, and save it as part of your Web site (be sure to specify in the Save As dialog box that FrontPage is to save the file as a Hypertext Style Sheet).

Linking the style sheet to the rest of your site

Now that the style sheet is tucked away in your site, the final step is to link the style sheet to those pages in your site to which you want the style sheet to apply.

To do so, follow these steps:

1. **In FrontPage, switch to the Folders View.**

2. **In the Contents list, while holding down the Ctrl key, click the pages to which you want the style sheet to apply.**

   If you want to apply the style sheet to the entire site, you can skip this step.

3. **Choose Format➪Style Sheet Links.**

   The Link Style Sheet dialog box appears.

4. **If you want the style sheet to apply to all the pages in your site, in the dialog box, mark the All Pages radio button.**

   Otherwise, FrontPage will apply the style sheet to the pages you selected in Step 2.

5. **Click the Add button.**

   The Select Hyperlink dialog box appears.

6. **Navigate your Web site to the location of the style sheet file, and then double-click the file.**

   (If you're not sure how to use this dialog box, see Chapter 6.)

   After you double-click the file, the Select Hyperlink dialog box closes, and the Link Style Sheet dialog box comes back into view with the style sheet file listed in the dialog box.

7. **Click OK.**

   The dialog box closes, and FrontPage applies the style sheet to the pages you specified.

You can apply more than one style sheet to selected pages. Here's where the *cascading* part of *Cascading Style Sheets* comes in: FrontPage applies the style sheet definitions, in order, to the page. In other words, if the first style sheet contains a background color and a typeface setting, and the second style sheet contains a different background color setting, the background color setting from the second style sheet takes precedence, but the typeface setting from the first style sheet appears as well.

Chapter 14

Cool Components

. . . .

In This Chapter

▶ Finding out what Components can do

▶ Integrating Components into your site

. . . .

*N*o longer satisfied with pages full of static text and pictures, the Web design community is figuring out ways to include interactive features in Web pages. FrontPage harnesses this new wave of Web development by transforming complex features into easy-to-use tools called *Components*. In this chapter, you discover what Components can do and how to use them in your Web site.

What's a Component?

A Component is a gizmo you insert into your Web page that simplifies certain Web publishing tasks or adds interactive features to your site.

Before the creation of Components, you had to do lots of mucking around with complicated HTML and server-based programs and then coordinate the whole process with your ISP or system administrator to add the following features to your Web site. Now you accomplish the same thing in a few deft mouse clicks.

FrontPage contains the following Components, each of which performs a different task:

- ✔ **Banner Ad Manager:** If you display banner advertising in your site, this Component simplifies the process.

- ✔ **Hit Counter:** This handy tool helps you keep track of the number of visits a page receives.

- ✔ **Hover Button:** This Component creates a customizable, hyperlinkable button.

- ✔ **Marquee:** This Component creates a scrolling text banner.

- ✔ **Confirmation Field:** This Component works in concert with an interactive form to confirm information visitors enter into form fields. (I explain how to use this Component in Chapter 10.)

- ✔ **Include Page:** This Component, added to a Web page, replaces itself with the contents of a second page.

- ✔ **Scheduled Include Page:** This Component works just like the Include Page Component, except that the inclusion appears only during a specified time period.

- ✔ **Scheduled Picture:** This Component works just like the Scheduled Include Page Component, except that it includes a picture instead of the contents of a Web page.

- ✔ **Substitution:** This Component enables you to display certain types of standard information in your Web pages.

- ✔ **Categories:** This Component streamlines creating links to new additions to your site. (I show you how to use this Component in Chapter 15.)

- ✔ **Search Form:** Add a keyword search to your site with the help of this Component.

- ✔ **Table of Contents:** This Component generates an automatically updated list of links to all the other pages in your site. (I cover this Component in more detail in Chapter 6.)

In the following sections, I show you how Components can simplify your life, and I demonstrate how to put the critters to work.

Several Components must team up with a web server outfitted with FrontPage Server Extensions to work properly (I talk about what FrontPage Server Extensions are and what they do in Chapter 16). I point out any specialized server requirements as I describe each Component.

Calling in the Banner Ad Manager

In the ongoing quest to turn a profit on the Internet, many Web sites help fund operations with *banner ads.* Banner ads are rectangular graphics that encourage visitors to buy a product or service. If your Web site attracts enough daily traffic, you may be able to sell the premium spot at the top of your home page (and other popular pages in your site) to advertisers. Many companies will pay a pretty penny for the chance to tout their wares to your visitors.

About Office 2000 Web Components

Microsoft Office 2000 — and with it, FrontPage 2000 — contains an exciting new feature called Web Components. Web Components enable you to insert interactive Office-like goodies into a Web page, such as a working spreadsheet, PivotTable, or chart. When a visitor browses the page, he or she can interact with the Web Component directly from within the web browser.

For example, say you want visitors to your site to be able to calculate the future value of an investment. You can use the Office Spreadsheet Component to design a spreadsheet that can calculate this information, and then insert the Component into your page. When visitors come to your Web site, they could plug their own numbers into the spreadsheet right from their own browsers.

To use Web Components, visitors must browse the Web using Internet Explorer 4.01 or later, and must have Office Web Components (an accessory that comes with Office 2000) installed

on their computers. For this reason, Web Components are best reserved for use on an internal network.

You can learn more about each Web Component by accessing its detailed Help system. To do so, insert a Web Component into your page, and then click the Help button inside the component's toolbar (the toolbar is visible inside the body of the Web page). To insert a Web Component in your page, place the cursor where you want the Component to appear, and then, in the Standard toolbar, click the Insert Component button. From the menu that appears, choose Office Spreadsheet, Office PivotTable, or Office Chart.

For more information about the Web-savvy features of Office 2000, pick up a copy of *Microsoft Office 2000 For Dummies* by Wallace Wang and Roger Parker or *Microsoft Office 2000 All in One For Dummies* by Bill Helling (both published by IDG Books Worldwide, Inc.).

The Banner Ad Manager helps you maintain a rotating display of ads in your site. You control the amount of time each ad appears on the page and the transition effect between ads.

For good examples of banner ads, take a look at these popular Web sites: Yahoo! at www.yahoo.com, CNET at www.cnet.com, and News.com at www.news.com.

FrontPage creates this effect by inserting a *Java applet* into the page. A Java applet is a mini-program written in the Java programming language, which means that the banner ad images appear only to your visitors who use Java-capable browsers (such as Internet Explorer Version 3.0 or later, or Netscape Navigator Version 2.0 or later). I talk more about Java applets in "Advanced Additions" on the CD.

To use the Banner Ad Manager, follow these steps:

1. **In the page, place the cursor where you want the banner ad display to appear.**

2. In the Standard toolbar, click the Insert Component button, and from the pop-up menu that appears, choose Banner Ad Manager.

The Banner Ad Manager Properties dialog box appears (see Figure 14-1).

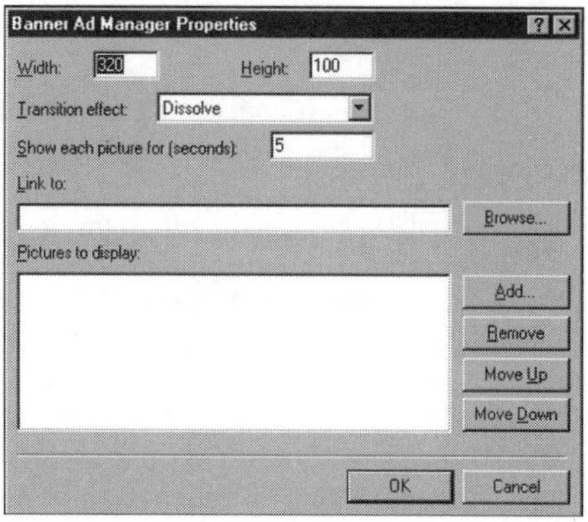

Banner Ad Manager Properties

Width: 820   Height: 100

Transition effect: Dissolve

Show each picture for (seconds): 5

Link to:

Browse...

Pictures to display:

Add...

Remove

Move Up

Move Down

OK   Cancel

Figure 14-1:
The Banner
Ad Manager
Properties
dialog box.

3. In the Width and Height text boxes, type the dimensions of the area in which the banner ad images are to appear.

The Banner Ad Manager creates an empty space in the page inside which images appear. The size of the space remains constant, even if the images are different sizes. For the Banner Ad Manager to look its best, therefore, each image should be the same size.

4. In the Transition Effect list box, choose the transition effect that governs how you want each image to look as it changes.

5. In the Show Each Picture for (Seconds) text box, type the number of seconds you want each image to appear on screen.

6. Optionally, in the Link To text box, type the URL of the destination you want visitors to visit if they click the banner ad display.

Unfortunately, this text box only lets you choose a single link destination for the entire display, even if the banner ads advertise products from different companies.

Now, you must tell the Banner Ad Manager which pictures to display.

7. Click the Add button.

The Add Picture for Banner Ad dialog box appears. (This dialog box works just like the Picture dialog box, which I explain in Chapter 7.)

8. **Choose the first picture you want to appear and then click OK to close the dialog box.**

   The Add Picture for Banner Ad dialog box closes, and the Banner Ad Manager dialog box becomes visible again.

9. **Repeat Steps 7 and 8 until you've added all the pictures you want to the Banner Ad Manager.**

   To change the order in which the pictures appear, click Move Up or Move Down.

10. **Click OK.**

    The dialog box closes, and the Banner Ad Manager appears in the page.

To see how the Banner Ad Manager works, preview your page using the Preview tab or by launching your Java-capable web browser. (Refer to Chapter 3 for directions on how to preview your page.) To change the Banner Ad Manager's settings, in FrontPage, double-click the banner ad on the page to open the Banner Ad Manager dialog box.

Tracking visits with a hit counter

A *hit counter* is an odometer-like row of numbers that sits in your page and records the number of visits or *hits* that the page receives. Each time someone visits the page, the number in the hit counter goes up by one. Hit counters let you brag to visitors about your site's popularity (plus, it's fun to watch the numbers increase every day).

To use a FrontPage hit counter, you must publish your Web site on a host web server that has FrontPage Server Extensions installed. For more information about FrontPage Server Extensions, see Chapter 16.

To insert a hit counter into your page, do this:

1. **In the page, place the cursor where you want the counter to appear.**

2. **In the Standard toolbar, click the Insert Component button, and from the pop-up menu that appears, choose Hit Counter.**

   The Hit Counter Properties dialog box appears (see Figure 14-2).

3. **In the Counter Style area, click the radio button next to the character style you want to use.**

   You can use your own image in place of FrontPage's preset counter graphics. To do so, click the Custom Picture radio button, and then enter the image's filename and location in the accompanying text box. You must choose a single graphic that contains the numbers 0–9, and the numbers must be evenly spaced inside the image.

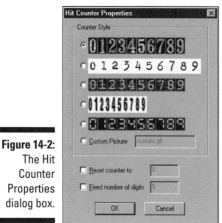

Figure 14-2:
The Hit
Counter
Properties
dialog box.

4. **Mark the Reset Counter To check box, and in the accompanying text box, type the counter's starting number.**

   If your Web site is new, leave the number at 0. If your site has already been around for a while, you can start the counter with an approximation of the number of visitors who came by before your counter was installed. (Or you can artificially inflate the number of folks who visit, but I know you weren't even considering that option.)

5. **If you want the counter to appear with a fixed number of digits, mark the Fixed Number of Digits check box and then type the number of digits in the accompanying text box.**

   For example, if you enter **5** in the text box, the counter will display hit number 1 as 00001.

6. **Click OK.**

   The dialog box closes, and a placeholder appears in the page (the place-holder looks like this: [Hit Counter]).

To preview and test the hit counter, you must use FrontPage in conjunction with a web server outfitted with FrontPage Server Extensions. To see the hit counter in action, you can either publish your Web site and preview the live version of the site, or you can use FrontPage together with a local web server. For more information about using a local web server, see Appendix A.

Inserting a hover button

A *hover button* is an animated button that, when clicked, activates a hyper-link. When the visitor moves the pointer over the button before clicking, the button changes color or shape. You can even specify a sound that plays when a visitor hovers over or clicks the button (or both).

By default, hover buttons are colorful rectangular boxes. If you prefer a differently shaped button, you can use this Component to place text on top of a graphic to turn the graphic into a button. You can even specify a second graphic that appears "on hover," resulting in an impressive effect.

The steps for creating a rectangular versus a graphic button are slightly different, so I describe each task separately in the steps that follow.

Hover buttons are actually Java applets and therefore require that your visitors use Java-capable browsers.

Creating a rectangular hover button

To create a hover button, follow these steps:

1. **In a page, place the cursor where you want the button to appear.**

2. **In the Standard toolbar, click the Insert Component button and from the pop-up menu that appears, choose Hover Button.**

   The Hover Button Properties dialog box appears (see Figure 14-3).

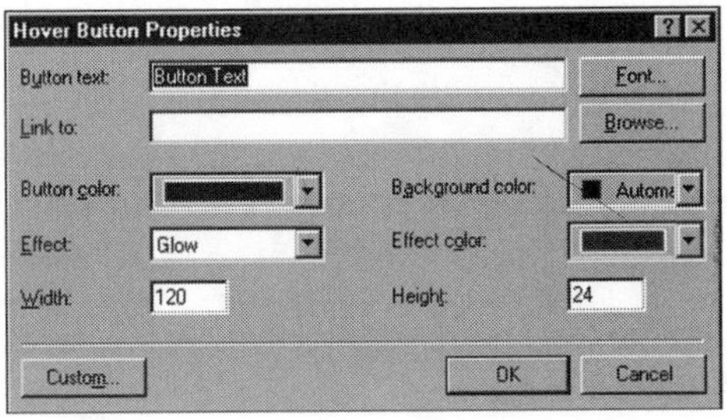

Figure 14-3:
The Hover
Button
Properties
dialog box.

3. **In the text box named B̲utton Text, enter the text label you want to appear on top of the button.**

4. **To change the appearance of the label text, click the F̲ont button.**

   The Font dialog box appears.

5. **Choose your desired font, font style, text size, and text color, and then click OK to close the Font dialog box.**

   (For detailed information about each font effect, see Chapter 5.)

   The Font dialog box closes, and the Hover Button dialog box becomes visible again.

6. **In the L̲ink To text box, enter the filename or URL of the page that appears when the hover button is clicked.**

   Or click Browse to choose a page from the Select Hover Button Hyperlink dialog box. This dialog box works exactly like the Create Hyperlink dialog box, which I describe in Chapter 6.

7. **In the Button Color list box, choose a button color.**

8. **In the Effect list box, choose the visual effect you want to appear when the visitor passes the pointer over the button.**

   I won't waste your time describing each effect here. Just pick the effect that sounds like what you want. After you're finished creating the button, you can preview the page to see how the effect looks. If you don't like the effect, you can change this setting.

9. **In the Effect Color list box, choose the color that you want to appear as part of the hover effect.**

10. **Enter the button's dimensions in pixels in the Width and Height text boxes.**

    You also can adjust button dimensions by leaving these text boxes alone and resizing the button later on by dragging its size handles.

11. **If you want to associate a sound with the hover button, click the Custom button. (If not, click OK to close the dialog box.)**

    The Custom dialog box appears.

12. **In the On Click text box, type the filename of the sound file you want to play after the visitor clicks the button.**

    Or click Browse to choose a sound file using the Select Sound dialog box.

13. **In the On Hover text box, type the filename of the sound file you want to play after the visitor passes the pointer over the button.**

14. **Click OK.**

    The Custom dialog box closes, and the Hover Button Properties dialog box becomes visible again.

15. **Click OK.**

    The Hover Button Properties dialog box closes, and the hover button appears in the page.

Creating a graphic hover button

To create a graphic hover button, follow these steps:

1. **Place the cursor in the page where you want the button to appear.**

 2. **In the Standard toolbar, click the Insert Component button, and from the pop-up menu that appears, choose Hover Button.**

   The Hover Button Properties dialog box appears.

3. **In the text box named Button Text, type the text label that you want to appear on top of the button.**

   If you don't want text to appear on the button, clear the contents of this text box and skip ahead to Step 6.

4. **To change the appearance of the label text, click the Font button.**

   The Font dialog box appears.

5. **Choose your desired font, font style, text size, and text color, and then click OK to close the dialog box.**

   The Font dialog box closes, and the Hover Button dialog box becomes visible again.

6. **In the Link To text box, type the filename or URL of the page that appears when the hover button is clicked.**

   Or click Browse to choose a page from the Select Hover Button Hyperlink dialog box (this dialog box works exactly like the Create Hyperlink dialog box, which I describe in Chapter 6).

7. **In the Background Color list box, choose a background color for the hover button graphic.**

8. **In the Width and Height text boxes, type the dimensions of the hover button.**

   The hover button feature creates an empty space inside which the button graphic appears. Chances are you want the hover button area to be the same size as the graphic you're using to create the button. If so, these dimensions should equal the width and height of the graphic.

9. **Click the Custom button.**

   The Custom dialog box appears.

10. **If you want to associate sounds with the button, enter the filenames of the sound files that you want to use in the On Click and/or On Hover text boxes.**

    Or click Browse to choose sound files using the Select Sound dialog box.

11. **In the Custom section of the dialog box, in the Button text box, type the filename and location of the button graphic.**

    Or click Browse to choose a picture from the Select Picture dialog box.

12. **In the On Hover text box, type the filename of the graphic you want to appear when the visitor passes the pointer over the button.**

    (Or click Browse . . . and I think you can guess the rest.)

13. **Click OK.**

    The Custom dialog box closes, and the Hover Button Properties dialog box becomes visible again.

14. **Click OK.**

    The Hover Button Properties dialog box closes, and the hover button appears in the page.

Test your hover button by previewing the page with the Preview tab or by launching your Java-capable web browser. To edit the hover button in FrontPage, double-click the button in the page to open the Hover Button Properties dialog box.

Creating a marquee

A *marquee* is a rectangular banner that contains scrolling text. Marquees are a fun and popular way to highlight announcements or other important information on your Web pages.

The big bummer is that marquees are visible only in Microsoft Internet Explorer. If you view a marquee in another browser, the thing just appears as regular text.

You can use other means to include scrolling banners in your page. For example, you can use a Java applet to add a scrolling banner to your page (at the end of this section, I talk more about this option). Unfortunately, Java applets also are visible in only a limited number of web browsers. Whatever method you choose, keep in mind that a portion of your visitors can't see marquees.

To insert a marquee, follow these steps:

1. **Place the cursor in the page where you want the marquee to appear.**

2. **In the Standard toolbar, click the Insert Component button and from the pop-up menu that appears, choose Marquee.**

    The Marquee Properties dialog box appears (see Figure 14-4).

3. **In the text box named Text, type the message that you want to appear inside the marquee.**

4. **In the Direction area, click the radio button next to the direction you want the text to scroll.**

    Choose the Left option if you want the text to begin at the right side of the marquee and scroll left, and choose the Right option if you want the text to do the opposite. Left is generally the better choice, because this direction enables visitors to read the marquee text from beginning to end as the banner scrolls by.

Figure 14-4:
The
Marquee
Properties
dialog box.

5. **In the Delay text box, type the number of milliseconds that the marquee text is to pause between each successive movement.**

   The smaller the number, the faster the marquee text scrolls by.

6. **In the Amount text box, type the amount of distance (in pixels) that you want the marquee text to move each time.**

   The smaller the number, the slower and smoother the marquee text scrolls.

7. **In the Behavior area, click the radio button next to the option that describes how you want the marquee text to move.**

   The Scroll option creates continually scrolling text (that is, text that scrolls to one side of the marquee until it disappears and then reappears again on the other side). The Slide option creates text that originates at one side of the marquee, scrolls to the other side, and stops there. The Alternate option creates text that scrolls from one side of the marquee and, after the text reaches the opposite margin, bounces back in the other direction.

8. **In the Align with Text area, click the radio button next to an alignment option.**

   These options control where the text sits inside the marquee boundaries. Your choices are Top, Middle, or Bottom.

9. **If you want to specify marquee dimensions, click the Width and Height check boxes and type a percentage or pixel value in the corresponding text box.**

   For information on how to set absolute versus proportional dimensions, refer to Chapter 9.

   The easier course is to leave this section alone and resize the marquee by hand. (I explain how to do so at the end of this section.)

10. **If you want the marquee text to repeat a limited number of times, clear the Repeat Continuously check box and then specify the number of repetitions you want in the scroll box underneath the check box.**

11. **In the Background Color list box, choose the marquee's color.**

    The Default option makes the marquee's background color the same as the page's background color. If you choose a different color, the marquee stands in contrast to the background color of the page. (You find out how to set your page's background color in Chapter 7.)

12. **Click OK.**

    The dialog box closes, and the marquee appears in your page (the marquee looks like regular text).

To see the marquee in action, preview the page using the Preview tab or Internet Explorer. To edit the marquee, in FrontPage, double-click the marquee to open the Marquee Properties dialog box.

To resize your marquee by hand, click the marquee, and then click one of its size handles (the square dots sitting along the dashed marquee boundary). While holding down the mouse button, drag the handle in the appropriate direction to change the marquee's height and/or width.

You may prefer to forgo the Internet Explorer-specific marquee option described here and instead use a Java applet to create a scrolling banner in your page. To do so, you must first download a scrolling banner applet from a public-use applet archive such as `javaboutique.internet.com/text.html`. Next, you must insert the applet into your page, and then configure the applet so that it works the way you want. For help, turn to "Advanced Additions" on the CD.

Include Page

The Include Page Component simplifies the process of inserting the same information in more than one page in your Web site. After you insert an Include Page Component into your page, the Component is replaced by the contents of a second page.

Here's an example: Say you want to display a list of news headlines in several pages in your Web site. Instead of typing the list of headlines into each page, you create a separate page that contains only the headlines. You then use the Include Page Component to include the contents of the headlines page in the other pages in your Web site. If you want to change the headlines later, you update the headlines page, and the Include Page Component reflects the update throughout the Web site.

The Include Page Component works very much like shared borders (for more information about shared borders, see Chapter 6). However, you can insert an Include Page Component in the body of your page, whereas shared borders stick to the page's margins.

Inserting the Include Page Component

To use the Include Page Component, follow these steps:

1. **Place the cursor in the page where you want the Component to appear.**

2. **In the Standard toolbar, click the Insert Component button, and from the pop-up menu that appears, choose Include Page.**

   The Include Page Component Properties dialog box appears.

3. **In the <u>P</u>age to Include text box, type the filename and location of the page in your Web site you want to include.**

   Or click Browse to choose a page from the Current Web dialog box.

4. **Click OK.**

   The Insert Component dialog box closes, and the contents of the included page appear inside the current page.

Try passing your pointer over the included information; the pointer turns into a little hand holding a piece of paper. This special pointer reminds you that the text is there courtesy of the Include Page Component.

Because the pages you include using the Include Page Component are often just fragments of information, meant only to be seen embedded in the "host" page, you may want to hide included pages from web browsers and from the Search Form Component. To do so, store the included pages inside your Web site's _private folder. (Refer to Chapter 2 for descriptions of the different FrontPage folders and how to store pages inside them.)

The _private folder is private only if you publish the Web site on a web server that supports FrontPage Server Extensions. For more information, see Chapter 16.

Updating included pages

To update a page that you've included inside other pages, simply open the included page in the Page View, make your changes, and save the page just as you would any other Web page. After you save and close the page, FrontPage updates the inclusion throughout the rest of your Web site the next time it *recalculates* the site's hyperlinks. When FrontPage recalculates hyperlinks, it refreshes the site, integrating any changes made to the site's system of hyperlinks. This process usually happens automatically as you update your site (you don't even notice), but you can also specifically tell FrontPage to recalculate your site's hyperlinks.

To do so, choose Tools⇨Recalculate Hyperlinks. The Recalculate Hyperlinks dialog box appears, warning you that recalculating hyperlinks may take several minutes. Click Yes to close the dialog box and proceed with the recalculation.

If remembering to recalculate hyperlinks every time you change an included page is a hassle, you can tell FrontPage to remind you when an included page has changed but hasn't yet been updated throughout the site. To do so, choose Tools⇨Options. The Options dialog box appears with the General tab visible. In the dialog box, click the Warn When Included Components Are Out of Date check box, and then click OK to close the dialog box.

Scheduled Include Page and Scheduled Picture

The Scheduled Include Page and Scheduled Picture Components work like the Include Page Component, except that the inclusion appears only during a specified time period. The Scheduled Include Page Component (like the Include Page Component) inserts the contents of a page into another page, and the Scheduled Picture Component inserts a single picture.

As an example of how the Scheduled Include Page Component can help you, suppose that you use your Web site to announce upcoming events. Instead of keeping track of event dates and making sure that you update your Web site before the event occurs, you can create a separate page for the announcements. Then you can use the Scheduled Include Page Component to include the contents of the page in other pages in your Web site, specifying the time period during which the announcements apply. After that time period is over, the announcements disappear.

The Scheduled Picture Component is handy if, for example, you flag additions to your Web site with a "New!" icon. Because things are new only for a limited time, you can use the Scheduled Picture Component to remove the icons after a week or so.

Both Scheduled Components work the same way, so I describe them together in the following steps:

1. **Place the cursor in your page where you want the Component to appear.**

2. **In the Standard toolbar, click the Insert Component button, and from the pop-up menu that appears, choose Scheduled Include Page or Scheduled Picture.**

    Depending on your choice, either the Scheduled Include Page Component Properties dialog box or the Scheduled Picture Properties dialog box appears.

3. **In the During The Scheduled Time text box, type the filename and location of the page or picture you want to include.**

    Or click Browse to choose a page or picture from your Web site.

4. **If you want to include a different page or picture before and after the inclusion period, type the filename and location in the text box named Before and After the Scheduled Time.**

    If you don't include an alternative page or picture, nothing appears at the location of the Component before and after the inclusion period.

5. **In the Starting area, choose the date and time you want the inclusion to first appear.**

    Specify the date by selecting options from the Year, Month, and Day list boxes. To specify the time, click the time notation inside the Time scroll box and click the up- or down-pointing arrows at the right side of the box to adjust the time.

6. **In the Ending area, choose the date and time you want the inclusion to disappear.**

7. **Click OK.**

    The dialog box closes, and the specified page contents or picture appears at the location of the cursor. If the inclusion period begins at a later time, the message [Expired Scheduled Include Page] or [Expired Scheduled Picture] appears in your page — unless you specified an alternative, in which case the contents of the alternative page or the alternative picture appears. The notice appears in FrontPage only to remind you that the Scheduled Component is present. People who view the page with a web browser can't see the notice.

If your host web server is located in another time zone (which is unlikely but possible if you publish your FrontPage Web sites by using an ISP or company server in another region), the times you specify must apply to the server's time zone, not yours.

Scheduled Include caveats

Using the Scheduled Include Page and the Scheduled Picture Components comes with a major catch. For the Components to work correctly, FrontPage must recalculate the Web site's links *during the scheduled inclusion time* to begin the inclusion and *after the scheduled include time expires* to cause the inclusion to disappear.

FrontPage automatically recalculates the site's hyperlinks whenever you update, move, rename, or delete a page containing hyperlinks. You can ensure that FrontPage recalculates your site's hyperlinks at the appropriate time in one of two ways: by updating and publishing your Web site every day or by manually recalculating hyperlinks in the live version of the site. In Chapter 16, I show you how to publish and update your Web site. To manually recalculate hyperlinks, open your Web site in FrontPage. (If you published the Web site on another web server, open it directly from the server on which it is published; I explain how to do this in Chapter 1.) Choose Tools⇨Recalculate Hyperlinks. The Recalculate Hyperlinks dialog box appears, warning you that recalculating hyperlinks may take several minutes. Click Yes to close the dialog box and proceed with the recalculation.

Substitution

The Substitution Component enables you to display placeholders in your page that replace themselves with bits of information called *configuration variables.* Configuration variables describe certain details about the page or contain snippets of information that you specify.

Similar to the Include Page Component, which includes the contents of another page in your Web page, the Substitution Component includes the value of the configuration variable you choose. Read on to find out how this Component can make your life easier.

Displaying standard configuration variables

FrontPage maintains a standard set of configuration variables for each page:

- **Author** is the user name of the person who created the page.
- **Modified By** is the user name of the person who most recently edited the page.
- **Description** is a description of the page.
- **Page URL** is the current location of the page.

Some Web sites created using FrontPage's Web site templates contain additional standard configuration variables.

Fixing a broken Component

If a Component isn't working properly, check the FrontPage Component Errors report. From there, you can repair the afflicted Component as follows:

1. **Choose View⇨Reports⇨Component Errors.**

   FrontPage switches to the Reports View and displays the Component Errors report. The report lists the pages that contain broken Components along with a diagnosis of the problem. (If you can't read the full description of the error, right-click the report entry and then choose Properties. The Properties dialog box appears, with the Errors tab visible. The Description box contains a detailed description of the problem.)

2. **Click OK to close the Properties dialog box and, depending on the problem outlined in the Description box, proceed to repair the Component.**

   Depending on the type of Component, you may need to open the page, double-click the Component to display its associated Properties dialog box, and then proceed with repairs there. Or you may need to perform a different task, such as correcting a configuration variable.

   After you complete repairs and save the page containing the Component, return to the Component Errors Report. The error entry should have disappeared.

To see the values for each of a page's standard configuration variables, in any of the FrontPage views, right-click the page's icon and, from the pop-up menu that appears, choose Properties. The Properties dialog box appears, with the General tab visible. In the dialog box, click the Summary tab. The author's name appears next to Created By in the Summary tab. (If no name appears next to Created By, the author did not use FrontPage to create the page.) The name of the person who last modified the page appears next to Modified By. The page description appears in the Comments text box. In the General tab, the page's current URL appears in the Location box.

To use the Substitution Component to display standard configuration variables, follow these steps:

1. **Place the cursor in your page where you want the Component to appear.**

2. **In the Standard toolbar, click the Insert Component button, and from the pop-up menu that appears, choose Substitution.**

   The Substitution Properties dialog box appears.

3. **In the Substitute With list box, choose the name of the configuration variable you want to display.**

4. **Click OK to close the dialog box.**

   The value of the configuration variable appears in your page.

If you use the Substitution Component to display the Page URL configuration variable, the URL that appears corresponds to the computer on which the page is *currently* located. If you later publish the page on another web server, the old, incorrect URL remains displayed inside the page.

To solve this problem, after you publish the Web site, open the Web site directly from the web server on which the site is published (refer to Chapter 1 if you're not sure how) and then open the page displaying the Page URL configuration variable. Click the URL and press the Delete key to delete the Substitution Component. Now reinsert the Substitution Component and set it up to display the Page URL configuration variable. (Follow the steps outlined in this section.) The correct URL appears. Save the page to make the change visible to the rest of the World Wide Web.

Creating and displaying your own configuration variables

You can create your own configuration variables to use as placeholders for standard bits of information throughout the Web site. Say, for example, you want to list your address in several Web pages. Instead of typing the address repeatedly, you can create a configuration variable named MyAddress. If you use the Substitution Component to include the MyAddress configuration variable in your page, your address appears in its place. Even better, if you move down the street, you simply need to update the configuration variable instead of editing your address in every single page.

To create your own configuration variables, follow these steps:

1. **Choose Tools➪Web Settings.**

   The Web Settings dialog box appears, with the Configuration tab visible.

2. **In the dialog box, click the Parameters tab.**

3. **Click the Add button.**

   The Add Name and Value dialog box appears.

4. **Type the name of the configuration variable in the Name text box.**

   Choose a one-word name that is brief and descriptive, such as **MyAddress**.

5. **Type the value of the configuration variable in the Value text box.**

   FrontPage substitutes this text whenever you display the configuration variable in your page. For the MyAddress configuration variable, for example, you enter your address here.

6. **Click OK to close the Add Name and Value dialog box.**

   The configuration variable's name and value appear in the box in the Parameters panel.

7. **To add more configuration variables, repeat Steps 3–6.**

   Modify or remove configuration variables by clicking their names in the list and then clicking the Modify or Remove buttons.

8. **After you finish creating configuration variables, click OK to close the Web Settings dialog box.**

To insert the newly created configuration variables in your Web site, follow the steps in the previous section.

Adding a keyword search to your Web site

A *keyword search* is to a Web site what a knowledgeable tour guide is to a big city: Both help you bypass the flotsam and get straight to the stuff you want to see. The Search Form Component enables you to add a keyword search to your Web site in as few as two mouse clicks.

With the Search Form Component nestled in a page in your Web site, visitors enter words or phrases into a text box and then click a button to activate the search. In a moment, a linked list of Web pages matching the search request appears. From there, your visitors need only to click a link to go to a particular page.

You can add a search form to an existing page or create a separate search page with the help of the Search Page template. To access the template, choose File⇨New⇨Page to open the New dialog box, and then double-click Search Page in the template list.

To use a FrontPage keyword search, you must publish your Web site on a host web server that has FrontPage Server Extensions installed. For more information about FrontPage Server Extensions, see Chapter 16.

To use the Search Form Component, follow these steps:

1. **In your page, place the cursor where you want the search form to appear.**

2. **In the Standard toolbar, click the Insert Component button, and from the pop-up menu that appears, choose Search Form.**

   The Search Form Properties dialog box appears.

3. **In the Label for Input text box, type the text label that prompts visitors to enter keywords.**

   The default label is Search for:.

4. **In the Width in Characters text box, type the width (in number of characters) of the text box into which visitors enter keywords.**

5. **In the Label for "Start Search" Button text box, type the text label that appears on the button that visitors click to start the search.**

   The default label is Start Search.

6. **In the Label for "Clear" Button text box, type the label that appears on the button that visitors click to erase the contents of the keyword text box.**

   The default label is Reset.

7. **In the dialog box, click the Search Results tab.**

8. **If necessary, specify the scope of the search by typing information in the Word List to Search text box.**

   The default value All causes the search to look through every page in your Web site. To restrict the search to a discussion group in your Web site, type the name of the discussion group directory here. (I show you how to create a discussion group — complete with a keyword search — in "Can We Talk" on the CD.)

   To hide pages from the Search Form Component, stow them away in the _private folder. (In Chapter 2, I show you how to move pages into folders.) For example, you may not want the search to extend to pages that aren't yet complete.

9. **Mark the check boxes next to the items you want to appear in the search results list.**

   After a visitor performs a search, the Search Form Component returns a linked list of matching pages. You can display additional information in the results page by clicking one or more of the following check boxes: Display Score (Closeness of Match) sorts the pages according to the closeness of the match; Display File Date shows the date that the page was last modified; and Display File Size (in K bytes) shows the page's file size.

10. **Click OK to close the Search Form Properties dialog box.**

    A search form appears in your page.

To preview and test the search form, you must use FrontPage in conjunction with a web server outfitted with FrontPage Server Extensions. To try out the keyword search, you can either publish your Web site and preview the live version of the site, or you can use FrontPage together with a local web server. For more information about using a local web server, see Appendix A.

If, after you test the keyword search, the search results seem out-of-date, make sure that you save all open pages in FrontPage and then recalculate your Web site's hyperlinks (choose Tools➪Recalculate Hyperlinks). Now republish your site and try your search again — it should be fit as a fiddle.

Part IV
Taking Your Web Site to a New Level

The 5th Wave   By Rich Tennant

Principal

"I found these two in the multimedia lab morphing faculty members into farm animals."

In this part . . .

*W*eb publishing can be a solitary task or can happen as part of a team, with many authors creating different chunks of the Web site. In this part, you discover how FrontPage helps you collaborate with a workgroup. You find out how to control who can access your Web site. You also discover how to publish your site on the World Wide Web.

Chapter 15

Sharing Access to Your Web Site

· ·

In This Chapter

▶ Streamlining teamwork with FrontPage collaboration features

▶ Controlling Web site access with permissions

▶ Changing access passwords

· ·

*F*rontPage gives you the power to control who can access your Web site. In this area of your life, at least, you can think of yourself as all-knowing and all-seeing.

By using FrontPage, you can regulate two types of site access: authoring access by members of your Web site-building team and browsing access by potential Web site visitors. FrontPage also contains a host of tools to make the collaboration process run smoothly. In this chapter, I show you how to use FrontPage workgroup and security features.

Collaborating with a Web-Building Team

Few Web sites are one-person operations. Even if you're the lucky staff member who got tapped to put together the company Web site, you probably need input and cooperation from other members of the team. If those team members are sitting in an office 50 miles away, collaboration can be tricky.

Fortunately, FrontPage is equipped to handle the job. Because FrontPage is able to work in conjunction with a web server, any team member with access to an internal network or Internet connection and a computer outfitted with FrontPage 2000 can work on the company Web site. The process goes like this:

1. You work with the team to plan the site's content and design.

2. **You create a core version of the site, which you then publish on a host web server (either an ISP's web server or a central company network server that's not accessible to the outside world).**

3. **All team members log on to the central server and use FrontPage to access the site to add and change pages.**

By using FrontPage to connect to a site stored on a central web server, more than one person can work on the site simultaneously, making collaboration among far-flung team members possible.

Of course, keeping track of the team's workflow is potential chaos. Fortunately, FrontPage comes with several features that help rein in the production process so everyone knows what's going on and what needs to happen next.

To use FrontPage's collaboration features, you must first publish your Web site on a web server that has FrontPage Server Extensions installed. (I talk more about FrontPage Server Extensions in Chapter 16.)

Assigning pages and setting review status

FrontPage enables you (and other site authors) to designate who's responsible for each page in the site and to specify the page's review status. To do so, follow these steps:

1. **Open the Web site directly from the central web server.**

   I explain how to open Web sites on remote web servers in Chapter 1.

2. **In the Folder List, right-click the page and then, from the pop-up menu that appears, choose Properties.**

   (You can set the same assignment and status for more than one page at a time. In the Contents section of the Folders View, while holding down the Ctrl key, first click each page to select it, and then right-click any of the selected pages and choose Properties from the pop-up menu.)

   The Page Properties dialog box appears.

3. **In the dialog box, click the Workgroup tab.**

   The Workgroup tab becomes visible (see Figure 15-1).

4. **In the Assigned To list box, type the name of the person responsible for the page, or choose a name from the list.**

   If the list is empty, add names by clicking the Names button. The Usernames Master List dialog box appears. In the dialog box's New Username text box, enter a new name and then click Add. When you're finished, click OK to close the dialog box and return to the Page Properties dialog box.

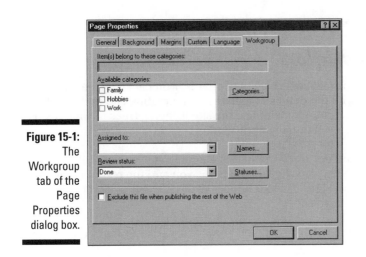

Figure 15-1:
The
Workgroup
tab of the
Page
Properties
dialog box.

5. **In the Review Status list box, type the page's status, or choose a status from the list.**

   The list box contains four preset status listings: Code Review, Content Review, Legal Review, and Manager Review. To change or add to the list, click the Statuses button. The Review Status Master List dialog box appears. To add an item to the list, in the dialog box's New Review Status text box, enter a status and then click Add. To delete an item from the list, click the item and then click Delete. When you're finished, click OK to close the dialog box and return to the Page Properties dialog box.

6. **Click OK to close the Page Properties dialog box.**

Each time an author updates a page, he can update the page's review status (for example, changing the status from *In process* to *Finished*), keeping the rest of the team abreast of the site's progress.

For a quick overview of who's responsible for each page and of your site's overall review status, take a look at the Assigned To and Review Status reports (choose View⇨Reports⇨Assigned To or View⇨Reports⇨Review Status).

Both reports enable you to change page assignments and review status without having to access the Page Properties dialog box. To do so, highlight the row that contains the file you want to change. Next, click the file's entry in the Review Status or Assigned To column to make the list box visible. Click the list box and then type in a different option or choose a different option from the list.

Using the Tasks View to keep track of workflow

The most challenging task for a Web publisher is, ironically, the most mundane: remembering all the details associated with creating and updating the Web site. If a team of authors maintains the site, keeping track of what needs to be done becomes even more complicated.

The creators of FrontPage understand this dilemma and thoughtfully included the Tasks View. The Tasks View helps you and the rest of the team keep track of unfinished tasks and is almost as easy to use as that pad of sticky notes sitting on your desk.

To see the Tasks View, in the FrontPage Views Bar, click the Tasks button (or choose View➪Tasks).

Creating tasks

You can create two types of tasks: tasks linked to specific pages and independent tasks (tasks that need to be done but aren't associated with a particular page in the Web site, such as writing a press release or phoning a consultant).

To create a linked task, select the page with which you want to associate a task. (For example, open the page in the Page View, or click a page icon in the Folder List.) Then, in the Standard toolbar, click the down-arrow next to the New Page button to display a pop-up menu. From the pop-up menu, choose Task (see Figure 15-2).

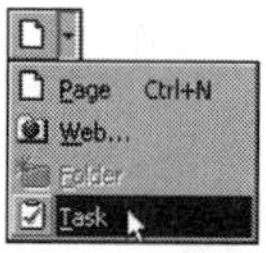

Figure 15-2: Creating a new task.

To create an independent task, without first selecting a page, follow the same steps as you do for adding a linked task.

When you create a new task, the New Task dialog box appears (see Figure 15-3).

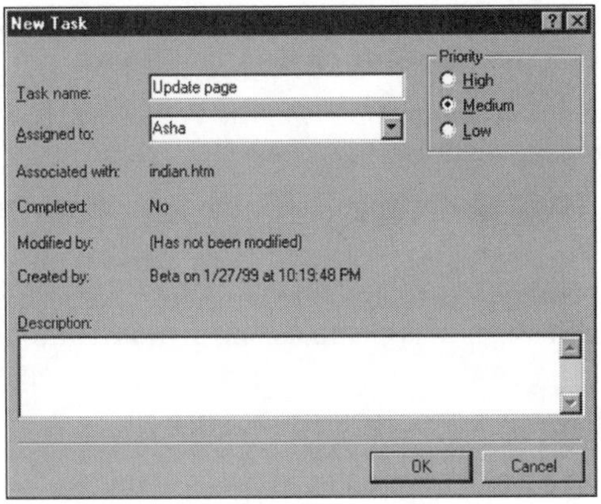

New Task

Task name: `Update page`

Assigned to: `Asha`

Priority:
- ○ High
- ● Medium
- ○ Low

Associated with: indian.htm

Completed: No

Modified by: (Has not been modified)

Created by: Beta on 1/27/99 at 10:19:48 PM

Description:

OK   Cancel

Figure 15-3:
The New
Task dialog
box.

To specify the task's details, follow these steps:

1. **In the Task Name text box, enter a brief, descriptive title.**

2. **In the Assigned To text box, enter the name of the person responsible for completing the task or choose a name from the list.**

   You set up the master list of names visible in the Assigned To text box by creating a username master list. For instructions, see "Assigning pages and setting review status" earlier in this chapter.

3. **In the Priority area, click the radio button next to the task's priority level.**

4. **If necessary, enter details or instructions in the Description box.**

5. **Click OK.**

   The dialog box closes, and the task appears in the Tasks View.

To modify a task, in the Tasks View, double-click the task. In the Task Details dialog box that appears, make any changes you want, and then click OK to close the dialog box.

Starting and completing tasks

When you are ready to begin working on a linked task listed in the Tasks View, FrontPage helps track your progress. When you're finished, FrontPage marks the task as completed, enabling you to maintain a history of site tasks. (If you simply want to mark an independent or linked task as complete, I include directions at the end of this section.) To start working on a linked task, do this:

1. **In the Tasks View, right-click the task you want to complete and then, from the pop-up menu that appears, choose Start Task.**

   The page associated with the task opens in the Page View. In the page, make whatever changes you want.

 2. **After you finish working on the page, click the Save button to save your work.**

   Because FrontPage remembers that you're working on a task, the Microsoft FrontPage dialog box appears asking if you want to mark the task as completed.

3. **If the task is complete, click Yes; otherwise, click No.**

   If you click Yes, in the Tasks View, the task's status changes from Not started to Completed. If you click No, the status changes to In progress.

To mark a linked or independent task as completed, in the Tasks View, right-click the task and then choose Mark As Completed from the pop-up menu.

Checking documents in and out

By turning on FrontPage *source control,* you can ensure that only one person at a time can edit a file — a crucial detail when several people are working on the Web site at the same time.

With source control turned on, authors must check out files before they can edit them. While a file is checked out, it can be opened and read by other authors but can only be edited by the author who checked the file out.

After the author is finished working on the file, she can save the changes and check the file back in, making the newly edited file available to the group again.

To turn on FrontPage source control, follow these steps:

1. **With the Web site open in FrontPage, choose Tools⇨Web Settings.**

   The Web Settings dialog box appears, with the General tab visible.

2. **In the dialog box, mark the check box called Use Document Check-In and Check-Out, and then click OK.**

   The dialog box closes and another dialog box appears, prompting you to recalculate the Web site.

3. **In the dialog box, click Yes.**

   The dialog box closes, and FrontPage turns on source control.

With source control activated, in the Folder List, little green dots appear next to the Web site's page icons (see Figure 15-4). Green dots indicate that the files are available to be checked out.

To check out a file, proceed as if you are opening the file; FrontPage pops open a dialog box asking if you want to check the file out. Click Yes. From there, the file opens as usual, and you can edit as you like. When you check out a file, the green dot is replaced by a red check mark in your FrontPage display. Any other authors who are logged on at the same time see a small padlock icon in place of the red check mark, indicating that the file is currently checked out by another author and cannot be accessed.

You can also check out files without opening them. By doing so, you "lock out" other potential authors while you're working on a group of files. To check out a page without opening the page, in the Folder List or in the Contents area of the Folders View, right-click a file (or selected group of files), and from the pop-up menu that appears, choose Check Out. After the files are checked out, you can open and close the files without having to worry about another author accessing the files.

When you are finished editing a file, save the changes and close the page. To check the page back in (making it available to the rest of the team), in the Folder List, right-click the page's icon, and from the pop-up menu that appears, choose Check In. In the Folder List, the red check mark is replaced by a green dot, and all is well.

Automating site updates with the Categories Component

When lots of people work on a Web site at the same time, keeping the site updated can be a major pain. After all, updating a site means more than just adding new pages; for those new pages to be accessible from the rest of the site, you must also scatter hyperlinks throughout the site that lead to the new pages.

FrontPage simplifies this process with the Categories Component. When inserted into a page, this Component creates a list of hyperlinks to every page that belongs to a particular category. (More about what a category is in a moment.) Each time a new page is added to the category, the Categories Component updates its list of hyperlinks with a link to the new page.

In FrontPage parlance, a *category* describes a subset of the information in your Web site. Depending on how your site is organized, you can set up whatever categories you like.

For example, say your Web site contains three main sections: What's New, Company Services, and Technical Support. You can set up three corresponding categories for your Web site, and then assign each page in the site to one of the categories. You can then insert the Categories Component into any page in your Web site. From then on, each time you add a new page to a category, a hyperlink leading to that page appears in the page containing the Component.

 If you are working in a multiauthor environment in which more than one person logs onto a central server to edit the site, that server must have FrontPage Server Extensions installed. If, however, you're creating your Web site on your own computer with no other authors involved, you can assign pages to categories and use the Categories Component whether or not your host web server has FrontPage Server Extensions installed.

Setting up and assigning pages to categories

To set up categories, do this:

1. **In the Folder List, right-click a page. From the pop-up menu that appears, choose Properties.**

   (It doesn't matter which page you choose; the categories you define apply to the entire Web site.)

   The Properties dialog box appears.

2. **In the dialog box, click the Workgroup tab.**

   The Workgroup tab becomes visible.

3. **To create a list of categories, click the Categories button.**

   The Master Category List dialog box appears.

4. **In the New Category text box, enter a new category name and then click Add.**

   The category appears in the category list.

5. **To add more categories, repeat Step 4.**

   To delete categories, click a category in the list and then click Delete.

6. **When you're finished, click OK to close the dialog box and return to the Properties dialog box.**

   The categories you created appear in the dialog box's Available Categories list.

7. **Click OK to close the Properties dialog box.**

To assign a category to a page, follow these steps:

1. **In the Folder List, right-click the page and then, from the pop-up menu that appears, choose Properties.**

   (To assign the same category to more than one page at a time, in the Contents section of the Folders View, while holding down the Ctrl key, first click each page to select it, and then right-click any of the selected pages and choose Properties from the pop-up menu.)

   The Properties dialog box appears.

2. **In the dialog box, click the Workgroup tab.**

3. **In the Available Categories box, click the category name(s) to which you want the page to belong.**

   You can choose more than one category.

4. **Click OK to close the Properties dialog box.**

Inserting the Categories Component

Now that you have assigned your site's pages to different categories, you are ready to insert the Categories Component into a page. When viewed with a web browser, the Categories Component replaces itself with a list of hyperlinks leading to pages in the category (or categories) you specify. To insert the Categories Component, do this:

1. **In the page, place the cursor where you want the Component to appear.**

2. **In the Standard toolbar, click the Insert Component button and then, from the pop-up menu that appears, choose Categories.**

   The Categories Properties dialog box appears (see Figure 15-5).

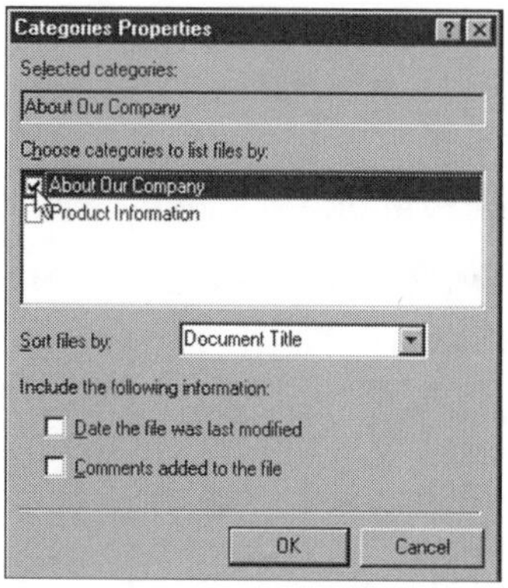

Figure 15-5:
The
Categories
Properties
dialog box.

3. **In the dialog box's C̲hoose Categories to List Files By box, mark the category or categories for which you want the Component to list hyperlinks.**

   If you choose more than one category, the Component will list hyperlinks to pages in each category but won't distinguish between the different categories.

   If you want the page to display links to separate categories in the same page, and you want those categories to remain distinct, you're better off inserting a separate Component for each category.

4. **Choose an option from the S̲ort Files By list box.**

   The Component can list pages alphabetically by title or sequentially according to the date the page was last modified.

5. **If you want the Component to list the date the page was last modified, or the comments added to the page, mark the appropriate check box.**

   I explain how to add comments to a file at the end of this section.

6. **Click OK.**

   The dialog box closes, and a placeholder for the Categories Component appears in the page.

To see the Component at work, preview the page by using a web browser. (The Preview tab doesn't do the trick for this Component.) When viewed with a browser, the Component is replaced by a list of links to the pages in the specified categories. FrontPage uses the page's title as the hyperlink text.

You can attach descriptive comments to any page in your Web site. To do so, in the Folder List, right-click the page's icon and, from the pop-up menu that appears, choose Properties. The Page Properties dialog box appears, with the General tab visible. In the dialog box, click the Summary tab. In the dialog box's Comments box, enter your comments, and then click OK to close the dialog box.

Keeping Your Web Site Secure

When I was a kid, I knew that I'd pushed my parents too hard if they said, "You live in our house — you live by our rules!" To this statement, I could offer no rebuttal — just resigned acceptance and a few minutes of serious pouting.

Well, this Web site is *your* home page — which means that *you* get to make the rules. You control who can update or change your Web site and even who can view it. The process is called *adjusting permissions,* and with FrontPage, you can perform the task with ease.

Permissions are different levels of Web site access. The Web site's host web server contains a list of usernames and associated passwords, along with corresponding levels of Web site access. By using FrontPage, you can access the web server's permission settings to add and change users and specify levels of access.

This feature is a blessing in a workgroup setting, because you can control who has authoring privileges. When each team member logs onto the central server to access the site, a FrontPage dialog box appears prompting them to enter a username and password, and FrontPage grants access based on the permissions you've specified.

Permissions also enable you to create a private Web site. When visitors try to access a private Web site, their web browser pops open a dialog box requesting a username and password. Unless they enter the name and password you specify, they are unable to browse the Web site.

FrontPage provides for the following three levels of access:

- **Administer:** Giving someone Administer access makes them an *administrator,* and an administrator can create, edit, and delete Web sites and pages and adjust a Web site's permissions. Every Web site must have at least one administrator.

- **Author:** An author can create, edit, or delete pages but cannot create or delete Web sites or adjust the Web site's permissions.

✔ **Browse:** A person with Browse access can only view a Web site with a web browser; that person can't edit the Web site or even open the site in FrontPage.

To adjust your Web site's permissions by using FrontPage, you must first publish the Web site on a web server that has FrontPage Server Extensions installed. (For more information about FrontPage Server Extensions, read Chapter 16.) Even then, some ISPs don't allow subscribers to adjust permissions settings. Be sure to check with your ISP or system administrator before working with Web site permissions.

Setting permissions

To control who may edit your Web site, you use FrontPage to specify administrators and authors. If you want your Web site to appear only to authorized visitors, you can also create a list of people with browsing access.

If the Web site for which you're setting permissions contains a subweb, the steps are slightly more complex. By default, all subwebs have the same permissions as their *Parent Web site* (the top-level Web site) and are visible to anyone with a web browser. Therefore, if you adjust the Parent Web site's permissions, you automatically change the permissions of all its subwebs as well. (If you're not sure what a subweb is, refer to Chapter 1.) In the following steps, I show you how to change the Parent Web site's permission settings, as well as how to give your Parent Web site and subwebs independent permission settings.

To access a server's permissions, the server must have FrontPage Server Extensions installed. Furthermore, permissions settings are conditional upon which web server program your ISP uses, as well as your own computer's network setup. The instructions in this chapter illustrate how permissions work for the Apache web server, a popular UNIX-based web server program used by many ISPs. If your host web server uses a different web server program or runs a different operating system, the steps will be slightly different. If in doubt about any of this information, check with your ISP or system administrator and refer to the FrontPage Help system by choosing Help➪ Microsoft FrontPage Help.

To set your Web site's permissions, follow these steps:

1. **Publish the Web site.**

   I explain how to publish in Chapter 16.

2. **Open the Web site directly from the host web server.**

   In Chapter 1, I explain how to open Web sites stored on remote servers.

3. **Choose Tools➪Security➪Permissions.**

   The Permissions dialog box appears.

   - If the Web site is a Parent Web site, you see two tabs at the top of the dialog box: Users and Groups (or Computers); skip ahead to Step 5.
   - If the Web site is a subweb, the dialog box contains a third tab: Settings. The Settings panel enables you to change the permission setting so that the Web site uses its own set of permissions instead of inheriting the Parent Web site's permission settings.

4. **If you want the subweb to have its own permission settings, click the Use Unique Permissions for This Web radio button and then click Apply.**

   FrontPage adjusts the Web site's permissions.

5. **Click the Users tab.**

   The Users tab becomes visible.

6. **To add a user, click the Add button.**

   The Add Users dialog box appears.

7. **In the Name text box, type a username.**

   Usernames and passwords are case sensitive, which means that FrontPage sees gonzo and Gonzo as two different names.

8. **In the Password text box, type a password.**

9. **Type the password again in the Confirm Password text box.**

10. **In the Allow Users To area of the dialog box, click the radio button for the level of access that you want the individual to have.**

11. **Click OK.**

    The Add Users dialog box closes, returning you to the Users tab of the Permissions dialog box.

12. **To restrict browsing access to authorized users only, click the Only Registered Users Have Browse Access radio button.**

    If you don't mark this radio button, anyone with an Internet connection and a web browser can browse your Web site.

13. **Click Apply to activate changes and continue adjusting permissions, or click OK to activate changes and close the Permissions dialog box.**

For details on creating group permission settings, refer to the FrontPage Help system by choosing Help➪Microsoft FrontPage Help.

Changing permissions

You can easily adjust your Web site's permissions. You can, for example, upgrade an author's access to administrator, or you can remove a user from the list of people authorized to browse the site. To edit a user's permissions, follow these steps:

1. **Open the Web site, and then choose Tools⇨Security⇨Permissions.**

   The Permissions dialog box opens.

2. **If it's not already visible, click the Users tab.**

3. **In the user list, click the name of the user whose permissions you want to change and then click Edit.**

   The Edit Users dialog box appears.

4. **In the Allow Users To area of the dialog box, click the radio button for the user's new permission setting, and then click OK.**

   The Edit Users dialog box closes, returning you to the Users panel of the Permissions dialog box.

5. **Click Apply to activate changes and continue adjusting permissions, or click OK to activate changes and close the Permissions dialog box.**

To remove a user from the permission list, follow the same instructions, but in Step 3, click the Remove button rather than the Edit button.

Changing your password

If you're serious about keeping your FrontPage data secure, changing your password every couple of weeks is a good idea, especially if you're a Web site administrator.

To change your password, follow these steps:

1. **Open the Web site, and then choose Tools⇨Security⇨Change Password.**

   Depending on the type of host web server or operating system, you may not be able to change your password by using FrontPage. If the Change Password command appears dimmed, it means that the person in charge of the server must change your password for you. Speak to your ISP or system administrator for details.

   The Change Password for User dialog box appears. (Where *User* is the username of the person currently accessing FrontPage — presumably that's you.)

2. **In the <u>O</u>ld Password text box, type your old password.**

3. **In the <u>N</u>ew Password dialog box, type your new password.**

4. **Retype your new password in the <u>C</u>onfirm Password dialog box.**

5. **Click OK.**

   The dialog box closes, and FrontPage updates your password.

To change another user's password, you must remove the user from the user list, add the user again, and then choose a new password for the user.

Chapter 16

Making Your Worldwide Debut

In This Chapter

▶ What *publishing your Web site* means

▶ The skinny on FrontPage Server Extensions

▶ Excluding unfinished pages from publishing

▶ Going public

▶ Keeping your site fresh

Drumroll, please! It's the moment you've been waiting for . . . time to unveil your painstakingly prepared, lovingly built Web site and make the site visible to the entire world.

In this chapter, I show you how to publish your Web site, and I give you tips on how to update your site to keep it fresh and interesting.

What "Publishing Your Web Site" Means

Publishing your Web site means making the site visible on the World Wide Web for all to see. For your site to be accessible on the Web, you must store all the site's files and folders on a computer called a web server. A web server is a computer running special web server software that maintains a high-speed, round-the-clock connection to the Internet. (In Chapter 4, I give you an overview of how the World Wide Web's client-server setup works.)

Most people gain access to a host web server by getting an account with an Internet Service Provider (ISP). Having an account at an ISP enables your computer and modem to establish a connection to the Internet. After you're connected, you can then use the Internet to send and receive e-mail, browse the Web, and transfer files between computers.

Most ISPs also provide a limited amount of publishing space on their web servers as part of your regular monthly fee. The amount of storage space varies (some ISPs provide as little as 5MB; mine provides 50MB); check with your ISP for details.

Not sure how much file space your FrontPage Web site takes up? Try this: In the Folder List, right-click the site's top-level folder and then choose Properties. The dialog box that appears displays the Web site's total file size (not including the size of any subwebs; you must open subwebs separately to check their size).

If your ISP doesn't offer the range of Web site hosting features you need, you may want to host your Web site with a separate company called a *Web presence provider* (WPP). WPPs rent out space on their web servers but don't offer dial-in Internet access or other Internet services, such as e-mail or newsgroups. Some WPPs offer a wider range of specialized Web site hosting features than do ISPs.

Before you shell out the extra money for the services of a WPP, be sure to read through your ISP's list of features. Your account may come with a bunch of Web site hosting features with which you're not aware.

Several innovative companies provide web server space for free. All you have to do is to register at the company's Web site and endure plenty of banner advertising. (These companies help fund their operations with the advertising revenue.) Popular choices include Tripod (www.tripod.com), Geocities (www.geocities.com), and Angelfire (www.angelfire.com).

If you're building a corporate Web site, your company may maintain its own web server and Internet connection. If so, speak to your company's system administrator for details about your network setup.

The Skinny on FrontPage Server Extensions

Having access to a host web server is only part of what you need to publish a FrontPage Web site. For some FrontPage features to work, the web server must have a set of auxiliary programs called *FrontPage Server Extensions* installed. FrontPage Server Extensions are a special set of programs that act as translators between FrontPage and the web server program.

What about Office Server Extensions?

Office 2000 contains a bunch of new Web- and intranet-enabled features that work with the help of a set of auxiliary programs called Office Server Extensions. Like FrontPage Server Extensions, Office Server Extensions work together with the web server program to power special tasks associated with Office.

If you're publishing your FrontPage Web site on a web server that has Office Server Extensions installed, you gain all of the benefits of FrontPage Server Extensions plus extra functionality for your Office documents. For more details about the Web-savvy features of Office 2000, pick up a copy of *Microsoft Office 2000 For Windows For Dummies* by Wallace Wang and Roger Parker or *Microsoft Office 2000 All In One For Dummies* by Bill Helling (both published by IDG Books Worldwide, Inc.).

Installing FrontPage Server Extensions on a web server is a big job, which is why many ISPs and system administrators have yet to fully support FrontPage. The number of FrontPage-friendly ISPs is growing every day, however, and as FrontPage becomes more widespread, the number is sure to increase. (I give you tips on finding an ISP to host your FrontPage Web site in the sidebar "Finding a FrontPage ISP," later in this chapter.)

The good news is that you can publish a FrontPage Web site on *any* web server — including servers without FrontPage Server Extensions installed — with certain caveats. You can use all FrontPage features except for the following, which rely on FrontPage Server Extensions:

- ✔ The _private folder
- ✔ Subwebs
- ✔ The Confirmation Field Component
- ✔ The Search Form Component
- ✔ The Hit Counter Component
- ✔ FrontPage workgroup features, including source control
- ✔ FrontPage discussion groups
- ✔ FrontPage user registration systems
- ✔ The Database Results Wizard and the Send To Database form handler
- ✔ Permissions

Finding a FrontPage ISP

The benefits of publishing your Web site with a FrontPage-friendly ISP are clear. But how do you find a FrontPage ISP? Check local computer magazines and newspapers, ask friends for recommendations, and lean on Microsoft for assistance. The Publish Web dialog box (available when you choose File⇨Publish Web) contains a button called WPPs that leads your web browser straight to the Microsoft FrontPage Web site, where you find an index of FrontPage Web presence providers (most of whom offer full Internet access as well).

If you're happy with your current ISP, consider publishing your Web site at Tripod (www.tripod.com). Tripod provides free Web space to anyone who registers . . . and, best of all, Tripod supports FrontPage Server Extensions.

Additionally, if you want to open or create a Web site on a remote web server, that server must have FrontPage Server Extensions installed.

The built-in FrontPage form handler works hand-in-hand with FrontPage Server Extensions but can be adjusted to work on any web server. See Chapter 10 for details.

If you attempt to publish a site that contains FrontPage Server Extensions-related features on a host web server that doesn't have FrontPage Server Extensions installed, FrontPage pops open a dialog box that lets you know the pages won't work properly and prompts you to change or remove the pages.

If you intend to publish your site on a server that doesn't support FrontPage Server Extensions, you can customize FrontPage to make available only those options that will work properly (see Chapter 5 for instructions). You must do this *before* you create your Web site. Changing FrontPage compatibility options does not remove features from your site; it simply instructs FrontPage to dim those commands and menu items that require FrontPage Server Extensions to be able to work.

One final hurdle: With the release of FrontPage 2000 comes a new release of FrontPage 2000 Server Extensions, which means that every ISP that supports FrontPage must upgrade from the older versions to the new 2000 version of the FrontPage Server Extensions. If you publish a FrontPage 2000-authored site on a host server running an older version of the FrontPage Server Extensions, the following features won't work properly:

- ✔ Subwebs
- ✔ FrontPage workgroup features, including source control
- ✔ The Database Results Wizard and the Send To Database form handler

If your ISP or company still uses an older version of the FrontPage Server Extensions, chances are it is in the process of upgrading. (Give your system administrator or ISP a call to make sure.)

Going Public

Time to take your show on the road. In this section, I show you how to publish your Web site.

Excluding unfinished pages from publishing

Before the curtain goes up, give your Web site the white glove test so that the site makes its debut with style and polish. Rev up the FrontPage spell checker (choose Tools⇨Spelling), make sure that your hyperlinks work properly (choose View⇨Reports⇨Broken Hyperlinks), and go through every inch of your site using a web browser — preferably more than one browser model.

If your site contains any pages that aren't yet ready for public viewing, you can tell FrontPage to hold those pages back while publishing the rest of the site. To do so, access the Publish Status report by choosing View⇨Reports⇨ Publish Status (see Figure 16-1).

Publish Status							
Name	Title	Publish	Modified Date	Review Status	Size	Type	In
index.htm	Welcome to my first Web S...	Publish	1/27/99 10:02 PM		7KB	htm	
photography.h...	Photography	Publish	1/27/99 10:55 PM	Done	1KB	htm	
hobbies.htm	My Hobbies	Publish	1/27/99 10:55 PM	Done	1KB	htm	
italian.htm	Italian Cooking	Publish	1/27/99 10:55 PM	In process	3KB	htm	
indian.htm	Indian Cooking	Publish	1/27/99 10:55 PM	Done	1KB	htm	
gallery.htm	Gallery	Publish	1/27/99 10:55 PM	Done	2KB	htm	
cooking.htm	Cooking	Don't Publish	1/27/99 10:55 PM	In process	6KB	htm	
contact_me.htm	Contact Me	Publish	1/27/99 9:56 PM		1KB	htm	
sunset_small.gif	images/sunset_small.gif	Publish	1/27/99 8:39 PM		3KB	gif	im
sunset.gif	images/sunset.gif	Publish	11/19/98 11:21 AM		23KB	gif	im
lightbulb.gif	images/lightbulb.gif	Publish	1/27/99 8:37 PM		3KB	gif	im
frontpage.gif	images/frontpage.gif	Publish	11/19/98 11:21 AM		4KB	gif	im
city_small.gif	images/city_small.gif	Publish	1/27/99 8:39 PM		2KB	gif	im
city.gif	images/city.gif	Publish	11/19/98 11:21 AM		14KB	gif	im

Figure 16-1:
The Publish Status report.

Inserting a time stamp

Some folks like their Web pages to display the date and time the page was last edited, so visitors know they are looking at timely information. FrontPage can automate this task for you, as follows:

1. **Place the cursor in the page where you want the time stamp to appear.**

2. **Choose Insert⇨Date and Time.**

   The Date and Time Properties dialog box appears.

3. **In the dialog box, choose a display option.**

   If you want the time stamp to reflect when you (or another author) last edited the page, choose Date This Page Was Last Edited. If you want the time stamp to reflect edits *and* automatic updates (such as if a Component automatically inserts information into the page), choose Date This Page Was Last Automatically Updated.

4. **In the Date Format list box, choose the date format you prefer.**

5. **In the Time Format list box, choose the time format you prefer.**

6. **Click OK to close the dialog box and insert the time stamp into your page.**

The Publish Status report lists details about every file inside your Web site, including the filename, title, the date and time the file was last modified, and more. The report's Publish column specifies whether the file is ready for publishing: *Publish* means that the file is ready to go and will be published or updated the next time the Web site is published, and *Don't Publish* means that the file is still in progress and will not be published or updated the next time the Web site is published.

To change a file's publish status, in the Publish Status report, highlight the row that contains the file you want to change. Next, click the file's entry in the Publish column to make the publish status list box visible. Click the list box and then choose Publish or Don't Publish.

If you exclude a page from being published that is linked to from another page in the site, that link will not work properly in the live version of the site. Therefore, before you publish, be sure to remove any hyperlinks that lead to unfinished pages. For instructions on how to do this, see Chapter 6.

Publishing your Web site

After you've given your Web site a thorough once-over, the next step is to find out your publishing URL. This URL tells FrontPage where in the host web server's file system to store your Web site. On servers that have FrontPage

Server Extensions installed, the URL may look something like `http://www.server.com` or `http://www.server.com/~username`. On servers that don't have FrontPage Server Extensions installed, the URL may instead begin with `ftp://`. (The difference has to do with the method or *protocol* FrontPage uses to connect to the web server and transfer the files.)

If in doubt, your ISP or system administrator can tell you your publishing URL. You must have the correct URL in hand in order to publish your Web site.

To publish your Web site for the first time, follow these steps:

1. **In FrontPage, open the Web site you want to publish.**

   If the site is already open in FrontPage, be sure to save any changes you have made to the site's pages.

2. **Activate your Internet connection.**

3. **Choose File⇨Publish Web.**

   The Publish Web dialog box appears (see Figure 16-2).

Figure 16-2:
The Publish
Web dialog
box.

Publish Web

Specify the location to publish your web to:

http://www.server.com   Browse...

WPP's... Click here if you don't have a web presence provider

○ Publish changed pages only
○ Publish all pages, overwriting any already on the destination

☐ Include subwebs
☐ Secure connection required (SSL)

Options ±   Publish   Cancel

4. **In the dialog box, type the Web site's publishing URL in the list box called Specify the Location to Publish Your Web To.**

   The URL you enter in this dialog box is specific to your web server and is different from what is pictured in Figure 16-2.

5. **If your Web site contains subwebs and you want to publish the Parent Web site and subwebs together, mark the Include Subwebs check box.**

   (If you don't see this option, click the Options button to expand the dialog box.)

   Note: Be sure to read the sidebar "Publishing a Web site that contains subwebs," later in this chapter, for important information about publishing subwebs.

6. **Click OK.**

   The Publish Web dialog box closes. A pause occurs as FrontPage contacts the host web server. If the web server contains security features (most do), the Name and Password Required dialog box appears.

7. **In the Name and Password text boxes, enter the username and password you chose at the time you established your account, and then click OK.**

   The dialog box closes, and FrontPage copies all your Web site files to the host web server. Depending on the size of your Web site and the speed of your Internet connection, this process may take a few minutes. (Watch your screen for messages explaining what's going on.)

   FrontPage takes care of file management and cleanup duties as it publishes your site. For example, if the host web server contains files at the publishing URL that are not part of the Web site you're publishing, FrontPage gives you the option of deleting those files from the host web server.

   If the host server has FrontPage Server Extensions installed and the host web server recognizes a default home page filename other than `index.htm`, FrontPage changes the home page filename on the host web server and updates any associated hyperlinks.

Publishing a Web site that contains subwebs

If you divided your Web site into a Parent Web and subwebs, when you publish the network of sites, you must maintain the identical file structure on the host web server in order for the hyperlinks between those sites to work. (If you are unfamiliar with the terms Parent Web and subweb, refer to Chapter 1.) If you publish the Parent Web and subweb at the same time, FrontPage takes care of everything, and you don't need to give the file system a second thought. If, however, you want to publish the subweb by itself, you need to keep a few details in mind.

Here's an example. Say you build a FrontPage Web site on your hard drive stored at `C:\My Webs`. The Web site contains a subweb stored at `C:\My Webs\subweb`. (The Web site at `C:\My Webs`, therefore, is the Parent Web.) Your publishing URL is `http://www.mysite.com`.

When you publish the Parent Web, you specify the publishing URL (`http://www.mysite.com`). You can choose to publish just the Parent Web, or you can publish the Parent Web and the subweb at the same time.

To publish just the subweb by itself, you must specify the publishing URL followed by a slash (/) and the subweb's folder name. In this case, you would publish the subweb to `http://www.mysite.com/subweb`.

If the host server recognizes a home page filename other than `index.htm` and *does not* have FrontPage Server Extensions installed, you must change the home page filename in the local copy of your Web site and publish the site again (see "Keeping Your Site Fresh," later in this chapter, for instructions). If you're not sure which home page filename your host server recognizes, ask your ISP or system administrator.

After the work is done, the Microsoft FrontPage dialog box pops up to tell you the publishing process was a success.

8. In the dialog box, click Done.

The dialog box closes.

Congratulations — your site is now visible to the world!

You're Live!

Pass the bubbly! Your Web site has joined the Internet community, and you can now call yourself a true-blue Web publisher. Using your web browser, visit your live Web site at its new URL and, just to be safe, give the site one last check. If all is well, set off those fireworks!

You might even want to line up a group of sympathetic testers who use different types of computers and browsers and ask them to give your site a run-through. Even if everything works perfectly when viewed with your computer and browser, a glitch might pop up when viewed from a different platform.

If something doesn't work properly, fix the problem on the *local* copy of your Web site — the copy stored on your computer — and publish your Web site again. I show you how in the following section.

Now that your Web site is open to the public, you need to let everyone know you're entertaining visitors. Whether your Web site sells products or showcases your Fabio photo collection, the site can benefit from publicity. How do you invite the world to your home page? Here are a few tried-and-true suggestions:

- ✔ **Search services:** List the page with popular search services, such as Yahoo! (`www.yahoo.com`), Excite (`www.excite.com`), and AltaVista (`www.altavista.com`). Each search service posts listing instructions on its Web site.

- ✔ **E-mail signature:** Include your Web site URL in the signature line of your e-mail messages. Most e-mail programs enable you to append a few lines of text to the bottom of every message.

✔ **Newsgroups:** Post a discreet announcement to newsgroups that discuss related topics. Keep your announcement low-key and respectful. If you blanket a newsgroup with advertising hype, not only will you irk the other newsgroup participants (hence, bad word-of-mouth), your publicity campaign may well backfire.

✔ **Traditional print advertising:** Add your Web site URL to business cards, letterhead, and print advertising.

✔ **Word-of-mouth:** Invite your friends and colleagues to visit your Web site and encourage them to spread the word.

For more promotion inspiration, check out the links in the Publicity Corner of my Web site, the Web Publishing Online Resource, at `www.ashaland.com/webpub`.

Keeping Your Web Site Fresh

Stagnant Web sites are as appealing as day-old pastry. On the World Wide Web, freshness counts, so keep your site vital by changing its content, updating its graphics, and adding new features regularly.

To update your site (or to correct any mistakes you find), you make changes on the local copy of your Web site and then publish the Web site again. To update the site's changed pages, a single button-click does the trick, as follows:

1. **In FrontPage, open the Web site you want to update and make (and save) whatever changes you want.**

2. **Activate your Internet connection.**

3. **In the Standard toolbar, click the Publish Web button.**

   If the host server supports security features, the Name and Password Required dialog box appears.

   If you update your site several times during a single FrontPage session, this dialog box only appears the first time you update the site.

4. **In the Name and Password text boxes, enter your username and password and then click OK.**

   The dialog box closes, and FrontPage copies the changed pages to the host web server.

Your site is now fresh as a daisy.

To republish the entire Web site (not just the changed pages) or to publish the Web site to a different location, follow the steps in the previous section called "Going public."

If your host web server supports FrontPage Server Extensions, you can use FrontPage in conjunction with Microsoft Internet Explorer (Version 3.0 or later) to quickly edit the *live* version of your site. To do so, launch Internet Explorer and use it to view your Web site at its live URL. In the Internet Explorer toolbar, click the Edit button. FrontPage launches and prompts you for your username and password. After you enter the correct username and password, the Web site opens in FrontPage, and the selected page opens in the Page View. Make whatever changes you want and then save the page. The changes are immediately visible on the World Wide Web. Be sure to make the same changes on the local copy of your Web site so that the next time you publish the Web site, your changes are preserved.

Part V
The Part of Tens

The 5th Wave By Rich Tennant

"OK LARRY, ENOUGH ABOUT THE ELECTION. LET'S TALK INTERNET BROWSERS. NEITHER ONE OF THE TWO BIG ONES ADEQUATELY REPRESENTS THE USER, WHICH IS WHY I PLAN TO LAUNCH A THIRD ALTERNATIVE—THE 'REFORM BROWSER.'"

In this part . . .

In the following chapters, I give FrontPage a rest and share some tips that help you expand your Web-publishing consciousness. I list ten things you can do with your Web site and ten Net spots you don't want to miss.

Chapter 17

Ten Things You Can Do with Your Web Site

• •

*W*eb sites are like rubber bands — if you put your mind to the task, you can think of a million ways to use them. To get you started, here are ten (minus one) of my favorite ways to use a Web site.

Make a Million Bucks

Some folks see flashing dollar signs as they think of the millions of potential customers surfing the Web. Secure credit card transactions and electronic commerce technology are giving rise to more and more virtual storefronts. So fire up the Corporate Presence Wizard (I show you how to use Wizards in Chapter 1) and create a slick business Web site. Who knows — maybe you're destined to become the next Net Rockefeller.

Keep in Touch

Your parents settled down in Miami. Your best friend is pursuing her dreams in Paris. Your brother works all the time and has no energy for phone calls. No problem! Use your Web site as a meeting place for friends and family. They can log on and share gossip 24 hours a day. Set up a password-protected discussion group that only registered loved ones can enter. (See "Can We Talk" on the CD for details on setting up a discussion group and Chapter 15 for information about password-protecting your Web site.) Post a family tree online with hyperlinks to the home pages of other wired (or should I say weird?) relatives. Devote a page to everyone's birthdays and anniversaries. Scan snapshots from the last family reunion and put them online for all to see.

Impress Potential Employers

A Web site is the perfect place to toot your own horn. Post your résumé online. List your accomplishments, talk about your goals, and point to the Web sites of past workplaces and your alma mater. Add your Web site address to your business card and present the card, along with a firm handshake, to people you want to impress.

Impress Geeky Friends

If you like to play "my hard drive is bigger than your hard drive" with your friends, use your Web site to become king or queen of the technical hill. Download obscure Java applets and ActiveX controls — or, better yet, write your own — and install them in your Web site. (Check out "Advanced Additions" on the CD to find out how to add Java applets and ActiveX controls to your Web pages.) Create a list of favorite Web destinations and include links to the home pages of Sun Microsystems, Microsoft, and the Official Star Trek Fan Club. Cultivate a vocabulary full of techie buzzwords and use them often. ("Yeah, I added a JavaScript to my IMG tags, but it wonked out after my friend ran it with Netscape 7.4026b and her box crashed.")

"Wire" Your Company

If your employees have Web access or are part of a company *intranet* (an internal network based on Internet technology but accessible only to company insiders), use a Web site as a central information hub. Publish company policies and the employee handbook. (Think of all the paper you save by updating these documents online.) Set up discussion groups for each of your departments. Start a Web-based company newsletter. Use the Guest Book page template to create an employee suggestion box. (See Chapter 3 for instructions on how to create a new Web page by using a page template.)

Spread the Word about a Good Cause

Can you think of something that you want the world to know? A Web site is potentially visible to millions of people, making your site one of the most effective ways to spread the word about an important cause. Create that Web site, publicize the site far and wide, and watch interested visitors start pouring in. (See Chapter 16 for promotion tips.) Create a feedback form or a discussion group so that visitors can ask questions. (For more information about forms, see Chapter 10, and for details about discussion groups, see "Can We Talk" on the CD.) Offer to send more information to those who are interested. Keep your site up-to-date so that your Web site becomes a well-respected resource for information and news. Insert a hit counter in your home page so that everyone knows just how many other people care about the issue you support (see Chapter 14 for information on hit counters).

Indulge Your Artistic Side

If you're a poet, artist, or musician, publishing a Web site is the next best thing to a local reading, a gallery showing, or a concert. Use your Web site to showcase your creativity. Transform your favorite poems into Web pages and invite feedback. Include sample clips of your music. If your work is on display somewhere else, tell visitors where to go to experience your talent.

Incite World Revolution

The photocopy machine put the power of the press into everyone's hands. Social activists produce reams of flyers and leaflets to help spread the word about important issues. The Web makes broadcasting information even easier — a Web page is visible to millions, and you don't need to staple it to telephone poles or hand it to passersby. So use your Web site to make a difference. Get on your virtual soapbox and issue a call to action.

Erect a Personal Monument

It's inherently thrilling to see your name in print or engraved on a plaque. Perhaps the permanence is the key — the idea that your words or ideas will always be there. A Web site can be the electronic equivalent of a personal monument — a place where you can immortalize the things most important to you. Scan your favorite vacation snapshots and create an online travel diary. Start an unofficial fan club for someone you admire (you'd be surprised by how many celebrities have e-mail addresses and participate in online chats). Use your Web site as a place to pay tribute to the things that inspire you.

Chapter 18

Ten Web Spots You Don't Want to Miss

*T*hroughout this book, I point you to Web sites that I find particularly helpful. In this chapter, I highlight ten must-see spots you really shouldn't miss (with a bonus site thrown in for good measure).

To make it easier for you to visit these sites, I include the *FrontPage 2000 For Dummies* Web Links Page on the CD that comes with this book. The Web Links Page contains links to every Web site mentioned in the book. For details, see Appendix B.

Microsoft FrontPage Home Page

This site is the place to go for all things FrontPage. Here you find FrontPage tips and information, free accessory downloads, and links to related resources. Most important, you can access online support and FrontPage help, including FrontPage newsgroups, a list of frequently asked questions, and much more.

Go to www.microsoft.com/frontpage to visit the Microsoft FrontPage home page.

Microsoft Support Online

Got a question? This site has answers. The mammoth online database contains thousands of articles that answer common software questions or explain annoying bugs. The Support Online site contains articles pertaining to all Microsoft products, including FrontPage.

Check out Microsoft Support Online at support.microsoft.com.

Netscape Web Site

Huh? Why am I pointing you to the home page of Microsoft's sworn enemy, you ask? Because Netscape Navigator is in widespread use, and if you want to design pages that look good to all your visitors, you need to stay abreast of Netscape developments. Better yet, install Netscape Navigator (it comes on the CD included with this book). Even if you don't use the program to browse the Web, use Netscape in combination with the FrontPage Preview In Browser button to preview your Web pages. The more browsers you use to preview your pages, the better you know how your pages appear to your visitors.

Browse the Netscape Netcenter at `www.netscape.com`.

Know the Code: HTML For Beginners

The surest way to beef up your Web publishing savvy is to learn HTML, the language behind every Web page. Plenty of good books on the subject are out there, but if you're fired up to get started, check out this straightforward, easy-to-take introduction to HTML basics.

You find *Know the Code: HTML For Beginners* at `www.builder.com/Authoring/Basics`.

Builder.com

If you like to keep on top of Web publishing happenings, make this Web site one of your regular stops. Builder.com contains practical how-to articles for all sorts of Web tricks.

Go to `www.builder.com` to check out Builder.com.

Webmonkey

The attitude-filled folks at HotWired bring you this in-depth Web site. Enthusiastic Web publishers can spend hours here; the site contains information on everything from basic Web page creation to advanced design and programming tips.

Go to `www.webmonkey.com` to see Webmonkey.

Learn the Net

If you just want to know how the Internet works, visit this well-organized Web site. You'll find tons of good, well-written information, but not so much that you'll be overwhelmed. Be sure to check out the excellent section devoted to Web publishing.

Start learning about the Internet at `www.learnthenet.com`.

Search.com

The Web contains information about the current political climate, pictures of African wild dogs, and several online dating services — the trick is finding these sites. By using Search.com, you can find just about anything, with links to the Web's most popular search utilities, an online Yellow Pages, an e-mail address directory, maps, flight information. . . . You name it — it's here.

Start your Internet exploration at `www.search.com`.

Download.com

Everyone keeps talking about the gigabytes of free software available on the Net, but where do you get all that stuff? This site groups shareware offerings into categories such as Business, Multimedia and Design, and Internet. Or you can look at a list of top picks or the most-popular titles.

Surf on over to Download.com at `www.download.com`.

Dummies.com

If you can't wait to get your hands on your next good read, check out the Dummies.com Web site (or the Web site of the creators of the *...For Dummies* series, IDG Books Worldwide). Find out which new books are about to hit the shelves, pick up some savvy tips, or order a title online.

Visit `www.dummies.com` and `www.idgbooks.com`.

Web Publishing Online Resource

In closing, I invite you to my little corner of the Web. I maintain this repository of interesting and useful Web publishing resources so that you can have a single place to visit when you're not sure where else to find the Web publishing answer you're looking for. If you visit, be sure to drop me a note!

By the way, I maintain the Web site using FrontPage. The Verify Hyperlinks command saves me hours of link-checking time, and the Page View's table-creation tools make it possible for me to lay out the pages nicely. I don't know how I ever got along without FrontPage. Really.

You find the Web Publishing Online Resource at `www.ashaland.com/webpub`.

Part VI

Appendixes

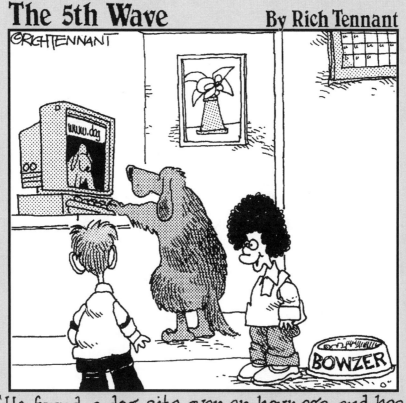

In this part . . .

The two appendixes contain extra info you may find helpful. If you want help with installing FrontPage on your computer, look no further than Appendix A. After you pull the CD out of the plastic cover on the back of this book, Appendix B helps you easily install all the CD goodies on your computer.

Appendix A
Installing FrontPage

*I*f installing FrontPage on your computer seems like a gargantuan task, help is here. In this appendix, I take you step-by-step through the FrontPage installation process. (For information about how to install the other programs included on the FrontPage program CD, refer to the documentation included with FrontPage.) I also talk about why and how to use FrontPage in conjunction with a local web server.

Microsoft FrontPage 2000 is not included on the CD that comes with this book. You need to purchase FrontPage at a software or computer store. See www.microsoft.com/frontpage for details. For information about the book's CD, refer to Appendix B.

System Requirements

The following list tells you what you need, hardware- and software-wise, to run FrontPage 2000. You may be tempted to skip this section, thinking, "I have FrontPage, so what else could I need?" Read it anyway. If you don't recognize something in this list, you may not have it.

If you intend to install the stuff on the CD-ROM that comes with this book, refer to Appendix B for additional system requirements.

To use Microsoft FrontPage 2000, you need

- ✔ Microsoft FrontPage 2000 (either the stand-alone version, or the version that comes bundled with Microsoft Office 2000 Premium Edition)
- ✔ Personal or multimedia computer with a 486 or higher processor
- ✔ Microsoft Windows 95/98 operating system, Microsoft Windows NT Workstation 4.0 or later, or Microsoft Windows NT Server 4.0 or later (will not run on earlier versions of Microsoft NT or on Windows 3.1)
- ✔ 16MB of memory for use on Windows 95/98; 32MB for use on Windows NT
- ✔ 167MB of available hard-disk space

- ✔ CD-ROM drive

- ✔ VGA or higher-resolution video adapter (Super VGA, 256-color recommended)

- ✔ A mouse or compatible pointing device

- ✔ An account with an Internet Service Provider or access to a company web server with at least 5MB of storage space for your Web site files. Preferably, your ISP's or company's web server supports FrontPage Server Extensions. (For information on FrontPage Server Extensions, flip to Chapter 16.)

If you intend to install the other programs that come on the FrontPage program CD, check the Microsoft FrontPage Web site at www.microsoft.com/frontpage for additional system requirements.

Installing FrontPage 2000 on Your Computer

FrontPage 2000 comes in two versions: the version bundled with Microsoft Office Premium Edition and the stand-alone version. I wrote the following steps using the version of FrontPage bundled with Office, but the Setup programs for both versions are very similar. If you're installing the stand-alone version, chances are these steps will give you all the help you need.

If not, remember that your licensed copy of Office or FrontPage gives you access to real, live Microsoft technical support engineers, either by telephone (it's a long-distance call, but you get help right away) or via e-mail (no long-distance charges, but you must wait one business day for an answer). For details about your support options, see www.microsoft.com/support.

To install FrontPage, follow these steps:

1. **Turn on your computer and CD-ROM drive.**

   If your computer is already on, exit any programs that are currently open.

2. **Insert the Microsoft Office CD 1 (or the Microsoft FrontPage 2000 CD), with the label facing up, into your CD-ROM drive.**

   In a moment, the opening screen of the Setup program appears. The Setup program takes you step-by-step through the installation process.

   If no opening screen appears, on your Windows desktop, double-click the My Computer icon to open a window that contains icons for each of your computer's drives. To launch the Setup program, double-click the CD-ROM icon.

3. In the opening screen, enter your customer information.

Enter your name, initials, organization, and the 25-digit CD key (you'll find the CD key on a sticker affixed to the CD case).

4. Click the Next button.

The End-User License Agreement dialog box appears.

5. Read the License Agreement. When you're finished, click the radio button next to I Accept the Terms in the License Agreement, and then click Next.

After you click Next, the Ready To Install dialog box appears.

You can, at any time, return to a previous dialog box to change your settings by clicking the Back button or exit the Setup program by clicking the Cancel button.

6. Click Install Now.

By clicking Install Now, you're telling the Setup program to perform a typical installation (this option works fine for most folks). If you want more control over the installation process and don't mind a few extra steps, click Customize, and then follow the Setup program's directions. When you're finished customizing the installation procedure, the Setup program presents you with an Install Now button.

After you click Install Now, the Installing dialog box appears. This dialog box stays in view as the Setup program installs Office (or the stand-alone version of FrontPage) on your computer. The setup process takes a few minutes, so sit back and relax. When installation is almost complete, a dialog box appears asking for permission to restart your computer in order to finish the setup process.

7. Click Yes.

The dialog box closes, and your computer restarts. The startup process may take longer than usual, because Windows is busy updating its system settings.

As soon as your Windows desktop appears, you're ready to begin using FrontPage.

8. To launch FrontPage, click the Start button, and then choose Programs⇨Microsoft FrontPage.

FrontPage launches, and you're ready to roll.

Using FrontPage Together with a Local Web Server

As you create your Web site with FrontPage, it's a good idea to *preview* the site using a web browser. By previewing your site, you give it a test run, making sure everything works perfectly before you publish the site on the World Wide Web. (I talk more about previewing your Web site in Chapter 3.)

To be able to test certain interactive features, however, your Web site requires the help of a web server. Without a web server running in the background, interactive forms, discussion groups, hit counters, and other server-based features can't work properly.

What do you do? You have two options, as follows:

✔ You can publish your Web site, and then preview and test the "live" version of the site (for directions on how to publish your site, see Chapter 16).

✔ You can test the site on your own computer by using FrontPage in conjunction with a local web server.

When I say *local web server,* I mean a web server program installed on your computer. That's right, you can install a web server on your own computer so that you can test all the capabilities of your Web site without having to make the Web site visible to the rest of the world. When you're satisfied everything is working as it should, you can publish the Web site to the "live" host web server.

By installing a web server on your own computer, you don't erase the need to publish your finished site on a web server hosted by your company or ISP. The local web server is there just for your own testing purposes, or to share the site with a few members of your workgroup.

Using the Microsoft Personal Web Server 4.0

FrontPage works with several types of web server programs, but for local testing purposes, I recommend using the Microsoft Personal Web Server 4.0 (*PWS 4.0* for short). PWS 4.0 is easy to install, easy to use, and it works hand-in-hand with FrontPage 2000. Better yet, it's free. PWS 4.0 in included on the Windows 98 CD, in the Windows NT 4.0 Option Pack, and can be downloaded from the Microsoft Web site at `www.microsoft.com/windows/ie/pws/default.htm`.

Note: If your computer is running Microsoft NT Server 4.0 or later, you already have a local web server installed. NT Server's built-in web server, called Internet Information Server 4.0 (IIS 4.0) also works with FrontPage. Refer to the NT Server Help system for more information about IIS.

If you decide to install PWS 4.0, make sure your computer measures up to the following minimum hardware and software requirements (in addition to those listed at the beginning of this appendix):

- ✔ 33 MHz 486 processor
- ✔ 16MB RAM
- ✔ 100MB hard drive space
- ✔ VGA monitor
- ✔ Microsoft Windows 95 or later, or Microsoft Windows NT Workstation 4.0 or later
- ✔ Microsoft Internet Explorer 4.01 or later

For directions on how to install PWS 4.0, refer to the Windows Help system by clicking the Start button and then choosing Help. If you download PWS 4.0 from the Microsoft Web site, follow the directions given there.

After you install PWS 4.0, the program launches automatically when you turn on your computer. To remind you that it's running, the PWS icon appears in the System Tray of the Windows Taskbar, next to the digital clock.

"Publishing" your Web site to a local web server

After your local web server is up and running, you can go back to using FrontPage as you always did. When you're ready to test your Web site's server-based features, you "publish" the site to the local web server.

When I say "publish" in this case, I don't mean that you make your site visible on the World Wide Web. You simply use FrontPage's publishing feature to store a copy of the Web site in the local web server's default folder or *home directory.* (For PWS 4.0, the default home directory location is `C:\Inetpub\wwwroot`.) The web server knows to look inside the home directory for the files that make up the Web site you want to test.

To publish your Web site to your local web server, follow the same steps as you would to publish your site on the World Wide Web with one difference: Instead of using the URL of your host web server as the site's publishing URL, you use the URL of the local web server.

In the steps that follow, I show you how to find out the publishing URL for PWS 4.0 (if you're using a different local web server, refer to the web server's documentation for instructions):

1. **In the System Tray of the Windows Taskbar, right-click the PWS icon, and from the pop-up menu that appears, choose Properties.**

   The Personal Web Manager launches (see the accompanying figure). The publishing URL is listed in the Publishing section of the dialog box, along with the location of the web server's home directory. (On my computer, the publishing URL is `http://beta`.)

Publishing URL   Home directory location

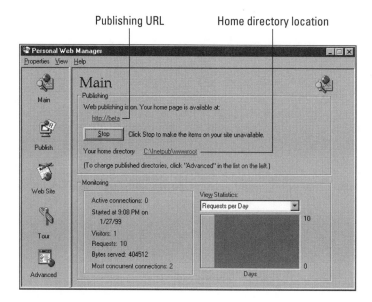

Note: For information about how to use the other Personal Web Manager options, in the Personal Web Manager dialog box, choose Help➪Personal Web Server Topics.

2. **Write down the publishing URL on a piece of paper, and then, in the upper-right corner of the Personal Web Manager dialog box, click the Close button (it looks like a little X).**

After you publish your Web site to the local web server, you can preview the site by entering the local web server's URL into your Web browser.

Publishing your Web site on PWS 4.0 simulates publishing your site on a host web server that has FrontPage Server Extensions installed. If your host server doesn't have FrontPage Server Extensions installed, when you first create the Web site, be sure to set FrontPage's compatibility options to disable any features that require FrontPage Server Extensions. I explain how to do this in Chapter 5.

Creating and opening Web sites directly from the local web server

If you find yourself having to constantly publish your site to the local web server to be able to test the site's capabilities, you may prefer to continue working on the version of the site stored on the server. That way, you don't have to go through publishing the site to test it; you simply use the FrontPage Preview in Browser command to preview the site. You can also create new Web sites using the local web server. Because the site is already "on" the server, you can test all of the Web site's features without first having to publish.

To create or open a Web site using the local web server, follow the directions in a sidebar in Chapter 1 about using the local web server's URL in place of the host web server's URL.

Appendix B

What's on the CD

*T*he CD-ROM included with this book contains goodies that make Web publishing with FrontPage easier and more fun.

Even better, the CD comes with its own interface that helps you easily install the programs onto your hard drive. In this appendix, I show you how work with the CD-ROM.

Microsoft FrontPage 2000 is not included on the CD that comes with this book. You need to purchase FrontPage 2000 at a software or computer store. See www.microsoft.com/frontpage for details.

System Requirements

Before you install the programs on the CD, make sure your computer meets the minimum system requirements listed below. If your computer doesn't match up to most of these requirements, you may have problems using the contents of the CD.

- ✔ A PC with a 486 or faster processor.
- ✔ Microsoft Windows 98, Windows 95, or Windows NT 4.0 or later.
- ✔ At least 16MB of RAM.
- ✔ At least 20MB of hard drive space available to install all the software from this CD. (You'll need less space if you don't install every program.)
- ✔ A CD-ROM drive — double-speed (2x) or faster.
- ✔ A monitor capable of displaying at least 256 colors or grayscale.
- ✔ A modem or network connection with a speed of at least 14,400 bps.

To check whether your computer requires the special installation named 16-bit in the interface, follow these steps:

1. **Right-click the My Computer icon located in the upper-left corner of your computer's screen.**

2. **Select Properties from the pop-up menu that appears.**

3. **Click the Performance tab.**

4. **In the Performance status group, look for the line labeled "File System:" If it says "32-bit," then select the 32-bit installation; otherwise, select the 16-bit installation.**

If you need more information on computer basics, check out *PCs For Dummies,* 6th Edition, by Dan Gookin or *Windows 95 For Dummies,* 2nd Edition, by Andy Rathbone (both published by IDG Books Worldwide, Inc.).

What You'll Find on the CD

Here's a quick overview of the stuff on this CD.

Several of the programs included on the CD are *shareware*, which means they are free for you to use for a limited evaluation period, after which you must either buy the software or delete the software from your system. If you decide to keep a shareware program, please support the software makers who so generously make their programs available in this way.

FrontPage 2000 For Dummies Web Links Page

Web site addresses or *URLs* can be long and cumbersome to type into your browser. To save you time and hassle (and to encourage you to visit the Web sites I mention throughout the book), I've placed links to all the sites I mention on this Web page. Simply open this page in a web browser and click away.

Bonus chapter: Can We Talk?

Turn to this chapter if you want to add a FrontPage discussion group to your Web site. This chapter explains the ins-and-outs of the Discussion Web Wizard, plus all the other details you need to know to customize and set up an interactive discussion group.

Bonus chapter: Advanced Additions

If you're ready for a challenge, read this chapter to find out how to add ActiveX Controls, Java applets, and plug-ins to your Web site. These add-ins enable you to integrate dynamic, interactive content into your Web site that, in some cases, goes beyond what FrontPage Components and Dynamic HTML can achieve. Check it out!

Custom-designed Web page templates

I designed a set of Web page templates especially for readers of this book. Examples include an online resumé, a personal homepage (one for adults and one for young people), a simple feedback form, and a form confirmation page. Check out the Readme file and the inerface on the Cd for details on accessing the files.

Internet tools

Netscape Communicator

Netscape Communicator is a suite of handy Web software, including Navigator, the most popular web browser available today. Chances are you're already using Navigator. If not, here's your chance to take the program for a spin. If you're already a Navigator user but haven't recently upgraded your copy, check out this version. You'll like what you see.

Microsoft Internet Explorer

Along with Netscape Navigator, Microsoft Internet Explorer is the high-end browser many people use to surf the Web. Internet Explorer is able to display different design goodies from those of Navigator, so I recommend installing both browsers on your computer and using them to preview your Web pages.

WS_FTP LE 4.6

FrontPage makes publishing your Web site a snap, but if you need to transfer other types of files or download software over the Internet, this intuitive FTP program gets the job done. WS_FTP LE is free to individuals for non-commercial home use; to students and faculty of educational institutions; and to U.S. federal, state, and local government employees. (Other users can try this version but must purchase WS_FTP Pro.)

Utilities

Quarterdeck CleanSweep

In this era of shareware and freeware mania, you may be tempted to fill your hard drive with freely available software programs. If you're not careful, your hard drive will soon be cluttered with unused files. Quarterdeck CleanSweep helps you manage this problem. CleanSweep logs every program you install on your computer, and later, if you decide to uninstall a program, removes the program without a trace.

Adobe Acrobat Reader

This free program enables you to view and print PDF files. (In fact, the bonus chapters on the CD are stored as PDF files, so you have a use for this program right away.) Many Web designers use PDF files to preserve the design of a particular document and also to make the document available across platforms and over the Web.

Paint Shop Pro

The stand-alone version of FrontPage comes with a graphics program called Microsoft Image Composer, and the Office-bundled version of FrontPage comes with Microsoft PhotoDraw. Both are excellent programs in their own right, but if you're looking for another option, use Paint Shop Pro to create and edit your Web graphics. This shareware graphics program contains drawing, cropping, screen capture, and painting tools, plus special effects such as drop shadows, chiseling, and tiling. Paint Shop Pro can also save just about any image format as GIF or JPEG, making it possible for you to use those graphics in your Web site.

WinZip

This shareware file-compression program "zips" several large files into a single, easy-to-transport file called a ZIP file. ZIP files are especially useful for sending files attached to e-mail messages — a common task for many Web publishers.

ThunderBYTE AntiVirus

It's essential to protect your computer from malignant Net-borne computer viruses. This program scans your hard drive for viruses and eradicates any it finds. Think of this virus-checking program as preventative medicine.

How to Use the CD

To install the items from the CD onto your computer, follow these steps:

1. **Insert the CD into your computer's CD-ROM drive and close the drive door.**

2. **In the Windows Taskbar, click the Start button and then choose Run.**

3. **In the dialog box that appears, type** D:\setup.exe.

   Your computer probably lists your CD-ROM drive as drive D (if you're not sure, double-click the My Computer icon on your desktop to see). If your CD-ROM drive uses a different letter, type the appropriate letter in the Run dialog box.

4. **Click OK.**

   A License Agreement dialog box appears.

5. **Read through the License Agreement, and then click Agree.**

   The CD Welcome screen appears.

6. **Click anywhere on the Welcome screen to continue.**

   The CD interface appears. The interface does all the work of installing the programs on your computer. On the interface, the CD contents are divided into categories, the names of which appear on the screen.

7. **To view the items in a category, click the category's name.**

   A list of items in the category appears.

8. **For more information about an item, click the item's name.**

   Be sure to read this information. Some programs may require you to adjust your computer's settings before you install, and this screen tells you where to go for that information, if necessary.

9. **To install the item on your computer, click the Install button. If you don't want to install the item, click the Go Back button to return to the previous category screen.**

   After you click Install, the CD interface drops to the background while the item installs on your computer.

   When installation is complete, the CD interface reappears. (If the interface remains hidden behind other windows, click once anywhere in the interface's window to bring it to the front.)

10. **To install other CD goodies, repeat Steps 7, 8 and 9.**

11. **When you're done installing CD items, click the Quit button to close the interface.**

    A final screen appears, asking if you're sure you want to quit.

12. **Click Yes.**

    The CD interface closes. You can remove the CD from your CD-ROM drive now.

If You Have Problems (Of the CD Kind)

I tried my best to compile programs that work on most computers with the minimum system requirements. Alas, your computer may differ, and some programs may not work properly for some reason.

Most likely, you don't have enough memory (RAM) for the programs you want to use, or you have other programs running that are affecting installation or running of a program. If you get error messages like `Not enough memory` or `Setup cannot continue`, try one or more of these methods and then try installing the software again:

- ✔ **Turn off any antivirus software currently running on your computer.** Installation programs sometimes mimic virus activity and can incorrectly trip your anti-virus program's alarm. When you are finished installing programs, be sure to turn the anti-virus program back on.

- ✔ **Close all running programs.** The more programs you run simultaneously, the less memory is available to other programs (including installation programs). Installers also typically update shared files and programs. If those files and programs are in use by another program, the installer may not work properly.

- ✔ **Have your local computer store add more RAM to your computer.** This is, admittedly, a somewhat time-consuming and expensive step. However, as a long-term solution, adding more memory can really help the speed of your computer and allow more programs to run simultaneously.

If you still have trouble installing the items from the CD, please call the IDG Books Worldwide Customer Service phone number: 800-762-2974 (if you're calling from outside the U.S., use this phone number: 317-596-5261).

Index

• A •

absolute measurements, 175–177
absolute positioning, 259–261
access levels, 301–302. *See also*
    permissions
Acrobat Reader (on the CD), 341
active graphics, 239–240
Active Server Pages (ASP), 214
ActiveX controls (on the CD), 340
Add Choice dialog box, 204
Add this page to the Navigation view...
    message, 242
Address style, 92
Administer permission, 301
Adobe Acrobat Reader (on the
    CD), 341
aligning
  graphics, browser offsets, 157
  graphics in web browsers, 157
  graphics with text, 140–141
  paragraphs, 96–98
  table cell contents, 179
All Caps effect, 88
ALT text, 146–147
AltaVista, Web site, 315
Angelfire, Web site, 308
animation. *See also* Dynamic HTML
  GIF, 131
antivirus software (on the CD), 342
ASP (Active Server Pages), 214
author of this book, e-mail and Web
    site, 6
Author permission, 301

• B •

backgrounds
  images, 156–157
  setting with themes, 240
  sounds, 252–254
  in tables, 183
Banner Ad Manager Component, 269,
    270–273
Banner Ad Manager Properties dialog
    box, 272
banner ads, examples (Web site), 271
banners, 241–242. *See also* marquees
  repeating across pages. *See* shared
    borders
Blink effect, 88
bold text, 88
bookmarks, 119–121
borders
  frames, hiding, 227
  paragraphs, 98–99
borders, on graphics
  adding/removing, 143–144
  beveling, 152
borders, on tables
  color, 183–184
  thickness, 175
brightness of graphics, 152
Browse permission, 302
browser compatibility, summary of
    (Web site), 84
browser offsets, 157
BrowserCaps, Web site, 84
browser-safe palettes, 132
Builder.com, Web site, 326

bulleted lists, 93–94
bullets, customizing, 94

● **C** ●

Capitalize effect, 88
captions
  graphics, 148
  tables, 182
Cascading Style Sheets (CSS)
  applying several to one page, 267
  applying to multiple pages, 266–267
  creating, 264
  cross-platform issues, 89
  defined, 263
  embedding in pages, 265–266
  and font effects, 88
  modifying, 264
  positioning objects, 257
  Web site, 264
categories
  assigning pages to, 299
  defined, 298
  reporting, 33
  setting up, 298–299
Categories Component, 270, 298–301
Categories Properties dialog box, 300
CD (with this book)
  ActiveX controls, 340
  Adobe Acrobat Reader, 341
  contents, 340–342
  Discussion Web Wizard, 340
  FTP software, 341
  installing, procedure, 342–343
  installing, system requirements,
    339–340
  Internet tools, 341
  Java applets, 340
  Microsoft Internet Explorer, 341
  Netscape Communicator, 341
  Paint Shop Pro, 342
  plug-ins, 340

  Quarterdeck CleanSweep, 341
  ThunderBYTE AntiVirus, 342
  troubleshooting, 343–344
  utilities, 341–342
  Web sites of interest, list of, 340
  WinZip, 342
  WS_FTP LE 4.6, 341
Cell Properties dialog box, 180
cells. *See* table cells
CGI (Common Gateway Interface), 214
chats. *See* discussion groups
check boxes, 199–200
checkout status, reporting, 33
Child Webs. *See* subwebs
CleanSweep (on the CD), 341
clients, 69
clip art gallery, 138–140
collaboration. *See* Web-building teams
collapsible outlines, 96
color palettes, 132
colors
  basing on another page, 113
  converting to black and white, 152
  defaults, 110
  hyperlinks, selecting, 112
  repeating across pages, 113
  tables, 182–184
  text, 89–91
  theme, changing, 242–245
  theme, vivid, 239
  web browser background, 157
columns. *See* table columns
comments on Web pages, 49
Common Gateway Interface (CGI), 214
component errors, reporting, 32
Components
  Banner Ad Manager, 269, 270–273
  Categories, 270, 298–301
  Confirmation Field, 270
  defined, 269
  Hit Counter, 269, 273–274
  Hover Button, 269, 274–278

Include Page, 270, 280–282
Marquee, 270, 278–280
and Office 2000, 271
Scheduled Include Page, 270, 282–284
Scheduled Picture, 270, 282–284
Search Form, 270, 287–288
Substitution, 270, 284–287
Table of Contents, 270
troubleshooting, 285
Confirmation Field Component, 270
confirmation fields, 216–217
Confirmation Form template, 216–217
confirmation pages
creating, 215–216
defined, 208
content pages
defined, 221
filling frames with, 223–224
contrast of graphics, 152
converting
color to black and white, 152
documents to Web pages, 54–57
folders to subwebs, 43
graphics formats, 134
paragraphs to lists, 94
spreadsheets to Web pages, 54–57
subwebs to folders, 44
text documents to Web pages, 56
text to tables, 170
copyright notices, repeating across
pages. *See* shared borders
copyright symbol, 101
Corporate Presence Wizard, 16
corporate Webs, 16
Create Hyperlink dialog box, 105
creating
bookmarks, 119–120
Cascading Style Sheets (CSS), 264
confirmation pages, 215–216
folders, 41–42
form fields, 192–193
forms, 189–191

frames pages, 221–223
hotspots, 161–164
links in navigation bars, 124
one-line text boxes, 193–195
scrolling (multi-line) text boxes,
198–199
subwebs, 22–23
Web pages from RTF files, 54–57
creating hyperlinks
within the current site, 104–106
destinations for, 104
to downloadable files, 107
to e-mail addresses, 108–109
to files on your computer, 108–109
sources of, 104
to the World Wide Web, 106–107
creating tables
by converting text, 170
by drawing, 169–170
with Insert Table button, 167–168
with Insert Table command, 168–169
creating Web pages. *See also* Web-
building teams
as a blank page, 49
comments, 49
from other documents, 54–57
from templates, 48–49
unexpected backgrounds, 49
creating Web sites. *See also* subwebs;
Web-building teams
corporate Webs, 16
customer support Webs, 14
discussion groups, 16
importing existing sites, 19–21
personal Webs, 14
project-tracking Webs, 14
from scratch, 18–19
from a template, 14–16
tracking workflow, 14, 39, 294–296
with wizards, 16–18
your first time, 10–13
cropping graphics, 151–152

cross-platform issues
  aligning graphics, 157
  browser offsets, 157
  browsers, 72–73, 83–85
  Cascading Style Sheets (CSS), 89
  computers, 72
  cultural differences, 74
  fonts, 87
  servers, 83–85
  special effects, 84
  speed, 73
  text size, 89
CSS (Cascading Style Sheets). *See*
    Cascading Style Sheets (CSS)
Customer Support Web template, 14
cut, copy, and paste, 82

● *D* ●

Dale, Chuck (Web site), 130
default target frames, changing,
    228–231
deleting
  files and folders, 44–45
  graphics, 153
  hotspots, 164
  table cells, 178–179
  table columns, 178–179
  table rows, 178–179
  tables, 185
  Web sites, 25–26
desktop customization, 83
discussion groups, 16, 340
Discussion Web Wizard
  on the CD, 340
  defined, 16
dithering graphics, 132
Dornfest, Asha (e-mail and Web site), 6
download speed
  cross-platform differences, 73
  estimating, 32
  graphics, 132–133

text alternative for graphics, 146–147
  thumbnails, 153–155
Download.com, Web site, 59, 327
drag and drop, 82
Drop-Down Menu dialog box, 204
drop-down menus, 203–206
Dummies.com, Web site, 327
Dynamic HTML, 254–256. *See also*
    HTML (Hypertext Markup
    Language)

● *E* ●

Edit Hyperlink dialog box, 117
editing
  graphics, 148–149
  Web pages. See Page View
editing hyperlinks
  color, basing on another page, 113
  color, default, 110
  color, selecting, 112
  destination, 109–110
  text, 109
editors, associating with file types, 51
e-mail
  author of this book, 6
  hyperlinks to, 108–109
  including URLs in, 315
  sending form results as, 211–213
external hyperlinks, 103

● *F* ●

fading graphics, 152
FAQs (frequently asked questions), 48
feedback forms, 189
file paths, 17
file types, associating with an
    editor, 51
file usage, reporting, 31
filenames
  conventions for, 61
  for home pages, 21

files and folders
  converting folders to subwebs, 43
  creating folders, 41–42
  deleting, 44–45
  file paths, defined, 17
  folders versus subwebs, 42
  images folder, 30
  importing to a Web site, 39–41
  private folder, 30
  renaming, 42
find and replace, 82
flipping graphics, 152
floating objects, 257–259
floating tables, 172–173
folders. *See* files and folders
Folders View, 28–29
Font dialog box, 86
font effects, 88
font tools, 85–87
fonts
  cross-platform issues, 87
  defined, 85
  formats, copying, 86–87
form fields
  See also check boxes
  See also drop-down menus
  See also one-line text boxes
  See also radio buttons
  See also scrolling (multi-line) text
    boxes
  creating, 192–193
  defined, 188
  making mandatory, 196–197
  names, 188
  passwords, 195
  restricting data entry, 195
  tab order, 195
  values, 188
form handlers, 188
Form Page Wizard, 189–191
Form Properties dialog box, 209

form results
  confirmation fields, adding to
    pages, 217
  confirmation fields, defined, 216
  Confirmation Form template, 216–217
  confirmation pages, creating, 215–216
  confirmation pages, defined, 208
  defined, 188
  Reset buttons, 206–208
  saving as a file, 208–211
  sending as e-mail, 211–213
  sending to a custom script, 214
  sending to database programs, 215
  specifying target frames for, 230
  Submit buttons, 206–208
  validation failure pages, 208
Format Painter button, 86–87
Formatted style, 92
Formatting toolbar, 11, 85–86
form-handling scripts, 214
forms
  adding to a page, 192
  creating, from templates, 189
  creating, with Form Page Wizard,
    189–191
  description, 187–188
  design tips, 194
  feedback, 189
  guest book, 189
  interactive, 187
  search page, 189
  testing, 218
  user registration, 189
  validating, 201
frame properties, changing, 225–227
Frame Properties dialog box, 226
framed Web sites
  previewing, 233
  saving, 232–233
frames
  adding to frames pages, 224–225

frames *(continued)*
  alternatives for incompatible
    browsers, 231–232
  borders, hiding, 227
  browser support for, 220
  content pages, defined, 221
  content pages, filling frames with,
    223–224
  default target frames, changing,
    228–231
  defined, 219
  deleting, 225
  initial pages, 221
  locking position of, 227
  names, 225–227
  and navigation bars, 221
  nesting, 229
  No frames message, 231–232
  and shared borders, 221
  sizing, 225–227
  spacing, 225–227
  target frame options, 229
  target frames, changing, 228–231
frames pages
  adding frames, 224–225
  creating, 221–223
  defined, 221
frequently asked questions (FAQs), 48
FrontPage 2000
  beta changes and errata, Web site, 6
  exiting, 26
  installing, 332–333
  Main window, illustration, 11
  starting, 11
  system requirements, 331–332
  Web sites about, 6, 22
FrontPage Server Extensions
  defined, 18
  and permissions, 302
  publishing your site, 308–310
  and subwebs, 22
FTP software (on the CD), 341

• *G* •

Geocities, Web site, 308
GIF format
  animation, 131
  defined, 130
  displaying gradually, 150–151
  interlacing, 150–151
  transparency, 149–150
graphics
  aligning, browser offsets, 157
  aligning with text, 140–141
  ALT text, 146–147
  background images, 156–157
  beveled borders, 152
  borders, 143–144
  brightness, 152
  browser-safe palettes, 132
  captions, 148
  collections of, Web site, 139
  color palettes, 132
  contrast, 152
  converting color to black and
    white, 152
  cropping, 151–152
  deleting, 153
  displaying gradually, 150–151
  dithering, 132
  editing, 148–149
  fading, 152
  flipping, 152
  hyperlinks from, 105–106. *See also*
    image maps
  launching a graphics program for, 152
  *Microsoft Image Composer For
    Dummies,* 134
  positioning with tables, 140–142
  resampling, 145
  rotating, 152
  saving on Web pages, 64
  sizing, 144–145
  smoothing rough edges, 145

spacing, 143
special effects, 152
speed of loading. *See* download speed
on Submit/Reset buttons, 206–208
text alternative for, 146–147
text labels on, 148
theme, changing, 245–246
thumbnails, 153–155
tiling, 156–157
trimming, 151–152
watermarks, 156–157
Web Graphics For Dummies, 133
Web site, 130
wrapping text around, 140–142
graphics, inserting in Web pages
from the clip art gallery, 138–140
from the current site, 135
format conversion, 134
from the World Wide Web, 137–138
from your computer, 136–137
graphics formats
See also GIF format
See also JPEG format
See also PNG format
converting, 134
graphics programs
launching, 152
list of, 134
guest book forms, 189

• **H** •

Headings style, 92
Helling, Bill (Web site), 309
help, 26
helper applications, 250
Hit Counter Component, 269, 273–274
Hit Counter Properties dialog box, 274
home pages
defined, 10
filenames for, 21
renaming, 42

horizontal lines, 102
hotspots
changing hyperlinks for, 162
creating, 161–164
defined, 160
deleting, 164
displaying, 162
drawing, 161–162
labeling, 162–163
moving, 163
resizing, 163–164
Hover Button Component, 269, 274–278
Hover Button Properties dialog box, 275
hover buttons
defined, 274
graphic, 276–278
rectangular, 275–276
htm(l) file extensions, 61
HTML For Dummies, 77
HTML (Hypertext Markup Language). *See also* Dynamic HTML
description, 76–77
tags, 79–80
Web site about, 326
hyperlinks
See also bookmarks
See also hotspots
See also image maps
to bookmarks, 120
choosing words for, 106
defined, 10
to deleted files and folders, 45
displaying a map of, 37–39
distinguishing markings, 105
external, 103
internal, 103
mailto links, 108
on navigation bars, 106
from pictures, 104–105
to renamed files and folders, 42
repairing, 114–115, 117–118

hyperlinks *(continued)*
  reporting information about, 31–32
  rollover effect, 113–114
  as tables of contents, 106
  unlinking, 118–119
  verifying, 31–32, 115–116
hyperlinks, creating
  within the current site, 104–106
  destinations, 104
  to downloadable files, 107
  to e-mail addresses, 108–109
  to files on your computer, 108–109
  sources, 104
  to the World Wide Web, 106–107
hyperlinks, editing
  color, basing on another page, 113
  color, default, 110
  color, selecting, 112
  destination, 109–110
  text, 109
Hyperlinks View, 37–39
Hypertext Markup Language (HTML).
    See HTML (Hypertext Markup
    Language)

• *I* •

image maps. *See also* hotspots;
    hyperlinks
  choosing a graphic for, 160
  default hyperlink, 164
  defined, 159
  specifying target frames for, 230
images. *See* graphics
images folder, 30
Import Web Wizard, 19–21
importing
  existing sites, 19–21
  files and folders, 39–41
Include Page Component, 270, 280–282
indenting paragraphs, 96–98
index.htm(l) files, 21

initial pages, 221
Insert Table button, 167–168
Insert Table command, 168–169
Insert Table dialog box, 169
installing FrontPage 2000, 332–333
installing the CD
  procedure, 342–343
  system requirements, 339–340
interactive forms, 187
interlacing GIF graphics, 150–151
internal hyperlinks, 103
Internet information, Web site, 327
Internet Server Application
    Programming Interface
    (ISAPI), 214
Internet Service Providers (ISPs)
  defined, 10
  finding, 310
Internet tools (on the CD), 341
intranets, 14
ISAPI (Internet Server Application
    Programming Interface), 214
ISPs (Internet Service Providers)
  defined, 10
  finding, 310
italics, 88

• *J* •

James, Steve, 77
Java applets
  on the CD, 340
  defined, 271
JPEG format
  defined, 130
  transparency, 150

• *K* •

keyboard shortcuts, menus, 2
Know the Code: HTML For Beginners,
    Web site, 326

• L •

links. *See* hyperlinks
lists
    bulleted, 93–94
    bullets, customizing, 94
    collapsible outlines, 96
    converting paragraphs to, 94
    definition, 94–95
    within lists, 95
    nesting, 95
    numbered, 93–94
    outlines, 95–96
    splitting, 94
Lists style, 92
logos, repeating across pages. *See*
    shared borders

• M •

mailto links, 108
Marquee Component, 270, 278–280
Marquee Properties dialog box, 279
marquees, 278–280. *See also* banners
Menu bar, 11
menus, 2
message boards. *See* discussion
    groups
Microsoft, Web site, 22
Microsoft FrontPage Home Page, Web
    site, 325
*Microsoft Image Composer For
    Dummies,* 134
Microsoft Images Gallery, Web site, 139
Microsoft Internet Explorer (on the
    CD), 341
*Microsoft Office 2000 All In One For
    Dummies,* 309
*Microsoft Office 2000 For Windows For
    Dummies,* 309
Microsoft Personal Web Server 4.0,
    334–335
Microsoft Support Online, Web
    site, 325

More Colors dialog box, 90
multi-authored sites. *See* Web-building
    teams
multimedia
    background sounds, 252–254
    defined, 250
    helper applications, 250
    music, 252–254
    video, 250–252
music, 252–254

• N •

navigation, design guidelines, 75–76
Navigation Bar Properties dialog
    box, 122
navigation bars
    and frames, 221
    hyperlinks on, 106
    inserting, 121–124
    links, creating, 124
    links, removing, 125–126
    reconfiguring, 124
    repeating across pages, 126–128
    text labels, 125
    troubleshooting, 124
Navigation toolbar, 36–37
Navigation View, 33–37
navigational structure
    defined, 33
    designing, 34–36
    displaying, 36–37
    navigation bars, 34
    Navigation View, 33–37
    page banners, 34
    parent pages, 37
    portrait versus landscape view, 37
    rearranging, 36
    removing pages from, 36
    subtrees, 37
    zooming in/out, 37
nesting
    frames, 229
    lists, 95

Netscape, Web site, 326
Netscape Communicator (on the
    CD), 341
Netscape Server Application
    Programming Interface (NSAPI),
    214
New dialog box, 15
New Tasks dialog box, 295
No frames message, 231–232
Normal style, 92
NSAPI (Netscape Server Application
    Programming Interface), 214
numbered lists, 93–94

• O •

Office Server Extensions, 309
one-line text boxes
  creating, 193–195
  defined, 193
  restricting data entry, 196–197
  validating, 196–197
Open File dialog box, 52
Options for Saving Results of Forms
    dialog box, 209
outlines, 95–96
Overline effect, 88

• P •

page banners, 241–242. See also
    marquees
page transitions, 256
Page View
  cut, copy, and paste, 82
  desktop customization, 83
  drag and drop, 82
  editing Web pages, 27–28
  find and replace, 82
  pop-up menus, 83
  red squiggly lines, 83
  redoing changes, 82

spell checking, 82–83
text, adding, 81–82
Thesaurus, 82
Tool Tips, 83
toolbars, 83
undoing changes, 82
Paint Shop Pro
  on the CD, 342
  Web site for, 130
Paragraph dialog box, 97
paragraph styles, 92–93
paragraphs. See also text
  aligning, 96–98
  borders, 98–99
  converting to lists, 94
  indenting, 96–98
  shading, 99–100
  spacing, 96–98
parent sites, 22
Parker, Roger, 76, 309
passwords. See also permissions
  changing, 304–305
  defined, 53
  in form fields, 195
PDF files, 55
permissions. See also passwords
  access levels, 301–302
  adjusting, 301, 304
  Administer, 301
  Author, 301
  Browse, 302
  default, 302
  and Server Extensions, 302
  setting, 302–303
Personal Web template, 14
personal Webs, 14
Picture dialog box, 135
Picture toolbar, 148
pictures. See graphics
plug-ins (on the CD), 340
PNG format, 130–131
pop-up menus, 83

Position dialog box, 258
positioning objects
  absolute positioning, 259–261
  and Cascading Style Sheets (CSS), 257
  floating objects, 257–259
  graphics, with tables, 140–142
  relative positioning, 261–263
  stacking order, 260
  with tables, 167
  z-index, 260
Preview in Browser dialog box, 59
Preview tab, 58
printing Web pages, 60–61
private folder, 30
Project Web template, 14
project-tracking Webs, 14
proportional measurements, 175–177
publicizing your site, 315–316
publish status
  changing, 312
  reporting, 33
Publish Web dialog box, 313
publishing Web sites. *See* Web sites,
    publishing

• *Q* •

Quarterdeck CleanSweep (on the
    CD), 341

• *R* •

radio buttons, 200, 202–203
red squiggly lines, 82–83
redoing changes, 82
relative positioning, 261–263
renaming files and folders, 42
Reports View, 29–33
resampling graphics, 145
Reset buttons, 206–208
Rich Text Format (RTF), creating Web
    pages from, 54–57
Richards, Linda, 133

rollover effect, 113–114
Root Webs. *See* parent sites
Rosenfeld, Lou, 76
rotating graphics, 152
rows. *See* table rows
RTF (Rich Text Format), creating Web
    pages from, 54–57

• *S* •

Save As dialog box, 62
Save Embedded Files dialog box, 136
Scheduled Include Page Component,
    270, 282–284
Scheduled Picture Component, 270,
    282–284
Scroll bars, 11
scrolling (multi-line) text boxes,
    198–199
Scrolling Text Box dialog box, 198–199
Search Form Component, 270, 287–288
search page forms, 189
search services, Web site, 315
Search.com, Web site, 327
security
  passwords, 53, 195
  sharing access. *See* permissions;
      Web-building teams
  user names, 53
Server Extensions. *See* FrontPage
    Server Extensions; Office Server
    Extensions
servers
  cross-platform issues, 83–85
  defined, 69
shading paragraphs, 98–100
shared borders
  and frames, 221
  and navigation bars, 126–128
shareware, Web site, 327
*Site Blueprints: The Key to Good Web
    Hygiene,* 76
sizing graphics, 144–145

Small Caps effect, 88
smoothing graphics edges, 145
software downloads, Web site, 327
sounds, collections of (Web site), 252
source control, reporting, 33
spacing
  characters, 91–92
  graphics, 143
  paragraphs, 96–98
special characters, 101. *See also*
      Dynamic HTML
special effects
  cross-platform issues, 84
  graphics, 152
speed, loading pages. *See* download
      speed
spell checking, 82–83
Split Cells dialog box, 181
spreadsheets, converting to Web
      pages, 54–57
stacking order, 260
Standard toolbar, 11
Status bar, 11
Strikethrough effect, 88
Style dialog box, 264
style sheets. *See* Cascading Style
      Sheets (CSS)
Submit buttons, 206–208
Substitution Component, 270, 284–287
subwebs
  converting to folders, 44
  creating, 22–23
  defined, 22
  examples, Web site, 22
  parent sites, 22
  publishing, 314
  and Server Extensions, 22

• *T* •

tab order, form fields, 195
table cells
  adding, 178
  aligning contents of, 179

defined, 165
deleting, 178–179
merging, 181
padding contents of, 173–174
selecting, 177
sizing, 179–181
spacing between, 174
splitting, 181
table columns
  adding, 178
  deleting, 178–179
  selecting, 177
  size, setting, 179–181
  size, warning about, 182
  sizing, 179–181
table of contents, 106, 111
Table of Contents Component, 270.
      See also Components
Table Properties dialog box, 171
table rows
  adding, 178
  deleting, 178–179
  selecting, 177
  sizing, 179–181
tables
  absolute measurements, 175–177
  aligning on the page, 171–172
  backgrounds, 183
  border color, 183–184
  border thickness, 175
  captions, 182
  color, 182–184
  deleting, 185
  floating, 172–173
  height and width, 175–177
  inserting stuff into, 170–171
  positioning graphics with, 140–142
  positioning page elements with, 167
  proportional measurements, 175–177
  purpose of, 165–167
  raised appearance, 184
  selecting parts of, 177
  shadow effects, 184
  within tables, 170–171

wrapping text around, 172–173
tables, creating
  by converting text, 170
  by drawing, 169–170
  with Insert Table button, 167–168
  with Insert Table command, 168–169
Tables toolbar, 177
Target Frame dialog box, 228
target frames, 228–231
Tasks View
  defined, 39
  tracking workflow, 294–296
teams, developing sites. *See* Web-
    building teams
templates. *See also* FrontPage Server
    Extensions; themes
  attaching to Web pages, 48
  Confirmation Form, 216–217
  Customer Support Web, 14
  forms, 189
  Personal Web, 14
  Project Web, 14
  shared, 65
  for Web pages, 48–49
  for Web sites, 14–16
text. *See also* fonts; paragraphs
  adding to Web pages, 81–82
  alternative for graphics, 146–147
  character spacing, 91–92
  color, 89–91
  converting to tables, 170
  cross-platform issues, 89
  line breaks, 142–143
  size, 88–89
  special characters, 101
  wrapping around graphics, 140–142
  wrapping around tables, 172–173
Text Box Validation dialog box, 196
text boxes. *See* one-line text boxes;
    scrolling (multi-line) text boxes
text documents, converting to Web
    pages, 56

text labels on graphics, 148
The Non-Designer's Web Book, 76
themes. *See also* templates
  active graphics, 239–240
  applying to Web sites, 240–241
  background pictures, 240
  colors, changing, 242–245
  defined, 87
  graphics, changing, 245–246
  page banners, 241–242
  previewing, 239
  text styles, changing, 246–247
  vivid colors, 239
Themes dialog box, 238–240
Thesaurus, 82
thumbnails, 153–155
ThunderBYTE AntiVirus (on the
    CD), 342
tiling graphics, 156–157
timestamping published pages, 312
Title bar, 11
Tittel, Ed, 77
Tollett, John, 76
Tool Tips, 83
toolbars, 83
tracking workflow, 14, 39, 294–296
transparency, 149–150
trimming graphics, 151–152
Tripod, Web site, 308
typeface. *See* fonts

• *U* •

underlined letters in menus, 2
underlining text, 88
undoing changes, 82
Uniform Resource Locators (URLs).
    See URLs (Uniform Resource
    Locators)
URLs (Uniform Resource Locators)
  on the CD, 340
  determining, 312–315

URLs (Uniform Resource Locators)
  (continued)
  including in e-mail signatures, 315
  used in this book. *See* Web sites of
    interest
user input
  See check boxes
  See drop-down menus
  See forms
  See one-line text boxes
  See radio buttons
  See scrolling (multi-line) text boxes
user names, 53
user registration forms, 189
utilities (on the CD), 341–342

• *V* •

validating
  forms, 201
  one-line text boxes, 196–197
validation failure pages, 208
video, 250–252
views
  editing Web pages, 27–28
  Folders View, 28–29
  Hyperlinks View, 37–39
  Navigation View, 33–37
  Page View, 27–28
  reporting site information, 29–33
  Reports View, 29–33
  site navigational structure, 33–37
  Tasks View, 39
  viewing files and folders, 28–29
  viewing Web pages, 27–28
Views bar, 11

• *W* •

wallpaper. *See* backgrounds
Wang, Wallace (Web site), 309
watermarks, 156–157
web browsers
  aligning graphics, 157
  background colors, 157
  browser offsets, 157
  cross-platform issues, 72–73, 83–85
  downloading, 59
  downloading, Web site for, 59
  frame compatibility, 231–232
  separating windows into sections.
    See frames
  TV analogy, 70–71
web clients. *See* web browsers
Web Components. *See* Components
*Web Design and Desktop Publishing
  For Dummies,* 76
Web Graphics 101, Web site, 130
Web Graphics For Dummies, 133
Web pages. *See also* Web sites
  attaching templates to, 48
  author's name, displaying, 284–287
  categorizing, 298–301
  comments, 101–102
  configuration variables, 284–287
  counting visits, 273–274
  defined, 10
  deleted, recovering, 32
  description, displaying, 284–287
  editing. *See* Page View
  hit counters, 273–274
  including in other pages, 270, 280–284
  keyword-search ability, 287–288
  modification history, displaying,
    284–287
  printing, 60–61
  saved status, displaying, 61
  saving to folders, 17
  speed of loading. *See* download
    speed
  URL, displaying, 284–287
Web pages, creating. *See also*
  Web-building teams
  as a blank page, 49
  comments, 49
  from other documents, 54–57

from templates, 48–49
unexpected backgrounds, 49
Web pages, opening
on an intranet, 52–54
in current Web site, 50
on the World Wide Web, 52–54
on your computer or network, 50–52
Web pages, previewing
with a local server, 334–337
with Preview tab, 58
with a web browser, 58–60
Web pages, repeating elements
color, 113
including pages in other pages, 270, 280–284
navigation bars, 126–128
shared borders, 126–128
Web pages, saving
to a different location, 63
erasing changes, 61
with graphics, 64
as a template, 65
to a Web site, 63–65
on your computer or network, 62–63
Web presence provider (WPP), 308
Web publishing, defined, 10
Web Publishing Online Resource, Web site, 327
web servers, 10
Web site reports
categories, 33
checkout status, 33
component errors, 32
download speed, 32
file usage, 31
hyperlinks, 31–32
publish status, 33
source control, 33
team status, 32
Web sites. *See also* Web pages
accommodating different environments. *See* cross-platform issues

automating updates, 298–301
backing up, 45
closing, 25
deleting, 25–26
mentioned in this book. *See* Web sites of interest
navigational structure. *See* navigational structure
previewing, 334–337
subsetting information. *See* categories
testing, 315
updating, 316–317
uses for, 321–323
Web sites, creating. *See also* subwebs; Web-building teams
corporate Webs, 16
customer support Webs, 14
discussion groups, 16
importing existing sites, 19–21
personal Webs, 14
project-tracking Webs, 14
from scratch, 18–19
from a template, 14–16
tracking workflow, 14, 39, 294–296
with wizards, 16–18
your first time, 10–13
Web sites, design guidelines
future growth, 76
image (look and feel), 75
navigation, 75–76
site purpose, 74
target audience, 75
Web sites, opening
from a list, 25
multiple sites, 24–25
on other computers, 24
single site, 23–24
Web sites, publishing to a local server, 334–337

Web sites, publishing to the World
    Wide Web
  defined, 307–308
  excluding unfinished pages, 311–312
  finding an ISP, 310
  FrontPage Server Extensions,
    308–310
  Office Server Extensions, 309
  publicizing, 315–316
  publish status, changing, 312
  with subwebs, 314
  testing, 315
  timestamping, 312
  updating, 316–317
  URLs, determining a, 312–315
  URLs, including in e-mail signatures,
    315
  Web presence provider (WPP), 308
  Web space, free, 308
Web sites of interest
  AltaVista, 315
  Angelfire, 308
  author of this book, 6
  banner ads, examples, 271
  browser compatibility, summary
    of, 84
  BrowserCaps, 84
  browser-safe palettes, 132
  Builder.com, 326
  Cascading Style Sheets (CSS), 264
  on the CD, 340
  color palettes, 132
  Dale, Chuck, 130
  Dornfest, Asha, 6
  Download.com, 59, 327
  Dummies.com, 327
  FrontPage 2000, 22
  FrontPage beta changes and errata, 6
  Geocities, 308
  GIF animation, 131
  graphics, 130
  graphics, collections of, 139

Helling, Bill, 309
HTML, 326
Internet information, 327
Know the Code: HTML For Beginners,
    326
marquees, 280
Microsoft, 22
Microsoft FrontPage Home Page, 325
Microsoft Images Gallery, 139
Microsoft Office 2000 All In One For
    Dummies, 309
Microsoft Office 2000 for Windows For
    Dummies, 309
Microsoft Personal Web Server 4.0,
    334–335
Microsoft Support Online, 325
Netscape, 326
PaintShop Pro, 130
parent Web site, example, 22
Parker, Roger, 309
PNG specification, 131
Rosenfeld, Lou, 76
search services, 315
Search.com, 327
shareware, 327
Site Blueprints: The Key to Good Web
    Hygiene, 76
software downloads, 327
sounds, collections of, 252
subweb, example, 22
Tripod, 308
Wang, Wallace, 309
web browsers, downloading, 59
Web Graphics 101, 130
Web Publishing Online Resource, 327
Web space, free, 308
Webmonkey, 59, 326
Windows NT 4.0 Option Pack, 334
Yahoo!, 315
Web space, free, 308
Web-building teams
  assigning people to pages, 292–293

automating site updates, 298–301
categorizing pages, 298–301
checking documents in and out,
     296–297
development process, 291–292
setting review status, 292–293
source control, 296–297
team status, reporting, 32
tracking workflow, 294–296
Webmonkey, Web site, 59, 326
Webs, 10. *See also* Web sites
What You See Is What You Get (WYSI-
     WYG), 57
Williams, Robin, 76
Windows 95/NT users, and this book, 2
Windows Explorer. See Folders View
Windows NT 4.0 Option Pack, 334–335
WinZip (on the CD), 342
wizards. *See also* FrontPage Server
     Extensions
  Corporate Presence, 16
  Discussion Web, 16
  Import Web, 19–21
  for Web sites, 16–18
worksheets, converting to Web pages,
     54–57
WPP (Web presence provider), 308
WS_FTP LE 4.6 (on the CD), 341
WYSIWYG (What You See Is What You
     Get), 57

Yahoo!, Web site, 315

• Z •

z-index, 260

Notes

Notes

Notes

Notes

Notes

Notes

Notes

Notes

Notes

From PCs
to Personal Finance,
We Make it Fun and Easy!

For more information,
or to order, please
call 800.762.2974.

www.idgbooks.com
www.dummies.com

Dummies Books™
Bestsellers on Every Topic!

TECHNOLOGY TITLES

INTERNET

Title	Author	ISBN	Price
America Online® For Dummies®, 5th Edition	John Kaufeld	0-7645-0502-5	$19.99 US/$26.99 CAN
E-Mail For Dummies®, 2nd Edition	John R. Levine, Carol Baroudi, Margaret Levine Young, & Arnold Reinhold	0-7645-0131-3	$24.99 US/$34.99 CAN
Genealogy Online For Dummies®	Matthew L. Helm & April Leah Helm	0-7645-0377-4	$24.99 US/$35.99 CAN
Internet Directory For Dummies®, 2nd Edition	Brad Hill	0-7645-0436-3	$24.99 US/$35.99 CAN
The Internet For Dummies®, 6th Edition	John R. Levine, Carol Baroudi, & Margaret Levine Young	0-7645-0506-8	$19.99 US/$28.99 CAN
Investing Online For Dummies®, 2nd Edition	Kathleen Sindell, Ph.D.	0-7645-0509-2	$24.99 US/$35.99 CAN
World Wide Web Searching For Dummies®, 2nd Edition	Brad Hill	0-7645-0264-6	$24.99 US/$34.99 CAN

OPERATING SYSTEMS

Title	Author	ISBN	Price
DOS For Dummies®, 3rd Edition	Dan Gookin	0-7645-0361-8	$19.99 US/$28.99 CAN
LINUX® For Dummies®, 2nd Edition	John Hall, Craig Witherspoon, & Coletta Witherspoon	0-7645-0421-5	$24.99 US/$35.99 CAN
Mac® OS 8 For Dummies®	Bob LeVitus	0-7645-0271-9	$19.99 US/$26.99 CAN
Small Business Windows® 98 For Dummies®	Stephen Nelson	0-7645-0425-8	$24.99 US/$35.99 CAN
UNIX® For Dummies®, 4th Edition	John R. Levine & Margaret Levine Young	0-7645-0419-3	$19.99 US/$28.99 CAN
Windows® 95 For Dummies®, 2nd Edition	Andy Rathbone	0-7645-0180-1	$19.99 US/$26.99 CAN
Windows® 98 For Dummies®	Andy Rathbone	0-7645-0261-1	$19.99 US/$28.99 CAN

PC/GENERAL COMPUTING

Title	Author	ISBN	Price
Buying a Computer For Dummies®	Dan Gookin	0-7645-0313-8	$19.99 US/$28.99 CAN
Illustrated Computer Dictionary For Dummies®, 3rd Edition	Dan Gookin & Sandra Hardin Gookin	0-7645-0143-7	$19.99 US/$26.99 CAN
Modems For Dummies®, 3rd Edition	Tina Rathbone	0-7645-0069-4	$19.99 US/$26.99 CAN
Small Business Computing For Dummies®	Brian Underdahl	0-7645-0287-5	$24.99 US/$35.99 CAN
Upgrading & Fixing PCs For Dummies®, 4th Edition	Andy Rathbone	0-7645-0418-5	$19.99 US/$28.99CAN

GENERAL INTEREST TITLES

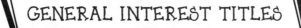

FOOD & BEVERAGE/ENTERTAINING

Title	Author	ISBN	Price
Entertaining For Dummies®	Suzanne Williamson with Linda Smith	0-7645-5027-6	$19.99 US/$26.99 CAN
Gourmet Cooking For Dummies®	Charlie Trotter	0-7645-5029-2	$19.99 US/$26.99 CAN
Grilling For Dummies®	Marie Rama & John Mariani	0-7645-5076-4	$19.99 US/$26.99 CAN
Italian Cooking For Dummies®	Cesare Casella & Jack Bishop	0-7645-5098-5	$19.99 US/$26.99 CAN
Wine For Dummies®, 2nd Edition	Ed McCarthy & Mary Ewing-Mulligan	0-7645-5114-0	$19.99 US/$26.99 CAN

SPORTS

Title	Author	ISBN	Price
Baseball For Dummies®	Joe Morgan with Richard Lally	0-7645-5085-3	$19.99 US/$26.99 CAN
Fly Fishing For Dummies®	Peter Kaminsky	0-7645-5073-X	$19.99 US/$26.99 CAN
Football For Dummies®	Howie Long with John Czarnecki	0-7645-5054-3	$19.99 US/$26.99 CAN
Hockey For Dummies®	John Davidson with John Steinbreder	0-7645-5045-4	$19.99 US/$26.99 CAN
Tennis For Dummies®	Patrick McEnroe with Peter Bodo	0-7645-5087-X	$19.99 US/$26.99 CAN

HOME & GARDEN

Title	Author	ISBN	Price
Decks & Patios For Dummies®	Robert J. Beckstrom & National Gardening Association	0-7645-5075-6	$16.99 US/$24.99 CAN
Flowering Bulbs For Dummies®	Judy Glattstein & National Gardening Association	0-7645-5103-5	$16.99 US/$24.99 CAN
Home Improvement For Dummies®	Gene & Katie Hamilton & the Editors of HouseNet, Inc.	0-7645-5005-5	$19.99 US/$26.99 CAN
Lawn Care For Dummies®	Lance Walheim & National Gardening Association	0-7645-5077-2	$16.99 US/$24.99 CAN

IDG BOOKS
WORLDWIDE

For more information, or to order,
call (800)762-2974

BESTSELLING
BOOK SERIES

Dummies Books™
Bestsellers on Every Topic!

TECHNOLOGY TITLES

SUITES

Title	Author	ISBN	Price
Microsoft® Office 2000 For Windows® For Dummies®	Wallace Wang & Roger C. Parker	0-7645-0452-5	$19.99 US/$28.99 CAN
Microsoft® Office 2000 For Windows® For Dummies®, Quick Reference	Doug Lowe & Bjoern Hartsfvang	0-7645-0453-3	$12.99 US/$19.99 CAN
Microsoft® Office 4 For Windows® For Dummies®	Roger C. Parker	1-56884-183-3	$19.95 US/$26.95 CAN
Microsoft® Office 97 For Windows® For Dummies®	Wallace Wang & Roger C. Parker	0-7645-0050-3	$19.99 US/$26.99 CAN
Microsoft® Office 97 For Windows® For Dummies®, Quick Reference	Doug Lowe	0-7645-0062-7	$12.99 US/$17.99 CAN
Microsoft® Office 98 For Macs® For Dummies®	Tom Negrino	0-7645-0229-8	$19.99 US/$28.99 CAN

WORD PROCESSING

Title	Author	ISBN	Price
Word 2000 For Windows® For Dummies®, Quick Reference	Peter Wererlet	0-7645-0449-5	$12.99 US/$19.99 CAN
Corel® WordPerfect® 8 For Windows® For Dummies®	Margaret Levine Young, David Kay, & Jordan Young	0-7645-0186-0	$19.99 US/$26.99 CAN
Word For Windows® 6 For Dummies®	Dan Gookin	1-56884-075-6	$16.95 US/$21.95 CAN
Word For Windows® 95 For Dummies®	Dan Gookin	1-56884-932-X	$19.99 US/$26.99 CAN
Word 97 For Windows® For Dummies®	Dan Gookin	0-7645-0052-X	$19.99 US/$26.99 CAN
WordPerfect® 6.1 For Windows® For Dummies®, Quick Reference, 2nd Edition	Margaret Levine Young & David Kay	1-56884-966-4	$9.99 US/$12.99 CAN
WordPerfect® 7 For Windows® 95 For Dummies®	Margaret Levine Young & David Kay	1-56884-949-4	$19.99 US/$26.99 CAN
Word Pro® for Windows® 95 For Dummies®	Jim Meade	1-56884-232-5	$19.99 US/$26.99 CAN

SPREADSHEET/FINANCE/PROJECT MANAGEMENT

Title	Author	ISBN	Price
Excel For Windows® 95 For Dummies®	Greg Harvey	1-56884-930-3	$19.99 US/$26.99 CAN
Excel 2000 For Windows® For Dummies®	Greg Harvey	0-7645-0446-0	$19.99 US/$28.99 CAN
Excel 2000 For Windows® For Dummies® Quick Reference	John Walkenbach	0-7645-0447-9	$12.99 US/$19.99 CAN
Microsoft® Money 98 For Dummies®	Peter Weverka	0-7645-0295-6	$24.99 US/$34.99 CAN
Microsoft® Money 99 For Dummies®	Peter Weverka	0-7645-0433-9	$19.99 US/$28.99 CAN
Microsoft® Project 98 For Dummies®	Martin Doucette	0-7645-0321-9	$24.99 US/$34.99 CAN
MORE Excel 97 For Windows® For Dummies®	Greg Harvey	0-7645-0138-0	$22.99 US/$32.99 CAN
Quicken® 98 For Windows® For Dummies®	Stephen L. Nelson	0-7645-0243-3	$19.99 US/$26.99 CAN

GENERAL INTEREST TITLES

EDUCATION & TEST PREPARATION

Title	Author	ISBN	Price
The ACT For Dummies®	Suzee Vlk	1-56884-387-9	$14.99 US/$21.99 CAN
College Financial Aid For Dummies®	Dr. Herm Davis & Joyce Lain Kennedy	0-7645-5049-7	$19.99 US/$26.99 CAN
College Planning For Dummies®, 2nd Edition	Pat Ordovensky	0-7645-5048-9	$19.99 US/$26.99 CAN
Everyday Math For Dummies®	Charles Seiter, Ph.D.	1-56884-248-1	$14.99 US/$22.99 CAN
The GMAT® For Dummies®, 3rd Edition	Suzee Vlk	0-7645-5082-9	$16.99 US/$24.99 CAN
The GRE® For Dummies®, 3rd Edition	Suzee Vlk	0-7645-5083-7	$16.99 US/$24.99 CAN
Politics For Dummies®	Ann DeLaney	1-56884-381-X	$19.99 US/$26.99 CAN
The SAT I For Dummies®, 3rd Edition	Suzee Vlk	0-7645-5044-6	$14.99 US/$21.99 CAN

CAREERS

Title	Author	ISBN	Price
Cover Letters For Dummies®	Joyce Lain Kennedy	1-56884-395-X	$12.99 US/$17.99 CAN
Cool Careers For Dummies®	Marty Nemko, Paul Edwards, & Sarah Edwards	0-7645-5095-0	$16.99 US/$24.99 CAN
Job Hunting For Dummies®	Max Messmer	1-56884-388-7	$16.99 US/$24.99 CAN
Job Interviews For Dummies®	Joyce Lain Kennedy	1-56884-859-5	$12.99 US/$17.99 CAN
Resumes For Dummies®, 2nd Edition	Joyce Lain Kennedy	0-7645-5113-2	$12.99 US/$17.99 CAN

Dummies Books™
Bestsellers on Every Topic!

TECHNOLOGY TITLES

WEB DESIGN & PUBLISHING

Title	Author	ISBN	Price
Creating Web Pages For Dummies®, 4th Edition	Bud Smith & Arthur Bebak	0-7645-0504-1	$24.99 US/$34.99 CAN
FrontPage® 98 For Dummies®	Asha Dornfest	0-7645-0270-0	$24.99 US/$34.99 CAN
HTML 4 For Dummies®	Ed Tittel & Stephen Nelson James	0-7645-0331-6	$29.99 US/$42.99 CAN
Java™ For Dummies®, 2nd Edition	Aaron E. Walsh	0-7645-0140-2	$24.99 US/$34.99 CAN
PageMill™ 2 For Dummies®	Deke McClelland & John San Filippo	0-7645-0028-7	$24.99 US/$34.99 CAN

DESKTOP PUBLISHING GRAPHICS/MULTIMEDIA

Title	Author	ISBN	Price
CorelDRAW™ 8 For Dummies®	Deke McClelland	0-7645-0317-0	$19.99 US/$26.99 CAN
Desktop Publishing and Design For Dummies®	Roger C. Parker	1-56884-234-1	$19.99 US/$26.99 CAN
Digital Photography For Dummies®, 2nd Edition	Julie Adair King	0-7645-0431-2	$19.99 US/$28.99 CAN
Microsoft® Publisher 97 For Dummies®	Barry Sosinsky, Christopher Benz & Jim McCarter	0-7645-0148-8	$19.99 US/$26.99 CAN
Microsoft® Publisher 98 For Dummies®	Jim McCarter	0-7645-0395-2	$19.99 US/$28.99 CAN

MACINTOSH

Title	Author	ISBN	Price
Macs® For Dummies®, 6th Edition	David Pogue	0-7645-0398-7	$19.99 US/$28.99 CAN
Macs® For Teachers™, 3rd Edition	Michelle Robinette	0-7645-0226-3	$24.99 US/$34.99 CAN
The iMac For Dummies	David Pogue	0-7645-0495-9	$19.99 US/$26.99 CAN

GENERAL INTEREST TITLES

BUSINESS & PERSONAL FINANCE

Title	Author	ISBN	Price
Accounting For Dummies®	John A. Tracy, CPA	0-7645-5014-4	$19.99 US/$26.99 CAN
Business Plans For Dummies®	Paul Tiffany, Ph.D. & Steven D. Peterson, Ph.D.	1-56884-868-4	$19.99 US/$26.99 CAN
Consulting For Dummies®	Bob Nelson & Peter Economy	0-7645-5034-9	$19.99 US/$26.99 CAN
Customer Service For Dummies®	Karen Leland & Keith Bailey	1-56884-391-7	$19.99 US/$26.99 CAN
Home Buying For Dummies®	Eric Tyson, MBA & Ray Brown	1-56884-385-2	$16.99 US/$24.99 CAN
House Selling For Dummies®	Eric Tyson, MBA & Ray Brown	0-7645-5038-1	$16.99 US/$24.99 CAN
Investing For Dummies®	Eric Tyson, MBA	1-56884-393-3	$19.99 US/$26.99 CAN
Law For Dummies®	John Ventura	1-56884-860-9	$19.99 US/$26.99 CAN
Managing For Dummies®	Bob Nelson & Peter Economy	1-56884-858-7	$19.99 US/$26.99 CAN
Marketing For Dummies®	Alexander Hiam	1-56884-699-1	$19.99 US/$26.99 CAN
Mutual Funds For Dummies®, 2nd Edition	Eric Tyson, MBA	0-7645-5112-4	$19.99 US/$26.99 CAN
Negotiating For Dummies®	Michael C. Donaldson & Mimi Donaldson	1-56884-867-6	$19.99 US/$26.99 CAN
Personal Finance For Dummies®, 2nd Edition	Eric Tyson, MBA	0-7645-5013-6	$19.99 US/$26.99 CAN
Personal Finance For Dummies® For Canadians	Eric Tyson, MBA & Tony Martin	1-56884-378-X	$18.99 US/$24.99 CAN
Sales Closing For Dummies®	Tom Hopkins	0-7645-5063-2	$14.99 US/$21.99 CAN
Sales Prospecting For Dummies®	Tom Hopkins	0-7645-5066-7	$14.99 US/$21.99 CAN
Selling For Dummies®	Tom Hopkins	1-56884-389-5	$16.99 US/$24.99 CAN
Small Business For Dummies®	Eric Tyson, MBA & Jim Schell	0-7645-5094-2	$19.99 US/$26.99 CAN
Small Business Kit For Dummies®	Richard D. Harroch	0-7645-5093-4	$24.99 US/$34.99 CAN
Successful Presentations For Dummies®	Malcolm Kushner	1-56884-392-5	$16.99 US/$24.99 CAN
Time Management For Dummies®	Jeffrey J. Mayer	1-56884-360-7	$16.99 US/$24.99 CAN

AUTOMOTIVE

Title	Author	ISBN	Price
Auto Repair For Dummies®	Deanna Sclar	0-7645-5089-6	$19.99 US/$26.99 CAN
Buying A Car For Dummies®	Deanna Sclar	0-7645-5091-8	$16.99 US/$24.99 CAN
Car Care For Dummies®: The Glove Compartment Guide	Deanna Sclar	0-7645-5090-X	$9.99 US/$13.99 CAN

IDG BOOKS WORLDWIDE

For more information, or to order, call (800)762-2974

FOR Dummies

BESTSELLING BOOK SERIES

Dummies Books™
Bestsellers on Every Topic!

TECHNOLOGY TITLES

DATABASE

Access 2000 For Windows® For Dummies®	John Kaufeld	0-7645-0444-4	$19.99 US/$28.99 CAN
Access 97 For Windows® For Dummies®	John Kaufeld	0-7645-0048-1	$19.99 US/$26.99 CAN
Approach® 97 For Windows® For Dummies®	Deborah S. Ray & Eric J. Ray	0-7645-0001-5	$19.99 US/$26.99 CAN
Crystal Reports 7 For Dummies®	Douglas J. Wolf	0-7645-0548-3	$24.99 US/$34.99 CAN
Data Warehousing For Dummies®	Alan R. Simon	0-7645-0170-4	$24.99 US/$34.99 CAN
FileMaker® Pro 4 For Dummies®	Tom Maremaa	0-7645-0210-7	$19.99 US/$26.99 CAN
Intranet & Web Databases For Dummies®	Paul Litwin	0-7645-0221-2	$29.99 US/$42.99 CAN

NETWORKING

Building An Intranet For Dummies®	John Fronckowiak	0-7645-0276-X	$29.99 US/$42.99 CAN
cc: Mail™ For Dummies®	Victor R. Garza	0-7645-0055-4	$19.99 US/$26.99 CAN
Client/Server Computing For Dummies®, 2ⁿᵈ Edition	Doug Lowe	0-7645-0066-X	$24.99 US/$34.99 CAN
Lotus Notes® Release 4 For Dummies®	Stephen Londergan & Pat Freeland	1-56884-934-6	$19.99 US/$26.99 CAN
Networking For Dummies®, 4ᵗʰ Edition	Doug Lowe	0-7645-0498-3	$19.99 US/$28.99 CAN
Upgrading & Fixing Networks For Dummies®	Bill Camarda	0-7645-0347-2	$29.99 US/$42.99 CAN
Windows NT® Networking For Dummies®	Ed Tittel, Mary Madden, & Earl Follis	0-7645-0015-5	$24.99 US/$34.99 CAN

GENERAL INTEREST TITLES

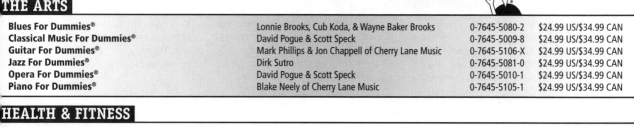

THE ARTS

Blues For Dummies®	Lonnie Brooks, Cub Koda, & Wayne Baker Brooks	0-7645-5080-2	$24.99 US/$34.99 CAN
Classical Music For Dummies®	David Pogue & Scott Speck	0-7645-5009-8	$24.99 US/$34.99 CAN
Guitar For Dummies®	Mark Phillips & Jon Chappell of Cherry Lane Music	0-7645-5106-X	$24.99 US/$34.99 CAN
Jazz For Dummies®	Dirk Sutro	0-7645-5081-0	$24.99 US/$34.99 CAN
Opera For Dummies®	David Pogue & Scott Speck	0-7645-5010-1	$24.99 US/$34.99 CAN
Piano For Dummies®	Blake Neely of Cherry Lane Music	0-7645-5105-1	$24.99 US/$34.99 CAN

HEALTH & FITNESS

Beauty Secrets For Dummies®	Stephanie Seymour	0-7645-5078-0	$19.99 US/$26.99 CAN
Fitness For Dummies®	Suzanne Schlosberg & Liz Neporent, M.A.	1-56884-866-8	$19.99 US/$26.99 CAN
Nutrition For Dummies®	Carol Ann Rinzler	0-7645-5032-2	$19.99 US/$26.99 CAN
Sex For Dummies®	Dr. Ruth K. Westheimer	1-56884-384-4	$16.99 US/$24.99 CAN
Weight Training For Dummies®	Liz Neporent, M.A. & Suzanne Schlosberg	0-7645-5036-5	$19.99 US/$26.99 CAN

LIFESTYLE/SELF-HELP

Dating For Dummies®	Dr. Joy Browne	0-7645-5072-1	$19.99 US/$26.99 CAN
Parenting For Dummies®	Sandra H. Gookin	1-56884-383-6	$16.99 US/$24.99 CAN
Success For Dummies®	Zig Ziglar	0-7645-5061-6	$19.99 US/$26.99 CAN
Weddings For Dummies®	Marcy Blum & Laura Fisher Kaiser	0-7645-5055-1	$19.99 US/$26.99 CAN

IDG BOOKS WORLDWIDE®

For more information, or to order, call (800)762-2974

FOR Dummies™
BESTSELLING BOOK SERIES

IDG Books Worldwide, Inc., End-User License Agreement

READ THIS. You should carefully read these terms and conditions before opening the software packet(s) included with this book ("Book"). This is a license agreement ("Agreement") between you and IDG Books Worldwide, Inc. ("IDGB"). By opening the accompanying software packet(s), you acknowledge that you have read and accept the following terms and conditions. If you do not agree and do not want to be bound by such terms and conditions, promptly return the Book and the unopened software packet(s) to the place you obtained them for a full refund.

1. **License Grant.** IDGB grants to you (either an individual or entity) a nonexclusive license to use one copy of the enclosed software program(s) (collectively, the "Software") solely for your own personal or business purposes on a single computer (whether a standard computer or a workstation component of a multiuser network). The Software is in use on a computer when it is loaded into temporary memory (RAM) or installed into permanent memory (hard disk, CD-ROM, or other storage device). IDGB reserves all rights not expressly granted herein.

2. **Ownership.** IDGB is the owner of all right, title, and interest, including copyright, in and to the compilation of the Software recorded on the disk(s) or CD-ROM ("Software Media"). Copyright to the individual programs recorded on the Software Media is owned by the author or other authorized copyright owner of each program. Ownership of the Software and all proprietary rights relating thereto remain with IDGB and its licensers.

3. **Restrictions on Use and Transfer.**

   (a) You may only (i) make one copy of the Software for backup or archival purposes, or (ii) transfer the Software to a single hard disk, provided that you keep the original for backup or archival purposes. You may not (i) rent or lease the Software, (ii) copy or reproduce the Software through a LAN or other network system or through any computer subscriber system or bulletin-board system, or (iii) modify, adapt, or create derivative works based on the Software.

   (b) You may not reverse engineer, decompile, or disassemble the Software. You may transfer the Software and user documentation on a permanent basis, provided that the transferee agrees to accept the terms and conditions of this Agreement and you retain no copies. If the Software is an update or has been updated, any transfer must include the most recent update and all prior versions.

4. **Restrictions on Use of Individual Programs.** You must follow the individual requirements and restrictions detailed for each individual program in Appendix B, "What's on the CD," of this Book. These limitations are also contained in the individual license agreements recorded on the Software Media. These limitations may include a requirement that after using the program for a specified period of time, the user must pay a registration fee or discontinue use. By opening the Software packet(s), you will be agreeing to abide by the licenses and restrictions for these individual programs that are detailed in Appendix B and on the Software Media. None of the material on this Software Media or listed in this Book may ever be redistributed, in original or modified form, for commercial purposes.

5. Limited Warranty.

(a) IDGB warrants that the Software and Software Media are free from defects in materials and workmanship under normal use for a period of sixty (60) days from the date of purchase of this Book. If IDGB receives notification within the warranty period of defects in materials or workmanship, IDGB will replace the defective Software Media.

(b) **IDGB AND THE AUTHOR OF THE BOOK DISCLAIM ALL OTHER WARRANTIES, EXPRESS OR IMPLIED, INCLUDING WITHOUT LIMITATION IMPLIED WARRANTIES OF MERCHANTABILITY AND FITNESS FOR A PARTICULAR PURPOSE, WITH RESPECT TO THE SOFTWARE, THE PROGRAMS, THE SOURCE CODE CONTAINED THEREIN, AND/OR THE TECHNIQUES DESCRIBED IN THIS BOOK. IDGB DOES NOT WARRANT THAT THE FUNCTIONS CONTAINED IN THE SOFTWARE WILL MEET YOUR REQUIREMENTS OR THAT THE OPERATION OF THE SOFTWARE WILL BE ERROR FREE.**

(c) This limited warranty gives you specific legal rights, and you may have other rights that vary from jurisdiction to jurisdiction.

6. Remedies.

(a) IDGB's entire liability and your exclusive remedy for defects in materials and workmanship shall be limited to replacement of the Software Media, which may be returned to IDGB with a copy of your receipt at the following address: Software Media Fulfillment Department, Attn.: *FrontPage 2000 For Dummies*, IDG Books Worldwide, Inc., 7260 Shadeland Station, Ste. 100, Indianapolis, IN 46256, or call 800-762-2974. Please allow three to four weeks for delivery. This Limited Warranty is void if failure of the Software Media has resulted from accident, abuse, or misapplication. Any replacement Software Media will be warranted for the remainder of the original warranty period or thirty (30) days, whichever is longer.

(b) In no event shall IDGB or the author be liable for any damages whatsoever (including without limitation damages for loss of business profits, business interruption, loss of business information, or any other pecuniary loss) arising from the use of or inability to use the Book or the Software, even if IDGB has been advised of the possibility of such damages.

(c) Because some jurisdictions do not allow the exclusion or limitation of liability for consequential or incidental damages, the above limitation or exclusion may not apply to you.

7. U.S. Government Restricted Rights. Use, duplication, or disclosure of the Software by the U.S. Government is subject to restrictions stated in paragraph (c)(1)(ii) of the Rights in Technical Data and Computer Software clause of DFARS 252.227-7013, and in subparagraphs (a) through (d) of the Commercial Computer–Restricted Rights clause at FAR 52.227-19, and in similar clauses in the NASA FAR supplement, when applicable.

8. General. This Agreement constitutes the entire understanding of the parties and revokes and supersedes all prior agreements, oral or written, between them and may not be modified or amended except in a writing signed by both parties hereto that specifically refers to this Agreement. This Agreement shall take precedence over any other documents that may be in conflict herewith. If any one or more provisions contained in this Agreement are held by any court or tribunal to be invalid, illegal, or otherwise unenforceable, each and every other provision shall remain in full force and effect.

Installation Instructions

To install the items from the CD onto your computer, follow these steps.

1. **Insert the CD into your computer's CD-ROM drive and close the drive door.**

2. **In the Windows taskbar, click the Start button and then choose Run.**

3. **In the dialog box that appears, type** D:\setup.exe **and then click OK.**

   Your computer probably lists your CD-ROM drive as drive D (if you're not sure, double-click the My Computer icon on your desktop to see). If your CD-ROM drive uses a different letter, type the appropriate letter in the Run dialog box.

4. **Read through the license agreement that appears, and then click Agree.**

   The CD Welcome screen appears.

5. **Click anywhere on the Welcome screen to continue.**

   The CD interface appears, on which the CD contents are divided into categories, the names of which appear on the screen.

6. **To view the items in a category, click the category's name.**

7. **For more information about an item, click the item's name.**

   Be sure to read this information. Some programs may require you to adjust your computer's settings before you install, and this screen tells you where to go for that information, if necessary.

8. **To install the item on your computer, click the Install button. If you don't want to install the item, click the Go Back button to return to the previous category screen.**

9. **To install other CD goodies, repeat Steps 7, 8 and 9.**

10. **When you're done installing CD items, click the Quit button to close the interface.**

    A final screen appears, asking if you're sure you want to quit.

11. **Click Yes.**

    The CD interface closes. You can remove the CD from your CD-ROM drive now.

If you still have trouble installing the items from the CD, please call the IDG Books Worldwide Customer Service phone number: 800-762-2974 (if you're calling from outside the U.S., use this phone number: 317-596-5261).

Discover Dummies™ Online!

The *Dummies* Web Site is your fun and friendly online resource for the latest information about *...For Dummies®* books on all your favorite topics. From cars to computers, wine to Windows, and investing to the Internet, we've got a shelf full of *...For Dummies* books waiting for you!

Ten Fun and Useful Things You Can Do at www.dummies.com

1. Register this book and win!
2. Find and buy the *...For Dummies* books you want online.
3. Get ten great *Dummies Tips™* every week.
4. Chat with your favorite *...For Dummies* authors.
5. Subscribe free to *The Dummies Dispatch™* newsletter.
6. Enter our sweepstakes and win cool stuff.
7. Send a free cartoon postcard to a friend.
8. Download free software.
9. Sample a book before you buy.
10. Talk to us. Make comments, ask questions, and get answers!

Jump online to these ten fun and useful things at
http://www.dummies.com/10useful

For other technology titles from IDG Books Worldwide, go to
www.idgbooks.com

Not online yet? It's easy to get started with *The Internet For Dummies*, 5th Edition, or *Dummies 101®: The Internet For Windows® 98*, available at local retailers everywhere.

Find other *...For Dummies* books on these topics:

Business • Careers • Databases • Food & Beverages • Games • Gardening • Graphics • Hardware
Health & Fitness • Internet and the World Wide Web • Networking • Office Suites
Operating Systems • Personal Finance • Pets • Programming • Recreation • Sports
Spreadsheets • Teacher Resources • Test Prep • Word Processing

IDG BOOKS WORLDWIDE BOOK REGISTRATION